The Changing Shape
of Government in the
Asia-Pacific Region

The Changing Shape of Government in the Asia-Pacific Region

Edited by John W. Langford and K. Lorne Brownsey

The Institute for Research on Public Policy/
L'Institut de recherches politiques

Legal Deposit First Quarter
Bibliothèque nationale du Québec

Canadian Cataloguing in Publication Data

Main entry under title:

The Changing shape of government in the Asia-Pacific
region

Prefatory material in English and French.
ISBN 0-88645-060-8

1. Comparative government.   2. Asia, Southeastern –
Politics and government.   3. East Asia – Politics and
government.   I. Langford, John W.   II. Brownsey, K.
Lorne, 1952-.   III. Institute for Research on Public
Policy.

JF51.C52   1988   320.3   C88-098540-2

The camera-ready copy for this publication was created
on a Xerox 6085 Desktop Publishing System.

The Institute for Research on Public Policy/
L'Institut de recherches politiques
P.O. Box 3670 South
Halifax, Nova Scotia B3J 3K6

Contents

Contributors

Chung-Si Ahn is an Associate Professor of Political Science, Seoul National University and the Associate Director of the Institute of Social Sciences, Seoul National University. He has published many articles and books on Korean politics and international relations in the Asia Pacific region. Professor Ahn was educated at Seoul National University and the University of Hawaii.

Zainah Mahfoozah Anwar is a researcher at the Institute of Strategic and International Studies in Kuala Lumpur, Malaysia. She has also worked as a political and diplomatic correspondent for *The New Straits Times*. Her areas of specialization include Malaysian politics and government and Islam and politics. Zainah Mahfoozah Anwar was educated at MARA Institute of Technology, Boston University and Fletcher School of Law and Diplomacy, Tufts University.

K. Lorne Brownsey is a researcher at the Institute for Research on Public Policy. His major areas of research include comparative governments and politics, and Sino-Canadian trade relations. Lorne Brownsey was educated at the University of Victoria.

Likhit Dhiravegin is currently an Associate Professor of Political Science at Thammasat University in Bangkok, Thailand. He has written a number of books and articles on the Thai bureaucracy, Thai politics, local government, regional politics, and modernization of Japan. Professor Dhiravegin was educated at Thammasat University, The Fletcher School of Law and Diplomacy, Tufts University and Brown University.

Mohammad Mohabbat Khan is a Professor in the Department of Public Administration, University of Dhaka, Bangladesh, and Chairman of the Centre for Public Affairs, University of Dhaka. He is the author of many publications in such areas as personnel management, administrative reform and public enterprises. Professor Khan was educated at the University of Dhaka, Syracuse University and the University of Southern California.

John W. Langford is currently the Director of the Asia-Pacific Workshop Series of the Institute for Research on Public Policy and the Director of the School of Public Administration, University of Victoria. His research and teaching areas include Canadian government and politics, public corporations, executive government, comparative administration and responsible administrative behaviour. Professor Langford was educated at Carleton University, Oxford and McGill University.

Lau Siu-kai is the Director of the Centre for Hong Kong Studies, The Chinese University of Hong Kong. He has published numerous works on social life and development and political reform in Hong Kong. Professor Lau was educated at the University of Hong Kong and the University of Minnesota.

John Nethercote is currently Deputy President of the Royal Australian Institute for Public Administration and editor of the *Canberra Bulletin of Public Administration*. Since joining the Australian public service in 1970 he has worked for numerous government boards and commissions and authored, or edited, many books and articles on Australian, British and Canadian public administration. Mr. Nethercote was educated at the University of Sydney, the Australian National University and the London School of Economics.

Paul E. Peterson is a Professor of Political Science at Johns Hopkins University, Baltimore. He is the former Director of the Governmental Studies Program of the Brookings Institution, and has also served as the Chairman of the Committee on Public Policy Studies, University of Chicago. His chief fields of research and publication include federalism, urban policy, education, and race relations. Dr. Peterson was educated at Concordia College and the University of Chicago.

Jon S.T. Quah is currently Associate Professor in the Department of Political Science, National University of Singapore. During 1986-1987 Professor Quah was on sabbatical leave and held the position of Research Associate, The Institute of Governmental Studies, University of California, Berkeley. His major areas of research and publication include ASEAN public administration, Singapore politics and family planning management. Professor Quah was educated at the University of Singapore and Florida State University.

Richard Simeon is the Director of the School of Public Administration and a Professor of Political Studies at Queen's University in Kingston. His writings include works on federalism, public policy and Canadian constitutional issues. From 1983-1985 Professor Simeon was Research Coordinator (Institutions) for the Canadian Royal Commission on the Economic Union and Development Prospects.

Habib Mohammad Zafarullah is the Executive Director of the Centre for Public Affairs, Department of Public Administration, University of Dhaka, Bangladesh. His major areas of research and publication include public administration, bureaucratic reform, and politics in Bangladesh.

Foreword

Recognizing the increasingly prominent political and economic roles played by the countries of the Asia-Pacific region in recent years, and their importance in many facets of Canadian development, the Institute for Research on Public Policy has made the establishment of an Asia-Pacific research agenda a priority. Research related to this region is underway in a number of the Institute's programs. Study of the economies of the ASEAN countries, and of Canadian trade with countries of the Pacific, falls within the international economic issues theme. Assessment of prospects for environmental quality and sustainable development will form part of the program of work within the environmental policy program. Other bilateral linkages or international discussion groups are organized within the general research program. It is, however, the governability theme that is the home of much of the Institute's Asia-Pacific activity, and it is under this theme that IRPP has undertaken to promote development of a network of Asia-Pacific policy institutes.

When the performance of governments is challenged — when their effectiveness in meeting the challenges of a rapidly changing environment while pursuing goals of economic growth, social justice, security, or collective services is questioned — nations may attempt to modify their political processes, their administrative structures, or the roles and responsibilities assumed by their governments. In particular the possible tension between economic performance and political participation is widely debated. But the link from the scale of government responsibilities to political blockages is also controversial.

Within the research program of the Institute dealing with problems of governability and institutions of governance, led by Professor John Langford (now Director of the School of Public Administration at the University of Victoria), it was recognized that it could be particularly fruitful to explore these questions in a comparative setting involving senior researchers from around the Pacific Rim, bringing Western perspectives on the challenges to governability inherent in the growing scale of government responsibilities together with Asian perspectives on the problems of guided development in the face of broadening political participation. The results revealed some surprising common elements along with some obvious contrasts.

The seminar for which the papers in this volume were prepared was the first in a series of workshops intended to link senior public policy researchers from around the Pacific Rim. This project reflects a perceived lack of research networking arrangements in the areas of government and administration in the region; the eagerness shown by research centres in the various countries to participate in a long-term, multi-lateral research relationship on the theme of governability suggests that this workshop series can provide a useful forum facilitating an exchange of views amongst observers from different nations.

The primary intent of this workshop series thus is to open up new channels of communication through which researchers from Asia Pacific nations can exchange views on problems and reforms in the area of governance and public sector management. But the publication of the workshop proceedings is intended also to be of benefit to policy-makers, businessmen and academics throughout the region.

This first workshop was characterized by a surprisingly frank and informative comparison of the major problems confronting the political and governmental systems of the participating countries, with respect to both institutional structures and political or administrative processes. The release of this volume setting out the papers and a brief summary of the discussion provides a fascinating overview of the state of play on these issues in the individual countries, and meets in a timely manner the general goal of disseminating the results of the discussion beyond the workshop participants themselves.

This discussion was intended to lay the groundwork for a longer term program of more detailed exchanges on specific governability issues, and the follow-up dissemination of these analytical exchanges through publication of similar proceedings volumes. Given the success which this first workshop seems to have achieved, there can be little surprise that participants have agreed to continue the dialogue at a second meeting this year. This second workshop is scheduled to be held in Bangkok, Thailand in December 1988, and will be devoted to examining more closely the relationships between political structures and economic development.

The Institute is pleased to publish this volume dealing with comparative administration and the changing shape of government in the Asia-Pacific region. We are also pleased to acknowledge the generous financial assistance given to the 1987 workshop by the Management for Change Program of the Canadian International Development Agency and from the University of Victoria. We hope that this publication and those from subsequent workshops will play an important role in raising the level of understanding of the problems that confront our respective societies. We hope also that they will contribute to the building of long-term multilateral linkages across the Pacific, links which will in turn break down cultural barriers and promote the peaceful competition and international harmony which is the goal of all the nations of the region.

Rod Dobell
President

January 1988

Avant-propos

Le rôle économique et politique joué, au cours des dernières années, par les pays de l'Asie du Pacifique prend de plus en plus d'importance, et l'influence de ces pays sur de nombreux aspects du développement canadien grandit de jour en jour. C'est pourquoi l'Institut de recherches politiques a fait de la recherche en ce domaine une de ses priorités. Plusieurs programmes de l'Institut y sont déjà consacrés. L'étude des économies des pays de l'ANSEA, ainsi que celle du commerce canadien avec les pays du Pacifique, entrent dans le cadre des questions d'économie internationale. L'évaluation des possibilités qui existent pour arriver à une qualité de l'environnement et à une croissance soutenable constituera une partie du programme de travail, dans le cadre du programme sur les politiques de l'environnement. D'autres rencontres bilatérales ou des groupes de discussion internationaux sont organisés dans le cadre du programme général de recherche. Toutefois, c'est le thème de recherche portant sur la capacité de gouverner qui accapare la plus grande partie des activités de l'Institut relatives aux pays de l'Asie du Pacifique, et c'est sous l'égide de ce thème que l'IRP a entrepris de favoriser le développement d'un réseau d'instituts politiques des pays de l'Asie du Pacifique.

Lorsque les actions entreprises par les gouvernements sont remises en question, c'est-à-dire lorsque le public doute que les gouvernements aient réussi à répondre aux défis d'un environnement en perpétuel changement au cours de leur quête de croissance économique, de justice sociale, de sécurité ou de services pour la collectivité, les pays peuvent essayer de modifier leurs méthodes politiques, leurs structures administratives ou les rôles et responsabilités assumés par leurs gouvernements. En particulier, la tension possible entre la performance économique et la participation politique est largement débattue. Mais le rapport entre l'étendue des responsabilités gouvernementales et les blocages politiques est également un sujet controversé.

Dans le cadre du programme de recherche de l'Institut consacré aux problèmes relatifs à la capacité de gouverner et aux gouvernements, dirigé par le professeur John Langford (actuellement directeur de l'école d'administration publique de l'Université de Victoria), il a été reconnu qu'il serait fructueux d'explorer ces questions d'une manière comparative, et d'impliquer des chercheurs de renom originaires de la zone du Pacifique. Cela devrait permettre de rapprocher les perspectives occidentales sur les défis relatifs à la capacité de gouverner, inhérents aux responsabilités grandissantes des gouvernements, avec les perspectives asiatiques sur les problèmes de développement dirigé, face à une participation politique de plus en plus importante. Les résultats de la première rencontre ont révélé certains éléments communs surprenants, ainsi que des contrastes évidents.

Le séminaire qui a donné lieu aux communications publiées dans cet ouvrage était le premier d'une série d'ateliers visant à réunir les meilleurs chercheurs en politique publique de la zone du Pacifique. Les activités de recherche relatives aux modes de gouvernement et d'administration de cette région étaient considérées déficientes et ce projet essaie de remédier à la situation. L'enthousiasme avec lequel les centres de recherche des différents pays se sont déclarés prêts à participer à une recherche multilatérale à long terme sur le thème de la capacité de gouverner indique bien que cette série d'ateliers peut servir de forum où les points de vue d'observateurs de différents pays pourront être échangés.

L'idée première de cette série d'ateliers est donc d'ouvrir de nouveaux moyens de communication qui permettront aux chercheurs des pays de l'Asie du Pacifique de confronter leurs opinions quant aux problèmes et aux réformes en matière de gouvernement et de gestion du secteur public. La publication prévue des actes de ces rencontres vise également à informer les législateurs, les hommes d'affaires et les universitaires de toute cette région.

Le premier atelier a été l'occasion d'un échange de vues d'une grande franchise et très éclairant sur les problèmes majeurs que doivent affronter les systèmes politiques et gouvernementaux des pays participants, que ce soit sur le plan des structures institution-nelles ou sur celui des pratiques politiques ou administratives. Le présent volume, avec une présentation de chaque communication suivie d'un résumé des discussions qu'elle a entraînées, offre une vue d'ensemble fascinante sur les facteurs en présence dans chacun de ces pays relativement aux questions analysées; il permet en outre, et d'une manière appropriée, de réaliser cet autre objectif général des rencontres, qui est d'en faire connaître les résultats à un public plus large.

Cette discussion avait pour but de préparer le terrain pour un programme à plus long terme d'échanges approfondis sur les questions spécifiques portant sur la capacité de gouverner, et également de dissémination de ces analyses au moyen de publications similaires au présent volume. Etant donné le succès que semble avoir rencontré ce premier atelier, on ne sera pas surpris d'apprendre que les participants ont convenu de se réunir à nouveau cette année, pour poursuivre le dialogue. Le second atelier se tiendra à Bangkok, en Thaïlande, en décembre 1988. Il sera consacré à l'étude détaillée des rapports qui existent entre les structures politiques et le développement économique.

L'Institut est heureux de publier ce volume sur l'administration comparée et sur le changement dans la forme de gouvernement des pays de l'Asie du Pacifique. Nous voulons également exprimer notre gratitude à l'égard des responsables du "programme de gestion pour le changement," de l'Agence canadienne de développement international, ainsi qu'à l'égard de l'Université de Victoria, pour leur généreuse aide financière à l'occasion de ce premier atelier. Nous espérons que le présent volume, et ceux qui résulteront des rencontres à venir, joueront un rôle important dans la prise de conscience des problèmes qui se posent aux sociétés en question. Puissent-ils contribuer à l'établissement de relations multilatérales à long terme autour du Pacifique, relations qui, à leur tour, permettront de supprimer les barrières culturelles et de promouvoir la concurrence pacifique et l'harmonie internationale qui demeurent le but ultime de tous les pays de cette région.

Rod Dobell
Président

Janvier 1988

The Changing Shape of Government in the Asia-Pacific Region

John W. Langford
K. Lorne Brownsey

The rapid economic growth experienced by the nations of the Asia Pacific region has resulted in western societies — particularly those on the Pacific Rim — paying an increasing amount of attention to that part of the world. Most of this scrutiny has focused on the changing economic environment. There has been much less discussion or analysis of the changing shape of the political and governmental systems of the region.

It is these changes which researchers from 10 Pacific Rim countries (Australia, Bangladesh, Canada, Hong Kong, Japan, South Korea, Malaysia, Singapore, Thailand and the United States) considered during a two and one-half day workshop organized by the Institute for Research on Public Policy and held at the University of Victoria in June, 1987. The papers that make up this volume were prepared for this workshop and revised in the wake of the workshop discussion.

The purpose of the workshop was to explore the nature of the institutional problems confronting the political and governmental systems of the participant countries, the nature of the steps being taken or proposed to deal with these problems, and the degree to which these problems and proposals share common characteristics or are unique to particular polities.

The success of this workshop was as much due to the remarkable economic growth of the region as anything else. Economic progress has given the research communities in countries around the Pacific

1

Rim a degree of confidence in their own experiences and models which makes the danger of intellectual domination by any western version of the good polity largely anachronistic. This does not mean that discussions at the workshop were never punctuated by exchanges about ideological bias or insensitivity to differences in political or administrative culture. These exchanges however, were not rooted in the presumption that there was only one road to salvation and that it followed a western route. In fact, discussions were founded in a collective consciousness of the fact that all societies on the Pacific Rim confront difficult problems of governance. It is no longer a question of some political and governmental systems being "developed" and others "under-developed" or "developing".

Typecasting the Participants

Three types of states are found around the Pacific basin: liberal-democratic states, most of which are parliamentary democracies and feature periodic mass elections, a pluralistic and competitive system of pressure groups and parties, and respect for basic political rights; bureaucratic-authoritarian states – also known as "guided develop-ment" or "semi-democratic" states – which may exhibit elements of the traditional liberal democratic model (e.g., elections and various degrees of pluralism and respect for human rights), but tend more noticeably to be characterized by strong man rule, a dominant party and heavy bureaucratic and possibly military intervention in decision-making; and finally, socialist states with Leninist institutions modelled on the communist regimes in the Soviet Union or China.

The experiences of the countries which participated in the workshop are all within the spectrum of the liberal democratic and bureaucratic-authoritarian models. Canada, the United States and Australia fit easily within the former. Japan, Singapore and Malaysia would appear to find a home there as well, but there are dis-senting voices on this typecasting. Japan has an established record of open parliamentary democracy, but it has an equally powerful tradition of one party rule and bureaucratic domination of the decision-making process. Both Malaysia and Singapore have success-fully adapted the British parliamentary model to local conditions over the last 30 years but both have done so in the context of single party rule or domination (and in the case of Singapore, one man rule), a powerful administrative apparatus and limitations on the rights of individuals, political parties, interest groups and the media. As these three polities, in a sense, straddle the line between liberal democratic and bureaucratic-authoritarian political systems it may be more appropriate to describe them as "controlled" or "soft authoritarian" systems.

Thailand, South Korea and Bangladesh are squarely within the bureaucratic-authoritarian or "guided democracy" model, with the military, military coups and the bureaucracy playing key roles in the governance of all three of these states. Liberal democratic form may be observed on occasion, but other more powerful societal and cultural forces have limited participation in political decision-making. Finally, Hong Kong, as a colony in transition, certainly exhibits the key attributes of bureaucratic-authoritarian regimes, namely "rule by the few in the name of the many" and a powerful role for administrators in the governance of the jurisdiction.

Pressures and Themes

From a global perspective, all of the states represented at the workshop and in this volume confront some common external and internal pressures on their political and governmental institutions. In a period of international economic instability and relative stagnation after a long run of often amazing economic growth, all governments stand accused of inadequate management and planning capacities to assure continued economic success or to lift their respective economies out of the doldrums, particularly in the face of growing concern as to the degradation of renewable resource bases and the sustainability of current policies. All governments face similar questions about the "correct" role of the state as an intervenor in the marketplace, as a coordinator of the economy's international competitiveness, and as a builder of safety nets for economically and socially disadvantaged citizens. Should governments dismantle their planning, regulating, spending and ownership institutions, do less and do it better, and leave the economy and the citizen to the fate of the marketplace? Or, at the other extreme, should they build even more sophisticated executive instruments for economic and social intervention and coordination?

Similarly, all of the countries on the Pacific Rim face increased pressures from groups within their society to share political and governmental power more widely. In almost all of these states (except perhaps the Philippines) such demands are evolutionary rather than revolutionary in nature. Parties, groups and sub-national governments want to participate in a reformed version of the existing system of government. They do not want to tear the system down and replace it with another. The middle class, women, aboriginal peoples, environmentalists, students, farmers, provinces and cities, etc., all express a desire to take part in decisions at the national level which affect them, and to reform political and governmental systems so that their participation is institutionalized. In a global sense all such groups and institutions face a common reaction from the existing power structures, be they democratic or authoritarian: we are sympathetic to your goals, but back off and slow down; the resources and capacities of the state are already stretched, and any substantial disruption of the status quo may endanger the society's capacity to maintain the existing level of economic and social development.

Conforming to these widely-felt pressures, the workshop discussion was organized around two broad themes. The first theme, the performance of executive government, focused on the issue of the capacity of modern governments to administer effectively the wide scope of tasks which they have taken on in recent years, and confronted the dilemma of designing institutions which are capable of planning, deciding, coordinating and delivering what they promise. Part of this discussion dealt with the notion that executive governance can be improved by shrinking the size of the governmental task through privatization, deregulation, downsizing and contracting out. Another part of this discussion took a more mechanistic approach to improving the performance of the executive branch of government. It was concerned with such issues as the capacity of the executive to direct and control the bureaucratic apparatus, the legitimacy of executive succession, the role of the military, and the modernization of bureaucratic processes (e.g., planning, budgeting, human resource management).

The second theme, enhancing participation in the political and governmental systems, followed naturally on the first in that there was widely observed to be a strong — though enigmatic — connection between executive effectiveness and participation. Active and vigorous legislatures, parties, interest groups and protest movements can, on the one hand, contribute enormously to the legitimacy and even the long-term stability of executive leadership. On the other hand, widespread participation in decision-making can also impair the short-term stability and effectiveness of the executive. These are issues which a few years ago had the potential to deeply divide Asian and western scholars. At this meeting there was little division. Awareness of the limitations of collective decision processes and the problems of governability in western democracies was too widespread for there to be any complacent certainty as to the true path to effective participatory government. The common purpose was to understand the context in which different societies were attempting to work out these vexing problems of institution building and to learn — where appropriate — from reform experiences in other societies.

The Challenge of Governability:
A Western Perspective

In recent years there has been much anxiety expressed about the institutions of governance in liberal democratic societies. The attack on western government starts with the size and scope of the edifice and goes on to question the integrity of all of its foundation stones including pluralism, electoral contestation, participation, executive responsibility and accountability. To many this all adds up to a crisis of "governability" – severe doubts about the capacity of liberal democratic governments to provide strong leadership and to govern effectively over a fragmented political system.

In the three western nations participating in this workshop the contemporary concern about governability has focused largely on the massive role which the state has staked out for itself since World War II. This has led to an intense debate about the need to reduce the role of government. In contrast to the Asian experience, in which the appropriate role of government is determined on the basis of pragmatic criteria, the debate in most liberal democratic states has been driven in recent years by a belief that less government is by necessity better government. Most western governments have been roundly criticized as ineffective and unaccountable and there have been many calls to reduce the size and functions of government and tighten the control and scrutiny of the activities which remain.

In Australia, the issue of the size and role of the state has been the subject of much debate in recent years. This debate has been punctuated by reforms of the public service in 1984, 1986 and 1987. These reforms have been intended in part to make the administration leaner and more efficient. There have also been calls for the privatization of Australia's many public enterprises. John Nethercote points out in his paper that the government has changed its approach to the question of privatization of public enterprises. It has moved from a position of attempting to "sustain their legitimacy" by injecting large amounts of capital into a number of the major enterprises, to one where, according the Prime Minister, the governing Australian Labour Party must "embark on a comprehensive debate of the issue of public ownership;" a debate in which "the question should be not 'Why should we sell a given enterprise?' but 'Why should we continue to tie up our resources in it?'"

In the United States and Canada there is also considerable debate about the need to reduce the degree of government intervention. At the national level, this debate has been transformed into some fairly significant reductions in the regulatory activities of both governments (particularly in the fields of transportation, communications, and finance); some limited reductions in services provided directly by government, either through eliminating or "downsizing" the service or contracting it out to the private sector; the devolution of some roles to state or provincial governments; and some privatization of public enterprises. As a signal of its continuing commitment to privatization, the Canadian government has established a Ministry of State for Privatization. Overall, in both the United States and Canada it should be noted that the intensity of the debate about "big" government has greatly exceeded the level of government action. Considering the argument that Richard Simeon makes in his paper about the negative impact of downsizing on the morale and performance of the public officials who remain, a slower than anticipated pace many not be all bad.

In the midst of this soul-searching about the appropriate role and scope of government, Western nations have not entirely lost faith in the notion that the direction, control and accountability of the executive agencies of government are values worth pursuing.

Richard Simeon suggests in his paper that the demand for increased control and accountability has given substance to a number of reform initiatives at the federal level in Canada. He notes that a number of legal restraints have been placed on the bureaucracy to ensure its accountability. For example, the Charter of Rights and Freedoms with its "requirements of non-discrimination, 'fairness,' 'due process,' and 'natural justice,' will be used to subject a wide variety of discretionary bureaucratic action to much greater judicial scrutiny." In addition, citizen's rights to privacy and access to information held by the federal government – at least in principle – have also been enshrined in legislation.

Parallel reforms in Australia have also resulted in the development of a new body of administrative law designed to increase bureaucratic accountability. Freedom of information legislation has been passed at the federal level, and Ombudsman's offices and an Administrative Appeals Board have been established.

At first glance liberal democratic states appear to be well endowed with institutions that facilitate effective participation in the political process. Elections are generally honest and held regularly, multi-party systems are in place, the media are free of government censorship, and there is a multitude of interest groups through which private citizens can make their feelings known. However, while it is true that there is no shortage of formal participatory institutions, effective participation is another matter. Political parties are considered by many to be dysfunctional; interest groups, while no doubt effective in representing the business community and other powerful groups, are not so readily able to demonstrate that they advance the needs of those who lack the resources or access to organize and lobby effectively; the media, while not directly censored, often demonstrate significant structural bias in favour of powerful interests in the society; and legislatures are suffering from declining authority and efficiency.

The workshop participants from the western democracies all noted that the political party systems in their respective countries are not serving as effective vehicles for the provision of widespread public participation in the governing process. In his paper on the United States, Paul Peterson writes that "the weakness of the party system has contributed to the growing disharmony between the executive and the legislature ...", and suggests that to redress this situation the process of choosing the presidential candidate must be altered so as to engender more party unity. Proposals to accomplish this include a "national primary, a series of regional primaries, increased representation for elected officials and conventions, and a nominating convention followed by a national primary."

In Australia there is also an apparent need to increase the democratic nature of the party system. Party leaders are presently chosen by parliamentarians. Nethercote argues that having the leaders chosen by delegates who have been chosen to do so by the party members would be more democratic.

The Canadian political system suffers from a long tradition of regional polarization. Although the current national government can claim to represent all regions of the country, a more typical situation in recent history has had the federal government surviving on the basis of its electoral support in central Canada. Simeon points out that the first-past-the-post, single member constitutency, electoral system has contributed to the inadequacy of electoral politics as a vehicle of participation. This system has been unable to translate percentage of electoral support into parliamentary seats. For example, the Liberal Party has consistently won 20-25% of the vote in western Canada, but seldom elects MPs from the region. Thus, western liberal supporters frequently feel that they have no direct access to the central government. Implementing a form of proportional representation has been touted as a way of resolving this problem, but there is no widespread support for electoral reform of this nature.

Although the legislatures in the liberal democracies are, in a formal sense, fulfilling their mandated duties (they pass bills, provide a forum for national and constituency issues and act as a censorial body on executive action) there is nevertheless much discussion of their declining importance. Concern about the Canadian parliament has focused on the diminution of the power of the House of Commons and its inability to adequately represent all regions. Simeon notes that reform of the parliamentary committee system has helped to lessen this first concern, but indicates that improving regional representation will confront many obstacles as it will inevitably involve the reform of the Senate, a process which now requires the unanimous approval of 11 legislatures (all provinces and the federal government) for the necessary constitutional amendment.

The operations of the Australian parliament have also been viewed in a less than favourable light. In Australia, the Senate is virtually co-equal in power with the House of Representatives and has the authority to withhold approval of budget legislation. Such a withholding occurred in 1975 and resulted in the fall of a government that enjoyed a majority in the lower house. Nethercote writes that this event was viewed with resentment by many Australians and prompted a number of reform proposals, the most dramatic of these being a plan which calls for the automatic dissolution of both houses if the Senate refuses to pass budget legislation.

In the United States, there is much concern about the operations of the Congress. In his paper, Peterson suggests that it has abdicated much of its responsibility to develop coherent and comprehensive policies to deal with the complex issues that confront the country. He points to the increasing fragmentation of Congress as the primary cause of this situation. He states that Congress has become so divided into partisan political, ideological and *ad hoc* policy factions that "it can only agree upon very broad definitions of purpose and resource allocation" with the job of filling in the blanks left to departments and agencies. Ironically, Peterson also notes "that at the same time that Congress is delegating major responsibilities to the executive, it is reserving for its members the capacity to shape many details that in other countries would become merely matters of administrative concern." Thus, Congress has to some degree traded functions with executive agencies, that is, it has assumed greater prerogatives in the area of administrative detail, but has passed off a great deal of its responsibility for substantive policy decisions.

Even more troubling to western liberal democracies than the limitations of elections, the party systems and legislatures as participative vehicles, is the role of interest groups. The immense power of groups has cast a shadow on the legitimacy of virtually every governmental institution except the judiciary. From being embraced as the salvation of liberal democracy, interest groups are now viewed by many observers as the major threat to the legitimacy of democratic governments and the economies of western societies.

In the United States interest groups have become an extremely powerful force. In his paper, Peterson suggests that their influence is particularly significant in Congress, as Congressional election campaigns subsist on the financial support of "interest-based political action committees." However, he also suggests that interest groups have had a pronounced impact on the activities of the bureaucracy which is often reluctant to take decisive action on issues for fear such action will offend a particular interest group.

Interest groups are also a very important component of the Canadian polity. In addition to the traditionally powerful interest groups representing business and labour, a plethora of other groups have surfaced in recent years. These new groups have exerted pressure on the government to deal with the problems associated with such issues as gender, race, or sexual orientation. Simeon suggests in his paper that the recently adopted Charter of Rights and Freedoms has also expanded the opportunity for individuals and groups to influence government policy in that the actions of the legislature, the political executive, and the bureaucracy are all "subject to the discipline of the Charter."

In the papers on the liberal democracies the federal government's sharing of power with sub-national level governments was also raised. Unlike most other federal states, Canada has experienced, in the post-war period, a pronounced shift towards a province-centered model of federalism. The most recent manifestation of this trend is the 1987 Meech Lake Accord on the Constitution. This agreement gave the provinces the right to veto any constitutional amendments affecting major national government and political institutions, a say in the appointment of Supreme Court judges and Senators, and limits on the federal government's exercise of its spending power. In his paper Simeon points out that the extent of decentralization in Canada can make it difficult for the national government to act effectively on the international level as it may be unable to implement any part of a treaty or policy that infringes upon provincial jurisdiction.

The United States currently has a highly centralized federal polity that is supported by an electoral system and an inter-governmental bureaucracy biased towards centralization. However, Peterson writes that this type of federalism is beginning to weaken and that lower levels of government are now sufficiently developed to carry out functions previously handled only by Washington. He suggests that there is some movement towards "a radical sorting out of responsibilities", on which could ultimately lead to reform of the United States federal system and the devolution of power to sub-national governments.

Australia is also examining the relationship between the national and sub-national levels of government in a federal system. An "expert" commission has been established to consider a host of constitutional issues, including a number which relate to the distribution of powers between the Commonwealth (federal) and State governments. In his paper, Nethercote notes that although there have been recommendations to allow the states to become more financially independent through increased taxation powers, the work of the commission has largely enhanced the power of the Commonwealth. For example, it has endorsed a new federal power dealing with "matters affecting the national economy" and "has proposed a range of new concurrent powers for the Commonwealth in navigation, shipping and civil aviation, nuclear energy and ionizing radiation, corporations and securities industry, trade practices of unincorporated entities and individuals, and 'the protection of consumers and their interests.'" Thus, quite unlike Canada, Australia is undergoing a process of significantly increasing federal powers.

By many measures the political systems of the liberal democracies fare well. They are stable, there is little suppression of freedoms, and they offer much opportunity for political and economic competition. Nevertheless these systems are under much stress. In recent years they have been battered by a host of problems and increasingly vocal demands. There seems little doubt that the shape of liberal democratic government in western nations must change in order to mitigate what amounts to a direct challenge to its ability to govern.

Guided Development – An Asian Perspective on Institutional Change

In most Asian polities the national government plays an all powerful role. At the national level, the political executive and the bureaucracy (and in some cases the military), wield most of the political power. This in turn diminishes the opportunities for wider public participation in the decision-making process. These characteristics are key features of the bureaucratic-authoritarian, soft authoritarian, or guided development style of government common in this part of the world.

In recent years there has been widespread and often strident criticism of many of these regimes. Much of this criticism has revolved around the issues of political instability, the failure or absence of participatory mechanisms, the suppression of basic human and political rights, and political and bureaucratic corruption. In many jurisdictions, these concerns have escalated into a powerful force for change.

Executive performance has proven to be a fundamental question in most jurisdictions. In some countries the issue is as fundamental as the legitimacy of executive succession, with reform efforts directed towards institutionalizing and stabilizing the process. For others the very activities governments engage in have been questioned and policies such as privatization, downsizing, and devolution of power to sub-national levels have been mooted. A third issue that has arisen is the need to reform the bureaucracy to improve executive control over it.

Executive succession is a major problem in Thailand where there have been 15 military coups since 1932. It has been proposed that the direct election of the prime minister would reduce the role that the military plays in determining who leads the government. Likhit Dhiravegin addresses this proposal in his paper and, while he acknowledges that the direct election of the prime minister would give the position "continuity" and "confidence," he warns of the hazards associated with such a change. Foremost among these is the concern that a prime minister who is directly elected by the people would become so confident that he would be reluctant to step down and could ultimately challenge the authority of traditional institutions. Despite the concern over the role of the military in government, it appears unlikely that its share of political power in Thailand will diminish significantly in the near future. And in fact, it may even increase, if a proposal to alter the constitution to allow government officials (including military officers) to concurrently hold political office, is implemented.

In Korea, like Thailand, much controversy has surrounded the question of executive succession. The 1980 Constitution called for the indirect election of the President by an electoral college. Opposition forces protested, often violently, that this system was easily manipulated by the President and the ruling party, and demanded direct elections. President Chun's ruling Democratic Justice Party (DJP) stonewalled this demand for a long time, but in July 1987, in a sudden and dramatic about face, the DJP introduced a reform proposal package that allowed for direct presidential elections. This reform was incorporated in a new Constitution that was ratified by national referendum in October 1987, just in time for the December presidential elections. This institutionalization of a widely acceptable process of executive succession is a most significant development in Korean politics, for as Chung-Si Ahn states in his paper "no previous President in the post-independent political history of South Korea has ever stepped down voluntarily from power."

In none of the countries represented in this volume is the issue of leadership legitimacy more critical than in Bangladesh. Since the country's independence in 1972, it has had two of its leaders assassinated and has experienced three successful and 35 unsuccessful military coups. The current Ershad regime assumed power in 1982, following a bloodless coup that toppled a civilian government.

Mohammad Mohabbat Khan and Habib Mohammad Zafarullah cite three reasons in their paper to explain the absence of a legitimate system for changing leaders: 1) the failure of political parties to develop into credible organizations; 2) the cooptation of the senior levels of the civilian bureaucracy by the dictatorship; and 3) perhaps most important of all, the enormous influence of the military, which views itself as the only force that can keep the country afloat. President Ershad has recently proposed that this concept of the military as the "safeguard of the nation" be institutionalized by constitutional amendment. Such a move would certainly further impede the development of a legitimate process for changing political leaders.

Clearly the institutionalization of an executive succession process that is free of military intervention is critical in countries like Thailand, Korea and Bangladesh. It is indeed a curious irony that while the *raison d'être* for the involvement of the military in the political process is to provide stability, exactly the opposite (military coups and political assassinations) have in the past been common occurrences.

Reform of the bureaucracy in order to improve executive control over it has taken place in a number of Asian countries. In Japan, the bureaucracy is an extremely important player in all facets of the policy-making process. Its senior leadership is in fact closely connected with the ruling Liberal Democratic Party and the major Japanese business interests. Despite the powerful position it enjoys, and a reputation for being extremely competent and free of corruption, the bureaucracy has recently been the focus of significant administrative reform. During the workshop discussion, Toru Yano noted that the management and coordination functions of government have been greatly enhanced, ministries agencies and bureaus have been reorganized, budget ceilings established, and a thorough review of existing programs carried out with the result that there have been many substantive changes in program areas. He also suggested that reform is still pending in an area that has recently been addressed by the liberal democracies; that is, the the protection and privacy of personal data and rights of access to government information.

In his paper on Thailand, Likhit writes that the focus of bureaucratic reform in that country is on "curbing the continued expansion of the system" which witnessed the formation of 25 new departments and over 500 new divisions in the period between 1969 and 1982. He notes that the Thai administrative structure is replete with duplication and although the government has given much attention to the problems of overlapping functions and coordination of government activities, a thorough reform of the bureaucratic system is "still pending."

Khan and Zafarullah describe a situation in Bangladesh where bureaucratic corruption is pervasive and the civil service is for the most part unresponsive to public demands. They note that there are provisions to exert a much tighter control over the actions of the civil service, but the implementation of these measures is often "counter-productive," if they are operationalized at all, and the prospect for improved bureaucratic performance is dismal indeed.

In Hong Kong, administrative reform has sought to bolster the role of the bureaucracy rather than diminish it. In his paper Lau Siu-kai notes that the Hong Kong government, faced with the uncertainties of the transfer of the colony's sovereignty, the diminished legitimacy of its rule, and the failure of Britain's efforts to reform the political system, confronts a severe governability problem. The government has responded to these pressures by increasing its reliance on the bureaucracy in order to maintain a stable polity and economy. This increased reliance has prompted a number of changes to enhance the bureaucratic environment. These measures include better pensions, better training, easier accessibility to private sector jobs after retirement, and postponement of the creation of a powerful ombudsman's office which could limit bureaucratic discretion.

There was also considerable discussion at the workshop about the appropriate role and functions of the public sector. A number of Asian governments, like their counterparts in the liberal democracies of the west, have implemented policies that deal with the size and scope of the state. Public enterprises have been privatized and positions eliminated from the national government.

Through reorganization and privatization, the Japanese government is moving to reduce the number of public enterprises to their 1965 level. Japan National Railway and Nippon Telegraph and Telephone, two of the country's largest public enterprises, have recently been taken over by the private sector. At the same time there have been major cuts in the number of public servants employed by the ministries of the central government. During the workshop, Yano noted that in the last five years the combined effect of privatization and downsizing has decreased the number of national and local government positions by over 220,000.

However, while these changes have been substantial, it should be noted that the basic structure, rules, or assembly of interests that make up the Japanese bureaucratic environment have not been challenged. Even the reduced level of state intervention resulting from such policies as privatization will be largely offset by other government initiatives. For example, Yano also pointed out that the recently promulgated Fourth Comprehensive National Development Program will provide a framework in which all economic development, both at the national and local level, will be conducted until the year 2000.

Malaysia has made extensive use of public enterprises as part of its strategy to reduce the serious communal conflict the country has experienced since independence. This conflict is largely a result of the economic subordination of the majority Malay population and the association of ethnic group with social occupation. In 1971 the government introduced the National Economic Policy (NEP), which has as its goal the raising of the Malay ownership of the economy to 30% by 1990 – a dramatic increase from the 1969 level of 1.5%. The vehicle most often used to achieve this objective has been the public enterprise. However, Zainah Anwar notes in her paper that the government has recently come to question this strategy. Most Malaysian public enterprises have a poor financial record and the government has been forced to divert an increasing amount of money that could have been earmarked for economic development (particularly Malay development) to servicing public enterprise debt loads. As a result, the government has begun to privatize a number of public enterprises. This will have the effect, at least temporarily, of reducing the degree of government intervention. However, it is unlikely that this is a permanent trend. The NEP continues to have as its goal the raising of Malay economic ownership (presently at 18%) to the target level of 30%. Such a goal will undoubtedly necessitate a high degree of government involvement in the economy.

The government of Bangladesh is currently pursuing a policy of wholesale privatization of public enterprises in the financial and industrial sectors – this policy being largely a response to the demands of foreign aid donor countries and agencies, upon which Bangladesh is dependent upon for survival. But, Khan and Zafarullah point out that privatization has been facilitated by a series of low interest, long-term government loans on easy terms. Thus, although the nature of government intervention has changed, there has been no significant reduction in the degree of intervention.

On the surface, the combined effect of these changes to executive government would seem to indicate a diminution of the role of national governments throughout the region. However, this would be a less than accurate impression as in virtually all Asian countries the central government retains firm control over the nation's helm. This dominance is facilitated by common cultural traditions that lend themselves to strong, elite-dominated government. Such policies as privatization are normally implemented solely for pragmatic reasons, and often reductions of government activity in one area are offset by increases in another. In fact, there is a common perception of *noblesse oblige* – almost an eastern version of Toryism – that makes inter-vention an obligatory function of government.

Perhaps the most significant criticism of Asian polities is the limited opportunity they present for citizens to participate effectively in the political process. In a sense, this is part and parcel of the government's role of guiding the development of the nation; such guidance, it is argued, requires that the executive be able to exercise its power without being impeded by what it perceives to be excessive demands for participation from a politicized and pluralistic citizenry.

Many Asian countries exhibit restrictions on the level of political participation that are antithetical to the liberal democratic model of government. Although these restrictions are normally state-initiated, the political culture of the region is again reflected in the make-up of the political system. Common cultural values such as deference, personalism and subordination also contribute to low levels of participation throughout the region.

Terms such as "controlled," "restricted" or "demi-democracy" were used by some Asian analysts at the workshop to describe their political systems. They refer to governments that are committed, albeit to varying degrees, to the principles of liberal democracy, but find it necessary to limit participation so as to ensure political and economic stability. Manifestations of restricted participation are found throughout the political and governmental systems of the region. The polity is frequently dominated by a single party or an elite group; electoral systems often favor the ruling party; the media may be censored; and for the most part, legislatures are little more than rubber stamp institutions designed to legitimize the political executive. In general, there is a shortage of institutions which facilitate meaningful mass participation in the political process.

This situation has prompted much call for political reform. In some countries these demands for reform have been expressed forcefully and even violently, and deal with such basic issues as the holding of free and open elections, or censorship of the media. In others, demands are more subdued, often focusing on the absence or ineffectiveness of participatory institutions.

Of all the Asia Pacific countries, Korea stands out as the one in which the demands for increased participation and openness are the most widespread and visible. The country has been wracked by massive and violent public demonstrations calling for greater democracy. The government's recent response to these demonstrations included releasing political prisoners, lifting the ban on political activities imposed on a number of important opposition leaders, relaxing media censorship, increasing local autonomy, and allowing for the direct election of the President. Ahn notes that these reforms will do much to increase the "fairness and accountability" of the political system, but cautions that "complete civilianization" of government remains an achievement for the future, as the state apparatus, particularly the military, will continue to dominate the relatively weak social and political organizations.

Jon Quah's paper describes Singapore as a polity in which decisions are made by a small political elite, and widespread public participation or pressure group activity is conspicuous by its absence.

He notes however, that the drop in electoral support experienced by the ruling People's Action Party in the 1984 election, can be viewed as a clear signal that the public expects "more participation and consultation in the policy-making process . . ."

To accommodate the desire for greater public involvement in the political system, the government introduced the National Agenda as means of ascertaining citizens' views on the major policy issues, and establishing a publicly-forged blue print for the future. The process involves a series of public forums, constituency walk-abouts by ministers, and dialogue with professional groups.

The Singaporean legislature is characterized by the lack of opposition members and highly centralized policy-making. The current government has expressed concern that as a result of these features backbench MPs are becoming lethargic. To redress the situation, it has formed a number of standing parliamentary committees to make these MPs more effective. The functions of these committees include evaluating and suggesting changes to policy, providing regular input to ministers, and assessing the effectiveness of policy implementation.

Quah suggests that although these reforms will increase the level of political participation and reduce the control of the ruling elite, they are "incremental" rather than "comprehensive" and do not threaten the "controlled" nature of Singapore's democracy.

Anwar notes in her paper on Malaysia that regional demands for increased participation have emerged as a challenge to the authority of the central government. This regional aspiration finds its home in the two east Malaysian states of Sabah and Sarawak. These states have greatly different ethnic, political and historical backgrounds from the rest of the country and resent the imposition of a Malay/Muslim dominated federal government. This has led to strained federal/state relations and pressure to reduce central authority. To combat this tension, several reforms to the administrative structure have been proposed including "recruiting more Sabahans and Sarawakians into the federal civil service . . . [and] encouraging greater social interaction of federal officers in Sabah and Sarawak with the local populace."

In Malaysia, there are also strong pressures insisting that the views of Islamic fundamentalists are to be reflected in government policy. The government's long-standing policy of secularism has recently eroded in the face of a widespread Islamic revivalism advocating the creation of a full Islamic state. To date the government's response to this pressure has been *ad hoc*, with change focused primarily in the education and financial sectors, and it has shown little support for the much more radical policies advocated by the "politicized Islamic revivalists." However, with the former

President of the Muslim Youth Movement of Malaysia, now occupying a senior position in the ruling UMNO party and the cabinet post of Minister of Education, this group has begun to participate in the decision-making processes at the highest level of Malaysian government. Anwar suggests that if Islamic fundamentalism continues to grow, the government could be forced to undertake a much more significant transformation of the polity in order to appease the "religious zealot's imperative mission to effect an Islamic social order."

The question of political participation in Hong Kong takes quite a different twist from that in other Asia Pacific nations. Political parties and other forms of participation have traditionally played a minor role in the polity and it is only very recently that there have been any elected officials in the government. Since 1982, when the issue of Hong Kong's sovereignty came to the forefront, there has been a noticeable increase in the demands for participation and the introduction of representative government. However, this heightened political activity is not widespread and is largely confined to a small group of middle class professionals.

Despite what would seem to be a powerful force in the creation of demand for participatory democracy — the fear of a communist-style government imposed on Hong Kong by the People's Republic of China (PRC) — most Hong Kong citizens do not support the democratic movement. In his paper Lau points to three explanations for this. First, as independence is not a possibility for Hong Kong, the only substitute for the present system of government is that found in the PRC, which is clearly an unacceptable alternative to most residents. Second, the sphere of activities performed by the government is small and the people do not require much in the way of participatory mechanisms to deal with it. Third, Hong Kong's economic prosperity presents many avenues of upward mobility and has acted as a salve for the potential problems that may arise from limited political participation.

The Hong Kong Legislative Council has been the focus of a number of recent reforms to increase its representativeness and powers vis-a-vis the executive. More of its members are now elected and its investigative powers have been increased. As desirable as these reforms may be to the nascent democratic movement, they have presented some difficulties to effective governance. The reformed legislature has become a factionalized assembly in which consensus has become increasingly difficult to achieve. Lau regrets that at such a critical juncture in its history, Hong Kong's administration is "curbed" by a "conflict-infested legislature" that lacks the "unity of purpose and action to constructively take part in policy-making or effectively oversee the work of government."

In Thailand, perhaps the key participatory issue is the ability of the system to accommodate both the old forces (the bureaucratic elite, both civilian and military) and the new forces (the emerging middle classes) in the political process. Likhit coins the term "demi-democracy" to describe the current power sharing arrangement in which the traditional component of the ruling elite is appointed to the Senate and the new element is elected to the House of Representatives. Although this system has been harshly criticized (largely because of the suspicion that politicians are buying their way into positions of power) Likhit suggests it is likely to continue for, as he states in his paper, "Thai society has become too complex for strong one-man rule calling all the shots. [And] at the same time, the demand for a full democracy in which the traditional bureaucracy is reduced to a passive role as executors of policy, is not foreseeable in the near future."

Likhit also suggests that democracy and political participation in Thailand would be enhanced by the devolution of power and the establishment of a system of effective local government. He notes that local government is "the foundation upon which the democratic process at the national level can develop." In his paper, he lists a series of proposals to strengthen sub-national government, including elections for provincial Governors and local leaders, and turning the Tambol Council, a commune-like unit that acts as an arm of the provincial government, into a unit of local government. However, Likhit points to a number of reasons why the centre is unwilling to devolve real power to provincial and local levels. Foremost among them are staunch opposition to such schemes from the central bureaucracy, particularly the Interior Ministry, and a fear that increased local autonomy will contribute to political fragmentation and threaten national security.

Demands for increased participation in the political process are numerous throughout the region and most governments are making some attempt to accommodate them. But increased participation is unlikely to spell the end of the rigid authoritarian style of government that is common in Asia and there will undoubtedly continue to be many examples of heavy-handed government action. However, criticism needs to be muted by the recognition of differing perspectives on the role of government. In Asia, there exists a kind of *quid pro quo* relationship between the governed and the government. In this relationship, restricted rights and elite domination may be accepted as the trade-off for economic prosperity. Most Asian governments have been remarkably successful in promoting rapid economic growth, the fruits of which have been enjoyed by a relatively large percentage of the population.

In this light, it must also be remembered that demands for increased participation are not always compatible with demands for more effective government. For example, governments in many Asian countries have facilitated rapid economic growth (effective executive performance) by assuming all-powerful roles (restricted partici- pation). Rapid liberalization of these polities is not without risk to continued economic growth. Western governments also face similar dilemmas when they are asked to accommodate the demands of an increasing number of groups in the context of fiscal restraint and conflicting demands for less government and the diffusion of political authority to sub-national levels of government. The reconciliation of such seemingly disparate claims represents a significant challenge to governments of all descriptions.

Conclusion

The most obvious fact which emerged from this forum on the evolution of political systems throughout the Pacific Rim is that while there are shared problems of governance amongst liberal-democratic and bureaucratic-authoritarian or soft-authoritarian states, there is little sign of shared solutions. In many western states inadequate executive performance is evoking calls for radical surgery to reduce the size of the administrative state; at the same time, concerns about partici- pation call forth proposals for elaborate institutional reform and cries of despair about the debilitating tendencies inherent in existing pluralist institutions. In most Asian states on the Pacific Rim, the concern about executive performance is focused on the inherent instability of regimes which depend on varying combinations of economic growth, strong bureaucracies, and armies for continuity and legitimacy. Wider participation seems, on the one hand, to offer a solution to the problems of unstable regimes and, on the other, to threaten their very existence and the economic prosperity upon which they often depend.

The clear message from the workshop discussion and the papers which follow is that the strategies which states on the Pacific Rim adopt to meet related pressures for effective executive performance and meaningful participation will depend on the particular combination of domestic and external circumstances in which they are working out these challenges. Observers in western states may envy the effectiveness of what they see as forceful executive governments in many Asian societies coupled with flexible, responsive economic institutions; similarly, analysts in many Asian states may long for the legitimacy and stability they see in the pluralist political systems of western societies. But the wide variety of economic, social and security environments in which the various polities are evolving virtually guarantees that convergence around one institutional model balancing effectiveness and participation is not in the cards.

Korean Politics in a
Period of Transition

Chung-Si Ahn

Introduction

South Korea today is in a period of rapid political transition. A political era characterized by firm authoritarianism ended abruptly in 1979 with the assassination of President Park Chung-Hee, who had ruled the country for eighteen years. Following his death, many different individuals and political groups vied for power during the short-lived interim government of President Choi Kyu-Hah. The so-called *Yushin* (Revitalization) constitution had been promulgated by President Park mainly to strengthen and prolong his presidency, and it left the country with a political framework that could not ensure an orderly succession of power. Nor did Park succeed in institutionalizing a political party system through which new leadership could emerge in a peaceful and orderly manner. With Park's departure from the scene, therefore, the social and political system of South Korea faced a state of potential explosion and acute polarization (Han 1986: 116-121).

It was these social and political conditions that enabled Major General Chun Doo-Hwan and his associates to step in and take over power. Chun retired from his military office and assumed the Presidency in August 1980 following the resignation of the interim President. Upon coming to power, he promised to carry out a series of social reform measures and he attempted to build new political institutions by replacing the *Yushin* constitution with a new amended one, which nevertheless retained the system of indirect presidential election. The new constitution, prepared in closed session by the Constitutional Amendment Deliberation Committee, was put to a national referendum on October 22, 1980. Ninety-five per cent of the electorate voted in this referendum and 91 per cent of those voting approved the new constitution. Thus Korea's Fifth Republic came into being.

Korea possesses the vigor of a dynamic society and an industrious people. The country has achieved a remarkable rate of economic growth in the last three decades. During the last twenty years, its population has achieved a literacy rate which is one of the highest in the world. The economy has matured and has created a substantial middle class which appears sufficient enough to provide the base for a stable democratic polity. The economic and social development which has taken place in the last quarter of the century is often the envy of other developing countries. However, the economic and social "miracle" has not yet been matched by a corresponding degree of progress in the political sphere. As a result, the country still suffers from serious ideological polarization, social unrest, political instability, and the potential for political upheaval.

Korea's political situation has been volatile for the last two years. It has been fraught with violent protests and major political confrontations between the ruling power group and the opposition forces. The country found itself on a collision course during the month of June 1987, until a dramatic compromise was reached between the government and the opposition forces over measures to settle the constitutional issue and speed up the democratization process. Following the announcement on June 29 by Mr. Roh Tae-Woo, then the chairman of the ruling Democratic Justice Party, of an eight-point democratization package, a new constitution has been written on the basis of bipartisan agreement for the first time in the nation's nearly 40 years of modern political history. If the political time-table is adhered to, a democratic political system based on the new constitution will succeed the Fifth Republic in early 1988. Will this process of transition lead the country to genuine democracy? Can the benefits of Korea's economic prosperity be supplemented by a "political miracle"? Will the country become the envy of the world for its political progress as well? The purpose of this essay is to shed some light on these crucial questions.

The current system of South Korean politics represents a mixture of elements including aspects of "strong state control," "restricted democratic processes," and a "mixed economy" with an emphasis on capitalist, export-oriented policy. These characteristics of the polity partly reflect the legacy of the country's past political history and its geopolitical setting, as well as the social and political changes it has undergone during the past several decades. In order to reveal the underlying causes of what is currently happening in the political life of the country, the following sections will provide an analysis of Korean political traditions and will trace the evolution of major events. I will also attempt to offer a broad outlook on where the system seems to be heading in the near and long-term future in light of prevailing social and political conditions.

The Rise of a Strong, "Developmental" State

Before Korea left its state of relative isolation and began to be exposed to the outside world in the late nineteenth century, it had been ruled by a monarchical authoritarian government with a highly centralized bureaucracy. The country had known a long tradition of centralized power and unitary government in which all the subnational political units were "created" by the state authority. All social and political organizations below the national level were "subordinate to the national government and subject(ed) to stringent control by the central regime." These sub-units possessed "only those powers and discretionary authority specifically given to them by the central government." (Ahn & Kim 1987: 33). The tendency to centralize and concentrate power in the government was reinforced in the twentieth century under Japanese colonial rule. For 36 years beginning in 1910, Japan ruled Korean society with a centralized colonial administration, and divide-and-rule tactics.

When the country was liberated in 1945, Korea inherited a system of centralized executive power. There were no countervailing social organizations to check the state's bureaucratic structure, nor were there any interest groups, such as labor unions, to institutionalize effective channels for articulating and aggregating popular demands through electoral participation. Instead, the "overdeveloped" state executive institutions such as the bureaucracy and the police were opposed by weak civil organizations unable to balance the power of the state. The division of the country into South and North, and the ensuing war (1950-1953), led to the establishment of a strong and large military presence within the country.

Representative democracy, which was introduced in the South for the first time in the nation's history during the First Republic, failed because of the charismatic leadership of Syngman Rhee, and the fact that the parliamentary system that followed Rhee's 1960 downfall at the hands of a student revolution, was not given enough time to take root. Ever since 1948, and particularly since the cease-fire in 1953, South Korea has faced a constant security threat from the North. This has required the nation to maintain a large military establishment and a capability to mobilize national resources for defence against both internal subversion and external attack. These requirements have favored the rise of a "strong state." Ideological rigidity and frequent abuse of the state apparatus to augment the oligarchical control by the ruling power bloc have been two of the major political consequences of Korea's strong state system. Progressive ideological movements and attempts to articulate demands for change through political organizations have often been suppressed under the pretext of preventing subversive political activities and consolidating national security against external threats. The process of nation-building, of industrialization and the need for authoritarian political control, have further contributed to the dominance of the state and its hegemony relative to local political units and other social groups and organizations (Ahn & Kim 1987: 34-40).

The existence of a strong state also implies the "politicization of social structure and processes." The concept of a corporatist state is often used to explain the characteristics of this kind of political process. A corporatist state has a special set of patterns and relationships between state and social groups in which "formally organized, non-competitive, officially sanctioned and coercive functional associations monopolize interest representation in given functional or occupational categories and in turn are supervised by agents of the state bureaucracy" (Choi 1984:26 and Schmitter 1979). Such a polity tends to show the following characteristics:

1.   The state apparatus enjoys relative autonomy vis-a-vis societal pressures and popular demands;

2.   The state can easily penetrate or dominate the society by means of state-guided official ideology, culture, etc;

3.   There exists a high degree of state bureaucratization and an overdeveloped coercive state apparatus vis-a-vis other social and political institutions such as political parties;

4.   The state elite is capable of mobilizing national resources and social groups, with less chance of facing organized resistance, in order to instill certain ideologies, policies and programs (e.g. economic development), and the decisions and priorities are usually made and set by top-down methods.

The political implications of the strong state system of Korea will be elaborated further in the next section.

In economists' terms, the strong state is equivalent to the "hard state" described by Gunnar Myrdal or the "developmental state" defined by the Institute of Development Studies at Sussex University

(White and Wade 1984), which is said to have the potential to provide strong leadership for economic growth. The regimes and leaders of both South and North Korea inherited pre-existing state systems capable of effectively controlling the societal sectors and implementing economic programs with relatively low levels of popular or organized resistance. Industrialization in Korea has been accompanied by active, often aggressive, government intervention. The importance of state action in promoting capitalist development becomes more prominent if one looks beyond economic policy to the spheres of culture, ideology, social structure, and politics. The historical development which provided Korea with a state system that is largely independent of any particular class base constitutes a crucial factor in understanding the political economy of industrialization and the characteristics of social and political change in Korea. As Clive Hamilton (1984: 43) concluded, the development of "Korean capitalism" by and large, has been "as much a political process as an economic one."

Korea's process of industrialization conforms to the model of the "hard," "corporatist," and "developmental" state in many respects, although it differs in many respects from Latin American cases. From the beginning, the government was capable of actively promoting fast-paced industrialization without serious resistance from either capitalist or working classes. Also, the government was powerful enough to intervene actively in the private business sector in terms of planning and direction, by means of a tightly organized economic policy developed in accordance with priorities set by the state elite. Thus, the advantages Korea has enjoyed are largely the result of deliberate state policies in the past to create new opportunities in the international marketplace and to exploit comparative advantages which existed at the time. The high rates of Korea's economic growth are also attributable to the fact that the government has been able to force capitalists, laborers, and farmers to follow the officially staged growth policy and to pursue their respective interests "within" the context of the national interest. As David C. Cole observed (1979: 81-82):

> First of all, the government has been effective in defining national priorities through the five-year plans and the annual development programs. Everybody has been made aware of the priorities given to exports, investment, savings, and hard work. Secondly, the government has been quick to perceive deviations from these national priorities and to take action against the miscreants. Thirdly, the government has had a powerful set of

instruments with which to reward good performance and penalize the failures of the greedy.

Other factors contributing to the rate of economic growth which are often cited as attributable to Korea's "developmental" state are:

1. The actions of the state to change class structures and establish political conditions conducive to industrialization in such areas as land reform, subordination of agriculture to industry, nationalist ideological mobilization, and political (and often repressive) control of labor;

2. The employment of technology appropriate for its factor endowment and level of development;

3. The efficient operation by government of public enterprises that the private sector is unable or unwilling to provide (e.g. in such areas as electric power, steel, transportation, fertilizer, communications, etc.);

4. The effective control of foreign investment and the regulation of foreign enterprises;

5. Favorable world market situations that enabled Korea to have access to foreign capital as well as to sell its exports.

(Cole 1979; Leudde-Neurath 1984; Enos 1984; Michell 1984; Hamilton 1984; Jacobsson 1984; Moore 1984).

Contrary to the theories of neo-classical economies, Korea's economy, like the economies of other Asian NIC's, "has grown rapidly as much in spite of as because of high-level government intervention" (Robison & Rodan 1986: 54).

One should not, of course, overlook the negative effects of the "hard state." State planning and excessive intervention often cause inefficiency and mismanagement of investment. It is also the case that state intervention has aggravated inequality and has produced "parasitic corporate groups, both private and public." State-initiated economic success, aided by outlawing strikes and suppressing labor movements, has also prevented the growth of independent labor organizations and their alliance for exerting political power. Family control of big corporations (*Jaebul*) does not seem to wane. The possibilities of corruption and the cooptation of business by political interests have often materialized. The approach of "growth first, distribution later" has often had high costs in terms of freedom and individual rights. The Korean economy began to show the signs of these strains during the later period of Park Chung-Hee's rule. In fact, the seeds of President Park's downfall took root, in no small part, as a result of economic achievements. The economic prosperity transformed the whole society, and along with the "Miracle of the Han River" came an explosion of political demands and rising expectations (Olson 1980), to which we will turn later on.

The basic structure of Korea's political economy has not been altered by the new Chun government. The modifications are largely changes of nuance. Whether the government's continued intervention in the economy will correct these negative elements or whether the new leadership that will emerge in 1988 will be effective and powerful enough to control them is not yet clear. The prospects are not very likely that the current features of the Korean economy will change in any significant way within the next five to ten years. In spite of the drawbacks, it remains true nonetheless that Korea's developmental state has proved, on balance, to be effective in getting the "fundamental" macroeconomic policies right.

Restricted Democracy and the End of the Park Era

The political system of South Korea can best be characterized as a "restricted democracy." This is a system in which formal democratic institutions and a legal order based on the principle of constitutionalism are officially proclaimed as the national ideology and source of legitimacy, but are only allowed to function conditionally, within a set of restrictions. The government is committed, at least in principle, to observing the rules of the democratic game and is expected to conform to the political procedures common to liberal democracy: to permit partisan politics; to refrain from censorship of the mass media; to honor popular demands; to allow multiple agents of socialization; and to encourage alternative channels for political inputs and the articulation of interests. However, these rules and procedures are only allowed to function "conditionally" in the sense that the ruling power bloc—be it a military junta or an alliance between international capitalism, the state and the local bourgeoisie—does not permit free contests for power to the point where they could result in its own defeat.

Under restricted democracy, the formal democratic institutions function to guarantee the core interests of the power bloc. In such a polity, the masses theoretically have the means to remove the top power holder through legally permitted institutional channels such as the electoral system. But in reality, political participation by the masses cannot exercise an influence strong enough to change the ruling party or the top leadership in the government. Such a polity

has a semblance of democracy but lacks a permanent institutionalization of its rules and procedures. Restricted democracy is unstable
because: (1) without firmly established legal norms and procedures,
political power is usually embedded in the charisma of a single leader
or in the factional elements among the ruling groups; (2) the processes
of political change and transfer of power are often carried through
with violence, coercion and repression instead of by peaceful means;
(3) the power bloc can easily resort to extra-institutional measures
such as cancelling the election when its core interest is perceived to be
threatened; (4) lacking legitimacy and coherence, the existing
political framework cannot effectively reconcile the differences among
rival political forces; and (5) attempts at institutionalization in such
cases, as exemplified by the recent political debates on constitutional
reform in South Korea, became themselves the object of major
political conflicts among opposing political groups. In fact, the system
can function in a democratic fashion "only if the ruling power bloc has
potential political support from broad segments of the population" so
that it is not in danger of losing power (Im 1987: 251).

Up to 1972, with the exception of the period 1960-63, South
Korea was under a restricted democratic political system. Despite the
Korean War and the necessity of retaining huge armed forces,
President Syngman Rhee provided considerable latitude for
democratic political processes to function, albeit within a framework
of authoritarian decisionmaking. It was only when Syngman Rhee
and his Liberal Party faced the prospect of being defeated that the
regime began to manipulate the state institutions in favor of the
ruling bloc. The Rhee regime was kicked out of power by the student
uprising of 1960 mainly because it had manipulated the democratic
institutions in its favor, especially through the amendments to the
constitution and the arbitrary changes in the electoral rules. South
Korea under Park Chung-Hee continued the state of restricted
democracy until 1972, except for the two years of military rule which
followed the coup of May, 1961. Lacking a sufficient base of popular
support and legitimacy to break with the tradition of civilian control,
the military regime had to abide by the national consensus on
democratic rules of governance. Therefore, the regime sought a
political framework that would allow restricted democracy and would
guarantee the core interests of the military power group. To cite one
example, the junta tried to retain power by winning the confidence of
the people through competitive elections. Park Chung-Hee had an
advantage over his civilian opponent from being the incumbent, and
his party won two presidential and parliamentary elections in 1963
and 1967 by considerable margins.

The Park regime also sought to resolve the legitimacy dilemma
by resorting to policies and programs that would provide an economic

base for popular support. The national drive toward modernization became the economic platform and the export-oriented policy was vigorously pursued. Taking advantage of Korea's lower wages relative to wages in the developed markets, this policy achieved considerable success in helping the regime to gain tacit approval among the masses as well as with the majority of the elite coalition. Even a substantial segment of the opposition political parties gave tacit approval to Park's modernization programs. The success was reflected in a greatly increased margin of support in the elections for the presidency and national assembly in 1967, compared to the elections in 1963. In the presidential election of November 1963, the recently retired General Park received 46.7 per cent of the votes cast, while his major opponent, Yun Bo-Sun, received 45 per cent. Park won the 1967 election by a more comfortable margin by receiving 51.4 per cent compared with Yun's 40.9 per cent.

However, the situation had changed by 1970. Distrust and disaffection with Park's authoritarian rule grew stronger. For example, Park narrowly defeated his opponent Kim Dae-Jung in the 1971 presidential election. In fact he lost in urban areas by 44.9 per cent vote to Kim's 51.4 per cent. The number of seats held by Park's Democratic Republican Party (DRP) in the national assembly also dropped. The DRP won 48.9 per cent of votes cast in 1970 over the New Democratic Party's (NDP) 42.5 per cent. In the 9th (1973) and 10th (1978) national assembly elections, support for DRP dropped to 38.7 and 31.7 per cent respectively, while the major opposition party (NDP) mobilized 32.5 per cent of votes in 1973 and 32.8 per cent in 1978 (Kihl, *et al.*, 1987: 56-61). At the same time, despite the remarkable rates of economic and export growth, Park's economic policy also began to be perceived negatively. A growth-oriented approach which increased disparities in income distribution became questionable in the eyes of many, especially the urban poor and industrial labor sectors. The increasing state intervention in industrial relations was viewed as collaboration between government and big business to divert a distributional conflict between capital and labor. Growing popular demands for wage increases and democratization were frequently met by a coercive and repressive use of force. The student movement, the opposition party and progressive intellectuals brought these issues onto the political battleground. The power bloc began to realize that the opposition forces and populist alliance had the potential to pose a fundamental challenge to the ruling group, even under the restricted democratic system. It was this sense of imminent crisis that precipitated the declaration of the *Yushin* Reform, following the declaration of martial law on October 17, 1972. Under the emergency powers, Park Chung-Hee imposed a new constitution which empowered him to control the legislature and judiciary more tightly. He was given the power of appointing one-third of the assembly members. The *Yushin* constitution also instituted indirect election of the president by an electoral college.

In 1978-79, demonstrations were mounted in protest at Park's pre-empting a fourth term and at his excessive control over the assembly with only a minority of popular support. Riots in Pusan and Masan and rivalry within the core power bloc resulted in a dramatic ending to Park's rule and many elements of the *Yushin* system when the president himself was assassinated on October 26, 1979. Korea once again reverted to a form of restricted democracy under the Chun government after the downfall of the Fourth Republic.

The Fifth Republic

Upon assuming power, the Chun government sought to relax Park Chung-Hee's tightly controlled regime and to return to a system of restricted democracy. The government restored in some measure the Western-style civil liberties of speech, assembly, and political activity. Unlike its predecessor, the Constitution of the Fifth Republic limited presidential tenure to a single term of seven years. It was also explicitly written into the constitution that there could be no amendment to enable the incumbent president to extend his term. In addition, President Chun also considerably reduced the political role played by the notorious KCIA and changed its name to the national Security Planning Agency. The power of the legislature was also increased somewhat over those granted by the 1972 constitution.

Nevertheless, the new constitution replicated some features of the earlier one imposed under President Park. Indirect presidential election, for example, was retained under the constitution of the Fifth Republic. According to Article 40, the president was to be selected by an electoral college of more than 5,000 electors who were to be "elected by universal, equal, direct and secret ballot by citizens." This electoral system was weighted unfairly in favor of the ruling power holders, as its critics claimed. Also, the presidency continued to enjoy extensive executive power and retained the right to dissolve the national assembly.

The method of seat allocation in the national assembly favoring the majority party was also left intact. According to the Fifth Republic Constitution, the two candidates gaining the highest number of votes in each of the 92 districts are elected. There was a high probability that one of the two would be a government candidate. In addition, the party obtaining the largest number of seats automatically received two-thirds of the 92 seats reserved for "national representation."

Nevertheless, a dozen political parties appeared during the earlier period of the Fifth Republic. Eight of them were able to win at least one seat in the 1981 general election, but only three parties were of substantial importance. The ruling Democratic Justice Party (DJP) won 35.6 per cent of the votes cast and took 151 seats. The major opposition party, the Democratic Korea Party (DKP) got 81 seats with 31.5 per cent of the votes. The Korean National Party (KNP), with links to the Park regime, was able to collect 25 seats with 13.2 per cent of the votes cast. The remaining five minority parties got one or two seats each.

The period up to mid-1985 was a period of limited but gradual liberalization and increasing relative freedom, albeit within the framework of restricted democracy. With the prospering economy the government's confidence also appeared to be growing. Opposition political activity was allowed within the confines of the "democratic" framework. The opposition parties did not pose serious challenges to the government and simply called for gradual democratization. The government pledged itself in a political blueprint to adopt a series of steps in order to steer the country eventually toward "full democratization." Then, the political atmosphere began to heat up again.

The general election held on February 12, 1985 was the first test of public confidence in the government. The results of this election brought about a rapid turn around in the overall political climate. The electorate gave surprising support to the newly formed opposition New Korean Democratic Party (NKDP), which had been created by those who had just been released from four years under a political ban. The opposition NKDP was hastily established shortly before the election of the National Assembly. Despite the short period it had to prepare for the election, it effectively mobilized millions of people against the ruling DJP, headed by President Chun Doo-Hwan, by campaigning for a constitutional revision requiring the direct popular election of the president.

The result of the 1985 general election came as a shock to the governing DJP. Although the DJP was able to retain its majority in the National Assembly, taking 148 out of the total 276 legislative seats (largely due to the disproportional system of representation), its share of the vote was only 35.3 per cent. The result implied that over 64 per cent voted for opposition candidates: the NKDP won 29.3 per cent of the vote; the Democratic Korea Party (DKP), which used to be second to the DJP, won 19.7 per cent; and the Korean National Party (KNP) 9.1 per cent. The NKDP obviously achieved the biggest success in this election.

The NKDP's initial response was to capitalize on its electoral success by absorbing the opposition parties. Accordingly, the DKP merged with the NKDP shortly after the election. The enlarged NKDP occupied 102 seats in the Assembly, with a combined support of 49 per cent of the electorate. However, the opposition's attempt to exploit its electoral success proved to be inept due to a number of factors. First, the unique system of representation gave the ruling party a disproportionate advantage. Under the system, two-thirds of the total seats in the assembly are filled by direct election, and the remaining 92 seats are allocated according to a formula for "national representation." Sixty-one seats are taken automatically by the party which wins the highest number of seats in the election. The remaining 31 are distributed proportionally among the parties that have won at least 5 seats. According to this formula, the NKDP received 17 seats, and the DKP and Korean *Kookmin* Party won 9 and 5 seats respectively. The DJP thus ended up with 148 seats, or 53.6 per cent of the total, with the support of only 35.3 per cent of those who had voted.

In the beginning, the strength of the enlarged NKDP was less prominent than expected because of internal divisions and regional rivalries. The party was formed and led by the united leadership of Kim Dae-Jung and Kim Young-Sam. Despite their proclaimed unity and apparent cooperation, the "two Kims" had been arch-rivals during their past political careers and quarreled openly over the leadership of the opposition movement. They are also known to hold substantially different opinions and positions with regard to the question of democratic reforms. Kim Dae-Jung was in fact still barred from official political activities. When the NKDP was formed in 1985, the "two Kims" had to compromise over the position of party president by appointing Lee Min-Woo, whose influence within the party was relatively weak.

Some dozen former DKP members were also overlooked after they were absorbed into the NKDP. When they recognized that the open displays of personal patronage and factional elements were to their disadvantage, these ex-DKP members withdrew from the merged NKDP to form the new Korean National ("Minjoong") Democratic Party. The governing party, of course, persistently attempted to exploit the internal divisions within the opposition camps and to reduce their ability to mobilize mass support.

Despite its internal cleavages, the NKDP's demand for direct presidential elections and its call for rapid democratic reforms mobilized support from a significant portion of the general population and from interest groups that were critical of the current regime and were demanding immediate constitutional reform to ensure more genuine democracy. The opposition party's position was strengthened in March 1986 when its top leaders joined in an alliance with several noted leaders of religious organizations to support the formation of a

National Coalition for a Democratic Constitution. The coalition organized a series of mass rallies in several provincial areas and continued to play a significant role in pressing the government and the ruling party to make concessions on the constitutional issue. Political and intellectual activists also began to organize themselves and join forces in calling for constitutional revision. Student demonstrators spilled into the streets again. Labor unrest started to grow at the same time.

Faced with these challenges and the potential for political instability, President Chun, who had previously held to the position that his successor would be the one to initiate a constitutional amendment after his retirement, made a political concession on April 30, 1986 by announcing that he would not oppose an amendment during his tenure, if both parties could reach a compromise in the national assembly and produce a negotiated settlement. Thus, a resolution was passed in the assembly to form a special committee on constitutional amendment.

The focus of the constitutional debate was the question regarding the power structure. The opposition insisted on a presidential system based on a direct popular vote, while the DJP opted for a parliamentary cabinet system. No practical progress was made towards a compromise, and the stalemate persisted until December 24, 1986, when the NKDP president, Lee Min-Woo, offered to negotiate over the DJP proposal if his so-called "seven-point package for democratic reforms" was accepted. The package included: guaranteed freedom of the press; the release of political prisoners; the restoration of civil rights for dissident figures like Kim Dae-Jung; the establishment of a two party system; the revision of the parliamentary election law along more democratic lines; and the early implementation of local autonomy throughout the country.

This proposal, which was widely viewed as a step forward, was however flatly rejected by the two "Kims" who saw that it would damage the NKDP's pursuit of the "unalterable goal of direct presidential elections." The issue widened the gulf between Lee and the two "Kims" and reinforced intra-party schisms. At the same time, the factions outside the mainstream who had been disillusioned by the "arbitrary and personal control of the party" by the two "Kims" revolted against the leadership. Having failed to expel the dissenters "who act in collaboration with the government to disintegrate the opposition front," the two Kims decided to split the party and form a new one with the members of the "mainstream factions." The Reunification Democratic Party (RDP) was inaugurated on May 1, 1987, with Kim Young-Sam elected as its president. The series of events which led to the "shattered hopes for compromise" precipitated President Chun's reversal of his earlier concession. On April 13, he declared his decision to postpone the constitutional revision until after the end of his term and the 1988 Seoul Olympics.

The announcement was met with vehement protests, foreign pressure, and appeals from various groups to reverse the declaration. Student radicals and political opponents poured onto the streets of the major cities in South Korea. On June 10th, president Chun compounded his mistake by nominating Roh Tae-Woo to be the DJP candidate for the net president. The incident was regarded by many people, including the country's burgeoning middle class, as a major setback to the prospects for national reconciliation. It triggered an explosion of violent protests for more than two weeks. Anti-government demonstrations drawing crowds as large as 50,000 flared up in more than two dozen cities. For the first time the protests received explicit support from many segments of Korean society other than students and opposition activists. The political situation deteriorated into the worst street violence since the beginning of the Fifth Republic. Rumors spread widely that martial law would be imposed.

The government faced its gravest political crisis – one that might lead to its eventual collapse. It had to make a difficult choice between finding some way of reaching a compromise on the constitutional issue, or taking extraordinary measures, including martial law, to control the situation. Either option appeared to be fraught with political risks and uncertainties. Then came the dramatic unilateral declaration on June 29th by Roh Tae-Woo, chairman of the DJP, which turned the political situation upside down by announcing an eight-point democratic reform program.

The Democratization Process

Roh's special declaration acceded to the people's demand for direct presidential elections. It laid the groundwork for political democratization as well as the restoration of the civil rights of dissident leader Kim Dae-Jung. Roh also said that if his requests were denied, he would step down as the DJP presidential nominee and as the party chairman. The eight point program contained the following formula for democratization:

1. Speedy amendment of the constitution to allow direct presidential elections and a peaceful transfer of power in February 1988.

2. Revision of the presidential election law to guarantee freedom of candidacy and fair competition.

3. Restoration of civil rights for Kim Dae-Jung and freedom for all political prisoners except those accused of treason and violent crimes.

4. Promotion and protection of basic human rights, including a drastic extension of *habeas corpus*.

5. Protection of press freedom and improvements to the press law.

6. Restoration of local self-government and autonomy of education.

7. Guarantees to allow the free and democratic growth of political parties.

8. Social reforms to stamp out crime and corruption.

On July 1 President Chun endorsed Roh's eight-point democratization formula. The government subsequently freed more than 500 convicted dissidents from jail and removed the names of 270 dissidents from the "political surveillance list". It also restored political rights to 2,335 opponents. Kim Dae-Jung was among those who rights were restored. On July 10, president Chun relinquished his leadership of the party by turning over the party presidency to Roh in order to assure him a full mandate in leading the DJP and in carrying out the task of democratization.

A new round of negotiations started soon afterward to amend the constitution. A presidential system based on direct voting, as demanded by the opposition groups, was adopted. Thus, a new constitution based on the consensus between the ruling DJP and the opposition RDP was approved by the national assembly on October 12. The new constitution was in turn put to a national referendum on October 27. Out of the 78 per cent of the electorate who voted in the referendum, 93 per cent approved the new constitution.

The new constitution adopted a unicameral parliament and broadened the scope of civil rights. It strengthened the power of the national assembly and curtailed presidential rights such as the emergency power. For example, the emergency power of the president has been limited to cover only economic and financial matters and events caused by natural disasters. The presidential term of office has been reduced from seven years to six years and remains a single term. The new constitution has also removed presidential powers to disband the National Assembly and to call for a new election. The constitution's General Provisions state for the first time that the armed forces should remain above politics. On the other hand, the powers of parliamentary members have been strengthened to provide better institutional checks and balances on the power of the administration. Complete immunity has been assured for actions inside the house. The total sitting days of the National Assembly have been increased from 90 to 100 a year.

The new constitution will be effective from February 1988. A new president will be elected in December 1987 to head the next government in February 1988. If the political time-table proceeds smoothly, South Koreans will have chosen their national leader by popular vote for the first time since 1971 and will host the 1988 Olympic Games under a new government.

The detailed background which led to the June 29th declaration and the government's stunning announcement of democratic reform and "grand national conciliation" has not as yet been revealed. However, one can conjecture that the following factors might have contributed to the turn of events. First of all, the memory of Park's failure and of the bloody Kwangju incident of 1980 (which caused at least 191 deaths) still haunts the leadership of the current power bloc. Therefore, the regime decided against the option of returning to the old, repressive, and militaristic policies.

Secondly, the international political and economic context in which the country finds itself is different from the Park era. This in turn provided an additional cause for cautious optimism that the crisis could be solved before it deteriorated to the extent of fundamentally threatening the ruling bloc's position of power and interest.

Thirdly, the current regime has suffered from a lack of legitimacy since its inception. This might have kept the ruling group from adopting a less pragmatic orientation to governing an increasingly complex and rapidly changing society. Korean society has matured, largely due to the expanding economy of the past two decades. There exists a substantial base among its population capable of maintaining social stability and responding to gradual political change. The country is evolving into a society which is increasingly difficult to manage by authoritarian measures. With less than a year left before transferring power to his successor, President Chun did not risk the danger of turning to a more radical style of leadership.

Finally, foreign pressures also played a significant role. The United States, for example, persistently urged the Korean government to take more positive actions to stimulate progress toward democratization. It pointed out through many channels that any move towards military intervention or a coup would be a threat not only to Korea but also to US security interests in Northeast Asia. In addition, the political crisis raised serious questions over the future of the 1988 Summer Olympic Games in Seoul. If they had not been held at all, national pride would have been gravely tarnished and the country's international credit would have been damaged forever.

Considering the progress made so far, one might be led to make optimistic predictions about Korea's prospects for democratic political development. However, the optimism must be qualified. First of all, the success of Korea's democratization process is contingent upon the strength, organization, and strategy of the opposition political forces. The opposition forces in Korea have been deeply divided and have failed in the past to present themselves as an attractive alternative to the governing party. Political dissent in Korea today takes many forms. It embraces many factions and a variety of ideological orientations as well. Those factions were able to unite in common cause as long as they opposed the government. But with the promise of democracy at hand, the unity and spirit of compromise tend to give away to the politics of division and rivalry. Infighting within the opposition is likely to endanger the process of democratization again as it did in the past. Kim Young-Sam and Kim Dae-Jung have failed to patch up their differences over the single candidacy in the presidential race against the ruling party. It remains to be seen whether the opposition leaders can avoid repeating their past mistakes.

Excessive demands from radical students and industrial workers may pose another danger in the way of democracy. The students and radicals are anti-government, but they do not necessarily support the opposition parties or their leaders. The more radical elements among the students and labor press both the opposition and the government too hard and too fast, or adopt methods which are too violent for society to accept. This could not only threaten the unity of the moderate opposition but also alienate the middle class who sympathized with the democratic opposition. It could also goad hardliners in the government into reverting to the old authoritarian crackdowns. Student radicalism and labor intransigence have frequently been used as pretexts for military intervention or harsh authoritarian measures in the past political history of South Korea (*Newsweek*, July 20, 1987: 18-19).

The second factor to consider is the propensity and capability of the military to play a political role or exert its influence in the political sphere. The military has an effective veto power, and will be ready to intervene whenever its basic interest is threatened. A heavy dependence by the past and present power blocs on the military's backing has left a legacy that still haunts South Korean politics. If the current ruling bloc finds that the alliance of various opposition groups poses a fundamental threat to the existing social and political system, it is likely that the group aligned with the military may take preemptive measures or exercise the veto power.

The third important variable affecting prospects for democracy is the capacity and willingness of the governing coalition to be more attentive and responsive to the wishes and demands of the people. Measures on the part of the government to support the movement towards democratic progress, social justice, and national harmony, and to expand the scope for public participation in the political process will be particularly important in this respect. There exists in Korea today a national consensus on the need to establish a more stable, legitimate and democratic political system and to broaden the basis of popular participation in the political process. Given the weakness of political institutions and effective opposition politics, it is the governing body which has the ability to initiate a genuine process of democratization and to facilitate the emergence of a political system which could lead to consensus and compromise among contending groups. The chances for a constructive dialogue with the opposition forces would also be greatly enhanced if the government moved unilaterally, if necessary, to implement democratic reforms. That would help convince both the general population and the people in the opposition camps that the government was indeed sincere in its desire and intention to move more rapidly towards genuine democracy.

Conclusion

Korea is now entering a crucial period of political transition. It faces the great challenge of achieving a democratic polity which is more accountable to its people. At this juncture, history has placed a heavy burden on Korea's politicians and especially on the leading power bloc to attend more closely to the hopes and desires of its people, who are calling for dialogue and compromise in order to institutionalize a more democratic political process. The nation's economic growth and social maturity show that its people are fully capable of reaching the goal they want to achieve. The majority of Koreans and their leaders are firmly committed to turn the economic miracle into a political success as well. Considering the state's dominance over society and the die-hard opposition critics arrayed against the current government, success in this regard will depend largely on the government's ability to induce various opposition groups to engage in dialogue and compromise. It will also depend on whether the ruling party and the government ensure a fair competition and free election for the president and prepare the ground for the democratization that was promised in the June 29th declaration by Roh Tae-Woo.

President Chun's repeated pledge to transfer power at the end of his term in February 1988 is an essential, though not sufficient, step towards a more open, liberalized, and legitimate political system. It is important in itself in view of the fact that no previous president in the post-independent political history of South Korea has ever stepped down voluntarily from power. The new constitution will be effective from February 1988. The government has already carried out a series of tasks directed at democratic reform. These include a blue-print for the implementation of a local autonomy system from early next year, measures to guarantee freedom of the press and protection of human rights, and plans to curb corruption. Many people feel that these are substantial steps and will be important factors leading to democratic change and to greater fairness and accountability.

An additional stimulus for positive political change comes from Korea's external relations. Korea's relationship with the outside world has become more extensive and more complex over the years. Korea now depends on trade for about 75 per cent of its GNP. This makes it inevitable that the country must pursue more intimate cooperation and interdependence with the international community. Korea is currently the seventh largest trading partner of the United States. The security relationship between Korea and the USA will continue to remain important. In spite of the dilemma posed by a growing anti-Americanism among students and some populist segments of Korean society, the US forces will continue to provide a shield against the threat of external aggression. Such protection will help Korea to develop into a prosperous economy and gradually into a more stable, democratic form of government.

With continuing economic growth, Korea will play an increasingly larger international role and will need to be more open and responsive to the outside world. The 1988 Olympics will provide additional momentum for Korea to move towards a more open and liberalized political economic system. This increasing level of interdependence constitutes an important element of optimism for Korea's political prospects. In view of these factors, Korea's open and basically liberal policy is likely to continue in the future. The logic of interdependence can also help Korean politics to avoid repeating the vicious circle of the past, and can enhance its ability to adapt to an increasingly dynamic, sophisticated, peaceful, and pluralistic world society.

Given the record of the past and the existing capacity of the society to cope with external pressure and manage the internal elements of change, and considering at the same time the much enhanced sense of power, self-confidence and national pride of its people, there is a good probability that Korea's future will evolve in the direction of social stability, sustained economic growth, and gradual political democratization. However, much remains to be done and a long span of time will be necessary for the country to achieve the goal of establishing a full-blown representative government and genuine liberal democracy. The authoritarian tradition of Confucianism still permeates nearly all aspects of political culture. Die-hard critics still hold to the idea that nothing but fundamental change will end the military authoritarian government and do the job of correcting social injustice. Solutions to substantive political issues which are based on compromise will require a longer span of time. Civilian social and political organizations are not strong enough or sufficiently institutionalized to strike a balance with the more powerful state political apparatus. The sheer size of the military establishment and the constant threat from the North make it impossible to foresee an easy and smooth return to a "complete civilianization" of politics in the near future.

Therefore, whoever assumes power in 1988, genuine social progress and political democratization in South Korea will occur gradually for the time being, and only within the framework of the restricted democracy whose characteristics have been discussed above. Because of this qualified optimism it is quite probable that for many critics, both inside and out, who hold to the classical ideals of liberal democratic theory, Korean political progress will remain less than satisfactory for some years to come.

References

Ahn, Chung-Si and Kim Kyong-Dong, "Korea," in Chung-Si Ahn, ed., *The Local Political System in Asia: A Comparative Perspective,* (Seoul: Seoul National University Press, 1987): 33-61.

Choi, Jang-jip, "A Corporatist Control of the Labor Union in South Korea," *Korean Social Science Journal,* 6 (1984): 25-55.

Cole, David C., "Free Enterprise vs. Government Regulation: Decisionmaking and Regulation in the Korean Economy," *Asian Affairs,* 7, 2 (November-December, 1979): 79-83.

Enos, John, "Governmental Intervention in the Transfer of Technology: the Case of Korea," Gordon White and Robert Wade, eds., *Developmental State in East Asia: Capitalist and Socialist,* The Institute of Development Studies, Bulletin No. 15 (1984): 26-31.

Hamilton, Clive, "Class, State and Industrialization in South Korea," in White and Wade, *op. cit.*: 38-43.

Han, Sung-joo, "Political Institutionalization in South Korea, 1961-1984," Robert A. Scalapino *et al.* eds., *Asian Political Institutionalization,* (Berkeley: Institute of East Asian Studies, University of California, 1986): 116-137.

Im, Hyug Baeg, "The Rise of Bureaucratic Authoritarianism in South Korea," *World Politics,* 39, 2 (January 1987): 231-257.

Jacobsson, Staffan, "Industrial Policy for the Machine Tool Industries of South Korea and Taiwan," in White and Wage, *op. cit.*: 44-49.

Kihl, Sung-Hum, *et al., The Study of Elections in Korea,* (in Korean) (Seoul: Dasan Publishing Co., 1987).

Leudde-Neurath, Richard, "State Intervention and Foreign Direct Investment in South Korea," in White and Wade, *op. cit.*: 18-25.

Michell, Tony, "Administrative Traditions and Economic Decision-Making in South Korea," in White and Wage, *op. cit.*: 32-37.

Moore, Mick, "Agriculture in Taiwan and South Korea: the Minimalist State?," in White and Wage, *op. cit.*: 57-64.

Olson, Edward A., "Korea, Inc.: The Political Impact of Park
    Chung-Hee's Economic Miracle," *Orbis*, 24, 1 (Spring 1980):
    69-84.

Robison, Richard and Gary Rodan, "In Defence of State Intervention,"
    Fareastern Economic Review, (October 23, 1986): 54-65.

Schmitter, Philippe C., "Still the Century of Corporatism?," P.C.
    Schmitter and G. Lehmbruch, eds., *Trends Toward Corporatist
    Intermediation*, (Beverly Hills, Ca.: Sage Publication, 1979):
    7-52.

The Unfinished Political Reforms of the Hong Kong Government

Lau Siu-kai

The way Hong Kong is relinquished as a colony marks a distinctive departure from British decolonization policy in the past. Instead of independence, Hong Kong is going to be restored to China in 1997. This will be done despite Britain's reluctance and misgivings, and after efforts at retaining certain forms of administrative presence or political influence after the reversion of sovereignty had failed. In the remaining period of British rule, "the Government of the United Kingdom will be responsible for the administration of Hong Kong with the object of maintaining and preserving its economic and social stability; and. . .the Government of the People's Republic of China will give its cooperation in this connection."[1]

This unprecedented way of surrendering colonial rule in British history confronts the British government with a political task which is both momentous and challenging. Instigated by a mixture of altruistic, ideological and pragmatic motives, Britain decided to introduce a series of political reforms in Hong Kong (whereas in the past significant reforms of any kind had not been made, and some had even been opposed upon their proposal) the primary concern of which was to develop a more participatory political system through devolution of power. Nevertheless, in view of the peculiar nature of Hong Kong, the general sequence of constitutional development which had in varying degrees informed political reforms in many former British colonies (consultative government – semi-representative government – representative government – semi-responsible

43

government – responsible government/self-government – (Dominion status) – independence) cannot be replicated faithfully in Hong Kong.[2] The impossibility of independence not only means that this seemingly 'logical' sequence cannot reach its final stage, it, by interacting with the unique character of Hong Kong as a colonial society and the dubious applicability of past decolonizing reforms to Hong Kong (and, for the matter, to other former colonies as well) would make it difficult for it even to go beyond the initial stages of this sequence.

Nevertheless, albeit with reservations, hesitancy, inconsistencies and haste, the reform proposals first broached by the Hong Kong government were obviously inspired by and reminiscent of past efforts to 'prepare' colonies for self-government (though not necessarily for independence). Within two years after the coming into force of the Sino-British Joint Declaration, however, it was obvious that Britain had back tracked and that further constitutional changes in Hong Kong could only be initiated by China or be introduced with China's blessing. Lacking the political will to confront China and increasingly aware of the threats associated with further reforms on the viability of the Hong Kong government, Britain has to all intents and purposes given up any significant reform attempt.

The abrupt termination of a reform process, strongly supported by a small group of vociferous democratic activists in Hong Kong (who deftly base their appeal on popular fear of communism), could not but produce political backlashes which appeared to have been only remotely anticipated by Britain. To escape from its political predicament, the Hong Kong government looks set on a path of political development which presupposes the primacy of the goal of maintaining a stable and sufficiently effective government. The steps that are likely to be taken in fulfilment of this primary goal will have significant political repercussions, and the course of development will in certain aspects be nondemocratic or even moderately authoritarian. It is thus ironical that political reforms which started off in a democratic direction would, when aborted, shift to a less democratic one.

Impossibility of Independence as a Constraint on Political Reform

In contrast with other former British colonies, Hong Kong is a highly modernized industrial city enjoying rapid economic growth in the post-war period. On the surface of it, the high literacy rate, the pervasive influence from the West, the growing middle-class sector and economic prosperity should provide a fertile ground for the transplantation of the Westminster parliamentary government.

Nevertheless, Hong Kong in the past had experienced even less constitutional advancement than other British colonies. One of the most significant factors that explain this paradox must be the decision of Britain, made known publicly in several occasions, that Hong Kong could never be independent because of its smallness, the opposition from China and the fact that even though a small part of Hong Kong was ceded to Britain permanently by the moribund Manchu regime in the nineteenth century, the bulk of the land area of Hong Kong has to be returned to China upon the expiry of a lease in 1997. In addition, in the past no nationalist demand for independence had even been made by the people of Hong Kong. The absence of nationalist agitation and the widespread acquiescence of the populace reflect the unique nature of Hong Kong as a colony. Hong Kong was wrung by force from China not out of a desire of Britain for territorial gain or for the natural resources that Hong Kong could offer. Rather it was the goal of Britain to obtain a foothold close to China which would allow her to develop Far East trade. Accordingly, Hong Kong as a barren and virtually nonpopulated island was turned into a British colony. *Unlike other British colonies, a colonial government was first set up in Hong Kong before the arrival of the colonial people.* In order to attract Chinese people to Hong Kong, particularly those with higher social status, colonial rule had perforce to be enlightened and benign even though colonial institutions looked otherwise. The Chinese people who moved to Hong Kong since the establishment of the colony came primarily for economic betterment or avoidance of political turmoil and persecution. They did not come to Hong Kong to launch a nationalist movement to topple colonial rule, particularly when the alternative to it was rule by the authoritarian Nationalist or Communist regimes. Consequently, up until the Sino-British negotiation over the future of Hong Kong, Hong Kong was governed formally in the most typical colonial fashion. Power was concentrated in the Governor, who acted as the plenipotentiary of the Crown. He was advised by the Executive and Legislative Councils (both appointed by him), but there was no legal obligation that he had to abide by their recommendations. In spite of the dignified position of the two Councils in the constitution of Hong Kong, in reality the government was a 'pure' bureaucratic government, where career officials, unhampered by forces coming from society, exercised autonomous power. (Incidentally, the society under colonial rule is atomistic and politically unorganized.)

Up till 1982, the elective principle as a means to recruit political leaders was not operative in Hong Kong. The only exception, though politically insignificant, was the partially elected Urban Council which was granted a small bunch of municipal functions.[3] The presence of some elected politicians did occasionally embarass the government, as a few of them did assume an inflated political role as the popular leader of the people.

The impossibility of ultimate independence had before 1982 precluded the transfer of the Westminster model to Hong Kong or the need to 'prepare' for it.[4] The only significant proposals for reform in the post-war period (in 1946 and 1966) came in the form of municipal councils,[5] which had been rejected by Britain as a way of constitutional advancement for her smaller colonies elsewhere.[6] Nevertheless, even these moderate reforms were eventually not adopted. The reasons for their abandonment revealed tellingly the constraints on political reform exerted by the impossibility of independence and all its implications. For it was largely the fear of opposition from China and the infiltration of pro-Communist elements into the government that cautioned both the government and the Westernized Chinese elites against even moderate reforms. Naturally, the fear of social and political instability produced by electoral politics (based only on a restricted franchise) also played a part in the strangulation of these early reform attempts.[7]

After the signing of the Joint Declaration, the absence of the prospect of independence looms even larger as a constraint on political reform. Now the successor regime is very much concerned with the 'content' or 'substance' of the sovereignty that it will eventually possess. China is not likely to see with magnanimity a returned sovereignty devoid of much substance as power has already been devolved to the people which can only be retrieved with difficulty.[8]

More specifically, the impossibility of independence as a constraint on reform makes its impact on several areas: the opposition to or even subversion of the reform by China and her supporters in Hong Kong (China's ascendant influence and her organizational presence in Hong Kong is beyond doubt), the difficulty of garnering support for the reforms when they are seen as only temporary arrangements and the difficulty of locating suitable collaborators to whom power can be transferred.

The reasons why China is opposed to political democratization (or, in the often-used terms of the Hong Kong government, 'the development of representative government') by Britain are legion:[9] (1) the fear that Britain will use it as an excuse to shirk its responsibility of administering Hong Kong until 1997; (2) democratization will release political forces of such magnitudes that continued rule of the Hong Kong government will be difficult or impossible; (3) the injection of elements of uncertainty which would wreck the stability and prosperity of Hong Kong before China is in a position to take over; (4) the possibility that power will be transferred to political groups which are pro-Britain, hostile to China or predisposed to place the interests of Hong Kong before those of China;

(5) China being compelled to openly organize politically in order to participate in the competition for the transferred power, thus bringing about detrimental consequences for Hong Kong; (6) democratization will disrupt the capitalist system of Hong Kong by scaring away local and foreign capital and by forcing the government to adopt excessive welfare measures and restrictive economic regulations; (7) the possibility of turning mass elections into occasions for the people of Hong Kong to periodically pass judgments on the popularity of China; and (8) the fear that the 'democratic forces' in Hong Kong will eventually become subversive of political tranquility in China by sheer demonstration effects and by their purposive promotion of Western-style 'democracy' in China. This list of reasons are by no means exhaustive, but they suffice to severely qualify the political formula of 'Hong Kong people ruling Hong Kong', which has been promised by China as a solution to its long-term future. After all, what is unequivocally specified in the formula is that the future government of the Hong Kong Special Administrative Region (SAR) will be formed by the local people. The way this government will be formed and the channels of political recruitment are however obscure and subject to diverse interpretations.

Not sure of Britain's intentions and unable to completely prevent some forms of power transfer from taking place, China for strategic reasons and out of an instinctual predisposition not to leave power to chance, feels compelled to compete in any power-grasping game.[10] In doing so China commands an overwhelmingly advantaged position because it is the future master of Hong Kong. As the new center of political gravity in Hong Kong, China is beginning to eclipse the authority of the incumbent government. Extending out from its official and unofficial organizations in Hong Kong, China has not only been able to attract to its side, and to create on its own, an increasing number of local leaders and organizations who are prepared to toe the line of China out of a multitude of motives (patriotism, expediency, selfishness or sheer power-worship), but China has also proven itself capable of 'penetrating' into the quasi-political bodies established by the Hong Kong government as the prop of colonial rule. Accordingly, the emergence of a 'dual' authority structure raises a great probability that, with time, power transferred by the departing government will be increasingly deposited in the hands of China rather than controlled by those favored by the British. While this scenario eventually is not avoidable, Britain would certainly be in no mood to speed up its appearance.

The coexistence of both the incumbent and future political masters makes it impossible to groom successors to her liking by Britain. The selection of collaborators in the decolonization process and grooming them into future rulers after the withdrawal of the colonial power had been standard practices of Britain.

As Wasserman (1976:174)* has suggested, decolonization consisted of two apparently contradictory processes. The first, the more discontinuous and visible, was the withdrawal of direct colonial authority by the metropole. This process involved a dramatic change of regime — a change in political institutions and in patterns of recruitment into decision-making roles. This was the process of democratization. Wasserman argues that this first process must be understood in terms of the second, which was characterized by continuity and consisted of the preservation of the colonial political economy and the integration of an indigenous elite into positions of authority in a way that would protect the economic and strategic interests of the metropole.[11]

In order to facilitate the rise and dominance of her favored indigenous elite, Britain might go as far as debarring the 'ineligibles' from entering into the political arena.[12]

For a variety of reasons, the exercise of grooming successor elites failed in many British colonies not long after their independence, as the victorious nationalist faction was unable to consolidate its power as a ruling group. What is pertinent here however is that Britain has even no chance to groom her own favored successors in Hong Kong as she is now confronted by an unprecedented situation. In a way the Hong Kong government is to be blamed for their past neglect, so that at the eve of the Sino-British negotiation, Hong Kong did not have a local leadership with organizational linkage to the masses. But what is of greater significance is the magnetic effect of the Chinese center of political gravity on the 'potential' elite that might 'normally' be groomed by the British. Not only are newly-arising leaders short in supply, but Britain cannot even be certain about the allegiance of her own supporters, as not a few of them are gingerly and meticulously playing the juggling act so as to maximize their chances with both political masters. In the run-up to 1997, Britain has to face the miserable fate of being a solitary and declining power, surrounded by people affiliated in varying degrees with the future political master.

Without the prospect of independence and confronted with the strident opposition from China, it would be difficult for the

---

* Wasserman, Gary. 1976. *Politics of Decolonization: Kenya Europeans and the Land Issue 1960-1965*. New York: Cambridge University Press.

constitutional changes initiated by Britain to have popular appeal, for it is always that these reforms would be dismantled later and that those who ardently support them would suffer from political reprisal afterwards. While earlier on concepts derived from past decolonization experience had been bandied by the Hong Kong government and some of its supporters (such as the ministerial system and two-party system), they hardly aroused public enthusiasm apart from raising the aspirations of a small group of democratic activists. Without widespread and determined public support, the transfer of institutions can only have a dim chance of success.

Nor is that all. By being bound by international agreement to be responsible for the administration of Hong Kong until 1997, yet under declining authority and in anticipation of increasing difficulties, Britain cannot do without the support of China in the governance of the place. The support from China is critical in at least several areas if effective and stable rule is to be maintained in the transitional period: (1) public policies devised by the Hong Kong government whose acceptance and success would be contingent upon the declared commitment of China after 1997; (2) policies and actions that require the active cooperation of China; (3) prevention of the occurrence of a situation where China, at loggerheads with Britain, would support actions against the government by some sections of the public; and (4) the need to bolster the authority of the government by the overwhelming power of China.

The absence of the prospect of independence in essence renders inapplicable the past decolonization procedures of Britain. Or equal, if not more, importance is the social-economic peculiarities of the Hong Kong society, which distinguish it as a very different entity from Britain's former colonies. In several critical aspects this uniqueness poses as an impediment to the introduction of 'democratic' political reforms in Hong Kong. And it reinforces the already potent impact of the impossibility of independence.

Socio-Economic Peculiarities of Hong Kong as a Colony

Decolonization in the former British colonies in the post-war era was largely forced upon her by the fervent nationalist movement, which galvanized almost all sectors of the colonial people into an anti-colonial campaign. The backdrop of the eruption of nationalist sentiments were largely the oppressive aspects of colonialism. (The indignities suffered by the colonial powers in the life-and-death struggle among themselves, the military defeat inflicted on them by the Japanese and their desperate reliance on the support and sacrifice of the colonial people to fight a total war also played a part in fomenting self-assertiveness among the colonized).

In contrast with former British colonies (and in fact all former colonies), the historical juncture where British felt obligated to embark upon a decolonization program in Hong Kong was one where nationalism was a fading force. The grievances that fed nationalist movements in other British colonies – ethnic discrimination, economic underdevelopment, meagre opportunities for upward social mobility and poverty of the masses – are not to be found, or found in only a mild form, in Hong Kong. Nationalism as a principle or an ideology also fails to find a sufficiently large audience there because the people have subscribed to colonial rule voluntarily. They are aware of the transience of colonial status and know that China can take over the place at any time. There is also of course the understanding that the denouement of a nationalist outburst would be Communist takeover. Without the intense pressure of a nationalist movement, the pace and content of decolonization orchestrated by Britain in Hong Kong naturally will be determined by considerations which have little to do with the imperative need to cater to nationalist demands. It turns out that these considerations would eventually point to a different mode of decolonization in Hong Kong.

In the past, both decolonization and nationalism had strong democratic implications, and hence both were essentially processes of democratization. By the same token, the push for democratization in the former British colonies was sustained and reinforced by the overarching nationalist movement and other movements encompassed by it: movements for independence, ethnic equality, economic development and cultural self-respect. The democratic movement gained force precisely because it was part of a larger, all-encompassing nationalist movement.

In Hong Kong, colonial rule as a school of democracy and the process of modernization have indeed given birth to a small group of democratic activists, who had registered their demand for democracy long before the appearance of the 1997 issue but who gained momentum only lately primarily due to the new political situation created by the scheduled departure of Britain, the intention of Britain to develop 'representative government' and the promise of China to allow the people of Hong Kong to govern themselves. The new situation even allows them to magnify their appeal for democracy by upholding it as a means to 'withstand communism or Communist China'. Despite these seemingly propitious conditions, the democratic activists however have not been able so far to force both the British and Chinese governments to accede to their demand for far-reaching democratic reforms, nor have they been successful in launching a democratic movement with mass participation. This failure of the democratic activists is of course explicable in terms of the opposition of China, the power of the pro-China elements in Hong Kong and the hesitancy and reservations of Britain about political reform. But a significant reason must be sought from the peculiar socio-economic character of Hong Kong society, which makes it extremely difficult to mobilize support for a large-scale democratic movement. Consequently, the democratic movement in Hong Kong can only be a solitary, isolated and small-scale movement. It is a movement that is led and participated primarily by middle-class intellectuals and professionals who lack sufficient organizational linkage or affective rapport with the common people. It is thus unavoidable that the role of the democratic activists is primarily the negative one of undermining and discrediting existing authorities (e.g. by selective interpretation of issues, public policies and decisions, and events, and by articulating unrealistic demands) through the highly developed and (largely) free mass media, where can be found a large contingent of young, idealistic and radicalized reporters and commentators. Overplaying the negative role, nevertheless, cannot compensate for the lack of political organization and power of the democratic activists. It might eventually backfire to the detriment of the credibility of the mass media. What is more serious is that it might even lead to psychological fatigue or aversion among an audience who are preoccupied with order and stability.

The masses, despite their apprehension about the future and mistrust of China, are in a state of political lethargy out of a sense of defeatism, powerlessness and aversion to politics.[13] They also suspect the motives of the 'leaders' in Hong Kong[14] and are skeptical about their political influence. Besides, they are quite satisfied with the status quo and supportive of the existing political system.[15] They do not see the relevance of democratic changes to their self-interests. Not a few of them are on the contrary worried that democratic reforms will place what they now have in jeopardy.

It is the opposition of the indigenous bourgeoisie and the middle classes to the democratization part of decolonization that dooms the movement of the democratic activists. Opposition to democratic reform coming from the indigenous bourgeoisie had been encountered in other British colonies, particularly from those who "recognize the fragility of their control locally and the interest they well may have in a European connection."[16] But in other British colonies the indigenous bourgeoisie as a class was tiny and weak. They were dominated by the economic interests of the colonial power or even by those of other foreign minorities (e.g. the Asians in East Africa). Their opposition to the nationalist movement hence did not pose a formidable obstacle to the nationalist movement. The indigenous bourgeoisie often found it politically advantageous to join forces with the nationalists to form a united anti-colonial front. As described succinctly by Emerson,

> The Western-trained intelligentsia and professional men were usually joined by the rising indigenous entrepreneurs and businessmen, as in India or in West Africa where the women traders must be included as well. Aside from other inducements to enlist in the nationalist cause, the local businessman was likely to find, or at least to be persuaded that he had found, his way blocked by Western economic interests which, better equipped with capital and the techniques of modern trade and enterprise, could also draw upon the support of the imperial and colonial governments.[17]

The desire of indigenous economic interests for more whole-hearted and extensive governmental support led them to make important financial contributions to the nationalist movements in India and some other countries.[18]

The indigenous bourgeoisie in Hong Kong is a totally different situation. The 'indigenousness' of the bourgeoisie of Hong Kong must be qualified by the fact that their predecessors came from outside (from China (such as the Shanghainese entrepreneurs) or from other advanced countries). While they have established roots in Hong Kong, the roots are by no means deep. Cosmopolitanism, a-nationalism, rationalism and predatoriness are the hallmarks of the indigenous bourgeoisie of Hong Kong. Intent on making profits and fully aware of the impossibility of controlling ultimate political power, they are willing to rely on the protection of the colonial government to provide a favorable environment for profit-making. (And this dependent disposition towards an authoritarian government is also to a certain extent shared by foreign capitalists.) In this aspect they have not been disappointed by the colonial government, whose professed doctrine of 'positive non-interventionism' has enabled the economy of Hong Kong to prosper. The indigenous capitalists are by now a formidable force which even the colonial government has to reckon with, for its interests are closely tied in with theirs. The dependent nature of the Hong Kong economy (dependent on foreign capital, markets and technology), and the need to maintain a competitive investment environment of low tax rate, minimal government regulation and labor quiescence have convinced the local bourgeoisie that an authoritarian government is indispensable to the economic viability of Hong Kong. Democratization feeds into the sense of political impotency of the indigenous capitalists and creates a feeling of panic. In addition to serving notice to the government on their opposition to democratization,[19] they also seek out China as their 'protector', knowing full well of their indispensability to the success of capitalist Hong Kong in the 'one country, two systems' model. As expected, the promise of protection comes promptly from China, who is eager to assuage their fears. In the mind of the local bourgeoisie, it is more expedient to rely on the all-powerful Chinese government to fulfil the promise of maintaining capitalism in Hong Kong (if China reneges on her promise, they are always free to leave) than to work with the weak and splintered local democratic activists who are presumed to be unsympathetic to business interests, prone to court the wrath of China and, in their search for social and economic justice, bound to play havoc with the economy. Since the Sino-British Agreement, the bargaining, or more appropriately, the veto of the local bourgeoisie has steeply increased because of the internationalization (and hence the mobility) of local capital (due to worldwide diversification of investment by local capitalists and growing proportion of them now holding foreign passports or rights of residence), the looming economic difficulties facing Hong Kong because of the gradual withdrawal of local capital and the increasing threats of international protectionism. Moreover, in their fight against democratization, the local capitalists find an ally also in foreign capital, whose sole interest in Hong Kong is as a place to invest. As the economy of Hong Kong is now in the critical stage of upgrading its industrial structure through the importation of advanced technology, direct investment by foreign, particularly multinational corporations, will be increasingly needed. In order to compete for foreign investment and high technology, it is imperative that Hong Kong maintain political stability and restrain popular demands that will inevitably grow with 'democratization.'

Another peculiar aspect of the weakness of the democratic movement in Hong Kong is the deplorable fact that, even though the middle class elements (intellectuals, lawyers, teachers, journalists, social workers, religious workers) provide the leadership for the movement, they fail to receive support from their own ranks. For one thing, through education and exposure to the workings of the western democracies, the middle classes in Hong Kong, like their counterparts in other developing countries, cherish democratic ideals and practices. Another thing is that it is almost a general rule that middle classes all over the world are inclined in varying degrees to participate in politics in order to achieve their goals, be they public-serving or self-regarding. A few examples from other places will make this 'need' for 'democracy' clear. In pre-independence Sierra Leone,

> [s]tripped to its essentials, the anti-colonial nationalism that emerged after World War I was merely the ideological

projection of the expanding appetite of middle class Africans for new jobs and related perquisites which only the government could provide. Inevitably, this nationalism confronted the sizable expatriate personnel, who claimed the most desirable posts in the colonial establishment, as the main barrier to its goal. This barrier, it was soon discovered, could be overcome only with the demise of the colonial regime itself. Hence the anti-colonial orientation of African nationalism.[20]

In the United States, collective choice made through the democratic procedure is a way of getting everyone else to subsidize the 'new' middle class, as stated satirically by Wildavsky:[21]

So let us assume that America's new class has money (though not the most money) but not corresponding status or power. Its defining existential condition is that high income and professional standing alone do not enable its members to maintain the status and privilege to which they aspire. Their money cannot buy them what they want; so their task, as they define it, is to convince others to pay collectively for what they cannot obtain individually. Thus government lies at the center of their aspirations and operations.

However, if the status quo is favorable to middle class interests, they will then become its staunch supporter, however 'undemocratic' it is. In Latin America, for instance, "the political alliances of the middle classes will depend on whether or not the social system proves capable of satisfying their minimum aspirations. Where that satisfaction is provided, the middle sectors will be likely to seek alliance with the powerful and privileged groups in the community, and will thus contribute to the maintenance of the existing order".[22] The orientation of the middle class in Hong Kong is basically similar of that in Latin America, but in an even more exaggerated form. The middle classes in Hong Kong have grown rapidly since the early 1970s, as a concomitant of the take-off of the economy. Since they still constitute only a small segment in a pyramidal class structure, their self-esteem and self-importance are grossly overblown. They have witnessed only a mild and diminishing form of ethnic discrimination in public employment, but that pales into insignificance when the grass in the private sector has grown even 'greener'. Of most importance in molding the social character of the middle classes are: that they do not find their path of upward social mobility blocked by an entrenched and closed upper class and that most of the middle class people have experienced upward mobility and rapid improvement of their standard of living *within their lifetime*. Naturally, the existing system is inordinately advantageous to them, and any proposal to restructure it is threatening.

To the middle class, 'equality of opportunity' is thus not an ideal to be attained in the future but a living reality and the *sine qua non* of Hong Kong's success. Such belief in and dedication to individual assertion, merit and equal participation have modeled the middle-class people into extreme individualists. The middle sector is by nature heterogenous (a result of diversity of social and economic origins and interests), hence its highly fragmented character. This prevents the formation of a compact social stratum constituting a bloc for purposes of political action. Consequently, "the political problem posed by these people is not so much what the direction may be as whether they will take any direction at all."[23]

The attitude of the middle class to the masses is one of snobbishness. Poverty is readily explained away as individual failures and should not be corrected by public welfare and assistance, the costs of which would have to be born by the self-reliant middle classes.[24] The intervention of the government to reduce social and economic inequalities will backfire, constrict equality of opportunities and dampen individual incentives. These attitudes, together with the absence of a need to ally with the masses to 'struggle against' a closed upper class, make the middle sector skeptical about democratic reforms.

The middle classes in Hong Kong are also a dependent stratum. They are dependent, due to the impossibility of independence for Hong Kong, on the colonial government for protection, and on both the government and the capitalists for employment. Because of the openness of Hong Kong society, successful capitalists are seen as those in the middle classes who have 'made it' much better than others. Instead of seeing the capitalists as an alien social entity whose interests are in conflict with theirs, they see them as but extensions of themselves and with whom they are proud to identify. This mentally reinforces the political conservatism of the middle classes. Moreover, as a significant component of the middle class sector is made up of civil servants, whose interests are bound up with those of the colonial government, the political lethargy of the middle classes is reinforced.[25]

The politically and economically dependent middle sector is basically materialistic, hedonistic, individualistic, snobbish, in many ways authoritarian, privatistic and self-seeking. It is organizationally and ideologically fragmented. Even the democratic activists are not immune from these middle class 'diseases', which are reflected in the timidity and disunity of their democratic movement. Despite

their deep-seated fear of communism, they have failed to unite into a
militant political force.   On the contrary, they are in the throes of
organizational and psychological disarray. In the typical style of the
Hong Kong middle classes, the most sought after solution to the 1997
malaise (viz. emigration) is individualistic in nature.

Political Reform in Hong Kong: Advance and Retreat

Even though fundamental political reforms had not been undertaken
before 1982, Britain had in the past built up an elaborate system of
consultation with expert and public opinion, which was made up of a
large number of advisory committees. This system had been
successful in co-opting the Chinese elite into the governmental
structure and in allowing the government to formulate reasonable
policies.[26]

The 1997 issue changed the situation. Whereas in the past,
political innovations represented 'change within tradition',[27]
incremental changes are no longer sufficient to cope with the new
environment. Despite reservations and past failures, Britain at first
was undaunted and announced, during the negotiation over Hong
Kong's future, that a package of political reforms would be introduced
stage by stage. There seemed to be a number of reasons for such a
hasty move: to transfer to the Hong Kong people so that they could
stand up against China after 1997, sweetening the Sino-British deal
over Hong Kong for the British Parliament by a promise to
'democratize', the need to share power with the ruled so that their
support could be obtained in the difficult transitional period ahead,
the imperative to buttress the declining authority of a departing
government, and possibly to enlist public opinion as a ploy to bargain
with China. The reforms suggested in the earliest reform proposals,
listed in the 1984 *Green Paper*, were grandiose. The main aim of the
reforms smacked of development into 'self-government': "to develop
progressively a system of government the authority for which is
firmly rooted in Hong Kong, which is able to represent authoritatively
the views of the people of Hong Kong, and which is more directly
accountable to the people of Hong Kong".[28] The path of constitutional
development as suggested in the Green Paper is reminiscent of the
'theory of preparation' for the Westminster model, which involves the
aggrandizement of the legislature as the center of power and the
source of legitimacy for other subordinate institutions.   As
summarized in the *Green Paper*:[29]

The Legislative Council

(a)   Arrangements should be introduced to provide for a substantial number of Unofficial members of the Legislative Council to be elected indirectly -

    (i)   by an electoral college composed of all members of the Urban Council, the New Regional Council and the District Boards (will be discussed later), and

    (ii)   by specified functional constituencies.

(b)   A number of appointed Unofficial members should be retained on the Council, for the time being.

(c)   The number of Official members of the Council should be gradually reduced.

(d)   To start with, these arrangements should be introduced in two stages — in 1985 and 1988 — following the District Board elections in those years.

(e)   The composition of the Legislative Council by 1988 should be -

    (i)   12 Unofficial members elected by electoral college,

    (ii)   12 Unofficial members elected by the functional constituencies,

    (iii)   16 appointed Unofficial members, and

    (iv)   10 Official members.

(f)   in 1989, after the 1988 elections to the Council have taken place, there should be a review of the position with a view to deciding what further developments should be pursued.

The Executive Council . . .

(g)   The majority of the appointed Unofficial members of the Executive Council should be replaced progressively by members elected by the Unofficial members of the Legislative Council from among their number, but a small number of members should continue to be appointed by the Governor and the four ex-officio members should remain as members of the Council.

(h)   These arrangements should be introduced in two stages — in 1988 and 1991 — following the elections to the Legislative Council in those years.

(i)   The eventual composition of the Executive Council by 1991 should be-

    (i)   at least 8 members elected by the Unofficial members of the Legislative Council.

    (ii)   2 members appointed by the Governor, and

    (iii)   4 ex-officio members,

although these members might be modified in the light of the review of the position of the Legislative Council in 1989.

The Governor . . .

(j)   In due course, the Governor should be replaced as President of the Legislative Council by a Presiding Officer elected by the Unofficial members of the Legislative Council after their own number. This change might be introduced in two stages.

Of even more momentous importance is the hint embedded in the *Green Paper* as to the possible change in the way the Governor was to be selected: "The future method of selecting candidates for appointment as Governor will also need to be considered. One possible development would be for the Governor himself, in his capacity as Chief Executive, to be selected, once the process described in this paper is complete, through an elective process, for example, through election by a college composed of all Unofficial Members of the Executive and Legislative Councils after a period of consultation among them."[30]

The process of constitutional development charted out by *Green Paper*, if completed, will definitely bring about fundamental transformation of the political system of Hong Kong. A quasi-Westminster apparatus will have been in place immediately before the Chinese takeover. This 'sneak attack' by the British, as China perceived it, alarmed and incensed her. But the democratic activists were not satisfied and complained about the sluggishness of the pace of reforms. The motives behind Britain's scheme to lay before the people of Hong Kong a long-term plan for constitutional development were difficult to gauge. Britain might have over-estimated the political need to seek the support of the people of Hong Kong for the forthcoming Sino-British Agreement; or she might aim at producing a *fait accompli* for China which would make disavowal of it difficult; or yet it might simply be a rash and ill-conceived decision of the British officials, over the head of the Hong Kong government, to replicate the past pattern of constitutional reform in Hong Kong. In any event, due to some obvious reasons (e.g. those obstacles to reform discussed before which were in part tacitly admitted in the *Green Paper* in its concern with 'instability' produced by 'adversarial politics'[31]) and some inexplicable ones, Britain suddenly underwent an abrupt turnabout. In the *White Paper*,[32] issued several months later, Britain undertook the first strategic retreat in her political reform 'offensive'. While some concessions were made to the democratic activists, the determination to institute medium- and long-term reforms effectively evaporated. Concessions were made by speeding up some short-term reforms: (1) instead of the 12 indirectly elected unofficial members of the Legislative Council (divided equally between the electoral college and the functional constituencies) proposed for 1985, the number was increased to 24 (with equal numbers for the two electoral modes); (2) the number of appointed unofficial members in 1985 would be reduced by one, from the 23 originally proposed to 22, thus providing for a larger number of elected unofficial members than appointed unofficial members; (3) the number of official members would be ten in 1985 instead of 13 in the *Green Paper*; and (4) the review of the development of the 'representative government' would be brought forward to 1987, in lieu of 1989 as proposed before. (All these reforms were duly implemented in 1985.) However, no definite promise was made as to future reforms.

What is glaring in the *White Paper* is the evident retreat by Britain. The enthusiasm for direct election, not strong in the beginning, was smoldered. The *White Paper* found that "[t]here was considerable general public concern that too rapid progress toward direct election could place the future stability and prosperity of Hong Kong in jeopardy. In summary, there was strong public support for the idea of direct elections but little support for such elections in the immediate future".[33] Plans to tamper with the composition of the Executive Council was suspended. The proposal for a ministerial system was shelved. There was no intention to change the role of the Governor nor the mode of his selection. From the silence of the *White Paper* on future reforms, it can be gathered that Britain had discarded any intention to initiate further reforms.

The hint for the British retreat was already suggested in the *White Paper*. Note the following sentence from the *White Paper*: "Since the Green Paper was published the Draft Agreement on the Future of Hong Kong has been initialled in Peking. Any proposals for change in the position and role of the Governor will need to take into account the provisions of the Joint Declaration and these important issues will be considered at the later stage."[34]

Since the implementations of the proposals of the *White Paper*, measures had been taken by China to take over the initiative in political reform. There was a two-pronged approach. On the one hand, China made explicit its objection to any attempt by Britain to turn the legislature into a center of real power and subordinate all other political and administrative institutions to it. To do so would be interpreted as an infringement of China's sovereignty over Hong Kong. Britain was asked to abandon any plans for further reforms until China's design for the future political system was made known, or unless they facilitated the 'convergence' between the present and future systems, and only if they were endorsed by China.[35] On the other hand, China immediately went into the drafting of the Basic Law – the future constitution of the Hong Kong SAR. The first draft of it will be available in 1988. The Basic Law drafting process provides the locus for the conservative forces in Hong Kong to congeal. Conservative forces were mobilized – particularly among business groups – to oppose 'premature' democratization by the Hong Kong government. In the meantime, China embarked upon an offensive and, through formal and informal channels, made known its intentions, or at least its reservations (particularly about party politics, direct elections and legislative hegemony), for the future political system of Hong Kong. As things stand, the political system in the future will be one centering upon a powerful chief executive, who will be independent of the elected legislature and will be checked by it only to a limited degree.[36]

The strategic offensive to pre-empt the initiative of political reform has landed Britain into a serious dilemma. To conform to China's intentions would erode the credibility of the Hong Kong government, which had already been ridiculed as a lame-duck. To do otherwise would run the risks of antagonizing China and having the reforms dismantled after 1997. Besides, given all the impediments to transferring a quasi-Westminster system to Hong Kong and the low probability of its successful operation, Britain did not really have too much confidence in her reform plans. At the end, the preponderant British interests in promoting long-term diplomatic and economic relationship with China took precedence. The statements by various British and Hong Kong officials all pointed to one direction: surrendering the reform initiative to China and playing the secondary role of preparing Hong Kong for the future system stipulated in the Basic Law.[37]

This strategic retreat by Britain was fully evident in the *Green Paper* issued by the Hong Kong government in May 1987.[38] This consultative document on future political reforms in Hong Kong must stand in history as the *last* attempt by the departing colonial regime to propose and introduce small-scale changes into the institutional structure in Hong Kong. In general, the *Green Paper* should be noted for its omissions rather than commissions. For glaringly omitted from the *Green Paper* are the role and composition of the Executive Council, the power relationship between the Executive Council and the Legislative Council, the advisory committee structure, the civil service, the 'ministerial system,' the role and ways of selection of the Governor and means to check bureaucratic power. Similarly absent from the *Green Paper* is any mention of the direction and the program of future institutional development, thereby rendering it primarily a one-shot attempt at tinkering with the system.

At the outset, the government confines its role in the reform process by restricting the scope of the 1987 review. The *Green Paper* makes it clear that the review will be conducted *within the framework of Hong Kong's existing constitutional arrangements*, thus ruling out significant constitutional changes. The *Green Paper* also claims to take *fully* into account the terms of the Sino-British Joint Declaration on the question of Hong Kong, which provides for Hong Kong to become a Special Administrative Region of China with effect from July 1, 1997, thereby admitting that the Basic Law will set the parameters for future political changes. The government further 'de-committed' itself by listing in the *Green Paper* only a battery of 'options' rather than concrete, solid proposals or recommendations. In asking the people to contemplate on these options, the *Green Paper* provides a confusingly large number of inconsistent and even contradictory criteria for evaluation, the overall effect being to encourage them to basically endorse the status quo while deliberating upon some 'harmless,' *ad hoc* changes in the system. These changes are geared primarily to deal with the incongruities in the less significant components of the political system of Hong Kong (the district boards and municipal councils and the practical aspects of elections), which result from the hesitant and largely non-programmatic nature of past political reforms by the government.

Perhaps the more significant options which the government is serious about are the introduction of a certain proportion of directly elected seats into the Legislative Council in 1988 and the Governor vacating from the post of president of the Legislative Council. Nevertheless, both options are significant more in terms of political psychology than in the institutional sense. However, both options are opposed by China and a substantial portion of the attentive public. How far Britain is prepared to 'confront' China, the business sector and the conservative forces in Hong Kong is not known. But it is quite unlikely that these more 'important' reforms will be introduced in 1988 if China, while steadfastly opposing these moves, is willing to provide Britain with certain concessions as a face-saving device.

While the plan to transform the viceregal structure of Hong Kong into a parliamentary government has been virtually abandoned, Britain was still able to introduce reforms in some less important areas which occasionally drew the suspicion and disapproval of China. However, these reforms were *ad hoc*, desultory and disconnected efforts, even though the overall direction was to open up further the political system. Some of the more important changes that have been made or will be introduced subsequently are:

(1)   the Hong Kong Act 1985, enacted by the British Parliament immediately after the signing of the Sino-British Agreement, was an Act to make provision for and in connection with the ending of British sovereignty and jurisdiction over Hong Kong. Section 3(1) of the Act reads: "Her Majesty may before the relevant date by Order in Council make such provision as appears to Her Majesty to be necessary or expedient in consequences of or in connection with the provisions of section 1(1) of this Act - (a) for repealing or amending any enactment so far as it is part of the law of Hong Kong; and (b) for enabling the legislature of Hong Kong to repeal or amend any enactment so far as it is part of that law and so to make laws having extra-territorial operation." Thus, through delegation of authority by the British Crown from time to time, the legislative power of the Legislative Council will be enhanced.

(2)   bolstering the power and status of the Legislative Council by enacting the controversial Legislative Council (Powers and Privileges) Ordinance in 1985. The ordinance, among other things, empowers the Legislative Council or a standing committee thereof to "order any person to attend before the Council or before such committee and to give evidence or to produce any paper, book, record or document in the possession or under the control of such person."[39] Even though the enlarged investigative power of the legislature is in some ways circumscribed, it still constitutes a potential powerful weapon for the legislature in its relationship with the Governor.

(3)   two indirectly elected Legislative Councillors were appointed to the Executive Council in 1986.[40] Though they are accountable to the Governor only, this move represented a strengthening of relationship between the 'closed' Executive Council and the elective elements in the legislature.

(4)   Legislative Councillors were more frequently appointed to consultative or advisory committees in an attempt to boost their status and influence. In addition, the government also seems to be making efforts to streamline the advisory committee structure, re-arrange a portion of the inter-related committees

into a quasi-hierarachical structure, and link some of the committees directly or indirectly with the Legislative Council, thus making them more amenable to legislative influence. There might also be long-term plans to develop specialized or select committees within the Legislative Council on a more or less permanent basis (and with the participation of outside experts) in order to augment the policy influence of the legislative Council on the executive.

(5) Steps have been taken to make the judiciary more independent of the government by drawing up judicial service regulations which will replace civil service regulations for judicial officers.[42]

(6) Immediately before their inauguration of the Sino-British negotiation over the future of Hong Kong, in a move reminiscent of the steps taken in former British colonies to use local bodies as the training ground of future leaders, eighteen (late nineteen) district boards were set up which were charged with consultative functions and had a partially elected membership. In 1985 the elective component was subsequently enlarged to two-thirds of the membership, and the chairmen of the boards also become elective.

Additional efforts were made or proposed to strengthen the district boards and to 'democratize' their structure, while retaining their basically advisory nature. In the mimeographed copy of a document "A Summary of the Recommendations of the Review of District Administration" distributed by the government in May 1987, the government tried to convince the district boards of their 'importance' by reiterating its 'commitments' to them through a number of relatively vague recommendations: (a) each DB (district board) may request a full briefing on subjects for which there are public consultative documents; (b) if government departments find it inappropriate to follow the advice of the DB, they should give it full explanations and wherever possible, suggest an alternative course of action or solution; (c) in cases where DBs and departments fail to agree on a solution to a particular problem, the matter should be referred to the Regional Secretary concerned for discussion with the relevant department heads, with a view to resolving the problem; (d) policy branches and department should provide DBs with regular briefings on their main areas of work and on the background to major policies and actions; (e) departments should, as far as practicable, provide an annual programme of their work in the district for consultation with the DB; (f) departments should continue to send senior and experienced officers to attend DB meetings to receive advice, provide information and respond promptly and definitely to DB's requests. If a reply cannot be given during a DB meeting, a written reply should be provided within two weeks. In the case of a positive reply, departments should advise the DB on the planned follow-up actions with expected dates of completion. Each DB may also request the attendance of representatives of departments other than those normally represented on the Board for discussion of matters related specifically to the district concerned; (g) all documents submitted to DBs for consultation should contain as much relevant background information as possible and should set out clearly the options available and the pros and cons of each option. Those documents in both Chinese and English should reach the DB members at least two weeks before the consultation; and (h) more DB members should be appointed to central advisory bodies.

It was also proposed that legal provisions should be made to allow DB members to vote the chairman of DB out of office. But the rules for that are stringent. A vote of 'no confidence' against a DB chairman must be moved by no less than two-thirds of the members concerned and would be carried only with the support of at least three quarters of the members.

(7)   At the semi-local level, there were the restucturing of the half-elected Urban Council and the establishment of a largely similar Regional Council in the New Territories. (It is possible that the Regional Council was originally conceived as an alternative to the introduction of an elective component in the Legislative Council, which, however quickly followed.)

(8)   Perhaps the most uncontroversial reform undertaken is the localization of the civil service, which is in fact a continuation of a past trend. The quickened pace of localization draws protestations from expatriate civil servants, which however is unavoidable. Starting from mid-1985, the government has stopped hiring expatriates for the elite administrative officers grade of the civil service.[43] Retirement age for expatriates was set at 57, and it was projected that by 1996, only three of the secretarial posts (equivalent to ministerial posts in other countries) out of a total of 18 (the figure for 1986) would be held by expatriates.[44] In 1986, "[i]n the senior management/ professional grades, local officers now hold over 70 per cent of the 1,500 posts whilst in directorate (i.e. most senior) ranks, the proportion has reached 50 per cent of the 940 positions."[45]

The Politics of Unfinished Reforms

The injection of new elements inevitably creates conflicts in the political system. Nevertheless, if the direction of change is clear and unalterable, and if the steps taken are appropriate and integrated, conflicts stemming from political reforms will only be temporary, for the old elements will be compelled to reconcile themselves to the emerging political order. Such, however, is not the case in Hong Kong. In the first place, with all the obstacles encountered in the reform process and the obvious reservations and vacillations of Britain, the initial reforms were largely *ad hoc*, incremental, disconnected and reactive extemporizations.[46] Moreover, the sudden abortion of the reforms not long after they had been installed made it unnecessary and impossible for the new and old elements to reconcile with one another, for without an ineluctable direction of change, no one is sure who would eventually be the loser. Thus, the aborted reforms of the British, instead of propelling the political system of Hong Kong toward a Westminster direction, in actuality turn a previously 'harmonious' system (however contrived the 'harmony' may be) into a conflict-laden one, which inordinately complicates the efforts of Britain to maintain a stable and effective government in her last decade of rule over Hong Kong.

Since the onset of the Sino-British negotiation, the Hong Kong government has found itself in a 'turbulent' environment,[47] which severely taxed its will and ability to govern. This turbulence is caused by a number of factors: the mistrust of China, the growing seriousness of social, political and economic problems, the volatility of public opinion, the unsettling feelings of pessimism and uncertainty, the rise of new political groups, the politicization of many socio-economic groups, the rivalries among these groups, the increasing resort to confrontational tactics to pressurize the government, the increasing sensitivity of the people to the conflict or potential conflict of interests between Hong Kong on the one hand and China or Britain on the other, as well as between the people and their government, and the increasing employment of populist appeals and oppositional tactics by the aggrieved and frustrated 'politicians' and leaders.

At a time of unprecedented turbulence, the power and resources at the disposal of the government are at their lowest point ever. The political autonomy of the government has been seriously curtailed by the entry of China and Britain into the decision-making arena. Never before has the government's direction been so constricted. Now it finds itself closely monitored by two superior governments whose interests it cannot ignore and whose support it cannot do without. The situation of the government is made even more difficult by the natural tendency for the people of Hong Kong to bypass it and seek directly the support of the British or the Chinese governments, particularly the latter. Even without the intrusion of Britain and China into the political scene, a departing government is bound to witness decline in authority. Various individuals and groups will become much bolder in challenging its authority. A transitional government is also victimized by a 'telescoping' process which leads the people to perceive it as the mistrusted future SAR government and to deal with it accordingly (for instance, to 'purify' it in a democratic direction by ridding it of its authoritarian powers so that they will not fall into the hands of the future government). The result is that the government will become increasingly hamstrung, in the process of policy formulation and implementation, by popular suspicions and objections, thus further undermining its increasingly tenuous authority and its ability to take decisive actions.

The hastily introduced reforms have aggravated the problem of 'ungovernability'. Instead of mobilizing support for the battered government, they have implanted a number of paralyzing contradictions into the political system which it is unable to control or to resolve. The formerly 'harmonious' system, centering on the Governor as the source of authority and legitimacy, has broken down, and in its place is a conflict-ridden, dissension-prone system, whose components base their power and influence on divergent, incompatible principles.

The gist of the matter is that the reforms undertaken by the Hong Kong government has, in an effort to pacify a variety of constituencies and in an attempt to politicize the vested interests so that they can fend for themselves in a new political game, so fragmented and dispersed the power it has devolved to the people (through a system of indirect elections by functional constituencies and local bodies) that a large number of political forces, all individually weak, have been unleashed. The resultant confusion can be testified to by the intensifying elite rivalries, polarization of opinions and increasing deployment of unconventional tactics to score political points. While the bulk of political power is still in the possession of the government, its declining authority position however would caution against its arbitrary use, for in a situation where the autonomy of the government has diminished, the repercussions of any misuse of power will be difficult for it to manage. Hence the government rapidly finds itself immersed in a political matrix dotted with numerous veto points. The rise of the veto groups may not suffice to throttle the government, but they are sufficient to block decisions which are interpreted as detrimental to a large-enough bloc of interests. The government will find itself in a situation where occasional resort to draconian measures, backed up by coercion, have to be made. But that would further erode its authority. Moreover, the closer is 1997, the less will be the government's capacity to assert itself in such manner. If nothing is done about it, and 'authority crisis' will ensue.

The most prominent contradictions in the reformed political system are located in the relationship between the Legislative Council and the executive institutions (the Executive Council and the civil service) headed by the Governor. Before the inclusion of elective elements in the Legislative Council, 'consensus' among the Councillors could be secured by the adroit manipulation of the appointment process to preclude the entry of discordant elements in the elitist legislature. The homogeneity of the Councillors was guaranteed by their largely shared socio-economic background and their uniform allegiance to the Governor. Despite the appeal to 'consensus' by some 'senior' (appointed) Councillors, the reformed legislature has become a new political entity characterized by: (1) divergent sources of recruitment of members; (2) heterogeneity of their socio-economic background; (3) different conceptions of legitimacy and accountability; (4) contrasting valuations of 'consensus politics'; (5) manifold definitions of the role of the legislator (with the 'trustee', 'representative' and 'spokesman' roles predominant); (6) penetration of outside forces into the legislature through the elected members and the increasingly politicized and militant appointed members; (7) mutually incompatible decision-making styles; (8) divergent political allegiances; (9) breakdown of the 'seniority' and 'disciplinary' system; and (10) the legislature becoming the arena for the assertion of Hong Kong interests *vis-a-vis* those of the Hong Kong, British and Chinese governments.[48]

Legislative politics becomes more open and sensational, as a growing number of legislators resort to public appeals through the mass media. Debates inside and outside the legislative chamber become more acrimonious. Personal attacks are not infrequent.

At a time when a strong and decisive government is needed, the Hong Kong government is curbed by a legislature which is its own creation. However, a conflict-infested legislature is bound to be a weak one, with a lot of veto power but without the unity of purpose and action to constructively take part in policy-making or in effectively overseeing the work of the government. A fractionized legislature cannot even effectively use the power at its disposal (such as the power bestowed on it by the Legislative Council (Power and Privileges) Ordinance), thus making a mockery of its power and rendering it superfluous. A legislature which has a lot of responsibility but not much power is susceptible to radicalization. Perhaps a way out of this impasse is to gradually transform it into the center of power as in the parliamentary system, but this alternative has already been foreclosed.

The relationship between the Legislative Council and the local bodies is far from cordial. Personal and institutional jealousies and mutual suspicions are the culprits for this state of affairs. So are feelings of status inferiority on the part of the district boards. Perhaps the most pertinent factors must be the ambiguous division of labor between the central and local bodies and the demand of the district boards for an enlarged jurisdiction as well as executive functions. The 'boycott' of the district board chairmen and many DB members of the consultative sessions of the Legislative Council was a vivid expression of the 'hostile' attitude of the local leaders.[49] It can also be interpreted as the outburst of the frustration of a group of leaders who have high hopes (instilled largely by the government in its extolment of the district boards) for their institutions and themselves, who now find themselves without real power and cast away into political oblivion.[50]

Out of a desire to reassert themselves and instigated by the overlapping of functions between themselves and the Urban and Regional Councils, the district boards are also embroiled in a 'turf war' with the two Councils, which are perceived as much better treated by the government (in terms of financial autonomy, executive responsibilities and the remuneration of the Councillors) and whose functions are deemed to be more effectively performed by the district boards themselves. What makes the conflict between the two Councils and the district boards difficult to resolve is the fact that the district boards can only become more politically significant if they can take over the functions of the two Councils. Conflict between them is hence unavoidable.[51] The recent decision of the political structure subgroup of the Basic Law Drafting Committee to basically 'freeze' the functions of the regional and local bodies after 1997 will exacerbate this conflict, as the parties are now locked in a zero-sum game.[52]

Possible Future Developments

How can the Hong Kong government, mired in a turbulent environment, presiding over an increasingly unwieldy and contradictory political system, and suffering from declining authority and autonomy, maintain effective and sufficiently stable rule in its last years? Past decolonization experience would suggest the forging of a loose alliance among democratic activists, traditional elements and pro-British groups to take over gradually power from the departing colonial master. But this option is out the question in Hong Kong. The weak and splintered democratic movement in Hong Kong cannot be compared with the all-encompassing nationalist movement in the former colonies, to ally with them will be contrary to the long-term interests of Britain and will lead to immediate confrontation with China. Under the existing circumstances, it is doubtful that the democratic activists can coalesce into a significant political force in the future. There are even signs that the government is distancing itself from them. Hong Kong as an urbanized and modernized society also does not provide the traditional elements (e.g. Indian princes, Malay sultans or African chiefs) who would act as a moderate and conservative force sympathetic with British rule. The pro-British groups (the co-opted elites, business interests and professional-managerial groups) are similarly not an appropriate ally. They do not have organizational linkage with the people, they are losing credibility as a result of their association with the declining colonial regime, their allegiance to Britain is dubious (many of them have gone over to the Chinese side) and they fail to demonstrate sufficient commitment to Hong Kong.

The Hong Kong government can of course relapse into *ad hocism* and incrementalism, which had been its hallmarks in the past, and which still are largely its decision-making style. But to stick to this style in a veto-infused environment can only lead to policy immobilism, which would be a source of instability in the extraordinary transitional period, where long-term planning and bold decisions are called for. A lame-duck government would ineluctably exacerbate the plight of 'ungovernability'.

Another option for the government, which is now being practised, is to establish a 'negotiated order' by accommodating the new political actors in an enlarged decision-making arena. These new actors obviously include China, Britain, the newly-emergent political groups and the increasingly politicized socio-economic interests. Compromising, bargaining and 'consensus-making' are the names of the game, and the government plays the central role in reconciliating diverse interests so that a semblance of effective governance can be maintained. But the government has been only partially successful so far with this strategy, and for several reasons: (1) the political arena is not opened up sufficiently to the satisfaction of most of the relevant interests; (2) some of the interests involved (such as China and Britain) are clearly more powerful than the Hong Kong government, and so their wishes will predominate, often to the chagrin of the minor interests; (3) political reforms by the government, with the fragmentation and dispersal of the power devolved, have already created such a large number of new interests that 'consensus-making' is very difficult, sometimes impossible; (4) some of the groups (particularly the more radicalized democratic groups) cannot really be accommodated into a conservatively-oriented 'negotiated order'; and finally (5) a government suffering from declining authority and possibly hampered by future economic difficulties simply does not have enough resources to satisfy a majority of the interests in the 'negotiated order', and ultimately it has to choose between interests more crucial to continued British rule and those less so. In the final analysis, a broad-fronted 'negotiated order', under existing circumstances, is bound to fail in the future, and in the end it is most likely that the democratic and uncompromisingly dissident elements will be excluded.

In order to preserve stable and effective rule, the most probable action that will be taken by the Hong Kong government will be made up of two components: (1) the reinforcement of the authority of the government by increasing reliance upon China as an informal 'partner' in the governance of Hong Kong; and (2) a reorganization of the power structure in the political system so that the role of the bureaucracy will be strengthened, and within the bureaucracy the leadership position of the hardcore officers (the elite administrative class) will be enhanced. Both components will point to the adoption of a moderate authoritarian orientation on the part of the government, which will be a departure from the previous trend of democratization. Further steps at formal democratization (e.g. the introduction of a small percentage of directly elected members of the Legislative Council) will not substantively alter this moderate authoritarian trend.

Increasing reliance on the participation of China in the Governance of Hong Kong will be sought because: (1) the ever-rising power of China will be needed to bolster the faltering authority of the departing regime; (2) the Hong Kong government can no longer 'take care of' the interests of China in Hong Kong *alone* without incurring irreparable damages to its tenuous ruling position; (3) only China can exert the necessary restraints on the opponents of the government; and (4) *only China can 're-assemble' the pieces of transferred power that have been dispersed by the Hong Kong government in its previous reforms.* An authentic alliance between Britain and China, backed up by the emerging 'united front' formed by China and composed of the business interests and other pro-China elements, should be sufficient to undergird stable and effective rule of the Hong Kong government in the run-up to 1997, particularly in view of the weaknesses of the democratic activists and the political immobilism of apathy of the masses. As this China-centered 'united front' will in time become the 'ruling coalition', it will be an element of continuity between Hong Kong as a British colony and Hong Kong as a Chinese Special Administrative Region.

Within the political system itself, the likely development will be that the Hong Kong government will gradually distance itself from bodies with elective and populist elements, bodies which have once been favored as target of power transfer. There are indications that the government, through the cautious and selective withdrawal of information, is trying to reduce the decision-making role of the

Legislative Council and the district boards.[53] However, in view of the declining authority of the government, it cannot resort to constitutional retrogressions to drastically strengthen the powers of the Governor, as happened in some former colonies such as Cyprus, Malta and British Guiana.[54] Nor can the Governor arbitrarily use the already formidable powers at his disposal, such as the power to dissolve the Legislative Council which was bestowed on him immediately after adoption of the decisions of the *White Paper*. Even so, the future relationship between the government and the partially elected bodies at both central and local levels is not likely to be a cordial or happily collaborative one.

The increasing dependence on the bureaucracy (the civil service) can be considered a logical phenomenon in the politics of unfinished reforms. Indications of 're-dependence' on the career civil service include efforts to appease civil servants and to fend off any attempts to curb bureaucratic discretion. Over the last two years, civil servants had been given an improved pensions scheme (with the endorsement of China),[55] more and better training facilities and opportunities,[56] and easier accessibility to private sector jobs after retirement.[57] A plan to install a powerful 'ombudsman' as a corrective for maladministration has been virtually shelved.[58] All these are measures taken to boost the morale of the civil servants, which has deteriorated as a result of the 1997 question and democratization.

A government under pressure would also try to exert more control over its resources and personnel and tighten up its supervisory practices. This the Hong Kong government seems to be doing by strengthening the 'ruling stratum' – the administrative officers – in the bureaucracy. The 'generalist', politically more sensitive administration officers are considered more loyal and more oriented to take the interests of the government *as a whole* into account. The administrative class has always been the main-stay of the bureaucracy, though in recent years its monopolization of top posts had been challenged by the professionals and specialists. Re-emphasis on the leadership role of the administrative class will inevitably intensify the conflict between the 'generalists' and the specialists.[59] Similarly, the process of 're-centralization' in the bureaucracy, as a means to enhance the solidarity of the civil service in a turbulent environment, will aggravate the conflict between upper and lower civil servants, a conflict that had plagued the administration in the past two decades. In any event, this attempt at 're-centralization' will encounter almost insurmountable obstacles since the civil service is now much more heterogeneous, more diverse in political orientations, more unionized and more prone to penetration by political influence from outside (including China). It is not inconceivable that in its efforts to strengthen and 're-centralize' the civil service, the Hong Kong government will feel compelled to seek the support of China, and the support will be forthcoming.

Conclusion

The decolonization process in Hong Kong must be entered into history as a very intriguing event in that it is afflicted with ironies and unexpected consequences. The initial British attempt to swiftly transplant a quasi-Westminster system of government to Hong Kong so as to enable the people there to stand on their own feet in the post-1997 era would in all likelihood end up differently: (1) the original trend of democratization will be taken over by a trend of moderate authoritarianism; (2) the expedient and compromising strategy of fragmenting and dispersing the power transferred results in a situation where only China will be in a position to 're-assemble' these scattered pieces of power and build a strong ruling coalition (not necessarily in the form of a visible political party) to dominate the political system, as the local forces are not in a position to consolidate into a potent ruling force in an electoral system dominated by indirect elections; (3) the participation of China in the governance of Hong Kong as a 'partner' of the incumbent government will be earlier than expected because of the growing inability of the Hong Kong government to control the veto power exercised by groups which are the creatures of its political reforms; and (4) the initial direction of building a parliamentary government will be shifted to an executive-centered system of government due to the re-dependence on the bureaucracy and its 're-centralization' and as a result of the takeover of the reform initiative by China (through the Basic Law drafting process).

These ironies and unintended consequences, in retrospect, can be easily explained. Decolonization in Hong Kong failed to provide a coherent foundation for development toward a clearcut institutional goal (a quasi-Westminster model). The lack of previous preparations, the absence of a political organizational infrastructure, the lack of determination on the part of Britain, the improvized nature of the reforms, the misfit between the reforms and objective conditions, the incongruities within the reformed institutional structure, the objection and pressure from China, the opposition of the vested interests (notably the business sector) and, most importantly, the impossibility of independence are the factors which readily come to mind. Consequently, raising of false hope of a parliamentary government only worked to unleash a large variety of political forces whose demands could not be met by the government and who could not be smoothly integrated into the existing system. In the process political conflicts multiplied while the institutional coherence of the original system could not be maintained. In the end, a backlash set in, culminating in the emergence of a moderately authoritarian and executive-centered government, buttressed by China, to restore political order while simultaneously producing political alienation and frustration.

The return to an executive-centered political system by the Hong Kong government will definitely facilitate the convergence between the system inherited from Britain and the future system imposed by China. Still, in order for convergence to occur, institutional refurbishments have to be made so as to remove the contradictions within the existing structure. In the final analysis, institutional continuity of the political system of Hong Kong will not be fundamentally disturbed by the tragicomical interlude of the unfinished reforms of the departing colonial government.

Notes

1. A Draft Agreement between the Government of the United Kingdom of Great Britain and Northern Ireland and the Government of the People's Republic of China on the Future of Hong Kong (Hong Kong: Government Printer, 26 September 1984).

2. 'Former British colonies' here refer to colonies making up the 'new' or 'second' British Empire and acquired after roughly 1815. They were colonies populated mainly by people of the non-British race.

3. See Norman Miners, *The Government and Politics of Hong Kong* (Hong Kong: Oxford University Press, 1986), pp. 166-179.

4. D.J. Morgan, *Guidance Towards Self-Government in British Colonies* (London: The Macmillan Press Ltd., 1980) pp. 62, 216, 228.

5. For both the 1946 and 1966 reform proposals, see Norman Miners, *The Government and Politics of Hong Kong* (Hong Kong: Oxford University Press, 1981), pp. 237-239.

6. For a summarization of *The Report of the Committee of Enquiry into Constitutional Development in the Smaller Colonial Territories* submitted to the Secretary of State in August 1951, see ibid, pp. 45-46.

7. N.J. Miners, "Plans for Constitutional Reform in Hong Kong, 1946-52", *The China Quarterly*, 107 (September, 1986), pp. 463-482.

8. An illustrative example of China's anxiety about taking over only a 'nominal' sovereignty from Britain was her interpretation (disclosed through informal channels) of the implications of the age-old The Colonial Laws Validity Act, enacted in 1865, for the future sovereignty of China over Hong Kong. Among other things, Section V of the Act granted to the representative legislature (any colonial legislature which comprised a legislative body of which one half were elected by inhabitants of the colony) "full power to make laws respecting the constitution, powers and procedure of such legislature, provided that such laws shall have been passed in such manner and form as may from time to time be required, by any Act of

Parliament, Letters Patent, Order of Council, or colonial law for the time being in force in the said colony." In 1865, the Act, which dealt with a longstanding issue about the validity of colonial laws when they were repugnant to the British common law and triggered off by the 'Boothby Affair' in South Australia, reflected an attitude toward legislative autonomy in the colonies of the Colonial Office that was described as "liberal and progressive" (D.B. Swinfen, *Imperial Control of Colonial Legislation 1813-1865* (Oxford: Clarendon Press, 1970), p. 178). To what extent this Act applies to Hong Kong is unclear, such as whether a legislature half of whose members are *indirectly* elected would become an *ispo facto* representative legislature. China's apprehension that the coming into force of the Act will mean that full legislative power would then be passed from the Governor to the legislature is also unfounded *in the strict legal sense,* as the legislature will still be restrained by a number of superior legal instruments. What China has in fact in mind however are: that the acquisition of the powers to change its constitution, powers and procedure would generate wide-ranging possibilities for the Legislative Council to acquire complete legislative power which would give it a supreme status in the political system; and , more importantly, out of suspicion of British intentions, the Hong Kong government will be unwilling to restrain the legislature by means of the superior legal instruments, or be conciliatory to the demands of the legislators, or be powerless or feel politically inexpedient to oppose the initiatives from the legislature, or worse still, be in conspiracy with the legislature by collaborating clandestinely with it in transforming it into the repository of the sovereign powers of Britain. Any of these scenarios would imply the transfer of power to the people of Hong Kong and reduce the power that will be returned to China in 1997.

9. See Lau Siu-kai nd Kuan Hsin-chi, "Hong Kong After the Sino-British Agreement: The Limits to Change", *Pacific Affairs*, 59, no. 2 (Summer 1986) pp. 214-236.

10. An example of small-scale Chinese participation in the electoral game can be found in the 1985 District Board Election. See Lau Siu-kai and Kuan Hsin-chi, "The 1986 District Board Election in Hong Kong: The Limits of Political Mobilization in a Dependent Polity", *Journal of Commonwealth & Comparative Politics*, 25, no. 1 (March 1987) pp. 82-102. Since 1985, a small number of pro-China leaders have also found their way into the Legislative Council.

11.   Collier, *Regimes in Tropical Africa: Change Forms of Supremacy, 1945-1975* (Berkeley and L.A., Calif.: University of Calfornia Press, 1982), pp. 29-30.

12.   A vivid example is Singapore where the British government suppressed the communists there to expedite the rise to power of the less radical faction of the People's Action Party led by Lee Kuan Yew. See John Drysdale, *Singapore: Struggle for Success* (Singapore: Times Books International, 1984).

13.   In a survey of a systematic sample (N = 767) of residents in Kwun Tong (an industrial community of Hong Kong) in 1985 by Dr. Kuan Hsin-chi and myself, only 31.5 percent of the respondents were trustful or very trustful of the Chinese government, and only 22.3 percent of them thought that China would allow the people of Hong Kong to manage their own affairs. Furthermore, a large proportion of them, 84.7 percent, regarded that their ability to influence the policy of the Hong Kong government was small or very small. In 1986, another survey of the residents of Kwun Tong was conducted by Mrs. Law Wan Po-san and myself (a systematic sample of 539), it was found that only 25.4 percent of the respondents were trustful or very trustful of the Chinese government. 50.3 percent of them expected the standard of living after 1997 to remain stagnant or decline; 60.3 percent thought that personal freedom would be reduced; 56.9 percent thought that there would be a diminution of human rights and 52.3 predicted decadence of the judiciary. As in 1985, a large proportion of them (87.9 percent) stated that they had no influence at all on the Hong Kong government.

14.   In the 1985 study mentioned in the last note, only 33.8 percent of the respondents disagreed or strongly disagreed with the statement that it was very likely that democratic politics would facilitate the rise of careerists set out to harm the public. As to their opinion toward the 'pressure groups', 58.5 percent said that they could find no trustworthy pressure group leaders; and 53.5 percent of them regarded the activities of the 'pressure groups' as endangering the stability and prosperity of Hong Kong. In the 1986 survey mentioned in the last note, only 22.7 percent of the respondents thought that the 'pressure groups' had made great or very great contributions to the improvement of the living environment of the people of Hong Kong.

15. See Lau Siu-kai and Kuan Hsin-chi, "The Changing Political Culture of the Hong Kong Chinese", in Joseph Y.S. Cheng, ed., *Hong Kong in Transition* (Hong Kong: Oxford University Press, 1986), pp. 26-51. In the 1985 survey mentioned in n. 13, 74.3 percent of the respondents considered the existing political system of Hong Kong as the best that could be found, given the existing circumstances. 72.1 percent of them were trustful or very trustful of the Hong Kong government. 66.8 percent of the respondents in the 1986 survey likewise were trustful or very trustful of the Hong Kong government. As to the performance of the Hong Kong government, the 1985 survey found that only 9.5 percent of the respondents accused the government of doing a bad or very bad job. In a poll commissioned by *South China Morning Post* (SCMP), "[on] a scale of one to 10, in which the top score indicated people thought the authorities were doing an extremely good job and the bottom of the scale that they were doing an extremely bad job, the government won an average rating of 6.3" (SCMP, December 12, 1986, p. 1).

16. Smith, "A Comparative Study of French and British Decolonization," *Comparative Studies in Society and History*, 20, no. 1 (January 1978), p. 91.

17. Emerson, *From Empire to Nation* (Cambridge, Mass.: Harvard University Press, 1960), p. 55.

18. Ibid, p. 56.

19. For the objection of the business sector to mass franchise, direct election and party politics, as well as their views of the future political system of Hong Kong, see for example, *SCMP*, June 1, 1986, p. 2; November 5, 1986, p. 2; December 2, 1986, p. 1; and *Ming Pao Daily News*, February 7, 1987, p. 2.

20. Martin Kilson, *Political Change in a West African State: A Study of the Modernization Process in Sierra Leone* (Cambridge, Mass.: Harvard University Press, 1966), p. 90.

21. Aaron Wildavsky, "Using Public Funds to Serve Private Interests: The Politics of the New Class", in B. Bruce-Briggs, ed., *The New Class?* (New York: McGraw-Hill Book Co., 1979), p. 148.

22.   Luis, Ratinoff, "The New Urban Groups: The Middle Classes", in Seymour M. Lipset and Aldo Solari, eds., *Elites in Latin America* (New York: Oxford University Press, 1967), p. 69.

23.   C. Wright Mills, *The White Collar: The American Middle Classes* (New York: Oxford University Press, 1951), p. xviii.

24.   See Harold L. Wilensky, *The Welfare State and Equality* (Berkeley and L.A.: University of Calfornia Press, 1975), pp. 54-58.

25.   The words used by Emerson to characterize local civil servants in former colonies are, probably to a lesser extent, equally apt in Hong Kong. "Even though the local civil servants are by education and background usually the kind of people whom one would otherwise expect to find enlisted in the nationalist movement, their general tendency has been to stand aloof from it and to view it with some of the same suspicion as do their imported fellow officials. The men who have been most successful in their official careers are likely to grant the colonial system the largest measure of acceptance or tolerance. They become imbued with the morale of the service and look askance at those who seek to take over a government without firsthand administrative experience. In the accustomed fashion of the bureaucrat, they, like the expatriate officials, have grave doubts as to the ability of the people to know their needs and manage their own affairs. The over-all consequence is, of course, that the local civil servants are often viewed with suspicion by the nationalists" (*From Empire to Nation*, pp. 249-250). For a discussion of the ambivalent attitude of the Chinese civil servants toward democracy, see Lau Siu-kai and Kuan Hsin-chi, *Chinese Bureaucrats in a Modern Colony: The Case of Hong Kong* (Occasional Paper No. 16, Centre for Hong Kong Studies, The Chinese University of Hong Kong, September 1986).

26.   See Ambrose Y.C. King, "Administrative Absorption of Politics in Hong Kong: Emphasis on the Grass Roots Level", *Asian Survey*, 15, no. 5 (May 1975), pp. 422-439; and Lau Siu-kai, *Society and Politics in Hong Kong* (Hong Kong: Chinese University Press, 1982).

27.   Brian Hook, "The Government of Hong Kong: Change Within Tradition", *The China Quarterly*, no. 95 (September 1983), pp. 491-511.

28. *Green Paper: The Further Development of Representative Government in Hong Kong* (Hong Kong: Government Printer, July 1984), p. 4.

29. Ibid, pp. 21-22.

30. Ibid, p. 20.

31. Ibid, p. 9.

32. *White Paper: The Further Development of Representative Government in Hong Kong* (Hong Kong: Government Printer, November 1984).

33. Ibid, p. 8.

34. Ibid, p. 11.

35. See, for instance, *Far Eastern Economic Review (FEER)*, 5 December 1985, pp. 12-14; *FEER*, 2 January 1986, pp. 10-11; *Asiaweek*, March 2, 1986, p. 26; *SCMP*, November 6, 1986, p. 1 and *SCMP*, February 12, 1987, p. 1.

36. *SCMP*, June 4, 1986, p. 1; *SCMP*, June 14, 1986, p. 1; *FEER*, 7 August 1986, pp. 24-25; *FEER*, 26 December 1985, pp. 14-15; *SCMP*, July 3, 1986, p. 1; *FEER*, 11 September 1986, p. 24; *FEER*, 19 February 1987, p. 48; *SCMP*, February 4, 1987, p. 1 and *Asiaweek*, February 22, 1987, p. 18.

37. *FEER*, 14 November 1985, p. 25; 12 December 1985, p. 21; 16 January 1986, pp. 37-38; 23 October 1986, p. 35 and 30 October 1986, p. 26; *SCMP*, 30 May 1987, p. 1.

38. *Green Paper: The 1987 Review of Developments in Representative Government* (Hong Kong: Government Printer, May 1987).

39. *Legislative Council* (Powers and Privileges) *Ordinance* (Hong Kong: Government Printer, 1985), p. 5.

40. *SCMP*, July 2, 1986, p. 2.

41. *Oriental Daily News*, March 31, 1986, p. 3.

42. *SCMP*, June 23, 1986, p. 1.

43. *SCMP*, July 8, 1985, p. 1.

44. *SCMP*, June 20, 1986, p. 1.

45. *White Paper on the Annual Report on Hong Kong 1985-86 to Parliament*, (Hong Kong: Government Printer, 21 February 1987), p. 8.

46. Lau Siu-kai, "Political Reform and Political Development in Hong Kong: Dilemmas and Choices", in Y.C. Yao et al, eds., *Hong Kong and 1997: Strategies for the Future* (Hong Kong: Centre of Asian Studies, University of Hong Kong, 1985), pp. 23-49.

47. Ian Scott, "Policy-Making in a Turbulent Environment: The Case of Hong Kong", *International Review of Administrative Sciences*, 52 (1986), pp. 447-469.

48. This can be seen in the furor over the Daya Bay nuclear plant in 1986 and the Public Order (Amendment) Ordinance in 1987.

49. See *SCMP*, November 18, 1986, p. 3; November 19, 1986, p. 1; November 20, 1986, p. 1 and November 26, 1986, p. 2.

50. See *SCMP*, November 23, 1986, p. 2; December 2, 1986, p. 30 and March 13, 1987, p. 6.

51. See *SCMP*, December 12, 1985, p. 2; December 13, 1985, p. 2 and February 8, 1985, p. 2.

52. See *Ming Pao Daily News*, March 17, 1987, p. 4.

53. See *SCMP*, July 20, 1986, p. 10 and November 23, 1986, p. 2.

54. See Martin Wight, *The Development of the Legislative Council 1606-1945* (London: Faber and Faber Ltd., 1946), pp. 78-81.

55. *SCMP*, December 6, 1986, p. 5.

56. *SCMP*, December 23, 1986, p. 4; January 12, 1987, p. 1; *Ming Pao Daily News*, March 12, 1987, p. 12 and March 19, 1987, p. 8.

57. *FEER*, 22 January 1987, p. 19.

58. See *SCMP*, August 21, 1986, p. 1 for a discussion of the government's intention to set up a weak Commissioner for Administration to investigate complaints against civil servants.

59. See *Pai Shing Semi-Monthly*, no. 136, January 16, 1987, pp. 40-41.

Demi-democracy: Thai Politics and Government in Transition

Likhit Dhiravegin

I. Introduction

The political system of Thailand since the revolution of June 24, 1932 is often incorrectly referred to as a democracy. During this span of fifty-five years, there are only about six years or one-ninth of the time which could be considered to be a period of democracy in the sense which the term is generally understood. The three years after World War II following the disgrace of the military and the approximately three-year interlude between October 14, 1973 when the military regime was toppled in a student-led upheaval and the bloodbath of October 6, 1976[1] which led to the military seizing of political power were the only two periods which saw full democracy in operation . The remaining years have witnessed military or military-dominated regimes governing in Thai society. The military bureaucrats have effectively been wielding political power since 1932. Indeed, this is not illogical when one examines the nature of the 1932 political change from absolute monarchy to a constitutional monarchy. That event resulted from a tussle for power between two political institutions, the monarchy and the military.[2]

It is ironical that the military bureaucracy, an institution created by the great monarch, King Chulalongkorn, in response to the need for reform (i.e. Westernization) in the fight against Western imperialism would itself become counter-productive for the monarchy. The need to avoid Western colonialism led to the reform campaign known as the Chakkri Reformation. This started in the early years after King Chulalongkorn's accession but came into full swing in 1892. The reform was to be continued by his son, King Vajiravudh.[3]

In the process of reform, a modern bureaucracy was created to replace the traditional structure built around the King's men. The new bureaucracy was to serve as the instrument to bring about a modern nation state with centralized political and administrative power. The Ministry of the Interior was charged with the function of provincial administration. It was enpowered to appoint governors, district officers and deputy district officers. This move was designed to create state power — a *state* building process sometimes referred to as "territorial integration". The Ministry of Education, as well as improving literacy among the people and providing technical and professional training, also had the function of assimilating the various regions and ethnicities into the fabric of the Bangkok based Thai nation-state. This process of *nation* building, sometimes referred to as "national integration", brought into being a Thai culture and nationalism which transcend ethnic origin and loyalties. The function of the Ministry of Finance was to increase the central government's economic power which provides a source of political power for the elite in Bangkok, and was also a requirement for centralization. The Ministry of Defence was to serve four functions: to create a modern military organization for national defence; to protect the institution of the monarchy; to provide positions for members of the royal family; and most importantly, to reinforce the centralized power of government.[4] Other ministries were to fill in the gaps for the administration of a modern, integrated nation-state which was replacing a traditional kingdom. But the emergence of the new bureaucracy with its modern functions led to the need to recruit new personnel, whose training in domestic institutions proved to be insufficient. Thus the practice came about of sending students to be trained overseas. It started with members of the royal families, but later extended to commoners. Exposure to Western liberalism would inevitably breed the desire to see the same principles prevail at home. Not surprisingly, it was the students returning from abroad (Paris) who staged the 1932 political upheaval against the age-old monarchical institutions.[5]

In light of this context, one could argue that what happened in 1932 was in fact a *coup d'etat* in which the monarchy was replaced by the bureaucracy which had come into existence as a result of the modernization or reform program launched by the monarchy. The bureaucrats, both military and civilian were already entrenched in positions of power. Their role was pervasive in all spheres. The institution has become omnipotent and omnipresent. Against this background, it was predictable that the new political process known as democracy, would encounter tremendous obstacles when introduced into Thai society. Within the generally apathetic and timid populace it was difficult for democracy to vie with a strong bureaucracy. After twenty-five turbulent years of struggle between the democratic and the bureaucratic forces during which the latter were dominant (See chart I), the political system became totally dominated by the bureaucracy following Field Marshal Sarit Thanarat's coup of 1958. From then on the military and civilian bureaucracy wielded real political power. Society drifted back to its traditional three-tier system of government, bureaucracy and people. The military wielded political power, while the civil service managed the routine operations of government and formulated and implemented policies. It was a bureaucratic polity par excellence.

A strongly institutionalized bureaucracy, within the centralized administrative structure which originated in King Chulalongkorn's reform program, led to a system of provincial administration controlled by the Ministry of Interior and other agencies and ministries of the central government. The supposed deconcentration of power in provincial administration by officials appointed from the various ministries, and most notably the Ministry of Interior, only served to buttress the power of the central government. The success of the modern nation-state was attributable to this administrative network of control.

One side effect of such a highly centralized system was the negative impact it had upon local government development. The octopus-like tentacles of the central government made it extremely difficult, if not impossible, for a genuine local system of government to flourish. Indeed, local government is usually viewed as local administration rather than as a devolution of power to the local level. Despite the multiplicity of organizational forms — municipal government, sanitation district, the Provincial Administration Organization, the Tambol (Commune) Council, the Bangkok Metropolitan Administration and the Special Local Government Model of Pattaya City — it is a well-known fact that local government in Thailand has left much to be desired. There is still a great need to develop or rectify the system. Domination by the Ministry of Interior, budget control by the central government, the meagre revenue base, the lack of incentives for qualified personnel, etc., are obstacles which are hard to overcome. In the final analysis, one can say that the *bureaucratic polity* and *Bangkok-centrism* which resulted from over-centralization of power have become antithetical to the *democratic process* and to *local self-government*.[6] Bureaucracy and democracy, Bangkok-centrism and local self-government represent polar extremes instead of different points along a continuum. One can argue that the intent of Thai political, governmental and administrative systems is directed towards democratic development and decentralization of power, a

Chart I

Prime Ministers of Thailand Between 1932-1957

		Background	Tenure in Office
1.	Phraya Manopakornnitithada	Civilian	11 months, 23 days
2.	Col. Phraya Paholpolpayuhasena	Military	5 years, 5 months, 23 days
3.	Field Marshal P. Pibulsongkram	Military	14 years, 11 months, 11 days
4.	Khuang Aphiwong	Civilian	1 year, 6 months, 17 days
5.	Tawee Boonyaket	Civilian	17 days
6.	M. R. Seni Pramoj	Civilian	10 months, 13 days
7.	Pridi Panomyong	Civilian	4 months, 17 days
8.	R. Admiral Tawan Thamrongnavasawat	Military	1 year, 2 months, 18 days

process which will serve to dilute the existing situation. Development over the years has led to a situation in which a compromise between, or a fusion of, the old and the new elements has come into existence. This is a Thai-style democracy known as the halfway democracy[7] to which we can now turn our attention.

II.   Demi-democracy: The Fusion of the New and the Old Elements

Demi-democracy, or in simple parlance the halfway democracy in operation at the moment, can be seen as reflective of the Thai political culture of accommodation and compromise. The genesis of halfway democracy can be traced back to the national development program launched by Field Marshal Sarit Thanarat and continued by his successors, Field Marshal Thanom Kittikachorn and Field Marshal Prapass Charusathien. It is interesting to note that the national development program is in essence a process for following the traditional political philosophy which places great emphasis on the people's welfare and well being. It is a sense of *noblesse oblige* but at the same time a process to gain legitimacy on the part of the political elite. This was especially necessary for Field Marshal Sarit, who came to power in a coup on October 20, 1958. This would have become a normal process had the event taken place during a traditional era such as Ayuthaya. But since the 1932 revolution which introduced the modern political system known as democracy, the legitimacy question has become a matter of concern in the event of a coup. To compensate for the lack of legitimacy provided by popular election, a national development program geared toward the concrete and immediate needs of the people, was the substitute for the abstract principle. Solid performance, in the concrete sense of the term, thus became the foundation for the Sarit regime whose development policy included building an economic infrastructure, offering inducements for foreign investment, creating new agencies including universities in the provinces in response to the development process, etc. It is a reform program similar to the one initiated by King Chulalongkorn. But Sarit and his successors could not foresee the result which would emerge from the national development process. The decade and a half of the national development program led to socio-economic changes which tool place within the traditional political system in which participatory politics became frozen. The socio-economic changes included the emergence of more urban centers, structural changes in the economy, increases in cash crops and the mushrooming of import-substitution industries. Even more important, new middle classes emerged. These were the import-export businessmen, white collar executives, industrialists, workers, bankers and financiers.

These people had been relatively small in numbers hitherto, when the dominant group in the middle class had been the public bureaucrats. The growth of this new class rendered the traditional political system, dominated by the military regime, unfit for the new socio-economic reality. The imbalance between the political structure and the (new) socio-economic structure was one factor which led to the uprising on October 14, 1973 which put an end to the military regime, sometimes referred to as the Sarit political system.[8]

The end of the military regime naturally led to some optimism that henceforth democracy would flourish. But this was not the case. After three years of open politics plagued by turbulence and political violence, the military staged a come-back in a bloody coup on October 6, 1976. The Thanin Kraivixien civilian government supported by the military only proved to be another nightmare because of its ultra-conservative policy and behaviour. The extremism of its anti-Communist campaign threatened to turn many more towards Communism. The social cleavages created by the tense political atmosphere and the political cynicism prevailing at the time threatened to tear apart the social fabric. The military coup of October 20, 1977 was welcomed with relief even by those who were staunch supporters of democracy. It has been argued that the civilian regime was only a stop gap measure to pave the way for a return to military power. At any rate, the new government under General Kriangsak Chomanan, which was considered more desirable than the dogmatic and ultra-rightist regime of his predecessor, was not spared the political troubles encountered by any leader in those years of turbulence. The oil shock was a factor which was easily exploited by the opposition. The Kriangsak regime was forced to give way to General Prem, who has continued to hold on to the reins of power for the last seven years.

But what is to be noted is the emergence of halfway democracy. It is a system in which there is a fusion of the old political elements with those of the new. The old elements were the bureaucrats, military and civil, who had wielded political and administrative power since the coup by Field Marshal Sarit in 1958, while the new elements consisted of the new middle class who emerged as a result of the national economic development program launched by Sarit and his successors. The old forces wanted to retain their position of power and if possible to maintain the *status quo*. The new forces exerted pressure for a more open political system in which they could participate in the decision-making process. This new social force, ironically, had come into existence as a result of the policy of national development adopted by the old element.

Against the backdrop of the October 14, 1973 uprising, which reflected the people's power and their demand for a role in the political process, and the numerous other coups, most notably the bloody coup of October 6, 1976, a compromise, or mutual accommodation, was worked out. This came about in the form of a system in which both elements were accommodated. The old element, consisting of military and civilian bureaucrats, were appointed Senators. More importantly, the premier, according to the constitution, did not have to run for election. As a result, he can be anybody who has the necessary support. The new elements, from the new middle class and the politicians can run for office as members of the House of the Representatives, and through this channel can assume ministerial posts. This is the arrangement in which both groups can share political power. The process of power sharing is such that it appears that a functional "democracy" has been operating in Thailand for almost a decade since the downfall of the Thanin regime.[9]

But the demi-democracy is faced with strong opposition from both the old element and other circles. The argument against it has been that the whole process has turned into one of business politics. Members of the House of Representatives have been accused of purchasing their way to power, starting with vote buying in the election to the buying of the Cabinet portfolio. The absence of hard evidence notwithstanding, these accusations are not groundless. The new businessmen who have turned to political ventures are not devoid of ulterior motives for protecting their business interests. Hitherto, businessmen, who were either first generation Chinese or naturalized Thai citizens, would seek political protection and business privileges through a patron-client relationship with high-ranking military and or civil bureaucrats. The relationship could even develop into marriage ties among their offspring. But a new situation has developed. The system has become more open. Present day businessmen also include members of the younger generation whose legitimacy as Thai citizens can no longer be questioned. They are educated and sophisticated. Moreover, their business ventures have become multi-national enterprises with large assets and thus have become directly linked to political stability. Inevitably they have to get involved personally in the political process. Politics and business have thus become intertwined. There are three methods by which these people seek to get involved in the political process. They support political parties, or whoever is in power, and thereby pull strings for their business interests. Second, they become executives of a political party and run for election to become members of the House of Representatives. Third, as a result of their financial power, they become Cabinet members.[10] Other means include developing patron-client relationships or screening appointments to the Senate.

Of late, complaints against such a political set-up have increased in magnitude. The system has been criticized for the growing influence of money in the process. One former deputy premier characterized it as a process of selling and buying. Buying votes, purchasing positions and earning money through the assumption of high positions, as well as the behaviour of many M.P.s who vie for the Cabinet posts have led to bickering in the parties, and a situation in which some have started to doubt the desirability of such a system. Meanwhile, the dominant role of the bureaucrats in the provinces continues to feature in the daily scene. Indeed, the situation is also true of the central agencies in which ministers are seen to be dominated by their permanent secretaries and directors-general, and this has led to unavoidable conflicts between political appointees and permanent civil servants or between politicians and bureaucrats, a clash between the old and the new elements in the halfway democratic set-up. Because of this situation, proposals for change or reform are made sporadically. These proposals can be summed up briefly below.

III.   Political Reform

The existing situation is plagued with problems over the succession to power. The fact that the premier and the members of the House of Representatives focus their attention on Cabinet positions rather than on serving as good M.P.s, is a concern for many who would like to see the democratic process mature. There is a strong feeling that Thailand cannot afford to go back to square one. Proposals for reform of the system comes in various forms; but the salient ideas can be summarized fairly briefly.

At the national level, with respect to the central government, the proposals are as follows.

First, is the proposal for the direct election of the prime minister. It is reckoned that direct election will give the prime minister the mandate and confidence to govern. It will also help to thwart the attempts of the military to seize power. A popularly elected prime minister will have continuity of tenure. The role of the prime minister would thus be similar to that of the American presidency, except that monarchy would continue to serve as the pillar of the nation and as the head of state, whereas the premier would serve as the Chief Executive.[11]

Reasonable as such a proposal may sound, there is opposition on two grounds. First, the idea is too advanced for the Thai political culture. If the elected premier won the support of a great majority of the people, ten million, for example, it would give him a mandate to hold on to political power and refuse to step down. Ferdinand Marcos, who won a landslide referendum, was a case in point. Secondly, the popularity of such an elected leader might cause a clash, symbolic as well as real, with traditional institutions. At best, the proposal is likely to remain a subject for academic discussion.

Second, it has been proposed that there should be a separation between the Executive and the Legislative Branches. Members of the House of Representatives would perform their legislative functions while Cabinet members would not be required to run for office as M.P.s before being appointed Cabinet members. This would make sure that M.P.s did not try to fight for portfolios. It is argued that this would end conflicts within and among political parties. Inter-party and intra-party bickering, which have resulted in disunity within the party and added to political instability, might thus be minimized.[12]

Logical as the proposal may sound, there are three questions to be answered. First, M.P.s vie for Cabinet posts because they are a source of power and wealth. If they are deprived of this incentive will there be good people to run for office as legislators? Secondly, there was an experiment with this kind of system in 1969 when Field Marshal Thanom Kitikachorn became premier with the support of the United Thai People's Party (Saha Pracha-thai), but political instability ensued despite the careful recruitment of party members. Members from the government party pressured the Thanom regime to grant them benefits and the situation was such that Thanom was forced to stage a coup in 1971. What guarantee is there that such a system would work at the present time?

Third, to ensure political stability, and improve efficiency and effectiveness and professional representation, it is proposed that there should be a national government supported by a dominant political party. The national government would consist of people from different professions, and would place great emphasis on national development. Conflict would be minimized because there would be consensus on the means and the ends. There might also be a national council, again with professional representation, along similar lines to the Latin American model known as corporatism.[13] But how a national government would be formed is still a big question mark, as is the issue of military dominance. This is because a national government would very likely follow the seizure of power by the military.

At the level of provincial and local government, the proposals are as follows.

First, there has been a recommendation that the provincial governor be elected in the same way as the governor of Bangkok. This would follow the American system which the state governor is an elected office holder.[14] But this proposal runs into three counter arguments. First, election results in Thailand are still predominantly dictated by money. Vote purchasing would become rampant, as is the case in the election of M.P.s. If such a system were put in place, it would be the rich Sino-Thai businessmen who would likely win the election. It is feared that administration of the province would be turned into a lucrative business venture instead of service for the common good of the community. The second argument is related to the inordinate fear of separatism. The old apprehensions of the colonial power continue to live on in the psyche of the Bangkok elite. If more autonomy were granted and control by Bangkok were loosened up, local leaders could become uncontrollable, and national security would be endangered. The third argument is that the Ministry of the Interior would never allow this move to an elected governorship because it would be a frontal attack on its power.

A second proposal is that the Tambol Council, a unit corresponding to the commune, be turned into a full local government unit with full jurisdiction at that level. The Tambol Councils, which cover a number of villages, have been carrying out the function of rural development, because they are the units which have been given special grants for dry-season development projects intended to put a check on migration. These six thousand units which cover the whole kingdom are taken as the basis upon which democratic development could take place. At the moment, despite the presence of some elected members in the councils, they still act as an arm of the provincial government. Indeed, they are pretty much under the influence, of the district officers or deputy district officers appointed from Bangkok.[15]

A related proposal is that the existing rule under which the village headman and the tambol headman have life tenure should be changed to allow for elections to these positions every five years. This would pave the way for changes in leadership and would give the younger members of the village and the tambol an opportunity to take part in village and tambol administration. It is also argued that such a system would promote the exercise of democracy and would lead to more impressive performance by the incumbents because of the need for re-election after five years. It would also encourage a closer relationship between office holders and voters. The counter arguments are that the frequency of elections might breed boredom and become a burden to voters in much the same way that they are to some American voters. There is also the fact that although political life might become more dynamic, this system could create cleavages in the village, and serious rifts between people on different sides. It could also create a conflict between provincial officials (i.e., the district officers and deputy district officers) and the elected office holders. Finally, elections at the village level would be a rather costly drain on the national budget.[16]

In any proposal for political reform it is to be expected that there will always be solid arguments on both sides. But one thing is clear. The Ministry of the Interior will be adamantly opposed to any scheme which will cut into its sphere of power directly.

IV.   Bureaucratic Reform

Bureaucratic reform still leaves much to be desired. This is due to the fact that most co-called reform programs are aimed only at short-term problem solving. The focus is on curbing the continued expansion of the system. It is to be noted that between 1969-1982, 25 new departments and 564 new divisions were established. Of these latter, 171 divisions had "bureaucratic reform" as the *raison d'être* for their establishment. This expansion only resulted in more problems which the government had to rectify. However, the government did attempt, with moderate success, to bring about bureaucratic reform. A committee for such a purpose was set up in 1959 and still exists. Efforts to bring about bureaucratic reform have been intensified under the present government. One important objective of the government is to provide an efficient and effective bureaucracy capable of delivering services to the people. This is to be done by improving the coordination of economic and social development, by curtailing the duplication of functions, by promoting decentralization of administrative power and encouraging a more autonomous and appropriate local government system.

The existing administrative system in Thailand is guided by two sets of legal provisions. The first provision which is a master administrative structure spells out the overall administrative structure of the country. Another provision is concerned with the establishment of ministries, departments. The two laws simply specify the power and functions of the ministries in broad terms without specifying the power and functions of departments. Expansion of the ministries was to be authorized by royal decrees. As a result, government agencies have been expanded at the department level with a considerable amount of duplication. Thus, while reform of the bureaucracy is given due attention, the prospect of genuine reform is still pending.

V.   Increasing the Efficiency of the Executive Through Structural Change

Attempts to bring about a more efficient executive were made through the introduction of a Committee for the Co-ordination of the Operation of Governmental Policy headed by the Secretary-General to the Prime Minister. The members of this Committee consist of the permanent secretaries of all the ministries or their equivalents, the chiefs of staff of the three armed forces, and the director-general of the Police Department. The Committee's mandate is to co-ordinate the policies of all the ministries. This covers a vast area; domestic policy, foreign affairs, economic and social development and national security. The

Committee is accused of being a duplicate of the Cabinet, and it has been dubbed a mini-Cabinet. The objective is to enhance the power of the executive branch, but it remains to be seen whether the Committee will be able to function effectively.

Another attempt at reform was the transfer of the Internal Security Operation Command from the First Army Region into the Office of the Prime Minister and the appointment of the Prime Minister as Chairman of the agency. Since the decision-making body in the agency consists of high-ranking military officers and civil servants, it is feared that it may become another mini-Cabinet, along the same lines as the Economic Cabinet which decides policy on economic matters and presents it for endorsement by the full Cabinet. So far, no serious negative consequences have resulted.

The two changes referred to above are attempts to strengthen the Executive. Their purpose was to counter the complaint that the existing executive was too weak. Strengthening the executive by reforming the administration structure represents an alternative to the proposal for the direct election of the prime minister, which was discussed earlier.

VI.   The Outlook for Significant Change

On the national level, there are two possibilities for change. The first scenario would see the existing demi-democracy or halfway democracy continue. In this case there is a real possibility that the constitution may be amended to allow more power to the bureaucrats. One likely amendment would be to allow permanent government officials to concurrently hold a political position, which would make it possible for a military officer, presumably the Commander-in-Chief of the Army, to assume the premiership. Meanwhile the process of sharing political and administrative power among the businessmen/ politicians and the government officials, military and civilian, will continue. Thus, the fusion of the old and the new elements will persist but greater political power will be granted to the bureaucrats.

The other possibility is that the halfway democracy becomes dysfunctional for the reasons discussed above. If there is enough pressure, real or manufactured, for a stronger executive, the idea of a national government may be adopted. In fact, such an idea has already been widely discussed, but, as was pointed out earlier, the establishment of such a system could only result from the direct seizure of power and the likelihood of this remains a question.

On the local level, because of the demand for greater autonomy, it is quite likely that in the industrialized areas — most notably the Eastern Seaboard — the Special Model of Local Government developed in Pattaya City will be adopted. Increased business activity, industrial development and urbanization will create the necessity for governmental and administrative change.

Whatever kinds of political or governmental reform take place within the next five to ten years, they must be able to combine the two features of participation and appointment. Participation by the new social forces born out of the new socio-economic milieu will have to go hand in hand with accommodation of the bureaucratic reality in Thai society. Thai society has become too complex for strong one-man rule calling all the shots. At the same time, the demand for a full democracy in which the traditional bureaucracy is reduced to a passive role as executors of policy, is not foreseeable in the near future. Any new political system will have to be in line with the nation's traditional culture, norms and values. Attempting to resist the tide of these forces would inevitably become self-destructive.

VII. Conclusion

If one attempts to forecast future developments in the political, governmental and administrative systems in Thailand and seeks to identify the areas where movement towards a viable political system is to take place, one must focus on three essential areas.

First, the national government and the political system will have to be such that participation by the new social forces can be accommodated. At the same time, there must be room for the old elements, the traditional bureaucrats, to have a part in the system. But whatever the form of government, participation will be an integral part. Gone are the days in which there could be strong rule by one dominant figure such as Sarit. Thai society has simply become too complex. The existing form of halfway democracy is in a sense a delicate combination of the traditional Thai system with that of the West. The hybrid seems to be functioning except that the people are somewhat impatient with the delays characteristic of an open political system. If the weaknesses of the present system can be rectified, if M.P.s are to have more discipline, if united political parties can be forged, then halfway democracy should continue to perform the minimum functions required of a political system.

Second, at the local level, there must be a genuine effort to develop self-government. This will serve as the foundation upon which the democratic process at the national level can develop. One can conceptualize the political system in Thailand at three levels: the superstructure, the intermediate structure and the infrastructure. The three structures are complementary. The superstructure consists of the constitution, the parliament and the government. The infrastructure, which serves as the foundation, consists of the people, who exercise their self government through local government units.

The intermediate structure serves to link the infrastructure to the superstructure, and consists of political parties and interest groups.[17]

Superstructure

(Constitution, parliament, government)

↑

Intermediate structure

(Political parties and interest groups)

↓

Infrastructure

(Popular participation and Local self-government)

Third, a viable political system will have to be nurtured by a sound economy. In order to develop the political system discussed above, Thailand must make progress with its economic development program. As Thailand approaches the 21st century it is developing slowly but inevitably into a member of the group of newly industrialized countries. It is becoming urgent for the country to mobilize its human and natural resources to achieve more efficient production in the agricultural, industrial and service sector. For this, the need to link human and natural resources is imperative. The two significant factors which will be instrumental in linking the human and natural resources are the political system and the level of technological expertise. The political system will have to be such that it will allow people of talent to come to the forefront and take part in the national development effort. In a socialist system, this would be accomplished through political mobilization. In our case, the system of halfway democracy with necessary modifications or the alternative of a "national government" may be the answer. However, reform of the political system alone will not be sufficient. Maoist China is a good case in point in which mobilization of the masses was efficiently done through the party mechanism but in which the neglect of the other important factor — science and technology — left China far behind its counterparts. This neglect has proved to be tremendously costly for China. Mobilization of the human element would have to be politicized and technologized.

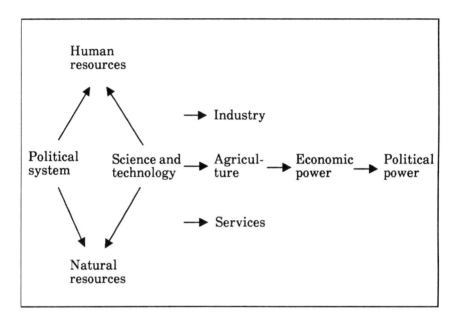

Such a concept is still a novelty in Thai society and it will take effort and time to communicate it. Very few leaders demonstrate insight and foresight about the future of the country. The political game is such that the short-term perspective dominates. This is another area in which progress will have to be made. There must be a guarantee that tenure in office will be long enough to complete the national development program but at the same time not too long to turn it into a permanent dictatorship. The desirable middle ground is hard to reach but this is the nature of the challenge which faces those who wish to bring about reform in Thailand.

Notes

1. For a discussion of the event, see Likhit Dhiravegin, *Thai Politics: Selected Aspects of Development and Change* (Bangkok: Tri-Sciences Publishing House, 1985, Part III, Section IV.)

2. For details, see Thawatt Mokarapong, *History of the Thai Revolution* (Bangkok: Chalermnit, 1972).

3. For a discussion of the reform, see Likhit Dhiravegin, *Demi-Democracy: Thai Politics in Transition*, (Bangkok: Tri-Sciences Publishing House, forthcoming.)

4. See Noel Alfred Battye, "The Military, Government and Society in Siam, 1868-1910 : Politics and Military Reform during the Reign of King Chulalongkorn, "Unpublished Ph. D. Dissertation, Cornell University, 1974.

5. See Mokarapong, *op. cit.*

6. See Likhit Dhiravegin, "Centralization and Decentralization: The Dilemma of Thailand," in Ernest E. Boesch, ed., *Thai Culture Report on the Second Thai-European Research Seminar 1982* (Saarbruecken, FRG., University of the Saar, 1983.)

7. For a discussion of the halfway democracy, see Likhit Dhiravegin, *Wiwathanakarn Karnmuang Karnpokrong Thai* (Evolution of Thai Politics and Government) (Bangkok: Samsart Publishing House, 1986, pp. 324-340.)

8. Thak Chaloemtiarana, *Thailand The Politics of Despotic Paternalism* (Bangkok: Social Science Association of Thailand and Thai Khadi Research Institute, 1979.)

9. This process of power sharing stems from the new political reality that the power pie has to be shared between the bureaucrats and the new social forces born out of socio-economic changes. For a discussion of the situation prior to the change, see David Morell and Chai-anan Samudavanija, *Political Conflict in Thailand, Reform, Reaction, Revolution* (Cambridge, Mass., Oelgeschlager, Gunn & Hain, Publishers, Inc., 1981.)

10. See Likhit Dhiravegin, "The Emergence of a New Politically Conscious Middle Class," *Thailand Business*, July 1985.

11. The most vocal individual who advocated this idea was Prapansak Komo-lapetch a former university professor who later resigned from his teaching career in order to run for election. The notion of a directly elected premier has now become an off-quoted proposal. But whether this idea will work in practice is still questionable.

12. It has been argued by many observers of Thai politics that bickering within, between or among political parties stems mostly from struggle over the Cabinet posts. If there is a separation between the Legislative and the Executive Branch in the sense described above, conflicts and hence political instability will be minimised.

13. See Somsakdi Xuto, *et al.*, *Strategies and Measures for Development of Thailand in the 1980's* (Bangkok: TURA and FES, 1983, pp. 153-159.)

14. This idea has been advocated by academicians but it is rejected by bureaucrats as being unrealistic and non-workable. It will allow merchants who have the means to purchase the position by vote-buying.

15. Cf. Xuto, *op. cit.*, pp. 146-152.

16. Likhit Dhiravegin, "Rabob Leuktang Kamnan Puasang Prachathipatai," (Election of Kamnan for Democratic Development) *Matichon*, October 8, 1986.

17. Dhiravegin, *Thai Politics. . . .*, Part IV, Section IV.

Government and Governance in Multi-Racial Malaysia

Zainah Anwar

I. Political and Governmental System

Compared to many other countries of the Third World, the political and governmental system of Malaysia is relatively well-established. The political system is a constitutional monarchy based on the Westminster model. The Yang diPertuan Agong (King) is Head of State and he is elected once every five years from among the Sultans, the hereditary Malay rulers of nine of the 13 states that make up Malaysia. A Prime Minister heads the government. Parliament consists of two chambers, the Dewan Rakyat (House of Representatives) and the Dewan Negara (Senate). The Dewan Rakyat has 177 members who are popularly elected once every five years or when Parliament is dissolved. The Senate has 69 appointed members, 26 appointed by the state legislatures, 43 by the King on the advice of the Prime Minister. The party system is dominated by the National Front (Barisan Nasional), a coalition of 13 largely communal-based parties, which forms the government. The main opposition parties are the Chinese-based Democratic Action Party

The Institute of Strategic and International Studies as an institute expresses no opinions and advocates no policies. The views expressed in this paper are entirely the author's own.

(DAP) and the Malay-based Islamic party, Parti Islam seMalaysia (PAS).

Malaysia is a multi-racial society where the Malays make up about 50 per cent of the population, the Chinese 31 per cent and the Indians some 10 per cent.[1] In religion, language, culture, food, customs, and values, they, in many ways, differ. The obstacles to integration are overwhelming. Many underlying tensions and much sublimated and open conflict pervade relations between Malays and non-Malays.[2]

Central to understanding Malaysian politics and government is the need to understand the complex forces of communalism, and to a lesser extent the forces of non-communalism and anti-communalism whose interplay shape the major institutions of the country and the objectives, functions and policies of government. But it is communalism which dominates Malaysian society. In such a society, political behaviour is often determined by communal interests. Communal considerations permeate a wide range of issues, politicising even non-political issues. The major political parties in Malaysia are communal-based, each championing the rights and interests of its own community. A background of the forces at work in Malaysian society is crucial to the understanding of the workings of its political and governmental system.

Malay political dominance is the central fundamental feature of the Malaysian political system. But it was not until after the May 13 1969 communal riots between the Malays and the Chinese[3], that this dominance was established and implemented unequivocally to ensure the political hegemony and socio-economic advancement of the Malays. The constitutional "bargain" struck by the leaders of UMNO (United Malays National Organisation), the MCA (Malaysian Chinese Association) and the MIC (Malaysian Indian Congress) – the parties that formed the Alliance coalition government – at the time of independence in 1957 was, after 1971, explicitly enshrined in the Constitution to protect the special position of the Malays and the legitimate interests of the non-Malays and to promote Malay socio-economic development.

The intercommunal contract negotiated among the Alliance leaders in 1957 had granted the non-Malays citizenship on the principle of *jus soli* for those born after independence and five-year residential status requirement for those above 18 years and born before 1957. It was also agreed that their property would be protected, their economic activity left unhindered, their culture respected and the private use of their mother-tongue assured.[4] In return, the leaders reached consensus that Malay would be the national language, the economically backward Malays should gain a proportionate share of the economic pie, that the delineation of constituencies which would facilitate a Malay majority in the legislatures should be legitimate.[5] "In order to advance decisively toward the time when the constitutional bargain was wholly fulfilled, the government was expected to pursue vigorously the goal of establishing Malay as a national language through its educational policy and the goal of increasing the Malay share of income through its economic policy. To assure that there would be no diversion from these goals nor a flagging of ardor by the government, it was agreed that these tasks should transcend the criteria of democratic politics."[6]

But twelve years after independence, the Malays felt that their side of the constitutional bargain had not been fulfilled, while the non-Malays have been granted their citizenship, took part in the political process, and pursued their economic activities unhindered. There was increasing Malay awareness that they were still backward, left behind in the country's development process. They saw an economic growth dominated by, and which benefited the urban, mercantile Chinese. They were led by a Malay-based government, but one that they believed was being manipulated by the Chinese. The 1969 riots were a culmination of increasing communal polarisation between the Malays and non-Malays, sparked off by Malay fears that their perceived political dominance was being threatened by the unexpected electoral gains by the Chinese opposition parties and the new air of confidence and euphoria, and in Malay eyes, arrogance, the Chinese exhibited in the victory parades that followed the May 10 general elections.

Fighting broke out on May 13 and hundreds of Chinese and Malays were killed. Even though the fighting was confined only to Kuala Lumpur, a national state of emergency was proclaimed. When Parliament was reconvened in February, 1971, it was clear to the new Prime Minister, Tun Abdul Razak Hussein, that "the indispensable requirement of a stable democratic system in Malaysia was the successful mobilization of the Malay community behind his government."[7] In having to win back the loyalty of the Malays, UMNO gravitated toward a more uncompromising championship of Malay communal interest and subsequently at the highest level, government was to be even more controlled by the Malays. The *New Economic Policy* was launched, designed to eradicate poverty and to restructure society by eliminating the identification of race with economic function. While this was supposed to be implemented irrespective of race, it was clear that the NEP was specially designed for the economically backward Malays. The modernisation of rural lives and the creation of a Malay commercial and industrial community meant affirmative action in favour of the Malays. By 1990, the end of the 20-year NEP period, it was targeted that Malays should own 30 per cent of the nation's share capital instead of a mere

1.5 per cent in 1969. This was to be done by cutting into the percentage (though not the absolute amount) of foreign share ownership, which would be reduced from 62 per cent to 30 per cent. Over the same period, non-Malay shares were also targeted to increase from 23 per cent to 40 per cent—all these objectives were to be achieved in the context of an expanding economy. There was to be no exercise in redistribution of the existing economic ownership, but rather, the creative development of the economic future to ensure a more equitable and politically tenable balance.

The NEP also stipulated massive government participation in the economy through the setting up of public enterprises which were designed to create opportunities for Malays to participate in the modern sector of the Malaysian economy—especially in commerce and industry—that was dominated by foreigners and the Chinese community. Thus government intervention in the economy to promote rapid economic growth is aimed not at growth for its own sake, but to restructure society toward a more racial balance in the distribution of income, employment and opportunity.

With the Malays controlling the government and policy-making at the highest level, and with the government adopting the institution of public enterprise as the key tool for restructuring society, the function and role of politics and government in Malaysia are very much intertwined. The idea of an independent and politically neutral bureaucracy does not apply as the political and administrative spheres of government become entangled. Thus, to some extent the function of government and its institutions in Malaysia are, since 1969, overtly designed to maintain Malay political dominance and to preserve and promote the special rights of the Malays as the indigenous people of the country.

The framework chosen to govern the country is still inter-communal. Political problems are thrashed out and decisions are reached in negotiations behind closed doors by the political elites of the ruling coalition. The course taken is still one that protects the legitimate interests of the non-Malays, but this time without sacrificing Malay political dominance. The tool chosen to manage ethnic conflict is a *grand coalition of parties*, drawing into the central government former opposition parties which represent all the important ethnic groups in the country.

Basically, the *National Front* coalition is an extension and expansion of the Alliance party. To the UMNO, MCA, and MIC coalition were attracted, the Chinese-based opposition party, Gerakan, the Islamic opposition party, PAS, and four other opposition parties, including three from the East Malaysian states of Sabah and Sarawak. There are now 13 member parties (PAS was expelled from the coalition in 1978), seven from Peninsular Malaysia, four from

Sarawak and two from Sabah. While the majority of the coalition members are non-Malay parties, the superior position of UMNO as the dominant political party in the country, is recognised.[8] Decisions in the National Front Supreme Council are made unanimously. Cabinet posts and electoral seats are allocated proportionately among member parties (currently, only eight member parties have cabinet representation). While the non-UMNO members continue to have access to cabinet positions (currently 14 to UMNO and nine to others), the pre-1969 MCA control of the strategic Finance and Trade and Industry ministries has been transferred to UMNO hands.

Despite the dominance of UMNO and its ability to form a federal government without power-sharing with any other party, it is clear that in its need for legitimacy and stability to govern a multi-racial society, the leadership is willing to share power with the non-Malays and to consult, bargain and compromise on divisive issues. The scope and extent may be more limited when compared to the Alliance system, but they are still practised. For in multi-racial Malaysia, there is a basic understanding among the political elites of the "need for consensus and wide representation in order to maintain legitimacy and political stability to avoid ethnic violence."[9] Recognition of the need for compromise and give and take – in an ethnically divisive society that sees one community's gain as the other's loss – is crucial to the nation's political survival.

Another central feature of the Malaysian political and governmental system is *executive dominance of Parliament.* The ruling National Front's control of an overwhelming 148 of the 177 seats in Parliament (giving it more than four-fifths majority) following the 1986 general elections means continued domination of the legislative branch of government by the executive. In Malaysia's parliamentary system, there is in fact a fusion of executive and legislative powers given the overwhelming strength of the ruling coalition and the whip it holds over its Members of Parliament. Since the Dewan Rakyat was fully elected in 1959, "all bills have been introduced by ministers or deputy ministers. The Government has never been defeated. The few, less than ten, Opposition bills which were introduced as private members' bills have all been rejected. The business of the House continues to be controlled by the Cabinet."[10]

The public perception of the Malaysian Parliament as a "rubber-stamp" institution that merely serves to legitimise the power of the executive is not without justification. The role of Parliament in providing checks and balances to the other branches of government, in being the bulwark of a country's democratic system and in being a source of governmental energy has not been put into much practice. In controlling and changing the rules and procedure of Parliamentary proceedings to limit the role of the Opposition in the legislative process, the government has often been accused of being less than democratic.

Malaysia is a *federation of 13 states*. But federalism in Malaysia has led to an evolution of centre-state relations where an increasingly *strong central government dominates states* which enjoy only limited autonomy. In the first place, the constitution provides for the dominant powers of the federal government over the states. If there are any inconsistencies between federal and state laws, federal law prevails, even if it was passed after the state law.[11] While the states have powers over land, mining, agriculture and forestry, the agricultural and forestry officers of the states (except in Sabah and Sarawak) are still bound to accept professional advice from the federal government. Members of the federal civil service occupy key positions at the state and local levels. Professionals working at the state and local levels are also federal employees. With the exception of matters such as land and Islam, 'state departments' are in fact 'operating agencies' of the federal government. One could safely go further by saying that state governments are implementors of federal socio-economic policies and programmes. Federal policy-makers exercise more *de facto* powers than formally provided for in the Federal Constitution."[12] The states' financial dependence on the federal government also means increased central influence over state policies.

The centralisation of power has historically been aided by the fact that except for certain periods, the political parties which ruled at the state level were all members of the National Front (and before that the Alliance).[13] 10 of the 13 states are under UMNO Chief Ministers who have been directly appointed by the Prime Minister. Although tensions can arise, they generally follow closely federal government policies and plans for development and political reforms. The states of Sabah and Sarawak, however, enjoy special rights under the federal system because of their different historical and political backgrounds and the fact that the majority population there are non-Malay and non-Muslim indigenes. In fact, the source of challenge to the federal government's dominance of the states comes from a newly emerging ethnic awareness in Sabah and Sarawak that has been politically mobilised to challenge the Malay-Muslim dominance of the states that is backed by the federal government.

II. Challenges and Trends

Managing ethnic relations

The greatest challenge to the Malaysian political system lies in the management of ethnic relations. Racial polarisation continues to be on the increase. If the 1960s, which was to have been a period of consolidation, ended with May 13 because of Malay fears, the 1970s—when the NEP implementation began in full swing—ended with non-Malay dissatisfaction.14 Ironically, the very policy that was designed to eradicate poverty and restructure society toward the overiding goal of national unity is now being held as one of the main causes for increasing racial polarisation in the country. For in the implementation of the NEP, the Malays have become more aware of their rights and privileges as the indigenous people of the country and the non-Malays, in particular the Chinese, feel they are being discriminated against and treated as second-class citizens.

The NEP was to be implemented within the context of an expanding economy. The economic boom of the 1970s which saw Malaysia's GDP growing at about eight per cent per annum had provided an expanding economic pie which was big enough to be shared by all. But since severe recession set in two years ago, the effects of the NEP's discrimination in favour of Malays, this within a shrinking economic pie, is felt much more acutely by the non-Malays. This has led to a more vocal Chinese challenge to the NEP and the overall concept of Malay dominance of the political system and its implications. If communal mass support is mobilised behind such a challenge, the fragile social harmony that exists today could be broken.

Race relations are still a delicate matter in Malaysia. In November 1986, tensions rose between the Malays and Chinese when the Selangor MCA passed a resolution questioning the indigenous status of the Malays.15 UMNO leaders demanded a retraction and an apology from the MCA. Following the established style of bargaining behind closed doors among the communal leaders, the cabinet solved the problem, but not without letting it drag on for over a week. The Prime Minister was quoted as saying that this was "because it (the cabinet) wanted Malaysians to be aware of the dangers of raising such issues."16 If the two sides had chosen to mobilise communal mass support behind each opposing position, the issue was emotional enough to seriously threaten the country's political stability. But as in this case, the political elites knew what the consequences would be if the matter was allowed to go out of hand and they turned to the established tradition of dealing with national problems in the cabinet or the National Front Supreme Council—behind closed doors. As in practice, only the settlement of the problem was announced to the public; the often heated and tough process of bargaining is kept secret. For as long as this process of elite accommodation works, then it can be expected that the simmering problem of race relations, while continuing to be on the front-burner of Malaysian politics, can remain largely under control. But if the elites choose to or are forced (to placate overwhelming grassroots sentiments) to mobilise communal mass support, then this delicate process in regulating conlict would break down, throwing the issue at hand to unbridled emotional appeals of communalism.

Executive dominance of Parliament

Malaysia is a highly centralised state where the federal government basically calls all the important shots. This extends to the function and role of the Malaysian Parliament which, like other major institutions of the country, is dominated by the executive branch of government. As a writer on Malaysians politics observed: "Under the Malaysian Constitution there are few institutional restraints on the exercise of power by the Federal Government so long as it commands a decisive majority in Parliament."[17] With the government controlling over four-fifths of the seats in Parliament (after the 1986 general elections) and thus further exerting its control of parliamentary proceedings to limit Opposition role and criticism, especially over sensitive and controversial issues, the Malaysian Parliament has failed to live up to its rightful role as the bulwark of the democratic system.

While the Government does tolerate the Opposition, it is "always on its own terms".[18] ". . . the strength of the Government side and the non-involvement of back-benchers in the determination and interpretation of Standing Orders has resulted in the views of the Government leaders being fully reflected in all changes. In short, procedures have increasingly been used to serve the interests of the Government with rare consideration given to the views of the Opposition."[19]

Through its control of the Standing Orders Committee, the government controls and limits the role of the Opposition in Parliament. Firstly, this is done through giving only limited time to the Opposition to take up issues. Question time, an important forum for MPs to make Ministers accountable for what their Ministries, departments or agencies are doing with the public money allocated to them, is limited to only one hour per day. Controversial questions submitted by MPS are placed at the bottom where they invariably remain unanswered as there is seldom enough time to go through all the questions on the Order Paper. The government's penchant for adjourning the House *sine die* on the completion of all government business also means that Opposition MPs are deprived of making their adjournment speeches. An adjournment speech is normally delivered once the House is to be adjourned and it is the last item of the day. For the Opposition, its importance lies in the fact that the government is required to answer matters raised in the speech. But this opportunity to make the government accountable is often denied.

Secondly, the government allows the MPs very little time to examine bills, either before the House meets or while the House is sitting. In one six-day sitting of the House, it dealt with 26 motions and 34 bills which were received by members either on the first day or subsequent days.[20] This practice continues till today. Such bulldozing tactics mean the Opposition has little time to study the bills carefully and to raise informed and responsible questions and criticisms of government proposals.

"The steady erosion of the time and grounds of debate (in adjournment speeches, oral and written questions, standing orders, etc.) has meant that the Opposition's role in the Legislative process has diminished. Indeed, where amendments have been made because of opposition, it is more as a result of pressure from outside the chamber."[21] The public perception of the Malaysian Parliament as a rubber stamp institution that serves to legitimise the power of the executive is not without justification.

Islamic revivalism

Yet another challenge to the Malaysian political system comes from the forces of Islamic revivalism. The use of Islam in a holier-than-thou battle for Malay votes by arch rivals PAS, the Islamic opposition party, and UMNO, has led to a cleavage within the Malay community of Malaysia. The present Muslim-secular dichotomy within the Malay community is one between devout Muslims who have found and understood the totality of Islam as a way of life and secular Westernised Malays whose priority lie with modernisation and development where traditional Islam is seen as a hindrance. Since independence, the latter group, as represented by UMNO, had always wanted to keep religion and politics separate, concerned that a narrow or traditional interpretation of Islam would only retard Malay economic development. But by the end of 1982, all efforts to keep Islam out of mainstream Malaysian politics were thrown out the window as UMNO, in the face of increasing challenge from PAS and under the pressure of Islamic revivalism, declared itself the biggest Islamic party in the world and announced an Islamisation process for the country.[22] Thus, a government which had tried hard since independence to separate religion from politics, appeared to have no option but to try and co-opt its critics and opponents by appealing to Islam for legitimacy, largely because the appeal of UMNO, a party of mainly secular Malay political elites, is now undermined by the new dominant factor in Malay politics, that of Islam.

The government's Islamisation process is a direct response to this new reality. Given the new religious fervour within the country, the appeal of Islam is not something that the government can ignore.

But its Islamisation policy designed to inculcate Islamic values like diligence and discipline within the administration and the population at large, to establish Islamic institutions like Islamic banking, insurance company, pawnbroking, and an International Islamic University, plus its introduction of Islamic Civilisation courses in all universities, have not won for the government the kind of approval it had sought, especially from the more radical forces of Islamic revivalism which remain in the opposition.

For the politicised Islamic revivalists who remain in the opposition, the introduction of the Quran and the Sunnah as the basis for a new constitution of the country and the implementation of Islamic law are *sine qua non* for the renewal of an Islamic society. But the government, pleading the multi-ethnic nature of Malaysian society, could never make this promise, focussing instead on Islamic institutions and other ad hoc programmes which are not designed to lead to the eventual formation of an Islamic state. PAS views it as "cosmetic Islamisation", a slow process aimed at momentarily pacifying and containing Islamic revivalism and to ensure that Malaysia never becomes an Islamic state.[23]

If this fundamentalist trend in Islamic revivalism continues to be a growing political force, then the strength and importance it holds in its ability to destabilise the government (by denying it the religious legitimacy it seeks) could force the political leadership to seek more changes in the institutions and policies of government in order to try and accommodate further the religious zealot's imperative mission to effect an Islamic social order.

Challenges to federal control

In Malaysia's highly centralised federal system, the special position of Sabah and Sarawak and their assertion of state and ethnic rights have posed challenges to territorial integration in what is a Muslim-dominated and Malay-dominated federation. Regional sentiments and state pride are high. The major indigenous groups in Sabah and Sarawak, the largely Christian Kadazan and Dayak respectively, are not found in other parts of Malaysia. They resent federal presence in the states, especially the domination of senior civil service positions by Peninsular Malaysians. Many feel that the federal government has made little effort to recruit East Malaysians to run the federal departments and agencies there. The fear of Malay-Muslim domination is further exacerbated by the fact that most of these federal officers are Malays. In Sabah, they have been accused of being insensitive to local customs and traditions and behaving like colonial masters ruling primitive natives.[24]

Secondly, regional sentiments in these two states are further reinforced by the territorial exclusiveness of their political parties. These state-based parties compete for supremacy between and within indigenous groups. The matter is further complicated by the fact that some of the parties align themselves with those in power at the federal level. "In particular, there has been a tendency for Muslim groups, or for parties with strong Muslim support, to establish a special relationship with UMNO, giving them an edge over their rivals in the resolution of local conflicts".[25] In the case of Sabah, the pro-Muslim policies and politics of the previous two state governments (and the strength they derived from their closeness with the federal government) led to the rise of Kadazan nationalism which eventually led to the ignominious routing of the ruling party at the 1985 elections, bringing into power a Kadazan-based communal party, Parti Bersatu Sabah (PBS). The PBS victory has naturally inspired Dayak nationalists in neighbouring Sarawak. In the April 1986 state elections, the Dayak nationalist party, the Parti Bansa Dayak Sarawak (PBDS), won 15 of the 21 Dayak majority seats in the state, emerging as the largest single party in the 48-seat state legislative assembly. This will of course increase its bargaining power, giving it a stronger platform to represent Dayak interests and to bargain for Dayak benefits with the Muslim-Malay-led state government.

The rise of ethnic awareness and ethnic nationalism among the indigenous non-Malay and non-Muslim groups in Sabah and Sarawak mean any further moves to control the states from the centre would be seen as a federal attempt to monopolise power and to assert Malay-Muslim domination, a notion acceptable in Peninsular Malaysia, but unwelcome in the Borneo states. It should serve as a warning to the federal government that rash assertions of the rights of the Muslims and the superiority of Malay/Muslim culture do not augur well for healthy federal-state relations between West and East Malaysia.[26] As it is, UMNO's plan to expand to Sabah, a move welcomed by most Malays there, but not by the Kadazans and other non-Malay indigenous ethnic groups, was forced to be put on hold partly because of such considerations.

Government intervention in the economy

In most Third World countries government agencies have become important tools in the development of the economy through direct participation in industrial and commercial ventures. In Malaysia, the use of the public enterprise (called Non-Financial Public Enterprises — NFPEs — where the government has majority equity ownership) to restructure the economy for a more equitable distribution of wealth has become an institution. In 1970 there were 17 NFPEs. In 1985 there were 683 companies in which the government held majority share. While the use of public enterprises to accelerate socio-economic development and in particular to open up opportunities for Malay businessmen in commerce and industry is unavoidable within the context of the New Economic Policy, the government has come to realise that this is not the most efficient means of achieving national objectives.

Of the total public sector development expenditure of the Fourth Malaysia Plan (1981-85), the NFPEs accounted for a high 34.5 per cent or M$27,743 million of the total expenditure. This expenditure does not include public enterprises where government equity ownership is below 50 per cent and annual revenue is below M$5 million. In 1986, the overall deficits of NFPEs widened from M$1.2 billion (1985) to M$3.5 billion. Of the estimated 900 companies with government equity (either as majority or minority shareholder), 80 per cent of them recorded overall deficits for 1986. For 1987, only a few agencies namely, Petronas, the National Electricity Board, the Malaysian Airline System and the Telecommunications Department are expected to register current account surpluses.[27] Among the hundreds of money-losing companies, wholly or partially owned by the government, worst hit are those set up by the Ministry of Agriculture with almost 90 per cent of them making losses and are no longer viable. Companies set up by the Ministry of Primary Industries and the Ministry of Land and Regional Development have also performed badly with most of them still surviving only because of the short-term cash advances from the government via their respective ministries, statutory bodies or holding companies.[28]

As the level and range of NFPEs activity expanded, so have the extent of their financing. Although a few of the public enterprises are self-financing, most of these agencies depend on the federal government for grants, equity, or loans, including domestic and external loans guaranteed by the government. The expenditure of these NFPEs has far-reaching implications and impact on the balance of payments and the external debt position of the country. Of Malaysia's M$51 billion external debt, NFPEs account for a hefty M$15 billion or 29 per cent of the total. The federal government had also extended substantial loans to these NFPEs which they are now unable to pay. Because of the recession, many of the NFPEs have requested that their outstanding loans be converted to equity — a situation that would merely transfer the debt problems of the NFPEs back to the federal government. As more and more money has to be put aside for debt servicing, less and less would be available for development. Because of the heavy financial burden these agencies place on the government and given the recession we are in, the government has cut back the funds allocated to the NFPEs and imposed stricter control over their expenditure and performance.

III. Reform Initiatives

Given the pervading strength and control of the executive over government machinery and the country's political system as a whole, any reform initiatives – other than those initiated by the government – to solve the problems discussed above can only succeed with executive support. The only serious concerted effort at reform that is being implemented now is in the *de-governmentalisation* of the economy through privatisation and deregulation and the stricter control over the NFPEs.

In trying to attract foreign investment to revive the country's economic growth, the government has relaxed foreign investment rules considerably. In the current temporary emphasis on growth rather than equity redistribution and restructuring, the government, for the first time since the New Economic Policy was implemented, has allowed 100 per cent foreign equity ownership for certain types of export-oriented projects. It has also embarked on a privatisation programme of NFPEs in order to reduce their financial burden on the public sector. The Port Kelang container terminal and Sports Toto (a numbers lottery) have been fully privatised. The Malaysian Airline System in late 1985 offered 30 per cent of its equity for public subscription. The Telecommunications Department has been privatised, but the shares are still held by the government and will be transfered to the private sector in stages. In January 1987, the Malaysian International Shipping Corporation offered 17 per cent of its equity for public subscription.

In the last three years, the government has also imposed stricter control over the NFPEs. A Central Information Collection Unit was set up to compile, process and analyse data on the operations of about 900 companies with government equity. This is to facilitate the availability of timely information for anlaysing the performance of these companies and their impact on the economy, especially the balance of payments. Technical assistance was also provided by the International Monetary Fund to design a new format for the regular collection of data on NFPEs which would provide an overall picture of their operations and means of financing for macro-economic analysis. All these form part of the "Early Warning System" designed to identify weaknesses and problems faced by the NFPEs so that early remedial action could be implemented.[29]

In the area of *ethnic relations*, government initiatives to alleviate the serious problem of racial polarisation are currently focussed on the school system. The new secondary school curriculum to be launched in 1988 will be focussed even more on promoting racial unity and integration among the students.[30] Schools are to ensure that extra-curricular activities like clubs, sports, work camps and uniform movements are not to be dominated by only one race. Malay students who today are not allowed to attend Chinese or Tamil language classes will be allowed to do so under the new curriculum. Teachers are to avoid using words, proverbs or sayings that are objectionable to the various communities. They are also to avoid using topics or items as teaching aids that could instil polarisation among schoolchilren. Certain textbooks containing words affecting the sensitivities of the different communities would be revised.[31]

There have also been calls for a review of the Constitution to spell out complete equality among the communities, thus ending the special privileges accorded to the Malays.[32] Politically, this would be untenable for a Malay-dominated government to implement in the forseeable future. While it can be expected that the New Economic Policy will eventually be phased out, the Malay history, Malay character and Malay nature of this country would be perpetuated. To eliminate the special position of the Malays as currently constitutionally protected would be seen by the Malays as an erosion of the Malay identity of Malaysia, a notion most Malays would find unacceptable.

In the area of *politics*, few reforms are being initiated. To be sure, there are exhortations from public interest groups and individual critics calling on the politicians to stop exploiting and manipulating racial sentiments to serve their own political interest. But as it is, the whole Malaysian political system has to live with the pernicious dictates of ethnicity. The political parties, though led by Malaysian-minded leaders, are communal-based. It serves their interest to remain so. While parties like the opposition DAP and the National Front coalition partner Gerakan call themselves multi-racial (as their membership is open to all communities), in effect, they are Chinese-based parties. Their members are overwhelmingly Chinese and the issues they champion reflect the interests of the Chinese community. Notwithstanding this, the Gerakan and Parti Bersatu Sabah (PBS), the Kadazan-based party that rules Sabah, are seriously negotiating a merger in an attempt to provide what they say is an alternative to communal political parties. It is their stated aim to provide an alternative party whose ideology would be based on Malaysian nationalism, as opposed to Malay nationalism or promoting non-Malay interests.[33] But their detractors see this move as more of an attempt to expand and strengthen the non-Malay base in facing the overwhelming power of UMNO within the National Front coalition.

In meeting the *Islamic challenge*, the government is embarked on a two-prong approach: accommodative and coercive. One of its earliest responses to the PAS threat was to amend the country's Penal Code and the Criminal Procedure Code in 1983, with new provisions aimed at controlling the then rapidly deteriorating relations between Malay-Muslims who supported UMNO and those who supported PAS. Under the new law, it is now an offence by fine or five years' imprisonment for those found guilty of causing "... disharmony, disunity, or feelings of enmity, hatred or ill-will" or whose actions prejudice or are likely to prejudice the maintenance of harmony or unity on grounds of religion between people of the same or different religions. It is also an offence to challenge anything lawfully done by the religious authorities or to allege that anyone professing a particular religion has ceased to profess that religion.

In the accommodative sphere, some analysts expect that the government's Islamisation policy will be expanded, this time the catalyst coming not just from PAS and the Islamic revivalists on the outside, but also from within the government. The ascendency of the former President of the Muslim Youth Movement of Malaysia (ABIM), Anwar Ibrahim, in the UMNO hierachy (he was recently elected vice-president) and his cabinet position as Minister of Education provide him with a strong base from which to translate his commitment to Islam into policy. As it is, the secondary school curriculum now under review is expected to reflect a more Islamic approach to education as against the present Western bias of the system.

In law reform, it can be expected that the purview of Islamic personal law will be expanded. Already the conservative state of Kelantan has introduced whipping of Muslims convicted of consuming alcohol. The southern state of Johore has drafted a similar law which will be up for debate at the next session of the State Legislative Assembly. There have also been calls to punish Muslims for apostasy and to ban Muslims from public places of entertainment.

In the area of *territorial integration*, numerous proposals have been put forward to minimise conflict and enhance harmony between Peninsular Malaysia and Sabah and Sarawak. A conference on national integration held in 1985 proposed a long list of reform initiatives which include:[34]

- refraining from equating the politics of Sabah and Sarawak with that of the Peninsula.

- reducing the identification, special position and perceived collusion between the Muslim political elite in Sabah and Sarawak with the Muslim elite in the Peninsula.

- recruiting more Sabahans and Sarawakians into the federal civil service and national organisations, particularly those involved in national planning.

- encouraging greater social interaction of federal officers in Sabah and Sarawak with the local populace.

- initiating a student exchange programme on a national scale.

- reducing the high cost of air travel between the Peninsula and the Borneo states.

Executive dominance of Parliament is an area where attempts at reform have not and will not go beyond mere calls on the government to promote a more just political system and to be more fair to the opposition parties on the rules of the game. For as long as the government has overwhelming control of Parliament, it is highly unlikely that the opposition could effect any change. Despite its strength, the government is in no mood to be magnanimous. It can be expected that the system will continue to be designed to perpetuate the ruling coalition party's dominance.

IV. Conclusion

Given the well entrenched power of the Malay-dominated government in Malaysia,[35] it is unlikely that any significant change would occur in the political and governmental system over the next five to ten years. The monarchy, a popularly elected Parliament with executive dominance, a ruling coalition of communal-based parties, a Malay-dominated political system are entrenched institutions that make up the system. What will continue to evolve and change are the dynamic forces that make up these institutions. The framework, the fundamentals, will not change, but the forces within will.

Change can already be seen in the *Malay political culture*. The Malay feudal mentality of according unquestioning loyalty and obedience to a leader has been substantially eroded. For the first time in UMNO history, the party President who is also the Prime Minister, was seriously challenged for the leadership of the party. He managed to scrape through with a majority of 43 votes in party elections held in April, 1987. The open challenge saw UMNO members split into two factions, one supporting the party president and the other supporting the then Trade and Industry Minister, Tengku Razaleigh Hamzah and his running mate, the former Deputy Prime Minister, Datuk Musa Hitam. For the first time in UMNO history, party members, including cabinet ministers and deputy ministers, declared publicly that they had lost faith in the party President. They criticised his economic policies and his leadership style. Such an unprecedented open attack against a party President who had just eight months before led the National Front to a resounding victory at the general elections has had a tremendous impact on the Malay political culture. The days of the publicly unchallenged UMNO leader could be over. Loyalty and obedience are not of right, but are to be earned or won. This new readiness to criticise, question and challenge the status quo augurs well for Malaysian politics as a whole as it forces the leadership to be more responsive in dealing with the issues raised, albeit this is only because of challenges from within the party, rather than from the outside.

In some ways, however, the government is at the same time getting increasingly authoritarian. Because of the power struggle, the party leadership is increasingly sensitive to criticisms, regarding critics as anti-government and anti-national or branding them as belonging to the rival camp. In fact, given the present disunity within UMNO, it can be expected that the Prime Minister would exert his control even more. Already the Ministers and Deputy Ministers who had supported the challengers have been sacked. The weeding-out process is expected to fall over into the public enterprises and other companies with UMNO business interests where political leaders had dispensed patronage by appointing their supporters to various managerial and board positions.

UMNO politics can be expected to continue to be in a state of flux. Given the uncompromising stance of Prime Minister Mahathir Mohamad against his challengers, a further challenge to his leadership should not be discounted. A process of reconciliation has not taken place. The wounds from the divisive party elections have not healed. In late June, 12 party members filed a suit in the High Court seeking to declare the elections null and void, claiming that the party had "deliberately/negligently" allowed 53 delegates from unregistered branches to attend divisional meetings where delegates to attend the crucial April general assembly were then elected. If the 12 succeed (exhausting the whole legal process may, however, take years), then fresh elections will have to be held for all posts, including that of president. This would mean another period of political uncertainty as UMNO members go to the hustings again for the high stakes involved.

The other dynamic force at work within the party system is the issue of *Chinese representation in government.* Pummelled by one crisis after another, the main Chinese partner in the National Front, the MCA, has lost much of its credibility in the eyes of the Chinese community. Thus in pushing for Chinese interest in the ruling coalition council, it negotiates from a weak base.

A two-year internecine power struggle led by millionaire Tan Koon Swan against the then MCA President finally saw the former's victory. But Tan was President for only two months. In January last year, the Singapore authorities charged and found him guilty of abetment in criminal breach of trust. He is now serving a two-year jail sentence. Seven months later, yet another crisis rocked the MCA. 24 deposit-taking cooperatives (DTCs), at least six of which were closely linked with the MCA, were suspended. Government-appointed inspectors found that the directors of the DTCs had siphoned off M$673 million of the total M$1.5 billion they had collected from depositers, many of whom were MCA members or supporters. Those arrested so far include the Deputy Minister for Culture, Youth and Sport, a former Deputy Finance Minister, the former MCA Youth chief who is also a former Deputy Trade and Industry Minister and also several Chinese business luminaries.

The weakening position of the MCA does not mean that Malay power would correspondingly rise. In fact it does not bode well for Malay interest or ethnic relations because the Chinese community might increasingly turn to the opposition DAP for recourse. If this continues, it could mean that the accommodative politics of the National Front would no longer be the main forum where the problems and demands made by the Chinese community are discussed and negotiated until an agreement is reached—behind closed doors. The DAP, as an opposition party, is not bound by these rules of the game and it would serve their political interest to outbid the MCA and loudly champion the interests of the Chinese community without having to take into consideration the effects on the other communities. Should the MCA further lose its influence among the Chinese and with the DAP picking up on these losses, then a snowball effect can be expected where the MCA would have to up the ante to restore its credibility as the protector of Chinese interests. In one attempt to bolster its emasculated image, the MCA had threatened to quit the coalition if its dollar-for-dollar refund scheme for the depositors of the collapsed deposit-taking cooperatives was not accepted by the government. In the past, communal aggressiveness has tended to arouse further communal aggressiveness. In a society where one community's gain is seen as a loss to the other, such a scenario, aggravated by sluggish economic conditions and the expected continuance of the NEP beyond 1990, could adversely affect the country's political stability.

It cannot be emphasised enough that the maintenance of inter-communal harmony is crucial for the government of a society which it believes is "precariously balanced on the razor's edge."[36] For as long as the political elites recognise the imperative need for inter-communal cooperation and compromise for the political survival and stability of the nation, then the National Front inter-communal governing framework will prevail. In a society that has so many forces going against it in its attempts to forge national unity and a national identity, the National Front system of power-sharing has worked to preserve the delicate balance of meeting the demands and needs of diverse and opposing forces.

A strong central government will continue to assert its authority in all aspects of the governing process. The New Economic Policy will be extended. But while restructuring is still a goal, the current emphasis has been temporarily shifted to growth. Through privatisation and deregulation, government intervention in the economy is expected to decrease. Public enterprises are better controlled and wastage is cut. On the economic front, there is a concerted effort on the part of the government to revive the economy. On the political front, a scene of continued flux can be expected, firstly because of the power struggle within UMNO and secondly over representation of Chinese interests and pacifying growing Chinese discontentment.

But when all is said and done, Malaysia remains a resilient society. After the May 1969 riots, several predictions of further racial upheavals following tense situations have come to nought. Compared to nation states like Sri Lanka and Fiji where similar problems of multi-racial governance have led to violence and instability, the Malaysian system of power-sharing, of elite accommodation, of give-and-take over divisive communal interests has worked. It may be imperfect and there are many moments of tension. But since 1969, the system has successfully kept the country in peace and stability. The government, following its well-tested tradition of negotiation and compromise behind closed doors — rather than an emotional public debate — has been able to put a tight lid over simmering political and communal problems. This prudent path, barring unexpected developments, can be expected to continue.

Notes

1.   Department of Statistics, Yearbook of Statistics, 1984. The figures for Sabah used to compile the total racial composition came from the Institute of Development Studies (Sabah). The population of the Borneo states of Sabah and Sarawak are dominated by indigenous groups that are not found in other parts of Malaysia. In Sabah, the Kadazans, Bajaus and other indigenous groups make up 56.94 percent of the total population of 1,217,000 (1986 IDS estimates). The Chinese form 16.22 percent of the population and the Malays, 5.57 percent. In Sarawak, the Ibans, Bidayus, Melanaus and other indigenous groups make up 49.17 percent of the total population of 1,408,790 (1984 Dept of Statistics). The Chinese make up 29.49 and Malays 20.08 percent.

2.   There are many inter-ethnic and intra-ethnic group conflicts and tensions, but the Malay/Chinese nexus is the dominant and by far the most crucial one.

3.   For more detailed accounts of the May 13 1969 riots, see: Karl Von Vorys, *Democracy Without Consensus: Communalism and Political Stability in Malaysia*, (Princeton: Princeton University Press, 1975) Chapters 13-16; Goh Cheng Teik, *The May Thirteenth Incident and Democracy in Malaysia*, (Kuala Lumpur: Oxford University Press, 1971); National Operations Council, T*he May 13 Tragedy*; Tunku Abdul Rahman, *May 13, Before and After*, (Kuala Lumpur: Utusan Melayu Press Ltd., 1969); Lau Teik Soon, "Malaysia: The May 13 Incident," *Australia's Neighbours* (July-August, 1969); A. Reid, "The Kuala Lumpur Riots and the Malaysian Political System," *Australian Outlook*, Volume 23, No. 3 (December 1969).

4.   See Von Vorys, *Democracy Without Consensus*, pp. 133-134.

5.   ibid. pp. 133-134.

6.   ibid. p. 134.

7.   ibid. p.425.

8.   The President of UMNO is Chairman of the National Front Supreme Council while the leader of each component party is a Vice-chairman. In the allocation of the 132 parliamentary

seats in Peninsular Malaysia in the 1986 general elections, UMNO as the dominant partner in the coalition was allocated to contest in 83 constituencies, MCA 32, Gerakan 9, MIC 6, and Hamim 2.

9. Diane K. Mauzy, *Barisan Nasional: Coalition Government in Malaysia*, (Kuala Lumpur: Marican & Sons (malaysia) Sdn. Bhd., 1983) p.137.

10. Michael Ong, "Government and Opposition in Parliament: The Rules of the Game", in Zakaria Haji Ahmad, ed., *Government and Politics of Malaysia* (Kuala Lumpur: Oxford University Press, 1987) p.40.

11. Article 75, the Malaysian Constitution

12. Elyas Omar, Policy Analysis and Development in Malaysia, (Kuala Lumpur: National Institute of Public Administration, 1974) (mimeograph) pp. 7-8.

13. From 1959 to 1974, the east coast state of Kelantan was under the rule of the Islamic opposition party PAS. PAS continued its rule after it joined the National Front coalition in 1974. It was expelled from the coalition in 1978 and lost its control of the state to UMNO in the subsequent general elections. The Chinese majority state of Penang is under the rule of Gerakan, a component party of the National Front. Sabah and Sarawak are ruled by state-based political parties which are also members of the National Front. Sabah is under the control of the Kadazan-based Parti Bersatu Sabah (PBS) and Sarawak ruled by a coalition of three ethnic parties that represent the Malay, Chinese and Dayak communities.

14. See The Star, Nov. 22, 1986.

15. The Selangor MCA resolution passed at its annual meeting stated that Malaysia's three major races originated from other countries and that none of them should brand the other as immigrants and claim themselves to be natives. There was an outcry from Malay groups and UMNO politicians who attacked the MCA for questioning the indigenous status of the Malays. They demanded a public apology from the Selangor MCA chief who is also the party's Deputy President, and his sacking from the cabinet. Several emotional gatherings were held

condemning the MCA action, while MCA grassroots leaders declared support for Datuk Lee Kim Sai. The issue was supposed to have been resolved behind closed doors at a cabinet meeting three days later. The cabinet was reported to have accepted the MCA explanation that the resolution was not intended to question the special status of the Malays as this was enshrined in the Constitution. It was also agreed that the labelling of non-Malays as immigrants should be stopped. But this agreement was not good enough for many Malay politicians. The calls for Datuk Lee Kim Sai's sacking continued. The newspapers, especially the Malay press, played up the issue. The controversy continued despite appeals by some national leaders to put the matter to rest. It was only finally resolved after the next cabinet meeting when it was announced that the MCA had withdrawn the offending resolution, following which the UMNO Youth leader then who had led the protest declared the matter was now closed.

16.   The Star, Nov. 22, 1986.

17.   Gordon P. Means, *Malaysian Politics* (London: University of London Press, Ltd. 1970) p.412.

18.   M. Ong: "Government and Opposition", in Zakaria, *Government and Politics*, p.42.

19.   ibid. p.42.

20.   ibid., p.48.

21.   Zakaria Haji Ahmad, "Continuity and Change", in Zakaria, *Government and Politics*, p.162.

22.   Islamisation in the Malaysian context does not mean the establishment of an Islamic state with the Quran and Sunnah as the constitution and the Shariah as rule of law. It means an inculcation of Islamic values like diligence and discipline and the establishment of Islamic institutions like Islamic banking, insurance company and pawnbroking and an International Islamic University.

23.   Zainah Anwar, "Islamic Revivalism in Malaysia: Dakwah Among the Students", unpublished Masters thesis presented to

the Fletcher School of Law and Diplomacy, Tufts University, Medford, Mass., U.S.A., 1986, pp.91-92.

24. See Mavis Puthucheary, *"Federalism at the Crossroads"*, (Kuala Lumpur: Institute of Strategic and International Studies, 1985) p. 23.

25. K.J. Ratnam, "The Political Dimension of Territorial Integration", in *The Bonding of a Nation*, proceedings of the First ISIS Conference on National Integration, Kuala Lumpur 1985, (Kuala Lumpur: Institute of Strategic and International Studies, 1986) p. 41.

26. M. Puthucheary, "Federalism", p. 28.

27. Bank Negara Malaysia Annual Report 1986, p.150.

28. Imran Lim Abdullah and Fadil Hashim, "Financing for Development — External Debt versus Direct Foreign Investment", a study prepared for the Harvard Business School Alumni Club of Malaysia, 1986, p.72.

29. See Bank Negara Malaysia Annual Report 1985, pp.129-130 and Annual Report 1986, p.148.

30. It is government policy to use the school system as the main manufacturer of racial harmony and unity and of Malaysian nationalism.

31. See New Straits Times, Sept. 15 1986 and Nov. 16, 1986.

32. In calling for a review of various provisions in the Constitution, Dr. Chandra Muzaffar, the President of Aliran, a public interest social reform group, said a new generation of non-Malays born after Independence would not tolerate any form of discrimination. But this non-Malay demand for equality, he said, could not be accommodated in the present Constitution which enshrines the special position and rights of the Malays.

33. See The Star, Nov. 22 1986.

34.   See Executive Summary of First ISIS Conference on National Integration, Kuala Lumpur, 1985.

35.   The composition of the 177-seat House of Parliament:

UMNO	83	seats
MCA	17	
MIC	6	
Gerakan	5	
HAMIM	1	
PBS	10	
USNO	5	
PBB	8	
SNAP	5	
SUPP	4	
PBDS	4	

	148	(National Front seats)
DAP	24	
PAS	1	
Independents	4	

	177	

36.   Mahathir Mohamad, "A Prescription for a Socially Responsible Press", in *Far Eastern Economic Review*, p.28.

Controlled Democracy, Political Stability and PAP Predominance: Government in Singapore

Jon S.T. Quah

Introduction

The Republic of Singapore attained its Independence 22 years ago, when it separated from the Federation of Malaysia on August 9, 1965. The present government, the People's Action Party (PAP) government, has been in power for the last 28 years, ever since it won the May 1959 general election.[1] During the first 25 years of PAP rule (1959-1984), there was a great deal of economic development as demonstrated in the rapid growth of the country's Gross National Product (GNP) per capita and the visible improvement in the standard of living of the population as a result of its successful public housing, family planning and industrialization programmes.[2]

However, two key events in recent years have increased more than ever the Singaporean political system's potential to change. First, the general election on December 22, 1984 was a watershed in Singapore politics as the PAP failed to repeat its electoral feat of winning all the parliamentary seats (as it had done in the 1968, 1972, 1976 and 1980 general elections) because it lost two of the 79 parliamentary seats to opposition candidates, and also experienced a swing of 12.6 per cent of votes against it.[3]

Singapore's GNP per capita grew by 11 times from S$1,330 in 1960 to S$14,653 in 1984.[4] However, in 1985 there was negative economic growth for the first time in two decades as a result of structural changes in the oil and marine-related industries, the increase in labour costs, and the weakness in domestic demand.[5]

125

Even though these three trends had originated in 1981, the government was caught by surprise by the 1985 economic recession, as these trends were masked by the exceptionally strong growth in construction which resulted from the accelerated public housing programme and the over-expansion in the private property sector. However, these trends became more visible in 1985 because of the slump in the construction sector.[6] To combat the economic recession, the PAP government formed the Economic Committee in April 1985 "to review the progress of the Singapore economy, and to identify new directions for its future growth."[7] The Economic Committee, which met 28 times and received contributions from over 1,000 persons, submitted its 234-page report entitled *The Singapore Economy: New Directions* to the Minister for Trade and Industry, Dr. Tony Tan Keng Yam, on February 12, 1986.

The purpose of this paper is to assess the extent to which the political system in Singapore will change, and in which aspects, as a result of the combined effects of the December 1984 general election and the 1985 economic recession. The main thesis of this paper is that, on the one hand, the results of the 1984 general election demonstrate the electorate's desire for a change in the paternalistic style of the PAP leaders, as well as their desire for more political participation. While the second-generation PAP leaders can satisfy the electorate's demand for more consultation and participation in the public policy-making process to some extent through the town councils and the formulation of the national agenda, the prerequisites for the city-state's economic survival necessitate, on the other hand, a tempering of the public's desire for more consultation and participation. In short, Singapore's political system will only change in a limited fashion because any fundamental change could lead to political instability and threaten its survival.

Central Features of the Political System

The Singaporean political system has been described in various ways by different authors. For example, the authors of the *Area Handbook for Singapore* have referred to Singapore as a "one-party administrative state par excellence."[8] Similarly, Robert Shaplen has described Singapore as "the technocratic state," while Dennis Bloodworth has called Singapore "an adhocracy."[9] More recently, a local scholar, Lau Teik Soon, has labelled Singapore as "an Asian democracy" i.e., a democracy which is "rooted in its Asian cultural traditions"; "adapted from the British parliamentary system"; and "focussed on national goals, particularly the building of a multiracial, non-communist and development oriented society,"[10] Instead of describing the political system in Singapore in the same way as these scholars have done, three of its key features will be identified and discussed in this section.

1. A Controlled Democracy

The first feature of Singapore's political system is that it is a "controlled democracy" i.e., it is a republic with a parliamentary system of government based on the British Westminster model, but which has been adapted to suit the local conditions.[11] According to the Constitution, the President is the head of state and is elected for a four-year term by the unicameral Parliament, which consists of 79 members elected from single-member constituencies by a simple majority vote.[12] Parliament has a maximum term of five years, unless it is dissolved earlier by the President. The latter also appoints the Prime Minister as head of the government on the basis of a majority vote of the Parliament. The Prime Minister and 14 other ministers constitute the Cabinet, which is the supreme policy-making body of the government.[13] However, while the Cabinet has the general direction and control of the government, it is collectively responsible to Parliament, which is the supreme legislative authority in the country.[14]

In his analysis of political systems, Douglas V. Verney contends that parliamentary government is concerned with *efficient* government, while presidential government emphasizes *limited* government.[15] This is certainly true in the case of Singapore, where the concern is with making government more efficient rather than with limiting its powers. Indeed, the constraints of the local environment have necessitated a modification of the original Westminster model of parliamentary democracy, which has resulted in "Democracy Singapore-style", i.e., a controlled or regulated democracy.

The first point to note about "Democracy Singapore-style" is that elections are free, fair and held regularly. General elections are usually held within three months of the dissolution of Parliament. In practice, general elections have been held about every four years from 1959 to 1984. The next general election is not due until 1989, but will probably be held in 1988, according to past practice. To prevent political parties from unduly influencing the voters in a general election, voting was made compulsory after the May 1959 general election.[16]

Secondly, in view of the racial, linguistic and religious diversity of the population,[17] any incumbent government in Singapore must formulate and implement policies which will encourage and promote harmony between the various ethnic groups. Another obligation of the ruling government in a plural society is to ensure that both public and private organizations in Singapore are fair and impartial in their treatment of their clientele, regardless of their ethnic group, language or religion. There is thus no room for discrimination of any sort in these organizations. Not surprisingly, there is also a Presidential Council for Minority Rights which examines bills presented in Parliament to ensure that the rights of the different minority groups in Singapore are not endangered.[18] In November 1984, Prime Minister Lee Kuan Yew contended that Singapore's success could be attributed not only to the six guiding principles of good government which he and his colleagues had relied on for the past 25 years but also to the tolerance and understanding among the different races, which provides the vital foundation for the implementation of these principles.[19]

Racial riots constitute the most serious threat to Singapore's survival because such riots can undermine the multi-racial basis of Singaporean society and also tear the social fabric apart. In a plural society like Singapore, racial riots are more likely to break out when there is no harmony, understanding and tolerance between the various ethnic groups. So far, there have been four racial riots in Singapore, viz., the Maria Hertogh riots of December 1950; the July and September 1964 racial riots; and the racial riots which occurred in Singapore as a result of the spillover effects of the May 13, 1969 racial riots in Malaysia.[20] The Maria Hertogh riots lasted for three days and resulted in 18 deaths and 173 injured persons.[21] After six days of communal violence in July 1964, 23 persons were killed and 451 injured. There were fewer casualties during the September 1964 riots as eight persons were killed and 60 persons were injured after two days of sporadic fighting.[22]

Needless to say, the PAP leaders' perceptions of the communal threat in Singapore have been influenced by the occurrence of the above racial riots. Accordingly, to prevent communalism from rearing its ugly head again to erode the racial harmony and understanding in Singapore, the PAP government has relied on a combination of positive and negative measures. Positively, the PAP government has embarked on a nation-building programme since 1959 when it established the Ministry of Culture. Its nation-building programme relies on economic development, public housing, national service, and periodic national campaigns to foster a sense of national identity among Singaporeans.[23]

In addition to its nation-building programme, the PAP government has also introduced some restraints on freedom of the press in Singapore in order to "immunize" the heterogeneous population from succumbing to the threat of racial riots by restricting individuals, groups, organizations and the press from sensationalizing and exploiting racial, linguistic and religious issues. For example, the

Printing Presses Ordinance, which was inherited from the 1948 Emergency Regulations, stipulated that it was unlawful to operate a printing press without an annual licence, which had to be renewed yearly and can be revoked at any time by the PAP government. Critics of the latter have contended that the Printing Presses Ordinance has curbed the freedom of the press in Singapore as newspaper editors have to exercise self-censorship in order to ensure the renewal of their yearly licences to publish their newspapers.

In May 1971, the PAP government revoked the licences of two English language newspapers, the *Singapore Herald* and the *Eastern Sun*, and detained (by means of the Internal Security Act) four directors and journalists of one of the Mandarin newspapers, the *Nanyang Siang Pau*.[24] The Printing Presses Ordinance was replaced in 1974 by the Newspaper and Printing Presses Act, which retained government licensing of printing presses and separated editorial control from financial ownership of a newspaper by issuing management shares to Singapore citizens approved by the PAP Government.[25] In 1986, the government amended the Act to restrict the circulation of foreign periodicals and newspapers which publish inaccurate or distorted reports on Singapore.[26]

Finally, the PAP government has employed the Internal Security Act (ISA) and the Criminal Law (Temporary Provisions) Ordinance (CLTPO) to detain without trial those persons who are involved in subversive or communist-related activities, drug traffickers, and criminals.[27] Perhaps, the use of the ISA and the CLTPO to curb the problems of communist subversion, drug trafficking and secret societies, is now less justified as the communists do not constitute a serious threat today, and the problems of the secret societies and drug trafficking have been dealt with quite effectively.[28]

2.   *Political Stability and Continuity*

The second main feature of Singapore's political system is its political stability and continuity. Singapore was a British colony for nearly 140 years and attained internal self-government peacefully in June 1959. This peaceful transfer of power is significant because it left intact the infrastructure developed by the British and spared the population from the bloodshed and turmoil that would have resulted from a violent transfer of power.[29] The PAP government has been in power since 1959, having been re-elected six times. Thus, apart from the Japanese Occupation (1942-1946) and the short rule of the Labour-Front government (1955-1959), Singapore has been governed by the British colonial authorities and the PAP government.[30]

The absence of natural resources on the small island has forced the PAP government to embark in 1981 on an industrialization programme which was dependent on foreign investment in order to promote economic development. In other words, foreign investment is needed for Singapore's continued economic development. Singapore's political stability is intimately linked with its level of economic development, which in turn, depends a great deal on foreign investment especially from the United States, Japan, Malaysia and other countries. If Singapore were politically unstable, foreign investors would not want to build factories or set up industries on the island for fear that they would lose their investment. Indeed, a 1985 *Straits Times* survey of 101 manufacturing firms in Singapore has shown that 24 per cent of these companies said that political stability was the most important reason for locating their operations in Singapore.[31]

Another survey conducted by the New York-based Association of Political Risk Analysts two years earlier placed Singapore among the top five countries as a safe haven for investment because of its political stability.[32] This implies that political stability in Singapore is thus a *sine qua non* for foreign investors to continue to invest in the city-state. The PAP leaders have always been aware of this and have repeatedly stressed to the population the need for political stability to ensure continued foreign investment. Indeed, in his election rally speech on December 19, 1984, the Prime Minister had urged the voters to "send the right signals" to foreign investors by supporting all the PAP candidates and by giving the ruling party a clean sweep once again in the December 22, 1984 general election.[33]

3.   PAP's Predominance

The PAP won the May 1959 general election and formed the government since it had won 43 of the 51 seats in the Legislative Assembly. The party system was competitive, with the PAP as the dominant party in the legislature and the Singapore People's Alliance and the United Malays National Organization-Malayan Chinese Alliance as the two opposition parties. The same trend was apparent in the September 1963 general election when the PAP captured 37 seats in the Legislative Assembly and the Barisan Sosialis became the opposition with 13 seats. However, in October 1966, the remaining Barisan Sosialis members of Parliament boycotted Parliament to discredit the ruling PAP government by demonstrating the absence of opposition in a parliamentary democracy.

The competitive party system in Singapore was thus transformed into a *de facto* one party dominant system, or more accurately, a "hegemonic party system" which is "one-party centred but does not preclude the existence of a periphery of secondary or 'second-class' minor parties."[34] The hegemonic party system acquired *de jure* status when the PAP won all the 58 parliamentary seats in the April 1968 general election. The PAP repeated its feat of winning all the parliamentary seats in the September 1972, December 1976 and December 1980 general elections. The PAP's monopoly of Parliament was broken when its candidate was defeated by the Worker's Party candidate, J.B. Jeyaretnam, in the October 1981 Anson by-election. In the December 1984 general election, the PAP won 77 parliamentary seats leaving only two seats for the opposition.

In short, the final and most important feature of the political system in Singapore is the predominance of the PAP in the political arena after 1959. What are the reasons for the PAP's predominance in Singapore politics? The PAP's pre-eminence in Singapore politics can be explained in terms of the following four factors.[35]

The first reason for the PAP's predominance in Singapore politics is the urgency of the survival issue especially after Singapore was separated from Malaysia in August 1965. To ensure Singapore's survival, the PAP government continued its policy of industrialization (initiated in 1961) and began the build-up of the armed forces with the introduction of national (or compulsory military) service in 1967. In 1968, the Employment Act was amended to ensure discipline among workers by preventing them from striking. Consequently, the number of manhours lost because of strikes dropped tremendously. During the same year, the Conservative government in Britain announced that it would withdraw its military forces based in Singapore by the end of 1971. This move threatened Singapore's survival as the British naval base employed about 40,000 workers and contributed to about 15 per cent of the Gross Domestic Product. Accordingly, the PAP government initiated several measures to minimize the economic effects of the withdrawal of the British forces, including the creation of a Bases Reconversion Unit to handle the conversion of the naval base into a commercial shipyard. In short, during the first five years after independence, the PAP government was able to garner the support of the people to tackle the various challenges to Singapore's survival.

Secondly, the PAP government acquired legitimacy in the eyes of the population because of its effective response to the communist and communal threats. Communism and communalism constituted two important threats to Singapore's survival during the 1950s and 1960s because, on the one hand, the communists wanted to destroy democracy and overthrow the incumbent government by force; and on the other hand, the communalists fermented racial riots to erode the multi-racial harmony in the country. However, communism and communalism are today no longer serious threats to Singapore's survival as a result of the effective measures taken by the PAP government. The PAP government relied on such positive measures as promoting economic development, nation-building, and the provision of relevant information to make the people aware of the dangers of communism and communalism and to prevent them from being unduly influenced by these threats. In addition, coercive measures were also employed by the PAP government to deal with those people involved in pro-communist and pro-communalist activities which endangered the security and survival of Singapore.[36] The PAP government's ability to deal effectively with the twin threats of communism and communalism has certainly reinforced its position in Singapore politics.

Thirdly, the PAP's predominance in Singapore politics can be attributed to its ability to deliver the goods and services to the population during its 28 years in power. When the PAP government first assumed power in June 1959, it was saddled with the twin problems of a serious housing shortage and a high level of unemployment. Accordingly, the PAP leaders created the Housing and Development Board (HDB) in February 1960 and the Economic Development Board (EDB) in August 1961 to deal with these two problems respectively. In 1960, only 9 per cent of the population was living in public housing, and the per capita GNP was S$1,330. By 1985, the proportion of the population residing in HDB flats has risen to 84 per cent, and the per capita GNP has increased to S$14,344 as a result of the HDB's success in solving the housing shortage and the EDB's ability to create more jobs through its industrialization programme.[37]

Another important achievement of the PAP government was its ability to curb the problem of corruption, which was a way of life in Singapore during the colonial period. The fact that corruption is no longer a way of life in Singapore today is a reflection of the effectiveness of the PAP government's anti-corruption strategy of reducing both the need and opportunities for corruption through the combined use of comprehensive anti-corruption legislation, an incorrupt anti-corruption agency, and constant improvement of the salaries and working conditions in the public bureaucracy.[38] Thus, the PAP leaders have been effective, responsive and incorrupt in delivering the goods to the population.

The fourth reason for the PAP's predominance in Singapore politics is the lack of a credible alternative to the PAP among the other 19 opposition political parties. Except for the Worker's Party (WP) and the Singapore Democratic Party (SDP), the other opposition political parties are quite weak organizationally, do not have adequate funds, and are unable to recruit professionals as members. Indeed, most of the opposition political parties are inactive during the interim period between general elections. According to Chan Heng Chee:

There is no tangible evidence to suggest that the opposition has sustained organizational operations that seek to nurture the ground between elections to build up support for the next electoral struggle. The shortage of manpower and finance and the structured dominance of the ruling party have virtually immobilized the opposition in the face of very great odds.[39]

Thus, although all the opposition candidates increased their votes in the December 1984 general election, none of the opposition parties, including the WP and SDP, constitutes a serious threat to the ruling PAP. Needless to say, whether the opposition political parties can make further inroads during the next general election depends not only on the performance of the two opposition members in Parliament, but also on whether these parties can upgrade themselves by attracting more capable and professional persons to join them.[40]

Overview of Major Problems

Until the 1985 economic recession, Singapore was frequently described as a success story. For example, Richard Clutterbuck has described Singapore as "the social and economic miracle" but its success story has given rise to controversy. According to him:

> Its [Singapore's] admirers point to the highest standard of living in Asia outside Japan, coupled with parliamentary government and social tranquility in a multiracial society. Its detractors say that these have been achieved by unacceptable erosion of civil liberties, by negation of parliamentary and trade union opposition, by detention without trial and by surreptious denial of freedom of speech and freedom of the press.[41]

No country or political system, no matter how successful, is immune from problems. Singapore is no exception. In this section, four major inter-related problems facing Singapore will be highlighted and analyzed.

1. High Degree of Government Intervention

The PAP government's predominance during the last 28 years, the environmental constraints (small size and population, heterogeneous population, and absence of natural resources) and the elitist nature of policy formulation[42] have all contributed to an unusually high degree of government intervention in Singapore. By government intervention is meant "the conscious and calculated action by government bodies to (1) distribute objective information on a given issue to a target population, (2) suggest a desirable or 'appropriate' pattern of behaviour towards that issue, (3) introduce incentives to reinforce the suggested pattern of behaviour among the target population, (4) introduce disincentives regarding alternative patterns of behaviour, and/or (5) introduce sanctions for those not following the suggested pattern of behaviour."[43]   These five steps imply a continuum in the degree of government intervention, from the mildest form (step 1) to the most intensive (step 5).

It is not difficult to document the high degree of government intervention in Singapore. Indeed, reference to the HDB's public housing programme, the PAP government's reliance on national campaigns, and its recent policies to reverse the "lop-sided pattern of procreation" by exhorting graduate women to get married and have more than to children, clearly illustrate the PAP government's high profile and highly interventionist style of governance in Singapore.

The PAP government's success in solving the serious housing shortage it inherited in 1959 has not only enhanced considerably its legitimacy in the eyes of the population, but is also one of the best manifestations of the high degree of government intervention in Singapore. It avoided the mistakes of the British colonial government and adopted a more positive and supportive approach towards public housing. Accordingly, the HDB was created as the *de jure* public housing authority and was provided with "governmental support, adequate financial resources, an efficient recruitment and selection policy, and the necessary legal powers for implementing the public housing programme."[44] The HDB's success story in public housing is quite well known now and does not require extensive documentation.[45] Nevertheless, the HDB's feat of providing low cost public housing for 84 per cent of the population during its first 25 years of its existence should be recognized, as it has not been repeated elsewhere in the world, and such a feat would not have been possible if the PAP government had not intervened in the area of public housing. In short, without the PAP government's support for, and intervention in public housing, the housing crisis in Singapore would not have been solved.

A second manifestation of the high degree of government intervention in Singapore is the PAP government's reliance on national campaigns to foster the development of a national identity among the population. From 1958 to 1984, 78 national campaigns (or an annual average of three national campaigns) have been held in Singapore.[46] In recent years, the PAP government has increased its reliance on national campaigns not only to change the attitudes and behaviour of Singaporeans, but also as an instrument for policy implementation. Each national campaign usually has three stages: (1) the identification by the political leaders of a social problem which requires corrective action, and their decision to rectify this problem by increasing public awareness through the launching of a nation-wide campaign; (2) the inauguration of the national campaign by a minister, who also explains the rationale for the campaign; and (3) the enforcement activities taken by the authorities to ensure compliance with the corrective measures suggested by the political leaders. Thus, the PAP government has relied on national campaigns to persuade the population to support its policies on the one hand, and disincentives have also been introduced to ensure compliance with such policies on the other hand.[47]

While such national campaigns as the "Keep Singapore Clean" campaigns have been very successful, the prevalence of and the frequency with which national campaigns have been held in recent years has led to an "overkill" effect on the population, which has been bombarded with so many campaigns that they might perhaps become immune to the messages and effects of such campaigns. National campaigns constitute a useful tool for the PAP leaders to communicate with the population to persuade them to change their attitudes and behaviour so long as such campaigns are used judiciously. If they continue to employ national campaigns indiscriminately to handle *all* problems, whether major or minor, the danger is that the population might become indifferent to such campaigns and ignore their messages. Indeed, the people might also resent being told constantly what to do by a paternalistic government and might perceive the holding of national campaigns as interference by the PAP government in their private lives.

Perhaps, the most sensitive area in which the PAP government has intervened in the lives of Singaporeans is population growth. The smallness of the island and its high rate of population growth after the Second World War forced the PAP government to establish the Singapore Family Planning and Population Board (SFPPB) in January 1966 to implement the national family planning programme. The SFPPB's population policy was designed to promote family planning among the population by employing a combination of incentives and disincentives, with emphasis on the latter.[48] The SFPPB succeeded in reducing population growth and also in persuading the majority of the population to accept the two-child family norm.[49]

However, the SFPPB's success in family planning has given rise to an unanticipated side-effect, which has only been recognized recently by the PAP government. In his national day rally speech on August 14, 1983, the Prime Minister identified the "problem" of the "lop-sided pattern of procreation" among graduate women in Singapore who had fewer children than their non-graduate counterparts. He argued that if such a pattern was not rectified, Singapore would not be able to maintain its present standards. Accordingly, he concluded that the government would encourage young educated Singaporeans to contribute to the expansion of the local talent pool by getting married and having more children.[50]

To rectify the lopsided pattern of procreation, the first Deputy Prime Minister and Minister of Education, Dr. Goh Keng Swee, announced on January 23, 1984 the priority scheme for Primary One school registration for children of graduate mothers, which was designed to encourage graduate mothers to have more than two children. Graduate women between 25 and 39 years of age in Singapore had an average of 1.3 children while their non-graduate counterparts in the same age group had an average of 2.9 children. Dr. Goh attributed this procreation pattern to the previous priority scheme for Primary One registration which gave priority to those with small families, especially those who had undergone sterilization after their first or second child, and to which the well-educated parents had responded much more than others. Thus, to rectify the imbalance, graduate others with three or more children were given top priority in registering their children for Primary One classes in schools of their choice.[51]

Needless to say, this new policy was criticized by members of the public, especially non-graduate mothers who felt that their children were discriminated against because their mothers did not have university degrees. The PAP government responded by saying that the number of graduate mothers who benefited from the new priority scheme represented a small minority.[52] In response to the widespread criticism of some of its policies during and after the December 1984 general election, the Minister of Education, Dr. Tony Tan, recommended the scrapping of the priority scheme to the Cabinet in May 1985.

Thus, unlike the public housing programme and the national campaigns, the PAP government's intervention in the area of population growth and population control was more controversial and was the target of much public criticism, especially the recent policies to reverse the lopsided pattern of procreation among graduate women. In fact, Prime Minister Lee Kuan Yew, who had been immune so far from public criticism, received an outpouring of public criticism for his graduate mothers policy because members of the public felt that the PAP government had gone too far this time in encroaching in such private and personal matters as marriage and procreation by suggesting whom they should marry and how many children they should have.[53]

In August 1986, the Prime Minister justified the PAP government's highly interventionist style by arguing that Singapore's success was the result of the implementation of unpopular policies which often interfered in the private lives of Singaporeans, but which have also contributed to the city-state's political stability and economic growth. He said: "I am accused often of interfering in the private lives of citizens. Yes, if I did not, had I not done that, we wouldn't be here today."[54]   In other words, without government intervention, Singapore's success would not have been possible.

While government intervention is an important prerequisite for the nation-building process in a country, it should be noted that a democratic political system cannot survive massive doses of government intervention. Prime Minister Lee is correct when he contended that government intervention was a *sine qua non* for Singapore's success. However, the results of the December 1984 general election demonstrate the need for the PAP government to modify its highly interventionist style of governing by tempering it with more consultation and participation from the electorate. In short, there are limits to government intervention in Singapore and these limits have been attained during the post-1984 general election period.[55]

2.   Low Degree of Political Participation

Political participation refers to either "the involvement in an activity that results in the reshaping and resharing of power" or "mobilization, as involving people in activity which may have no impact on the reshaping or resharing of power as far as the participants are concerned."[56]   Viewed in both senses, the highest level of political participation was experienced in Singapore during 1955-1959, when the PAP was able to mobilize (through its left-wing faction) the Chinese-educated masses and the trade unions against the incumbent Labour Front government, and to capture power by winning the May 1959 general election.[57]   However, according to Chan Heng Chee, "After 1959 the tendency has been to move away from participation in the first sense and to encourage participation in the second."[58]   More specifically, the PAP leaders reduced political activity by taming the trade unions, detaining their communist and pro-communist political opponents, and curtailing the activities of the student unions and the mass media. In short, the PAP government replaced the "competitive and conflictual political style" of the 1950s and 1960s with "the establishment of the administrative state in which politics is seen to be a matter of management."[59]

Perhaps, the best indication of the low level of political participation in Singapore is the elitist nature of policy formulation.

According to the Constitution, the Cabinet is the supreme policy-making body of the government and formulates most, if not all, of the public policies in Singapore.[60]   Each minister has control and direction of a staff of civil servants in his ministry. When politics are formulated at the political level by a minister or by the cabinet as a whole, the civil servants' role is to provide the required information, advice and past experience to the Cabinet, which will then discuss and evaluate such information before recommending an appropriate policy.[61] The Prime Minister, who is *primus inter pares* among his colleagues, is in reality the dominant figure in the Cabinet and his influence prevails in the formulation of public policies in Singapore, even though he has kept a low profile in recent years and has left the day-to-day running of the government to Goh Chok Tong and his colleagues. Indeed, many of the public policies formulated in Singapore bear his imprint.[62]

However, when public policies are not formulated at the Cabinet level (which is very rare), such policies can result from the initiative of civil servants, who are responsible for defining the problem and for suggesting how to deal with it. Thus, civil servants in Singapore usually behave as "a trained apolitical body of professionals giving expert advice on, and carrying out the efficient implementation of, policy."[63]

The various elite groups in Singapore participate in policy formulation in two ways. First, as members of statutory boards and advisory committees they provide technical information and assistance, "review and make recommendations regarding proposed policy and program changes, and suggest new measures for official consideration."[64] Secondly, the elite groups influence policy formulation through "their participation in chambers of commerce, trade associations, professional societies, and other organizations that represent aggregations of economic and social power."[65]

There are many professional organizations in Singapore such as the Singapore Medical Association, the Law Society of Singapore, the Singapore Institute of Architects, and the Institution of Engineers, Singapore, to name a few examples. However, the scope of these associations' influence and effectiveness in lobbying for "legislative changes, additions or omissions beneficial to their professions" has been restricted by government intervention.[66] In other words, these professional associations are not effective pressure groups. Nevertheless, they "are consulted by policy-makers from time to time, and asked for their views and suggestions on problems falling within their realm of expertise."[67]

During the 1950s and early 1960s, trade unions were the most important pressure groups in Singapore which exerted influence on the incumbent government and political parties. The situation was radically changed in 1968 with the enactment of the Employment Act and the introduction of the concept of the tripartite alliance between the government, workers and employers in industrial relations for the purpose of improving the economy through the attraction of foreign capital and the provision of jobs.[68] Although trade unions are well organized groups in Singapore today, with the advent of the tripartite movement and the close ties between the National Trades Union Congress (NTUC) and the PAP government, they are no longer pressure groups.[69]

Finally, like the trade unions, intellectuals do not play an active role in the formulation of public policies in Singapore. Chan Heng Chee has identified four roles for intellectuals in Singapore: (1) become intellectual-politicians; (2) legitimize the established order; (3) become mandarins of the established order; and (4) remain as independent critics who influence public discussion and shape public opinion.[70] As the first three roles have been dealt with above in considering the role of the political leaders, elite groups and senior civil servants in policy formulation, only the fourth role of intellectuals as independent critics will be discussed here.

Independent intellectuals can contribute to policy formulation by formulating economic and cultural goals, increasing the political awareness of the population, serving as the critic of power and the conscience of society, and providing "an alternative source of ideas to be tapped."[71] A decade ago, Chan Heng Chee concluded that "the views of an independent intellectual receive no favour and if his views are critical of governmental power his function is not recognised as legitimate" by the PAP government because "his claim to the right of criticism is an alien tradition borne of Western liberal thought."[72] Her assessment of the role of intellectuals in policy formulation in Singapore remains quite accurate today as the PAP government is still not very tolerant of independent critics, whether local or foreign. Indeed, in May 1985, the Minister without Portfolio, Ong Teng Cheong, described those who were critical of public policies as "dissenters" and in August 1985, the Prime Minister referred to these critics as "wiseacres."

The need for wider participation in the formulation of public policies becomes more obvious as Singaporeans become more affluent, better educated and informed, well-travelled, and have higher expectations. When the basic needs for survival have been met, people become more concerned with higher-level needs, such as the need for greater control over decisions involving their personal lives. Furthermore, according to a local sociologist:

> One by-product of higher levels of education is a keener awareness of the negative effects of an over-regulated

society where policies may determine the children's career path and the relations between family members. People would like to see the institutional channels of participation in decision-making being expanded beyond elections in order to arrive at policies that reflect faithfully the common will, particularly in matters of an intrinsic and higher-level nature.[73]

The 1984 general election results demonstrated, *inter alia*, that 37 per cent of the voters who voted for the opposition candidates (and perhaps even many of those who voted for the PAP) wanted a change in both the style of government and the substance of some of its policies. Singaporeans resent increasing government control over their lives, and they do not want controversial policies that affect them personally to be formulated and implemented without taking their views and sentiments into account. The problem is not the explanation of such policies, but discussion of whether the policies are acceptable or necessary in the first place. If controversial policies such as the priority school registration scheme are introduced without parliamentary debate and without taking into consideration the feelings of the population, it is not surprising when disgruntled voters demonstrated their personal dissatisfaction either by voting for opposition candidates regardless of their credibility or by casting spoilt votes, as 26,000 of them (2.9 per cent of the voters) did on December 22, 1984.[74]

In short, the low degree of political participation is reflected in the elitist nature of policy formulation and the absence of effective pressure groups in Singapore. However, as the 1984 general election results have shown, there is now a great demand by the population for more participation and consultation in the policy-making process in Singapore.

3.   Ineffective and Weak Opposition

When the PAP government assumed power in June 1959, there were eight opposition members in the Legislative Assembly together with its 43 members. In February 1963, the Internal Security Department (ISD) launched "Operation Coldstore" which resulted in the arrest and detention of many communists and pro-communist sympathisers, many of whom were members of the Barisan Sosialis (BS). However, in spite of "Operation Coldstore," the BS managed to win 13 seats in the September 1963 general election. Together with a member of the United People's Party, the BS constituted the opposition with 14 members against the 37 PAP members of the Legislative Assembly. So far, this is the largest number of opposition members in the legislature. There was no longer any opposition member in Parliament by October 1966, as all the BS members decided to boycott Parliament. This was a serious tactical error by the BS, one from which it never recovered.

Apart from damaging its own credibility as a party, the BS's boycott of Parliament also contributed to the "clean sweep" phenomenon in the April 1968 general election where the PAP won all the 58 parliamentary seats. Without the participation of the BS, the PAP easily won the seven contested seats after winning the other 51 uncontested seats on nomination day. When the PAP repeated the "clean sweep" phenomenon again during the September 1972 general election, it prompted an American correspondent to write an article entitled, "How to Win a Clean Sweep in Free Elections."[75] Prime Minister Lee Kuan Yew was also concerned about the lack of parliamentary opposition in spite of the fact that 31 per cent of the voters had voted for opposition candidates. He even suggested that university dons could be appointed to provide opposition in Parliament, but this idea was not pursued any further. The PAP repeated its electoral feat for the third time in the 1976 general election. After winning all the 75 parliamentary seats for the fourth time in the December 1980 general election, the PAP leaders began to view their success in a general election in terms of winning *all* the parliamentary seats and reducing the percentage of opposition votes.[76]

The lack of an opposition in Parliament after the April 1968 general election created a dilemma for the PAP because the "repeated re-election of the PAP has only brought the party a bad reputation and tarnished the fair name of the Republic abroad."[77] However, the PAP leaders have always believed that the "real" opposition in Singapore is the illegal Malayan Communist Party and its members who are bent on overthrowing the incumbent government by violent means.

When J.B. Jeyaretnam of the Worker's Party won the October 1981 Anson by-election, he not only broke the PAP's monopoly of Parliament during the last 15 years but also "illustrated to the Singapore electorate that the PAP was neither invincible nor infallible."[78] During the 1984 electoral campaign, the PAP became aware that the population wanted an opposition in Parliament from feedback obtained from its branches, the grass-roots organizations, and the ministerial walkabouts. On July 24, 1984, the Prime Minister introduced the Non-Constituency Member of Parliament (NCMP) scheme to allow for the seating of the three opposition candidates who had received the highest percentage of votes (exceeding 15 per cent) in their constituencies. This means that there would be at least three opposition members in parliament even if the PAP had won all the 79 seats. He gave three reasons for introducing the NCMP scheme: (1) to educate younger voters (who constituted 60 per cent of the electorate) on the myths about the opposition's role in Parliament since they had not experienced the political conflicts of the 1950s and 1960s; (2) to sharpen the debating skills of the younger ministers and MPs in Parliament; and (3) to provide a means of giving "vent to any allegation of malfeasance or corruption or nepotism" in order to "dispel suspicions of cover-ups of alleged wrongdoings."[79] However, the NCMP scheme was not well received by either the opposition political parties or the public because the restrictions imposed on the NCMPs would make them "second-class" MPs.[80] The election of the two opposition MPs in the December 1984 general election, and the rejection of the remaining NCMP seat by two eligible opposition candidates meant that the NCMP scheme never got off the ground.[81]

Although there are 20 registered political parties in Singapore, only nine – the PAP and eight opposition political parties – participated in the 1984 general election. Unlike the PAP which fielded candidates in all the 79 constituencies, the eight opposition parties and three independent candidates contested 49 constituencies on nomination day on December 12, thus leaving 30 constituencies uncontested and giving walkovers for the PAP candidates. Moreover, unlike the PAP, the eight opposition political parties "do not have any rigorous selection systems because they do not have the means, nor candidates of sufficient calibre."[82]

Indeed, the opposition political parties find it extremely difficult to attract capable and well qualified individuals, especially professionals, to join their ranks. This fact becomes obvious when the background of the 51 opposition candidates in the 1984 general election is analyzed. The opposition candidates were likely to be male Chinese in their late forties and who had a secondary school education. Only 14 opposition candidates (27 per cent) were university graduates and of these, six were lawyers, one was a medical doctor and another was a dental surgeon. The opposition candidates had a total of 19 different occupations, ranging from bookkeeper to tax assistant; but one third of them were "businessmen."[83]

If the PAP with all its resources has found it difficult to recruit professionals, the obstacles facing the opposition parties in their search for capable candidates appear to be insurmountable. Indeed, few professionals are prepared to enter politics, let alone join the opposition political parties and jeopardize their career prospects. In this connection, Chan Heng Chee has observed that:

In-built structural disadvantages for the effective organization of opposition politics dissuaded the educated and the professional elite, who in any other context would have been the natural pool for the recruitment of political leadership, from joining the opposition parties.[84]

In short, the opposition political parties in Singapore are weak and ineffective because of inadequate finances, poor organization, and their inability to recruit professionals as members.

4. Economic Recession

In 1985, the Singapore economy fell into a serious recession as the real Gross Domestic Product declined by 1.7 per cent for the first time in two decades and after averaging an annual growth rate of 8.5 per cent for the past five years. Initially, the PAP government did not realise how serious the recession was, and until March government officials were still predicting a 5 per cent GDP growth rate. What was even more surprising was the suddenness of the economic decline and by June 1986, the unemployment rate had gone up to 6.3 per cent.[85]

According to the Report of the Economic Committee, the 1985 economic recession in Singapore was the result of the combined influence of both external and internal factors. Externally, low petroleum prices and the reduction in demand for petroleum affected not only the oil refining and petrochemical industries, but also dealt a severe blow to the shiprepairing and shipbuilding industries, which made up one quarter of the manufacturing sector in Singapore. Moreover, the reduction in the growth rate of the U.S. economy affected Singapore adversely because of its trade with the U.S. in computer peripherals and electronics. To make matters worse, there was also a decline in trade with the other ASEAN countries and a drop in the number of tourists from these countries because of the exit taxes imposed by Indonesia, the Philippines and Thailand, and the 50 per cent tax introduced by Malaysia on goods brought in from Singapore by residents.[86]

Internally, the increase in operating costs, especially labour costs, was the result of a continuous trend of high wage cost increases which were not matched by productivity growth. Thus the high costs of doing business had adversely affected Singapore's international competitiveness and the profitability of its companies. Furthermore, domestic demand was weakened not only by the slump in construction, but also by a continued high rate of national savings which could not be channelled into productive domestic investments. The national savings rate of 42 per cent of the GDP is the highest in the world. Finally, such rigidities in the economy as the absence of adjustment mechanisms in the wage structure and the preference of some Singaporeans to remain unemployed instead of accepting less well paid or harder jobs, had also contributed to the economic recession.[87]

Overview of Reform Initiatives

In response to the problems discussed above, a host of reforms were introduced by the PAP government viz., the introduction of Town Councils (TCs), the establishment of the Government Parliamentary Committees (GPCs), the formulation of the National Agenda, the proposed Team Members of Parliament (MPs) scheme, and the prescription for economic recovery by the Economic Committee. These reform initiatives will be discussed below, beginning with the TCs.

1. Town Councils

The idea of setting up TCs in the HDB estates was first mooted in 1985 by Lim Boon Heng, the MP for Kebun Baru, for the purpose of tapping the existing pool of community leaders and involving them in some decision-making.[88] On September 1, 1986, three TCs covering nine constituencies in the Ang Mo Kio area were established on a six-month trial basis.

It is surprising that the *raison d'être* of the TCs has not been clearly spelt out yet by the PAP government. In an interview with the *Straits Times*, Dr. Chan Yan Chong, a research and organization manager with a local company, identified two possible reasons for creating TCs:

> The primary aim is to encourage greater participation in
> social service, especially community service. It can also be
> a useful base from which the Government can talent-spot
> potential and future political leaders.[89]

On March 17, 1987, S. Dhanabalan, the Minister for National Development clarified the purpose of TCs during the parliamentary debate on his ministry's estimates. He said:

> The basic aim of setting up town councils in Housing Board
> estates is to allow residents to manage their own
> surroundings. They must learn to make the kind of
> decisions that everybody has to make to allocate scarce
> resources. They must plan what they want for their area.
> ... When people managed their own estates, they would
> have to make the kind of difficult decisions which the HDB

now has to make and which some people grumble loudly about. But when they make their own decisions, they have to defend and live with their decisions.[90]

By the end of the fourth month of the trial period (December 1986), the chairmen of the three TCs indicated that they would request an extension of the trial period from six months to a year because it was "premature to make a decision on whether or not to implement such councils based on six months' showing."[91] On February 1, 1987, the First Deputy Prime Minister Goh Chok Tong identified the extension of the TC concept as one of the two top priorities of the PAP government in 1987.[92] One week later, he met 80 town councillors from the three pilot TCs in Ang Mo Kio New Town to discuss their achievements and the teething problems they had encountered so far. These town councillors informed Goh that they were still unclear about their roles and responsibilities and that they were plagued by such problems as "the limited powers given to them, a lack of funds and the short trial period which made it difficult for them to reach out to residents."[93] Thirty residents of Ang Mo Kio New Town interviewed by *Straits Times* reporters indicated they were also in favour of an extension of the six-month trial period for the three pilot TCs as it was "too short to enable the three councils to make any significant impact."[94]

Goh granted the town councillors their request and announced that the trial period for the three pilot TCs would be extended by another six months to August 1987. In spite of the problems faced by the town councillors so far, it is surprising to note that Goh went on to announce that the PAP government was proceeding with its plan to form more TCs to allow Singaporeans to manage their public housing estates because it was convinced that it was "on the right track." He further indicated that a proposal describing the main features of a TC would be presented to Parliament within the next three to six months. Such a proposal would help to define the role and powers of a TC and to solve the teething problems encountered by the three pilot TCs in Ang Mo Kio New Town. The decision to extend the TC concept to other constituencies would be made after August 1987.[95]

A *Straits Times* reader, K.C. Tan, suggested in his letter to the Forum Page that more information on the TC concept and the Team MPs proposal should be provided by the PAP government to enable whose who are interested to discuss these ideas further.[96] After his walkabout of Changkat constituency on March 29, 1987, the Minister for Community Development, Wong Kan Seng, acknowledged that "Singaporeans did not have a clear idea about the responsibilities and workings of the (town) councils and said this was because not enough information was available to them." However, he was confident that

Singaporeans would accept the TC concept once they were better informed.[97] Needless to say, this would depend not only on the amount of information provided on the TCs, but also on how they would actually function.

2.   *Government Parliamentary Committees*

Goh Chok Tong first suggested that committees should be formed to improve parliamentary debate in 1986. His suggestion led to the formation of informal PAP parliamentary groups to deal with specific subjects. In January 1987, he indicated that "It is now time to formalise the PAP parliamentary groups and convert them into government parliamentary committees."[98] According to Dr. Hong Hai, who prepared a paper on the topic for Goh, MPs in Singapore "do not play a role that is commensurate with their numbers and abilities" because they do not provide adequate or effective inputs which affect the outcome of legislation. To rectify this undesirable situation, MPs who are not Cabinet members should be given more opportunities to evaluate proposed legislation. Thus, the formation of Government Parliamentary Committees (GPCs) "could be an effective way by which ministers' decisions can take into account the views of their colleagues in Parliament and those people who are directly affected by these decisions."[99]

In the same paper, Dr. Hong also identified the following functions of the GPCs:

1.   To evaluate a proposed policy change or legislation, determine feedback from other MPs and from citizens affected by the proposals and seek opinions from advisers.

2.   To suggest changes to a proposed Bill and hold several private meetings with the minister and/or his colleagues before the Bill is put in its final form.

3.   To defend any proposed legislation which it endorses in Parliament.

4.   To provide ideas and feedback on a regular basis to the various ministers on current issues.

5.   To provide a formal channel for evaluating the effectiveness of policy implementation.[100]

Finally, he concluded the paper by suggesting that the GPCs would help the PAP government to "know even better" because "it had the full benefit of counsel from MPs outside the Cabinet and their advisers."[101]

In his speech to senior civil servants on February 10, 1987, Goh Chok Tong gave three reasons for introducing GPCs. First, the formation of GPCs would correct the public's "misconception that the MPs had little or no influence over policies and were not capable of taking an independent stand." The second reason for introducing GPCs was that participation in such committees would provide the younger and better qualified MPs with opportunities to influence government policies. The third and "most compelling" reason for establishing the GPCs was "the need for a new political formula that would take Singapore into the next century." As the present reliance on Cabinet dominance might not be healthy for the future, it should be modified by introducing GPCs, which provide a new "formula of continuing Cabinet dominance coupled with more effective backbenchers" that would satisfy the demands of younger Singaporeans "who want to see more action from their elected MPs."[102]

Each GPC has between five to six members, who are appointed for two years. Of the nine GPCs that were created, only two (the Finance, Trade and Industry Committee and the Health and Environment Committee) have six members, while the rest have five members each.[103] A resource panel of 12 independent experts provides advice in their areas of expertise to members of a GPC. This means that there are nine resource panels of experts, one for each GPC.[104]

The Chairmen of the nine GPCs identified credibility as an important ingredient for their effectiveness. Indeed, "for the GPCs to be perceived as credible, they must not appear to collude with the Government, party and the civil service."[105] The *Straits Times* supported the formation of GPCs in its editorial of February 14, 1987, because such committees would enhance the quality of debate in Parliament. It viewed the introduction of the GPCs as "a response to the electorate's call for greater participation in decision-making and more active backbenchers." As such, GPCs "offer a balance between maintaining strong and decisive leadership and greater debate on national policies."[106] Finally, in the view of a local political scientist, GPCs can be effective and credible if their activities result in more responsive government, and better Bills and laws.[107]

3.   *The National Agenda*

In his speech to cadres at a closed-door party conference on November 23, 1986, Goh Chok Tong provided the first inkling of the National Agenda when he said that the PAP leaders would discuss their party manifesto with a cross-section of the population in 1987.[108]   The debate on the National Agenda was launched on February 18, 1987 with a press conference by the Chairman of the PAP's Manifesto Committee, Lee Hsien Loong, at the PAP headquarters. According to him, the purpose of the seven-month long debate was to enable all Singaporeans to participate in formulating the means for attaining the goals set by the PAP's Vision of 1999.[109]

More specifically, a long list of questions has been formulated for Singaporeans to answer. The first set of 27 questions deals with the challenges facing the country and how its goals are to be·achieved. The answers provided by Singaporeans participating in small meetings, dialogue sessions and public forums will help to shape the National Agenda. Another set of questions, to be released in May 1987, will deal with the challenges of population trends, the limits of growth, and the economic, social and cultural objectives of the nation.[110]

Three types of activities have been organized in connection with the National Agenda. First, a new series of seven constituency walkabouts was launched on February 22, 1987 to enable the younger ministers to meet residents in these constituencies and to seek their views on various items on the National Agenda through the dialogue sessions. Secondly, the Feedback Unit organized, during February-April 1987, seven dialogue sessions with professionals to obtain their views on the National Agenda. Finally, the Ministry of Community Development conducted national education seminars for thousands of grassroots leaders to explain and discuss the political and other issues affecting Singapore.[111]

The first draft of the National Agenda will be presented at the PAP Youth Wing Convention in September 1987. Its final draft will be presented at the PAP Convention for endorsement in November 1987. Describing the National Agenda as "a people's manifesto", the *Straits Times* stressed that the "litmus test" of the National Agenda's success "will be how dissenting views are accommodated."[112] During his walkabout of Yuhua constituency on February 22, 1987 Lee Hsien Loong stated explicitly that the purpose of the debate on the National Agenda was to formulate "a correct and inspiring manifesto for the nation."[113] Another objective for inviting public discussion on the National Agenda, according to Goh Chok Tong, was to encourage more Singaporeans through such discussion to assume responsibility for the country's future when Prime Minister Lee Kuan Yew retires.

In short, "the responsibility for looking after Singapore's future . . . should rest on all Singaporeans."[114]

4. *Team MPs*

The MP for Kebun Bahru, Lim Boon Heng, outlined his proposal on Team MPs when he inaugurated a senior citizens' club in his constituency on January 24, 1987. Instead of the present system of voting for an MP in each constituency, voters in the three adjacent constituencies constituting a town council would, under the new scheme, vote for a team of three candidates from the various teams put up by the political parties contesting a general election. The team that garners the highest number of votes wins the election, and its three members will become MPs and be held collectively responsible for running their TC.[115]

Lim gave two reasons for introducing the Team MPs proposal. According to him, the "underlying message" was "that voters must vote wisely because they have to live with their choices." It must be remembered here that the PAP leaders were shocked not only by the 12.6 per cent swing of votes against it during the 1984 general election, but also by the fact that "all the opposition candidates increased their votes, not because of their credibility or their manifestoes, but because of voter dissatisfaction with the government's controversial policies."[116] Thus, the Team MPs proposal can be seen as the PAP's response to the 1984 general election results. Lim went on to say:

> If you want to have an opposition, then the opposition should have the possibility of being credible to the extent that it could develop into an alternative Government. If voting is purely on the basis of selecting an individual candidate, I don't think this, in itself, gives anybody the confidence that a particular party has got any basis to claim that it could provide an alternative Government.[117]

The second reason for implementing the Team MPs plan was that it would help to improve the calibre of election candidates, especially those from the opposition political parties. Since the elected Team MPs will be responsible for running their TC, candidates standing for election must demonstrate "some form of administrative ability if they want to get elected and run the town councils." Furthermore, they must also have "the vision and foresight to envisage what are the problems the town councils will face in order to formulate the right policies."[118]

Lim's proposal for Team MPs generated a great deal of public discussion, as it was intended to do.[119] One month later, Goh Chok Tong announced in a television interview on February 27, 1987 that the government would introduce the Team MPs plan for the next general election.[120]

5.   *Prescription for Economic Recovery*

On the basis of its thorough diagnosis of the causes of the 1985 economic recession in Singapore, the Economic Committee recommended a comprehensive set of policy changes to deal with the internal causes of the recession. More specifically, it recommended the following policy changes:

1. To reduce operating costs, the present employer CPF (Central Provident Fund) contribution rates should be immediately reduced by 15% points, for a period of 2 years in the first instance.

2. For households whose mortgage payments will be affected, the government should make special arrangements to enable them to reschedule their housing loans.

3. Meanwhile, the government should review the CPF scheme from a longer-term perspective, to decide on the appropriate long term rate and structure of contributions that would meet the basic needs of the CPF scheme.

4. In addition to the CPF reduction, there should be, as a matter of national policy, no increase in overall wage levels in 1986 and 1987.

5. The public sector should take the lead on wage restraint.

6. It is necessary to make fundamental reforms to our wage payment system as soon as possible.

7. The corporate tax rate should be reduced immediately from the present 40% to 30%. A further reduction to 25% should be considered as soon as the revenue position permits.

8. Personal income tax rates should also be brought down as soon as possible, with the maximum marginal rate reduced to 30%, in line with the corporate tax rate.

9. To encourage greater investments in equipment and machinery, an across-the-board investment allowance of 30% should be introduced for expenditure on machinery and equipment.

10. The government should aim to lower statutory board charges to the greatest extent possible. The budget policies of statutory boards should form an integral part of government's fiscal policy, and statutory board revenues and expenditures should be considered as part of the government budgetary position.

11. The government should find non-recurrent ways to increase development spending, and be prepared to allow an overall public sector deficit, in 1986 and 1987.

12. The Singapore dollar exchange rate should continue to be set by market forces, but its impact on our export competitiveness and tourist costs should be taken into account. The dollar should, as far as possible, be allowed to find its own appropriate level, reflecting fundamental economic trends.[121]

According to the Economic Committee, the above recommendations are "immediate policy adjustments" that are required for restoring the Singapore economy to a growth path and are consistent with its long term development.[122]

Conclusion

Will the reform initiatives solve or minimize the four major problems discussed above? To what extent will the three central features of the Singaporean political system be modified by the proposed reforms? These two questions will be dealt with in this concluding section.

Of the five reform initiatives identified in the previous section, the Economic Committee's prescription for economic recovery appear to be the most thorough and the most likely to succeed, judging from the recent performance of the Singapore economy. The PAP government accepted the Economic Committee's Report and implemented its recommendations. The economy is on the mend now, albeit in a lop-sided manner as three sectors (construction, commerce, and financial and business services) remained depressed during 1986, in contrast to the growth in the manufacturing, and transport and communications sectors.[123]   Indeed, according to the Ministry of Trade and Industry's economic survey of 1986, there were three indicators that the economy was recovering:

> Singapore's real GDP grew by 1.9 per cent in 1986, after falling by 1.8 per cent in 1985; 11,000 jobs were created in 1986 – a major improvement over 1985, when 102,000 jobs were lost.   And thanks to an astutely-managed Singapore dollar, cost-cutting and wage restraint, total investment commitments in manufacturing went up by 27 per cent, after falling by 38 per cent in 1985.[124]

On January 9, 1987, the Minister for Trade and Industry, Lee Hsien Loong, indicated in a television interview that Singapore would be able to achieve a long term target of 4-6 per cent economic growth, judging from the experience of other countries such as Japan.[125] About two and a half months later, he predicted, on the basis of "rough estimates", that the economy would have grown by 6 per cent in the first quarter of 1987, and would perhaps grow by 5 per cent in the second quarter.[126] The recovery of the economy is important for the PAP government as it will ensure its predominant position and maintain political stability and continuity. The PAP would probably lose votes if the economy has not fully recovered by the next general election.

The setting up of the GPCs is an excellent idea and a move in the right direction.   Apart from giving the younger MPs more opportunities to influence the outcome of proposed legislation, the GPCs also help to rectify the elitist nature of policy formulation in Singapore by seeking the advice of their resource panels and consulting those people that would be affected by the proposed policy changes. Given the absence of an effective opposition both within and outside Parliament, the effective performance of the GPCs could result in the public perception that an opposition in Parliament was unnecessary. Indeed, the impressive performance of the chairmen of the nine GPCs during the recent parliamentary debates on the 1987 Budget estimates led some grassroots leaders to say that the GPC chairmen were "making up for the lack of an effective opposition in Singapore."[127] A grassroots leader from Yuhua constituency said:

> The Government should now take the views aired by them [the GPC chairmen] seriously and it will be clear that there

is no need for an Opposition to tell us what is right or wrong.128

Needless to say, the continued effectiveness of the GPCs in Parliament will increase the pressure on the remaining opposition MP (Chiam See Tong) to prove his worth as the GPC chairmen and their members will be competing with him to evaluate proposed legislation in Parliament.

Like the GPCs, the formulation of the National Agenda is also a good idea. The PAP's Vision of 1999 was formulated for the December 1984 general election by the younger leaders.129 The National Agenda will help the PAP identify, through the views of Singaporeans, the various means of attaining the goals specified in the Vision of 1999. Thus, this exercise can be viewed as an attempt by the PAP leaders to obtain more accurate feedback from the public about what they want. However, the acid test of the success of the National Agenda would be the fate of dissenting views. How would such views be incorporated in the National Agenda? Or would such views be simply dismissed as being "impractical", "not suitable for the local context", or "against the national interest". The seven-month long public debate on the National Agenda and its related activities are appropriate responses to the electorate's call for more participation and consultation in national policy-making in the 1984 general election. However, a final judgment of the national Agenda's efficacy has to be postponed until the contents of its final draft are presented at the PAP Convention for endorsement in November 1987. Another question that can be asked is: Will the National Agenda be a one-time effort by the PAP to consult the views of the public and encourage their participation? Or will the PAP leaders revert to their pre-1984 general election leadership style of not consulting the population after the National Agenda exercise has been completed?

The TCs and the Team MPs plan constitute a "joint package" that is designed to correct and prevent Singaporeans from voting for those candidates who lack credibility and the administrative ability to run the TCs. In other words, the PAP leaders want to prevent "freak" election results and to ensure long term political stability.130 According to Goh Chok Tong:

> Our concern is not the opposition taking seats away from us. Our concern is a different kind of people who might, through some freak results, end up controlling the country.131

The public reaction to these twin proposals has been less than enthusiastic, if not negative.132 *Straits Times* reporters interviewed

88 residents in 10 constituencies and found that almost two-thirds of them had not heard or read about the Team MPs proposal. "Of those who had heard of it, many said they did not understand it fully. Six were for it, 17 against, and eight, undecided."[133] Among those who were not in favour of the Team MPs idea, Michelle Foo, an administrative executive, was particularly astute when she said that:

> It is another way of making sure the PAP stays in power. It is clear that the move is to make it more difficult for opposition parties to get in. We don't have many opposition parties and they can't even agree among themselves. So how can they team up against the PAP?[134]

She is right because, contrary to what Goh Chok Tong has said,[135] the Team MPs plan favours the PAP as it is a political party with a proven track record and has put up competent election candidates because of its rigorous eight-stage selection process.[136] On the other hand, the opposition political parties because of their problems would find it extremely difficult to form credible teams of candidates to contest the general election. While the Team MPs proposal will undoubtedly encourage the opposition political parties to put up more credible candidates, it also constitutes another obstacle to the development of an effective opposition in Singapore.

Another disadvantage of the Team MPs plan is that it might discourage qualified and interested Singaporeans from participating in politics either as PAP or opposition candidates because of the increased workload of the Team MP. Being an MP in Singapore is supposedly a part-time job because he also holds a regular job simultaneously. Thus, in reality, the MP has to cope not only with his own career, but also perform constituency work. If the Team MP proposal is implemented, MPs will be saddled with an additional burden: that of running the TC. Two of the MPs interviewed by *Straits Times* reporters were concerned about this increase in their workload and one of them said: "Right now, MPs are really being stretched. I don't know how much more they can be stretched."[137] Unless being an MP becomes a full-time job, it is unlikely that many Singaporeans would want to enter politics because of the triple demands of holding a regular job, doing constituency work, and running a TC.

So far, the PAP government has provided very little information on the TCs and Team MPs plan. Indeed, it has not responded to the question raised by many Singaporeans: Why change the present system? Moreover, what will happen to the various Residents' Committees (RCs)? Will the RCs become white elephants with the emergence of the TCs? Will the TCs be able to manage the HDB estates more efficiently and effectively than the HDB's Area Offices? Most important of all, as a *Straits Times* reader has asked: Why is there no national referendum to find out from the electorate whether it is in favour of the TCs and Team MPs proposal?[138] This question was simply dismissed by Lim Boon Heng, who contended that "there is no need then to resort to a referendum" because the TC concept and Team MPs system are not fundamental changes affecting the Constitution.[139]

The Team MP proposal assumes that the voter will only vote for the team of MPs that he or she perceives is capable of running the TC. In other words, those candidates who are viewed to be incompetent and unable to manage the TC, will be rejected at the polls. The real test, of course, will be the next general election, the results of which will demonstrate whether this assumption is warranted or not. In this connection, the leaders of the opposition political parties have expressed the view that "there was a chance that the [Team MP] scheme might backfire on the PAP — if people voted for an entire team of Opposition candidates just to make sure that the best man won."[140]

In sum, of the four major problems identified in the third section of this paper, it is unlikely that the problem of the high degree of government intervention and the problem of the ineffective and weak opposition will be solved or minimized in the near future. The level of political participation has been increased especially with the recent formation of the GPCs and the public debate on the National Agenda. The problem of economic recession has been successfully tackled by the implementation of the Economic Committee's recommendations.

Finally, what effect will the five reform initiatives have in terms of changing the three central features of the Singaporean political system? Probably very little since the PAP government will continue to rule in Singapore, barring unforeseen circumstances and the emergence of effective opposition political parties during the next 5-10 years.

Two future events in particular will determine to a very great extent the future shape of the political system in Singapore. The first event will be the next general election in 1988 or 1989. The results of this election will demonstrate: (1) whether the PAP can reduce the percentage of anti-PAP votes; (2) whether the opposition political parties can increase their representation in Parliament; and (3) whether the Team MPs plan would work or be rejected by the electorate. There is no question that the PAP will win the next general election. What is less clear however, is the number of parliamentary seats that will be retained by the PAP MPs, and the extent of the inroads that will be made by the opposition political parties. Above all, the election results will demonstrate to the PAP whether the electorate endorses its post-1984 general election policies, especially its recent reform initiatives.

The second event that will have a bearing on the future of the Singapore political system is, of course, the actual timing of Prime Minister Lee Kuan Yew's retirement and departure from Singapore politics. During his national day rally speech on August 19, 1984, the Prime Minister announced his intention to retire in 1988 at the age of 65, following the practice adopted by major U.S. corporations.[141] One possibility, which he himself has not ruled out, is that Lee would retire as Prime Minister in 1988 as announced and become the President. Obviously, as *Newsweek* magazine has so aptly pointed out, he would be "A Hard Act to Follow."[142] The $64,000 question is now no longer: "Who will succeed LKY?" Barring unforeseen circumstances, the First Deputy Prime Minister, Goh Chok Tong, will succeed Lee Kuan Yew when he retires as Prime Minister in 1988 (or later). Rather, the new $64,000 question is: "*When* will Brigadier-General (Reservist) Lee Hsien Loong become Prime Minister?" Whoever succeeds Lee Kuan Yew has to convince not only Singaporeans but also foreign investors that he and his colleagues have the intelligence, capability and stamina to preserve and enhance the prosperity and political stability which Singapore has enjoyed since 1959.

In conclusion, the three central features of the Singaporean political system — a controlled democracy, political stability and continuity, and PAP's predominance — will remain unchanged so long as the PAP government is in power. Whatever changes are made will be incremental and not comprehensive changes. There might be some lessening of control in the political system after the departure of the remaining Old Guards in the Cabinet as the younger PAP leaders prefer a more consultative style of leadership. However, whether the younger PAP leaders will adopt such a leadership style when they are fully in-charge of the country is still unclear. This reservation is prompted by the following remarks by Goh Chok Tong regarding the Team MP plan if it is rejected by the majority of the population:

> We've got to convince them that the [Team MPs] scheme is meant to benefit the residents, not the party. If large numbers of people, meaning *70 or 80 per cent,* opposed the idea, the Government would take a little more time to persuade them that the system was in their favour. We must, however, be convinced ourselves that this will work in the interest of the country and the people. And that must be our criterion for deciding whether the scheme works in the interest of the nation and the people.[143]

If the above remarks by Goh are taken seriously, his refusal to drop the Team MPs plan in the face of overwhelming public resistance does not augur well for the loosening of political control under the reign of the younger PAP leaders. If the Team MPs proposal is actually implemented in spite of public opposition, then such reforms as the TCs, National Agenda and Team MPs, are merely changes in the *form* but not the substance of the leadership style of these leaders. In short, it would appear that the younger PAP leaders, like the proverbial leopard, cannot change their spots.

Notes

*   I have been on sabbatical leave as a Research Associate at the Institute of Governmental Studies, University of California, Berkeley, from September 1986 to May 1987. As a result of my absence from Singapore during this period, I had to rely on newspaper cuttings sent to me from Singapore to enable me to keep up with the latest developments there. In this connection I am most grateful to Ms. Jill Quah, Head of the Cataloguing Department, Central Library, National University of Singapore, for sending me all the relevant newspaper cuttings. Without her help, it would have been quite difficult for me to write this paper.

1.   See Ong Chit Chung, "The 1959 Singapore General Election," *Journal of Southeast Asian Studies*, Vol. 6, No. 1 (March 1975), pp. 61-86, for an analysis of the PAP's campaign and performance in the 1959 general election.

2.   See You Poh Seng and Lim Chong Yah, eds., *Singapore: Twenty-five Years of Development* (Singapore: Nan Yang Xing Zhou Lianhe Zaobao, 1984) and Peter S.J. Chen, ed., *Singapore: Development Policies and Trends* (Singapore: Oxford University Press, 1983).

3.   Jon S.T. Quah, "Singapore in 1984: Leadership Transition in an Election Year," *Asian Survey*, Vol. 25, No. 2 (February 1985), pp. 226-227.

4.   Republic of Singapore, *Economic Survey of Singapore 1985* (Singapore: Ministry of Trade and Industry, 1986), p. ix.

5.   Republic of Singapore, Report of the Economic Committee, *The Singapore Economy: New Directions* (Singapore: Ministry of Trade and Industry, 1986), pp. 37-38.

6.   *Ibid.*, p. 38.

7.   *Ibid.*, p. iii.

8.   Nena Vreeland *et al.*, *Area Handbook for Singapore* (Washington, D.C.: Foreign Area Studies, American University, 1977), p. 77.

9. See Robert Shaplen, *A Turning Wheel* (London: Andre Deutsch, 1979) and Dennis Bloodworth, *An Eye for the Dragon: Southeast Asia Observed* (Harmondsworth: Penguin Books, 1975).

10. Lau Teik Soon, "The Political System and Nation-Building in Singapore," (Paper presented at the Workshop on "The Political System and Nation-Building in ASEAN," Department of Political Science, National University of Singapore, January 23-25, 1986), p. 1.

11. This term was used by Clark Neher to describe the political systems in Malaysia, Singapore and Thailand. See Clark D., Neher, *Politics in Southeast Asia* rev. ed. (Cambridge: Schenkman Books, Inc., 1987), pp. 3 and 7. See Arend Lijphart, *Democracies* (New Haven: Yale University Press, 1984), pp. 4-6 for a description of the Westminster model of democracy.

12. In 1959 the Legislative Assembly had 51 seats. In 1968, the number of parliamentary seats was increased to 58. The shift of population from the city to the new towns has led to further increases in the number of parliamentary seats: 65 seats in 1972; 69 seats in 1976; 75 seats in 1980; and 79 seats in 1984.

13. Jon S.T. Quah, "The Public Policy-making Process in Singapore," *Asian Journal of Public Administration*, Vol. 6, No. 2 (December 1984), p. 113. For details of the composition of the present Cabinet, see *Straits Times* (Singapore), December 30, 1986, p. 1.

14. K.I. Sudderuddin, ed., *Singapore 1986* (Singapore: Information Division, Ministry of Communications and Information, 1986), p. 39.

15. Douglas V. Verney, "Analysis of Political Systems," in Harry Eckstein and David E. Apter, eds., *Comparative Politics: A Reader* (New York: The Free Press of Glencoe, 1963), p. 190.

16. If a voter fails to vote in a general or by-election in Singapore, his name will be taken off the electoral register if he cannot provide a good reason for not voting. He has to pay S$5 to have his name re-instated in the electoral register.

17. For details of the racial, linguistic and religious diversity of the population in Singapore, see Sudderuddin, *Singapore 1986*, pp. 8-15.

18. More specifically, the Presidential Council for Minority rights has two functions: (1) to review any Bill or subsidiary legislation passed by Parliament to ascertain whether the rights of any ethnic or religious community have been discriminated against, or whether any of the constitutionally guaranteed fundamental liberties have been contravened; and (2) to provide advice on matters affecting persons of any racial or religious community referred to it by Parliament or the government.

19. *Straits Times*, November 19, 1984, p. 1.

20. Jon S.T. Quah, "Meeting the twin threats of communism and communalism: The Singapore response," in Chandran Jeshurun, ed., *Governments and Rebellions in Southeast Asia* (Singapore: Institute of Southeast Asian Studies, 1985), p. 193.

21. Mohammed Ansari Marican, "The Maria Hertogh Riots, 1950," (B.A. Hons. academic exercise, Department of History, University of Singapore, 1973), Chapters 5-6.

22. Foo Kim Leng, "The 1964 Singapore Riots," (B.A. Hons. academic exercise, Department of History, National University of Singapore, 1980).

23. Jon S.T. Quah, "Singapore: Towards a National Identity," *Southeast Asian Affairs 1977* (Singapore: Institute of Southeast Asian Studies, 1977), pp. 207-219.

24. Richard Clutterbuck, *Conflict and Violence in Singapore and Malaysia 1945-1983* (Singapore: Graham Brash, 1984), pp. 341-342.

25. See *ibid.*, pp. 341-342, and Patrick Nathan, "Democracy in Singapore: An Assessment," (B.Soc.Sci. Hons. academic exercise, Department of Political Science, National University of Singapore, 1985), pp. 32-33.

26. The Newspaper and Printing Presses (Amendment) Bill, which was introduced in Parliament on May 5, 1986, empowers the

government to restrict the sale and distribution of foreign publications which interfere in Singapore's politics.

27. Nathan, "Democracy in Singapore," pp. 43-45.

28. See Ho Tai Yan, "The Origins and Application of the Internal Security Laws of Singapore 1945-1977," (B.A. Hons. academic exercise, Department of History, University of Singapore, 1978) for more details on the ISA; and Jon S.T. Quah, "The Police and Law Enforcement in Singapore: Problems and Prospects" (Paper presented at the Annual Meeting of the Academy of Criminal Justice Sciences, Philadelphia, March 11-14, 1981), pp. 14-15 for details of the CLTPO.

29. Quah, "The Public Policy-making Process in Singapore," p. 111.

30. See C.M. Turnbull, *A History of Singapore 1819-1975* (Kuala Lumpur: Oxford University Press, 1977).

31. N. Balakrishnan, "Political stability the key: Survey," *Straits Times*, August 12, 1985, p. 17.

32. Jon S.T. Quah, "Singapore in 1983: The Continuing Search for Talent," *Asian Survey*, Vol. 24, No. 2 (February 1984), p. 184.

33. Quah, "Singapore in 1984," p. 226.

34. Chan Heng Chee, "Political Parties," in Jon S.T. Quah *et al.*, eds., *Government and Politics of Singapore* 2nd ed. (Singapore: Oxford University Press, 1987), p. 146.

35. This analysis of the PAP's predominance in Singapore politics is based on Jon S.T. Quah and Stella R. Quah, "The Limits of government Intervention: Learning the Hard Way," in Kernail S. Sandhu and Paul Wheatley, eds., *Singapore: The Management of Success* (Singapore: Oxford University Press, forthcoming), pp. 3-7 of chapter.

36. Quah, "Meeting the twin threats," pp. 186-212.

37. *Yearbook of Statistics Singapore 1985/86* (Singapore: Department of Statistics, 1986), p. 144; and *Economic Survey of Singapore 1985*, p. ix.

38. Jon S.T. Quah, "The Public Bureaucracy in Singapore, 1959-1984," in You and Lim, eds., *Singapore: Twenty-five Years of Development*, pp. 295-298.

39. Chan, "Political Parties," p. 169.

40. Quah, "Singapore in 1984," p. 227.

41. Clutterbuck, *Conflict and Violence*, p. 319.

42. Quah and Quah, "The Limits of Government Intervention," in Sandhu and Wheatley, *Singapore: The Management of Success*, p. 16 of chapter.

43. Stella R. Quah, "Social Discipline in Singapore: An Alternative for the Resolution of Social Problems," *Journal of Southeast Asian Studies*, Vol. 14 (1983) p. 281.

44. Jon S.T. Quah, "Public Housing," in Quah *et al.*, *Government and Politics of Singapore*, p. 254.

45. See Jon S.T. Quah, "Singapore's Experience in Public Housing: Some Lessons for Other New States," in Wu Teh-yao, ed., *Political and Social Change in Singapore* (Singapore: Institute of Southeast Asian Studies, 1975), pp. 113-154; Stephen H.K. Yeh, ed., *Public Housing in Singapore: A Multidisciplinary Study* (Singapore: Singapore University Press, 1975); and Aline K. Wong and Stephen H.K. Yeh, eds., *Housing a Nation: Twenty-Five Years of Public Housing in Singapore* (Singapore: Maruzen in Asia, 1985).

46. This total is compiled from Tham Kok Wing, "National Campaigns in Singapore Politics," (B.Soc.Sci. Hons. academic exercise, Department of Political Science, National University of Singapore, 1983), pp. 92-94, and data provided by the Information Division in the former Ministry of Culture.

47. Quah, "The Public Policy-making Process in Singapore," p. 120.

48. For details of these incentives and disincentives, see Quah, "Social Discipline in Singapore," p. 281, fn. 76.

49. *Ibid.*, pp. 283-285.

50. Quah, "Singapore in 1983," p. 179.

51. *Straits Times*, January 24, 1984, p. 1.

52. Quah, "Singapore in 1984," p. 221.

53. Quah, "Singapore in 1983," p. 180.

54. *Straits Times*, August 18, 1986, p. 1.

55. See Quah and Quah, "The Limits of Government Intervention," in Sandhu and Wheatley, *Singapore: The Management of Success*, pp. 2 and 25-29 of chapter.

56. Chan Heng Chee, "The Political System and Political Change," in Riaz Hassan, ed., *Singapore: Society in Transition* (Kuala Lumpur: Oxford University Press, 1976), p. 39.

57. *Ibid.*, pp. 40-41, 44-45.

58. *Ibid.*, p. 45.

59. Chan Heng Chee, "In Middle Passage: The PAP faces the Eighties," (Singapore: Department of Political Science, University of Singapore, Occasional Paper No. 36, 1979), p. 13.

60. Republic of Singapore, Reprint of *The Constitution of the Republic of Singapore* (Singapore: Singapore National Printers, March 31, 1980), Article 24 (2), p. 14.

61. Quah, "The Public Policy-making Process in Singapore," pp. 113-114.

62. *Ibid.*, pp. 114-115.

63. Kawin Wilairat, "Singapore's Foreign Policy: A Study of the Foreign Policy System of a City-State," (Ph.D. dissertation, Georgetown University, 1975), p. 335.

64. *Ibid.*, p. 355.

65. *Ibid.*, p. 354.

66. Stella R. Quah, *Balancing Autonomy and Control: The Case of Professionals in Singapore* (Cambridge: Center for International Studies, Massachusetts Institute of Technology, 1984), p. 118.

67. *Ibid.*, p. 119.

68. Lee Boon Hiok, "Public Sector Labour Relations in the Singapore Context," (Singapore: Department of Political Science, University of Singapore, Occasional Paper No. 37, 1979), p. 13.

69. The Minister without Portfolio, Ong Teng Cheong, is also the NTUC's Secretary-General, and several NTUC officials are also PAP members of Parliament.

70. Chan Heng Chee, "The Role of Intellectuals in Singapore Politics," in Wee Teong Boo, ed., *The Future of Singapore – the Global City* (Singapore: University Education Press, 1977), p. 41.

71. *Ibid.*, pp. 45-46.

72. *Ibid.*, p. 46.

73. Quah, "Social Discipline in Singapore," p. 287.

74. Quah, "Singapore in 1984," p. 227.

75. Willard A. Hanna, "How to Win a Clean Sweep in Free Elections," *AUFS Reports*, Vol. 20, No. 11 (November 1972), pp. 1-10.

76. Quah, "Singapore in 1984," p. 226.

77. G.S. Muthukrishnan, "Focus on Singapore: Dilemma of the PAP," *Pacific Community*, Vol. 2, No. 1 (October 1970), p. 202.

78. Chan Heng Chee, "Politics in Singapore, 1984-1986," in Quah *et al.*, *Government and Politics of Singapore*, p. 312.

79. Quah, "Singapore in 1984," p. 223.

80. The NCMPs would differ from the elected MPs in that they would not be able to "vote in Parliament on any motion relating to a Bill to amend the Constitution, a Supply Bill or Supplementary Supply Bill, a Money Bill or a vote of no

confidence in the government." See *Straits Times*, July 25, 1984, p. 10.

81. Lee Boon Hiok, "Non-constituency MPs – A place for the opposition in Singapore?" *The Parliamentarian*, Vol. 66, No. 3 (July 1985), pp. 124-125.

82. Lee Kim Chew, "The Making of an Opposition Candidate," *Sunday Times* (Singapore), September 2, 1984, p. 2.

83. This profile of the opposition candidates is culled from data obtained from "Who's fighting whom and where," *Straits Times*, December 13, 1984, p. 18; and Ho Chin Beng, *et al.*, "Why this table is incomplete," *Straits Times*, December 15, 1984, p. 22.

84. Chan, "Political Parties," in Quah *et al.*, *Government and Politics of Singapore*, p. 163.

85. Economic Committee, *The Singapore Economy*, p. 38; and Chan, "Politics in Singapore, 1984-1986," in Quah *et al.*, *Government and Politics of Singapore*, p. 318.

86. Economic Committee, *The Singapore Economy*, pp. 4-5; and Chan Heng Chee, "Singapore in 1985: Managing Political Transition and Economic Recession," *Asian Survey*, Vol. 26, No. 2 (February 1986), p. 164.

87. Economic Committee, *The Singapore Economy*, pp. 5-7.

88. "Goh on when town council concept will not work," *Business Times*, January 17, 1987.

89. Dr. Chan Yan Chong, "Pros and Cons of town councils and team MPs," *Straits Times*, February 27, 1987, p. 19.

90. "Dhana explains aim of setting up town councils," *Straits Times*, March 18, 1987, p. 12.

91. Low Mei Mei, "MPs want six months' extension," *Straits Times*, December 30, 1986.

92. Paul Jacob, "Two top priorities this year," *Straits Times*, February 2, 1987, p. 1.

93. "Councillors still not sure about roles and responsibilities," *Straits Times*, February 10, 1987, p. 14.

94. "Let town council trial run go on longer, say residents," *Straits Times*, February 10, 1987, p. 14.

95. Ahmad Osman, "Town councils: Govt 'on the right track'," *Sunday Times*, February 1987, p. 1.

96. K.C. Tan, "More info needed for discussion," *Straits Times*, March 26, 1987, p. 22.

97. "Town councils will be more widely accepted," *Straits Times*, March 30, 1987, p. 10.

98. Chuang Peck Ming, "Committees to spur parliamentary debate," *Business Times*, January 17, 1987.

99. Dr. Hong Hai, "How parliamentary panels can play a greater role," *Straits Times*, January 17, 1987.

100. *Ibid.*

101. *Ibid.*

102. Ahmad Osman, "PAP MPs to have more say," *Straits Times*, February 14, 1987, p. 1.

103. The other seven GPCs are: the Communications and Information Committee, the Community Development Committee, the Defence and Foreign Affairs Committee, the Education Committee, the Home Affairs Committee, the Labour Committee, and the National Development and Housing Committee. For details of the composition of the nine GPCs, see "Who's who," *Straits Times*, February 14, 1987, p. 14.

104. "A sounding board for ideas from Govt, S'poreans," *Straits Times*, February 10, 1987, p. 14.

105. Paul Jacob, "Credibility vital for panels to be effective," *Straits Times*, February 14, 1987, p. 14.

106. "Quality of Debate," *Straits Times*, February 14, 1987, p. 18.

107. "NUS don on how GPCs can be effective and win credibility," *Straits Times*, February 21, 1987, p. 11.

108. Paul Jacob, "Five ways to let voters have say," *Straits Times*, December 11, 1986.

109. Patrick Daniel, "PAP reaches out for consensus," *Straits Times*, February 19, 1987, p. 1.

110. "Questions for the People," *Straits Times*, February 19, 1987, p. 14.

111. Daniel, "PAP reaches out for consensus," p. 1.

112. "A People's Manifesto," *Straits Times*, February 20, 1987, p. 18.

113. Patrick Daniel, "Debate begins on National Agenda," *Straits Times*, February 23, 1987, p. 1.

114. "Why we're inviting public discussion — Chok Tong," *Straits Times*, February 23, 1987, p. 1.

115. Ahmad Osman, "Vote MPs by team system proposed," *Sunday Times*, January 25, 1987, p. 1.

116. Quah, "Singapore in 1984," p. 227.

117. Ahmad Osman, "Proposed changes won't affect one-man-one-vote, says MP," *Sunday Times*, January 25, 1987, p. 13.

118. *Ibid.* p. 13.

119. See for example the letters in the forum page of the following issues of the *Straits Times*: February 6, 10, 12, and 21; March 11, 13, 20 and 21, 1987.

120. "Team MPs in next polls," *Straits Times*, February 28, 1987, p. 1.

121. Economic Committee, *The Singapore Economy*, pp. 49-50.

122. *Ibid.*, p. 54.

123. Patrick Daniel, "Recovery is lop-sided, survey shows," *Straits Times*, February 28, 1987, p. 1.

124. Vikram Khanna, "The economy has turned the corner," *Straits Times*, March 4, 1987, p. 16.

125. "4-6% growth set as target," *Straits Times*, January 10, 1987, p. 1.

126. "5-6% likely in first half," *Straits Times*, March 26, 1987, p. 1.

127. "GPC chairman win praise for good show in Parliament," *Straits Times*, March 30, 1987, p. 1.

128. *Ibid.*, p. 1.

129. The six PAP ministers who formulated the statement, "Singapore, City of Excellence – A Vision for Singapore by 1999," were: Goh Chok Tong, Ong Teng Cheong, Dr. Tony Tan, S. Dhanabalan, Prof. S. Jayakumar, and Dr. Yeo Ning Hong. See "The men who came up with the concept," *Straits Times*, December 12, 1984, p. 16.

130. "Team MPs proposal is to ensure stability in the future: BG Lee," *Sunday Times*, March 22, 1987, p. 1.

131. "Team MPs system is politically neutral, says Goh," *Straits Times*, February 28, 1987, p. 11.

132. See for example the following letters to the *Straits Times*, forum page: David Chan, "Group system will deal blow to democracy," *Straits Times*, February 6, 1987, p. 20; Wong Joo Seng, "System will lead to MPs voters didn't choose," *Straits Times*, February 21, 1987, p. 22; HKN, "Team MPs will lead to undemocratic system," *Straits Times*, March 11, 1987, p. 20; and Robert Craiu, "Proposal is an unwieldy marriage of 2 systems," *Straits Times*, March 20, 1987, p. 26.

133. "What the men in the street has to say," *Straits Times*, February 12, 1987, p. 10.

134. *Ibid.*, p. 10.

135. "Team MPs system is politically neutral, says Goh," *Straits Times*, February 28, 1987, p. 11.

136. As the PAP's selection process is a rigorous one, it is not surprising that only 21 per cent of those invited to participate in the selection process are actually selected. See Philip Lee and Christine Khor, "Few stumble on the home stretch," *Sunday Times*, July 1, 1984, p. 20.

137. "Many favour it because of economies of scale," *Straits Times*, February 12, 1987, p. 10.

138. "It is essential that the Government holds a referendum on this important issue [Team MPs] and the issue on town councils as it must necessarily have grave repercussions on the voters for many years to come. The silence of the majority must not be taken as assent by the minority." HKN, "Team MPs will lead to undemocratic system," *Straits Times*, March 11, 1987, p. 20.

139. Lim Boon Heng, "Proposed system not a fundamental change affecting Constitution," *Straits Times*, March 21, 1987, p. 22.

140. "Idea is vague and may backfire on the PAP," *Straits Times*, February 12, 1987, p. 10.

141. Quah, "Singapore in 1984," p. 224.

142. William Burger with Melinda Liu, "A Hard Act to Follow: Singapore's Lee Kuan Yew prepares to pass the torch – but what comes next?" *Newsweek*, February 23, 1987, pp. 8-13.

143. "Team MPs in next polls," *Straits Times*, February 28, 1987, p. 1. Emphasis added.

Entrenched "Strong Man" Rule: The Governmental System in Bangladesh

Mohammad Mohabbat Khan
Habib Mohammad Zafarullah

Introduction

Since independence in 1971, the political system of Bangladesh has been in a state of flux; it has yet to achieve the stability which comes from being institutionalized. The last fifteen years have been marked by the following features: frequent changes in government; tampering with the fundamental provisions of the Constitution; manipulation of Parliament to suit the parochial interests of the regime in power; coups or attempts to topple governments through political assassinations; fragmentation of the major political parties into a myriad of small factions or splinter groups; creation of political parties by military rulers to mobilize popular support for their regimes; manipulation of the electoral process to 'legitimize' the person in power; policy failures by successive regimes in the economic and social fields leading to recession, political unrest, and escalating levels of political and bureaucratic corruption; failure to tap and mobilize domestic resources resulting in the almost total dependence on foreign aid; absence of effective structures for popular participation at both the national and local levels; arrogance on the part of higher bureaucrats towards politicians and the public; and the growth of intra-bureaucratic and inter-agency conflicts.

In the following sections of this paper, we will attempt to outline and explain the principal characteristics of the governmental system in Bangladesh, to analyse the major institutional and organizational problems of the political system, to examine a number of reform proposals and initiatives, and to provide an outlook on the likelihood of significant political and governmental changes in the immediate future.

Central Features of the Political and Governmental System

The Awami League (AL) government led by Sheikh Mujibur Rahman (Mujib) which came to power at independence, achieved the distinction of framing a Constitution for the country within a year. The political system was to be based on "the high ideals of nationalism, socialism, democracy and secularism, which inspired our heroic people to dedicate themselves to, and sacrifice their lives in, the national liberation struggle."[1] These four basic principles were designed to be the underpinning for all the political, administrative, social and economic objectives of the nation. The Constitution aimed at the creation of a "socialist-economic system" which had, as its basic feature, the concept of an egalitarian ethic.[2] Democracy would be the guarantor of the people's fundamental rights as well as the instrument to ensure popular participation in governance.[3] The government was to be responsible for meeting the basic needs of the people, and for creating society free of exploitation.[4] State ownership of the means of production and distribution was to be the basis of the economic system, although cooperative and private ownership of property was also permitted within prescribed limits.[5]

The governmental system was intended to adhere to the basic tenets of parliamentary democracy. Thus, the cabinet, representing the political party with a majority in the unicameral legislature, would exercise control over the governmental machinery and would be responsible for its actions to the legislature. Parliament was legally to be supreme. The President, on the model of the British monarch, was to be the nominal head of state, performing ceremonial functions only. However, as in many other republics, he was to be elected by the members of Parliament. An independent judiciary was to safeguard the supremacy of the Constitution and preserve the fundamental rights of the citizens.

Though the Constitution imposed certain restraints and limitations on governmental power, in fact, the country was ruled capriciously by a single man – the Prime Minister.[6] This was possible because of Mujib's immense popularity initially among the people who placed their trust in his leadership. However, the government's failure to solve a multitude of pressing domestic problems which emerged in the wake of the war of liberation rapidly caused a decline in the credibility of Mujib's leadership. Instead of consolidating the political gains which he achieved during the war of liberation and which he could have utilized in uniting the people and in galvanizing them in the task of nation-building, Mujib chose extra-constitutional means to suppress growing discontent among the politically conscious sections of the society. By the end of the first year of independence, organized opposition to his regime emerged outside Parliament. Mujib responded by using deceit and brute strength in his bid to eliminate opposition. He created his own personal security force composed mostly of party workers who had been trained in guerilla warfare during the war. The members of this force were directly accountable to Mujib and operated independently of the army and police. This aroused fear and apprehension among the people as this force regularly and systematically tormented innocent people and operated above the law. Also, the members of the armed forces became suspicious of the government's attempt to equip this force with sophisticated weapons and technical equipment at the expense of their own development. The ill-feeling this created would later prove fatal to Mujib.

On the economic front, the task of developing a viable infrastructure within a socialist framework remained unattended. Nationalization of the major segments of the industrial sector proved to be a bane for the economy. Widespread corruption among state enterprise personnel, labour unrest, and ineffective management resulted in poor performance. A devastating famine, large-scale smuggling along the border, insufficient attention to the agricultural sector, an unfavourable balance of payments, and a rapid rise in the prices of essential commodities and the cost of living index created a "difficult economic situation [that] seriously affected the daily lives of [the] people particularly the landless rural workers and generally the urban population . . . [this] generated widespread social and political tension".[7]

Being unable to redress this situation, Mujib opted for a complete transformation of the system of government. The rationale behind this move was basically to entrench himself and his party in power despite mounting opposition. Even the "massive"[8] victory of the Awami League in the parliamentary elections of 1973 failed to quell the growing dissension, distrust and dissatisfaction of the people towards the regime. In early 1975, after ruling the country for some time under a state of emergency, Mujib replaced the multi-party parliamentary system with a one-party presidential type of government where all powers were concentrated in his hands. All parties were banned except the Awami League, which was renamed and reorganized as the Bangladesh Krishak Sramik Awami League (BKSAL). Members of the other parties were urged to join the new party. BKSAL, in reality, became a monolith whose tentacles spread into the army and the bureaucracy.

Within a short time, the Mujib regime was overthrown in a coup led by some disgruntled mid-ranking army officers. They installed a senior member of the Mujib cabinet as the President. BKSAL was disbanded. Parliament was retained and a new cabinet composed of prominent Awami Leaguers was formed. The Constitution was put in limbo and the country was placed under martial law. This regime was shortlived; a couple of counter-coups, both of which had overt political overtones, brought to the fore Major General Ziaur Rahman (Zia), the Army Chief of Staff. Although initially there was a civilian President (a former Chief Justice of the Supreme Court), it was Zia who was the *de facto* ruler.

Zia ruled the country for five and a half years.[9] During the first part of his regime (November 1975 to February 1979), he made systematic efforts to legitimize and stabilize his rule. Organized political activities were permitted from July 1976 when an ordinance was proclaimed to regulate the re-emergence and operation of political parties. This was followed about a year later with a country-wide referendum through which Zia sought the people's vote of confidence in his leadership and their support for the policies and programmes of his government. The following year he was elected to the presidency[10] directly by the people on the basis of universal adult franchise. This gave immense credibility to his position. In response to demands from the political parties, the parliamentary elections of 1979[11] were preceded by a proclamation that repealed certain "undemocratic" provisions incorporated by Mujib into the Constitution in early 1975.[12] In the parliamentary elections, Zia's Bangladesh Nationalist Party (BNP) won an absolute majority.[13] This can be attributed to Zia's personal appeal as an honest, sincere and hard-working person, to improved economic conditions, to an improved law and order situation, and to his vigorous campaigning before the elections.

During the second part (February 1979 to May 1981) of Zia's regime, the country made the transition from martial law to civilian rule. However, all the actions of the martial law period were legitimized by Parliament through an amendment to the Constitution in April 1979. The form of government that emerged was somewhat different from Mujib's on three counts: first, the democratic framework of governance was to operate within a multi-party system; second, checks were put on certain executive and legislative powers of the President that had been conferred by Mujib's amendment of the Constitution; and third, the independence of the judiciary, which had been curtailed by Mujib, was restored. The fundamental principles of state policy were also given a new direction. First, nationalism was now to connote Bangladeshi nationalism, rather than the Bengali nationalism enunciated in the original Constitution of 1972. This reflected Bangladesh's separate identity as a nation *vis-a-vis* the state of West Bengal in India.[13a] Second, the Constitution was given an Islamic basis by omitting secularism and putting "absolute trust and faith in the Almighty Allah [as] the basis of all actions". Third, socialism was defined as economic and social justice.[14]

The return to civilian rule did not bring stability on the political and economic fronts. The ruling BNP, composed of heterogeneous elements with diverse and contradictory ideological leanings, was plagued by intra-party schisms. Democratic norms failed to establish themselves within the party and almost all major decisions on governmental affairs were taken unilaterally by Zia without taking into confidence senior party leaders.[15] The party leaders made little fuss about Zia's high-handedness for they depended upon him for patronage and protection. Zia took the support of his followers for granted and began to extend his web of control to the villages. A new institution — *Gram Sarkar* (village government)[16] — was introduced to further broaden his support base.

During the initial years of his rule, Zia succeeded in improving the economy. A 7.8 per cent growth in GDP and a 4.4 per cent increase in per capita income during 1977-78 manifested the relative success of the government's economic policies. However, by the end of 1981, the GDP growth had significantly declined from 6.1 per cent in 1980-81 to 0.9 percent.[17]

Zia's assassination in May 1981 by a section of the Bangladesh army in an abortive attempt to capture power showed clearly the fragile nature of the BNP without its creator. Justice Sattar, who had been a handicapped Vice President under Zia, succeeded him by winning a presidential election held in late 1981. He faced a more difficult situation within both the party and the government. He was overthrown by the Army Chief of Staff, Lt.Gen. H.M. Ershad, within a short time of his installation as President. Sattar's fall can be attributed more to the greed and lust for power by senior members of the armed forces than to any policy failures on the part of his government. In fact, in the midst of an uncertain political climate, Sattar initiated a number of actions designed to stabilize the political and economic situation of the country. He tried to curb corruption by sacking a number of ministers and attempted to maintain discipline and orderliness in the banking sector.

Ershad moved swiftly to consolidate his power. All political activities were banned, Parliament was dissolved, and the Constitution was placed in abeyance. A number of BNP ministers were arrested on charges of corruption and tried by specially constituted military tribunals. Many political figures were put behind bars without specific accusations.

From the very beginning, the military government wanted to label itself a "reformist" regime. This resulted in the establishment of high-powered committees to inquire into a wide array of issues. The Committee for Administrative Reorganization and Reform (CARR) looked at ways of decentralizing the administration. Expert committees dwelt at length on the formulation of a national drug policy, a decentralized judicial system, a new industrial policy, a new education policy and a land reform policy.

The Ershad regime followed in the footsteps of the earlier military rule of Zia by organizing a "new" type of administration. All powers were vested in the office of the Chief Martial Law Administrator (CMLA), a position occupied by Ershad. He was assisted by two Deputy CMLAs (the Chiefs of the Navy and Air Force). A motley group, composed of serving generals, senior bureaucrats and professionals,were chosen as advisors to look after various ministries and divisions. The field administration at various levels became the responsibility of the members of the military. For this purpose, the entire country was divided into zones and sub-zones and placed under zonal and sub-zonal martial law administrators wielding considerable authority.

In course of time, Ershad ventured to civilianize his rule and consolidated his hold on power. He lifted the ban on political activities, entered into negotiations with politicians, inducted some of those who chose to support him into his "cabinet", elevated himself to the presidency by dismissing the titular President whom he had himself installed, held a referendum to seek approval of his rule, organized parliamentary elections in order to form a legislative body and used it to give legal cover to all actions and activities of four and a half years of military rule, and, finally, staged a presidential election to put the seal of legitimacy on his accession to power.

The governmental system in Bangladesh today represents a somewhat strange combination of both the British and the American systems. The President, as head of state and government, exercises enormous authority and influence over all spheres of governmental affairs. His election to the presidency by the direct vote of the people lends credence to his position. He is assisted by a chosen Vice President who, like his superior, holds office for a five-year term. A Council of Ministers (Cabinet) composed of the Prime Minister (the leader of the House in Parliament), three Deputy Prime Ministers and a large number of ministers, state ministers and deputy ministers, links the presidency with the Parliament. Ministers do not necessarily have to be members of Parliament; the President is empowered to appoint up to one-fifth of his ministers from among non-parliamentarians. Advisors, with the rank and status of cabinet ministers, assist the President on various policy matters. Although they actively participate in its deliberations, ministers are not accountable to Parliament; rather they are responsible to the President who exercises his discretion in hiring and firing them.

Three hundred members of Parliament are directly elected by the people. They, in turn, elect, or rather select by simple majority, thirty women members. Formally, the Parliament performs all the functions of a modern legislature: initiating bills, deliberating upon their contents, and passing them; scrutinizing administrative action; discussing and approving budgets; and impeaching the President.[17a] However, a number of provisions in the Constitution curtail the pre-eminence normally enjoyed by modern parliaments. For instance, although the President lacks the power of final veto over bills passed by Parliament, their re-enactment would be difficult as it would require the support of the majority of all members and not only of those voting. Second, amendment of certain provisions in the Constitution cannot be made by Parliament unless ratified by popular referenda. Third, the President is empowered to override money bills.[17b]

The Supreme Court, comprised of a High Court Division and an Appellate Division, is the highest level of the judicial system. The High Court Division has original, appellate and other jurisdictions and powers as well as the power to enforce constitutionally guaranteed fundamental rights. All other courts are subordinate to it. The Appellate Division hears and determines appeals against judgements, decrees, orders or sentences of the High Court Division. Its other important function is to serve as a legal advisor to the President.

The administrative structure[18] of the government consists of line and staff agencies at both the national and local levels. A large number of ministries consist of a central secretariat with branches extending to the field. Each ministry consists of one or more self-contained units called divisions, performing a specific set of functions. A ministry operates under the direction and guidance of a cabinet or state minister who is advised by a senior official with the rank and status of a secretary. The latter is the administrative head of the ministry or division and is responsible for carrying out in an appropriate manner any business assigned to his ministry/division. The other principal officers working in a ministry/division include additional secretaries, joint secretaries, deputy secretaries and assistant secretaries. Their number varies according to the volume of business a particular ministry/division has to handle.

Execution of government policies is the responsibility of attached departments or subordinate agencies. Attached departments implement policies formulated by a ministry and act as repositories of technical information for the latter to draw upon. Subordinate agencies function as field offices for detailed execution of governmental programmes. Other types of public organizations performing specialized functions of an industrial, commercial, regulatory, developmental or promotional nature include public corporations, boards and authorities. These are established under specific legislative or administrative authority and are given relative freedom from governmental control in the performance of their routine activities. However, such public bodies operate under the administrative jurisdiction of a relevant ministry and, for all practical purposes, have little operational autonomy. "There is hardly any aspect where the government does not encroach."[19]

At the subnational level, the structure of public administration extends through three tiers: division, district and *upazila* (sub-district) hierarchically arranged in that order. The divisional administration guides and supervises the activities of district administrative units under its jurisdiction. Coordination of developmental activities and deciding upon questions of revenue administration are two of its major functions. District administration, since the days of British imperial rule, has been the cornerstone of local administration. Its crucial role encompasses a wide-range of activities: land revenue administration, correctional services and development administration. In recent years, the coordination of the operations of local units (*upazila*) under its control has proved to be the most intricate and crucial responsibility of district administration.[20]

At the local level, *upazila* is the only unit where a representative body exists alongside a centrally-directed and centrally-controlled bureaucratic apparatus. The representative body (*upazila parishad* or sub-district council) consists of a directly elected chairman, chairmen (also elected) representing union *parishads* (councils) located within the *upazila*, nominated members (including women) and a representative of the *upazila* central cooperative association. In addition, there are members who represent the bureaucracy at that level. They have voice but no vote in council meetings. The national government has retained the control over all regulatory and major developmental functions. Indeed, development administration is the *raison d'être* of the *upazila* system. Their functions encompass formulation, implementation, monitoring and evaluation of all development projects and coordination of the activities of the officials of line ministries located at that level.[21]

Among the staff agencies of the government at the national level, the Planning Commission plays a preeminent role. It performs three broad sets of functions: preparation of annual and long- and short-term plans; deliberating upon and recommending policy prescriptions and institutional changes pertaining to the implementation of these plans; and serving as a central agency to coordinate short- and long-term economic policies of various ministries.[22]

The highest policy-making body, headed by the President, is the National Economic Council (NEC). It provides guidance in the formulation and adoption of economic policies, plans and programmes and reviews the progress of their implementation.[23]

Overview of Major Institutional and Administrative Problems

The major institutions of a political system are the executive, the legislature, the judiciary, the political parties, and the electorate. The system that has developed over the years in Bangladesh through trial and error exhibits the effects of political adventurism — by democrat-turned-dictator, and by overambitious army generals. This has resulted in attempts to develop political institutions around a particular individual — the President — with the support of the military, the bureaucracy and unprincipled politicians. As a result the development of the presidency as a viable democratic and credible institution has been jeopardized. The lack of restraints and limitations on the authority of the President and the concentration of powers in his hands has, in effect, made the presidency an autocratic institution. Presidential elections to regularize and "civilianize" the rules of a military dictator have not been openly competitive. Typically they have been a formality to consolidate the incumbent's already entrenched position. Once elected, he becomes omnipotent. He is not accountable for his actions to Parliament. Theoretically, the Parliament exhibits all the characteristics of legislative preponderance over the political system. In practice, however, parliaments have been made impotent by ambitious presidents. Members of Parliament, especially those belonging to the ruling party, show little inclination to use the parliamentary forum to criticize the policies of the government. This is mainly due to two reasons. An anti-government stance, however justified it might be, could lead to a reprimand from the party chief, who happens to be the President himself, and secondly, members refrain from voting against the government lest they should act contrary to the "interest" of the party they belong to. If they oppose the government they are liable to lose their seats in Parliament. In reality, it is the President who wields total control over Parliamentary affairs. Parliamentarians belonging to the ruling party have been carefully hand-picked by the President for their loyalty and commitment. Political parties like the BNP and Jatiyo Party (JP) were organized by Zia and Ershad respectively to bring together an assortment of individuals, irrespective of their political affiliations or beliefs, so that they might strengthen the support base of their founders.

The President uses the bureaucracy to implement his policies and programs.[24] He relies upon a select band of senior generalist civil servants and military generals to design policies whose implementation will help strengthen his position. For instance, his moves to reorganize the administration at the local level and to denationalize state enterprises and promote the private sector have been directed to broadening his power base in the rural areas and obtaining the support of the urban moneyed class.

State control of the media at the behest of the President has served as a deterrent to the expression of public opinion. The extensive nature of media control can be gauged from the fact that even privately-owned newspapers with supposedly neutral editorial policies provide extensive coverage for the minutest of details concerning the President's actions and whereabouts in order to obtain government patronage in the form of official advertisements. Radio and television, both of which are wholly state-controlled, spend most of their air time extolling the "achievements" of the President and his regime.

The servility of the media has a negative influence over the electorate during elections. Opposition political parties are given very limited space and time in state newspapers, radio or television to express their views. The electoral process, in itself, is far from foolproof.[25] Instances of bogus-voting, ballot box snatching, violence and corruption by some civil servants acting in collusion with locally deputed officials of the Election Commission to manipulate election results in favour of the President or his party, have been too many to be dismissed lightly. The rigging of elections has not only undermined the credibility of the Election Commission but also adversely affected the image of the President, members of Parliament and representatives of local bodies. The people's confidence in the electoral process has reached its lowest ebb.

Originally, the Constitution envisaged an independent judiciary. Though the Chief Justice and other judges of the Supreme Court were to be appointed by the President, judges of the subordinate courts were to be appointed by him on the advice of the Prime Minister in consultation with the Supreme Court. Similarly, magistrates were to be appointed on the recommendation of the Public Service Commission and the Supreme Court. The Supreme Court was to be responsible for the control and discipline of all personnel in the judiciary and the magistracy, and was to oversee all matters relating to their conditions of service and career planning.

Attempts to undermine the independence of the judiciary began under the parliamentary democratic system in existence during the

Mujib era. On the pretext of curbing the activities of political parties/groups on the radical left, the government created special tribunals with extensive powers. There was no provision for any appeal against their judgement.[26] This executive act was followed by a constitutional measure that further weakened the position of the judiciary. Accompanying the transformation of the political system in early 1975 was a measure that vested all powers over the judiciary and the magistracy in the President.[27] He could now remove or dismiss a judge of the Supreme Court by a memorandum providing clarification as opposed to the previous requirement for an indictment proceeding by two-thirds majority in Parliament. In spite of a further amendment to the Constitution under the Zia regime in 1978, restoring the earlier status of the judiciary, the executive still holds sway over the judicial system by retaining the authority for the appointment of judges and controlling the magistracy through the Ministry of Establishment.[28]

In Bangladesh, the bureaucracy, to a large extent, conforms to the Weberian model. Decision making patterns and working relationships are dictated by highly formalistic rules and regulations apparently leading to an impersonal style of administration. In other words, impersonal adherence to the application of these rules is considered important for ensuring uniformity of procedures and operations and minimizing discrimination among clients. A fixed hierarchy defines and delimits superior-subordinate relationships, with each level representing a different degree of authority and control. Division of labour is based on differentiation of tasks. However, bureaucrats are not always assigned specific positions on the basis of their specialization or expertise, but rather on the basis of belonging to a particular civil service cadre. Rationality is conceived in a narrow sense. It is primarily equated with administrative efficiency and economy, both of which are considered ends in themselves rather than means to an end – effective delivery of public service.

The civil service is, by and large, based on the concept of a closed career system, although in recent years there have been cases of variations. The focus of classification is on the individual, who is a member of a corps (functional cadre) recruited at the entry level on the basis of his general educational background and performance in open competitive examinations. There is permanency of tenure except for reasons of gross misconduct. A civil servant is not separated until he attains retirement age. Members of the super cadre – Senior Services Pool (SSP) – at the apex of the structure are usually rotated throughout the administrative system during their careers to hold a series of key positions whose scope may vary considerably.[29] The SSP is almost exclusively dominated by members of a single cadre –

administrative — composed of people with a generalist background. The other twenty-nine cadres, some of which are purely technical, like engineering, health, agriculture and telecommunications, resent the administrative cadre's undue domination over senior positions in the civil service. An upshot of this has been organized moves by the non-administrative cadres to resist the preeminence of the administrative cadre. Consequently, inter-agency coordination has suffered, leading to procrastination in decision making and execution. Suspicion and mistrust between the generalists and specialists have had a baneful influence over efficiency and effectiveness.

Although the closed career system does not envisage lateral entry into the civil service structure, a pattern has developed where the career progression of civil servants is being impeded by the induction of military personnel into key positions. Supporters or hangers-on of the regime have been given lucrative diplomatic assignments in Bangladesh missions abroad in total disregard for the claims on those positions by career foreign service personnel. The practice was begun by Zia and institutionalized by Ershad. This form of patronage has had a pernicious effect on the morale of civil servants. Also, the perpetuation of a promotion system obsessed with seniority impedes recognition of proven competence and demonstrated innovativeness on the part of bright and highly qualified mid-level civil servants (some with MAs and PhDs from foreign universities). One consequence of such a situation is an exodus of talents from the civil service to the private sector, and to regional and international organizations.

Another effect of the obstacles to career progress has been a decline in the willingness of the brightest university graduates to enter the civil service. Unlike the past, when competition was keen among the best graduates of the top universities, a career in the civil service is now placed low in the range of options. The private sector (banks, financial institutions and trading concerns) and multinational corporations vie with each other to attract the most talented young people.

The recruitment and selection process[30] itself is beset with problems, largely due to the absence of a comprehensive and well-defined recruitment policy. Employment planning, both short- and long-term, is not undertaken. Other features are *ad hocery* in appointments, lack of objectivity and reliability of selection tests, misinterpretation and ineffective implementation of the affirmative action policy of the government and actions by the Ministry of Establishment, exclusively manned by members of the administrative cadre, hindering the Public Service Commission from playing its intended role as a central personnel agency.

Training in public administration has problems of both a qualitative and quantitative nature. There has been a shortage of training opportunities for the majority of civil servants and the quality of training imparted in the existing institutions has been unsatisfactory. This has been due, in part, to the dearth of a well-trained professional corps of trainers. Training methods are archaic as most programs are lecture-based and no effort is made to introduce modern methods and techniques. Course content is based on western ideas and precepts, which are modified, if at all, by taking cognizance of environmental realities. Bureaucratic politics and patronage are key factors in the selection of trainees rather than perceived need or relevance. Most trainees, particularly those belonging to the higher echelons of the civil service, are found to show little interest in training and have demonstrated a contempt for institutional training. Junior and mid-level civil servants have also been apathetic towards training primarily because it is not linked with their career development. Follow-up of training programmes or their proper and timely evaluation have been conspicuous by their absence. No effort is made to measure the effects of training or changes in the knowledge, attitude, behaviour and job performance of trainees. These inadequacies of administrative training have not been remedied because of the absence of a clear and innovative national training policy.[31]

Large-scale corruption has become endemic at all levels of society. The bureaucracy is no exception. Corruption has become institutionalized with civil servants relying on a variety of corrupt practices to provide them with "a life style far beyond their actual means."[32] Almost every public dealing, in one way or another, is tinged with corruption. The public image of civil servants generally is one of inertia, indolence, inefficiency and corruption. Measures to tackle these problems have proved to be counter-productive. There have been many cases of insubordination within the bureaucracy as well as allegations of malfeasance. Though institutional mechanisms exist to discipline and control civil servants in order to improve administrative performance and eliminate bureaucratic red tape and obstructionism, these have rarely been utilized. Indeed, the bureaupathologies are too numerous to identify. They range from simple administrative oversight, arbitrariness, lack of courtesy and arrogance to serious maladministration. Eventually, the ordinary citizen has to bear the brunt of a bureaucratic misrule whose prevalence can be attributed to failure of effective political control. Parliament has failed to demand accountability from bureaucrats for their actions. The judicial system is constrained to take action on its own to correct the injustices or irregularities suffered by the citizens.

A constitutional provision for the office of ombudsman does exist but no government has deemed fit to operationalize it.

Political parties in Bangladesh must shoulder the major blame for the lack of political development in the country. Major parties till now have failed to agree on an acceptable system of governance. Each has its own idea of a political system, irrespective of whether it is compatible or not with the peculiarities of the country and its people. As we have indicated before, the basic conflict has been between proponents of the presidential system and adherents of the Westminster model. In addition, there are those whose preferences are for either an Islamic or a communist state. Almost all political parties, when in opposition, have been plagued with internecine conflicts and feuds among the top leaders, not over questions of principle but ways to safeguard their personal interests. This has resulted in parties breaking into hostile and quarrelsome factions with the ensuing erosion of their strength and credibility. The Awami League suffered several splits after independence in spite of its extensive organizational network and a cadre of dedicated workers. Many top leaders in the Mujib government, who had been central to the party's existence before independence, not only deserted the party but also formed their own political organizations with objectives similar to those of their parent party. The BNP, the other major party which was in power before Ershad came to power, also broke into factions which, in turn, splintered into even smaller groups.

The cult of personality rather than issues matters most in Bangladesh politics today. Mujib and Zia symbolize the Awami League and the BNP respectively despite their demise. When they were alive their image strengthened the power base of the parties they led. There was no controversy about their stature among party workers and no one really challenged their authority. Mujib's daughter had to be brought from exile outside the country six years after his death to save the party from disintegration due to a leadership crisis. For similar reasons, Zia's widow was elevated from looking after her own household to the top leadership position in the BNP. Both of these women were newcomers to politics; yet they were considered the most acceptable leaders by their respective party workers. In the case of both parties, the dominance of a single leader has not augured well for the functioning of a democratic polity. Compliance on the part of followers is taken for granted by the leader and he or she becomes capricious not only about handling party matters but also about controlling democratic tendencies. As President, Mujib persuaded his party to lend its support for his action to transform the governmental system. In a similar manner Zia, as the Chairman of BNP, concentrated extraordinary powers in his hands and thwarted moves by some party members to ensure accountability for his actions.

Opportunism has been another feature of Bangladesh politics. Short-term partisan and individual interests outweigh long-term national interests. The consequence has been the adoption of short-sighted policies and the betrayal of people's trust. Politicians have, in many cases, used political parties to bargain with the person-in-power (Zia and Ershad, for instance) for ministerial positions for themselves. After being known for their entrenched "ideological" leanings and political beliefs, they were not loth to abandon their parties along with some of their followers and rally behind the ruler. This sort of support became necessary for the replacement of military by civilian rule and both Zia and Ershad have made good use of it. The contribution by self-seeking politicians in bringing about a reform to civilian rule is significant because, as members of Parliament, they ratify all actions taken under martial law prior to its lifting. They are thus instrumental in encouraging the military's usurpation of state power.

Most political parties suffer from organizational deficiencies – an ineffective chain of command and a lack of mechanisms to hold leaders accountable. At times, party reorganizations are effected only to perpetuate the hold of a particular group over party matters. Leadership changes are carefully avoided, leaving little scope for grooming young party workers for key party positions. In effect, the fate of everything seems to depend on a single person and his coterie.

Overview of Reform Initiatives

Since independence, successive governments in Bangladesh have attempted to bring about reforms in various fields. Most of these efforts have not been successful. Those which were, brought only marginal changes to the *status quo*. Most reform efforts failed at the crucial implementation stage of the reform cycle. Lack of strong political commitment and concomitant bureaucratic support, organized resistance by those affected by the changes and general apathy on the part of the people at large towards reform measures were instrumental in frustrating reform efforts.

The present regime has initiated several reform measures to bring about far-reaching changes in many areas. Not all the measures are directly relevant for the purpose of this paper, and only those with direct implications for the governmental system are discussed here.

Political and administrative reforms were attempted in the past. Political reform efforts were primarily directed at the subnational level but had implications for national politics as well. The creation of the one-party state in 1975 was followed by the planning and adoption of a scheme providing for the appointment of political people as heads of district administration. These people, to be known as district governors, were given extensive powers and were to be directly accountable to the President. This new form of local administration was to work hand-in-hand with the district branches of the only "legally recognized" political party – BKSAL. This proposed system was an innovation in the sense that it was designed to do away with the inherited colonial pattern of local governance where bureaucrats reigned supreme. Obviously however, it was also intended to further strengthen Mujib's hold over the country. With the fall of the regime in August 1975, the scheme could not be launched.

A similar, but much more innovative attempt, was made by Zia in 1977. It focused on the grassroots and its aim was to make villages centres of development. The genesis of this reform emanated from a movement for self-reliance – government-sponsored nation-wide experiment aimed at making each stratum of the society self-reliant – that had been launched in late 1975. A micro-governmental system known as *Gram Sarkar* (village government) was "designed to meet the basic needs of the rural people and remove rural poverty by the rural people themselves entirely on the basis of self-help."[33] A *Swanirvar* (self-reliant) *Gram Sarkar* (SGS) consisted of a *Gram Prodhan* (village chief) and eleven *Gram Montris* (village ministers) representing various occupational groups. They were chosen through consensus by a *Gram Shava* (village assembly) which was comprised of all adult members of the village.[34] The SGSs were linked with the other levels of government. The control of the national government over the SGSs was extensive. It also became clear that SGSs were used to extend the influence of the ruling party (BNP) to the villages.[35]

During the first decade (1972-1982) after independence several attempts were made to reform bureaucratic structure and processes.[36] The Administrative and Services Reorganization Committee (ASRC) and the National Pay Commission (NPC) appointed by Mujib made a number of recommendations. His dislike of the inherited elitist bureaucratic system was widely known and so he wanted the ASRC to give a new model of administration in keeping with the fundamental principles of state policy. Some far-reaching proposals of the Committee were: to create a single classless unified civil service structure; to develop a personnel system emphasizing merit and equity; and to decentralize the administration. Its service classification was accepted by the NPC in formulating a pay structure that considerably reduced the disparity between the highest and lowest scales of pay in the civil service. The recommendations of the ASRC were not accepted, while the less significant ones of the NPC were implemented. This was due to organized resistance by senior members of the generalist civil service.[37]

Zia's interest in administrative reform was reflected in his initiating a series of measures. He appointed a Pay and Services Commission (P&SC) whose central thrust was that the bureaucracy should be subordinate to the political leadership and that civil servants should be politically neutral and responsive to societal demands. The amalgamation of all existing services and the creation of an all-purpose service was its most significant recommendation. The recruitment system was to be based on the merit principle and competency would determine advancement in the service. Zia distinguished himself by accepting a number of the major recommendations of the P&SC and gradually implementing them. The government's actions included the creation of twenty-eight services under fourteen main cadres, the establishment of a Senior Services Pool (SSP) and the introduction of new national grades and scales of pay.[38] His other reform measures included: elevating the Establishment Division (the central personnel agency) to a fully-fledged ministry; rationalizing the recruitment and selection system; streamlining public administration training; improving administrative procedures by framing new rules and designing manuals and guidelines for the use of administrative agencies.[39]

As soon as he came to power, Ershad asserted on repeated occasions his intention "to take government nearer to the people" by a process of political and administrative decentralization.[40] The process began with the institution of a reform planning body (Committee for Administrative Reorganization/Reform – CARR). Identifying several major inadequacies in the existing political and administrative structure of the country, CARR recommended the creation of representative bodies with wide powers and supporting bureaucratic staff at two subnational levels – *zila* (district) and *upazila* (subdistrict). Popular participation was singled out as the principal basis of a democratic sub-polity based on devolution of power and authority. The major function of each of these subnational entities was to undertake developmental activities within its respective jurisdiction through a process of local level planning without governmental intervention.

Though the government accepted the major recommendations of CARR, their implementation was carried out in a haphazard manner. *Zilas* have been left untouched, leaving no scope for infusing the representative element at that level. *Zila* administration still continues to be run by bureaucrats. *Upazilas* have come into existence and people's representatives have been elected to run them, but it is becoming increasingly difficult for them to manage the affairs of the *upazila* independent of governmental intervention. By controlling financial grants, the national government is, in effect, dictating how developmental plans should be formulated and implemented by local representatives. Another encroachment into *upazila* affairs by the government has been in the area of public personnel administration. Civil servants assigned to the *upazila* are controlled by and responsible to their respective line ministries. All these features have stifled local autonomy and considerably lessened opportunities for popular participation at the *upazila* level.[40a]

The government's claim that its decentralization policy broke new ground by providing opportunities for the people to participate in governance at the local level is rhetoric. As was the case with Zia's SGS scheme, Ershad's aim was to use *upazilas* to further tighten his hold over the country. The election of *upazila* chairmen, professed by the regime to be non-partisan, was, in reality, an exercise to install party members in the *upazila* administration. Using governmental facilities indiscriminately and unabashedly, Ershad campaigned in favour of his *protegés*. The boycott of the elections by all major parties, however, proved to be to his advantage.

In the realm of central administration, a martial law committee (MLC), almost wholly composed of army personnel, emphasized departmental reorganization, retrenchment and economy in administration. It also focused on efficiencies to be achieved through improvement of the bureaucratic process. The recommendations of the MLC were introduced incrementally and resulted in genuine cutbacks in administration. But, in course of time, to gain short-term political goals, the Ershad regime increased the number of ministries/divisions and lifted the embargo on recruitment.[41]

Proposals by politicians and academics for reshaping the governmental system have been few and far between. So far, only one political party – Jatiyo Samajtantrik Dal (Rab faction) – has proposed a framework for a new political system. The idea is premised on providing representation of professional groups in Parliament. According to this prescription for political participation at the national level, Parliament will consist of three hundred members elected from general constituencies and two hundred members representing thirteen professional/occupational groups (the military and bureaucracy, for instance).[42] This idea has lately found favour with Ershad and it appears that the military-bureaucratic alliance which calls the shots in Bangladesh is very eager to institutionalize the role of the military and the bureaucracy in the politics of the country. JSD's proposal has, understandably, found appreciative audience in Ershad and his cohorts in the party. Ershad's insistence on a constitutional role for the military in politics is now new. In fact, after the demise of Zia in mid-1981, he lost little time before publicly expressing his opinion in favour of this role. At that time he was Chief of Army Staff and had not yet taken over power and his views raised a lot of controversy but gave clear indications of his ambitions. It is not surprising then that JSD (Rab)'s idea is finding favour with him. The proposal has been actively opposed by the two major opposition parties – Awami League and BNP.

Though many academics have analyzed the predicaments of the existing political and administrative system and made rather vague propositions for change, only a few have outlined an alternative to the existing system; still fewer have presented concrete proposals which merit serious consideration. A. and R. Ahmed (a husband and wife team both with higher degrees from the United States and both teaching at a tertiary institution) have presented a conceptual framework for political and administrative reorganization to facilitate the structural transformation of the country's governmental system. Their model has several features: first, a unicameral legislature of five hundred members, of whom three-fifths would be elected members representing territorial constituencies and two-fifths would represent different professional/occupational groups; second, a greatly enlarged National Economic Council (NEC) of seven hundred to nine hundred members, comprising the chairmen of all *upazilas*, officials of the Planning Commission and line ministries, heads of sector corporations/autonomous bodies and representatives of professional groups, with responsibility for reviewing national development plans and approving development programs; third, a People's Consultative Council (PCC) consisting of eminent personalities selected by the executive and approved by the legislature, who would advise the Planning Commission in preparing short-term, medium-term and long-term plans; fourth, the Planning Commission which would be placed above all ministries and headed by the President; fifth, *zilla parishads* (district councils) which would coordinate the activities of the national government and *upazilas*.[43]

The ideas of both JSD (Rab) and of A. and R. Ahmed look attractive. But institutionalizing them would, indeed, be a difficult task. There is lack of consensus on the number and kind of professional/occupational groups. The process of choosing their representatives would allow political parties to further extend their influence over them thereby negating the idea of pure and simple professional/occupational representation.

The Ershad regime has attempted to decentralize the judiciary by establishing civil and criminal courts at the *upazila* level, by appointing benches of the High Court in six district headquarters, by simplifying the codes of criminal procedure, and by expediting the process of disposing of cases. The Law Reforms Committee and the Civil Procedure Reforms Commission advised the government on these measures.[44]

The creation of permanent benches of the High Court Division of the Supreme Court in the district headquarters and their subsequent conversion into Circuit Benches have been a gross violation of the Constitution. This has raised certain institutional complexities as it is considered *ultra vires* by an overwhelming majority of lawyers of the Bar Association. The Chief Justice, in vindicating this move of the regime and in acting on orders of the President, has not only undermined the neutrality of his office but also failed to protect the Constitution. All these moves have left the judicial system in disarray as lawyers have virtually paralysed its working. Consequently, people's confidence in the judiciary has waned as the controversy over the governmental reform measures persists. The judiciary today is, unfortunately, politics-ridden.[45]

On the economic front, the Ershad regime has been pursuing a policy of denationalization and privatization of the industrial and banking sectors. While the primary emphasis has been to encourage private entrepreneurism to "revitalize" the economy, the existing state industrial enterprises have been subjected to procedural reforms intended to increase their efficiency and productivity. Following the recommendations of the Committee for Reorganization of Public Statutory Corporations (CRPSC), the operational autonomy of the enterprises have been expanded, their internal organization has been restructured, their managerial and operative functions streamlined, performance evaluation and monitoring techniques somewhat improved, and financial discipline and accountability procedures strengthened.[46]

However, the crude privatization moves by the government have had a baneful impact on the working of state-owned financial institutions (SFI). Huge amounts of money, borrowed at low rates of interest and on easy terms by prospective industrialists from these institutions, have become extremely difficult to recover because of built-in deficiencies in the process. In spite of the negative impact this has had on the economy, the government continues to make regular repayment of loans to foreign donors and, consequently, the burden of repayment has to be shouldered by the general public. The shortfall in foreign assistance, because of the dismal recovery situation and the poor performance of state enterprises, has also hindered the government in making investments in new developmental projects in various sectors of the economy. Non-recovery of loans has strained not only the liquidity of SFIs but has also created manifold problems for the public sector.[47]

Major political parties including the Awami League and BNP have been very critical of the Ershad government's policy in the industrial sector. The Awami League, which had nationalized all major industries in 1972 while in power, has publicly vowed to reverse the denationalization policy when it is returned to power.

One group of academics is opposed to privatization. They believe that it will lead to a further widening of the gap between the common man and the urban moneyed class. Another group considers it imperative to promote entrepreneurism in the private sector to offset the poor performance of the public sector.

Future Outlook

Bangladesh remains volatile nation. The fervour of independence was quick to evaporate; the strong nationalistic support for the state being above everything soon fizzled out. Committed democrat though he was, Mujib, within a short time, found that he was abhorred by the people for his authoritarianism. Military rule was accepted with enthusiasm when it came because many people believed that it would redeem the nation. After some years, however, its real nature became apparent and the people began to crave for democracy once again.

In a span of only fifteen years, the country has seen many upheavals in the political arena and changes and reversals on the economic front. The form of government has been subjected to often drastic changes, to accommodate the idiosyncrasies of the strong man in power. Economic and social policies have been affected by these changes. The political parties and the intelligentsia are divided over how the polity should be governed and over the modes of political participation. Until now, no consensus could be reached about whether the nation should have a parliamentary or a presidential system or a mixture of the two; whether there should be a free economy or greater governmental intervention or a balance between the two.

Thus it is difficult as well as hazardous to make realistic projections about the significant changes that might occur in the next five to ten years in the political and governmental system of Bangladesh.

In the foreseeable future, there seems little possibility of a constitutional transfer of power to an opposition political party or alliance which were to win an election held free and fairly. Winning elections (presidential or parliamentary) for such a party or alliance would be an impossibility, primarily because of the ruling party's unyielding desire to hold on to the reins of power by any means, fair or foul. Widespread rigging of elections and other forms of electoral manipulation by the ruling coterie have prevented the true manifestation of the popular will; there is no likelihood of the situation changing soon. Moreover, the sharp decline in voter turnout at the polls is clear indication of the voters' lack of confidence and trust in the validity of elections in Bangladesh.

Unless there is a change of regime by force, Ershad will be in power for the next five years, until the time of the next presidential election. During this period what we can expect to see is the maintenance of the *status quo*, or even a reversal of changes already initiated. Ershad's desire to retain total control over government and party matters will be achieved through frequent shuffling of ministerial positions, rotation of senior civil servants from one department to another, induction of military personnel into key public service positions and continued changes in party positions at different levels. This would further consolidate his position in both party and government. As politics revolve around him, ministers and members of Parliament belonging to his party will generally play the role of his henchmen. This will deter the Jatiyo Party from developing into a true political party.

Because of the predominance of individual and factional interests within them, the opposition political parties are likely to continue to remain divided and ineffective in launching and sustaining democratic movements. Their activities will be restricted to making statements and holding public meetings. As a result they are likely to lose the people's confidence as viable alternatives to the present regime.

The firm establishment of a decentralized administrative structure to cover the district level will be used to the existing regime's advantage. Already there is evidence of a move towards re-centralization. The national government's control over resource allocation in the form of distribution of grants to the local units for development purposes is likely to contribute to this tendency. This is because of the country's almost total dependence on foreign aid and on the donor countries/agencies' insistence on its effective utilization. The deployment of national government officials in increasing numbers at local levels would stultify local initiative and popular participation in development.

The bureaucracy, especially at the senior level, can be expected to become increasingly dependent on the President and will heed his advice without question as far as policy planning is concerned rather than advising him on policy alternatives. Generally, the bureaucracy will probably continue to be faction-ridden, unresponsive to societal demands and inaccessible to the common people unless attitudinal changes are brought about through behavioural training. Because of the peculiarities of an authoritarian political system, civil servants will continue to remain mere instruments of autocratic action, insulated from the people and disdainful of their real needs. There is no likelihood of any major institutional reforms being effected during the next five to ten years if this regime continues. Whatever changes occur in the governmental system will be geared to entrenching the regime further.

Conclusion

The emerging political and administrative culture of Bangladesh has been influenced by its peculiar historical experience and social ethos. The authoritarian nature of its present political system has been due to the failure of the party in power to adhere to democratic values and by the people's desire to epitomize power within a single personality. This has led to the acceptance by the people of an autocrat without questioning the basis of his usurpation of power, to an unassailable and rigid bureaucracy, and to a fragmented party system preventing the growth of a realistic opposition in the legislature even if opportunities for such opposition existed. Added to these is the inertia of age-old traditions and beliefs which have made the entire system lose any momentum for change.

The institutional and administrative problems which confront the governmental and political institutions in Bangladesh today are numerous and diverse. Furthermore, there is no indication that these problems will be remedied through reform measures in the foreseeable future.

The rise and fall of people's expectations have been recurring phenomena. Two military regimes, since the fall of the Awami League government, each promised initially to rescue the people from the influences of unscrupulous politics, economic mismanagement and social decay as well as to pave the way for 'clean' politics and greater popular participation in state affairs, but the regimes themselves gradually became masters of political manipulation, promoters of affluence for the few, and false custodians of democratic institutions. This is the irony of Bangladesh.

Notes and References

1.   Government of the People's Republic of Bangladesh (GPRB), *The Constitution of the People's Republic of Bangladesh.* (Dhaka: Government Printing Press (GPP), 1972), Preamble.

2.   GPRB, *Constitution*, Article 10.

3.   GPRB, *Constitution*, Article 11.

4.   GPRB, *Constitution*, Articles 14 and 15.

5.   GPRB, *Constitution*, Article 14.

6.   See T. Maniruzzaman, *The Bangladesh Revolution and its Aftermath.* (Dhaka: Bangladesh Books International, 1980), pp. 154-98; T. Maniruzzaman, *Group Interests and Political Changes: Studies of Pakistan and Bangladesh.* (New Delhi: South Asian, 1982), pp. 126-75; R. Jahan, 'Bangladesh in 1973: management of factional politics' in M.M. Khan and H.M. Zafarullah eds. *Politics and Bureaucracy in a New Nation: Bangladesh.* (Dhaka: Centre for Administrative Studies, 1980), pp. 56-71.

7.   GPRB, Planning Commission, *Annual Plan, 1973-74.* (Dhaka: GPP, 1973), P. 1.

8.   There were allegations of large-scale rigging of elections in favour of the Awami League candidates. Of the 300 seats in Parliament, the party won 292.

9.   For details see, M. Franda, *Bangladesh: The First Decade.* (New Delhi: South Asian, 1982), pp. 219-335; Maniruzzaman, *Group Interests and Political Changes*, pp. 229-59; Maniruzzaman, *Bangladesh Revolution*, pp. 199-234.

10.   M.M. Khan and H.M. Zafarullah, 'The 1978 presidential election: a review', in S.R. Chakravarty and V. Narain eds., *Bangladesh: Domestic Politics.* (New Delhi: South Asian, 1986), pp. 100-10.

11.   M.M. Khan and H.M. Zafarullah, 'The 1979 parliamentary elections in Bangladesh,' *Asian Survey*, 19, No. 10 (October 1979), pp. 1023-36.

12. The salient features of this proclamation were: appointment of a prime minister who must be a member of Parliament and should enjoy the confidence of majority members of the House; provision for the inclusion of non-members in the Cabinet, their number not exceeding one-fifth of its total strength; the President having no power to veto any bill passed by Parliament; and the holding of referenda for making major changes in the Constitution and the method of electing the President. *Bangladesh Times*, 16 December 1978.

13. Khan and Zafarullah, '1979 parliamentary elections.' pp. 1030-33.

13a. M. Anisuzzaman, *Bangladesh Public Administration and Society*. (Dhaka: Bangladesh Books International, 1979), pp. 16-36.

14. GPRB, *The Constitution of the People's Republic of Bangladesh*. (As modified up to February 1979) (Dhaka: GPP, 1979), Preamble.

15. M.M. Khan, 'Political parties in Bangladesh, 1978: a trend analysis,' *Asian Affairs*, 1, No. 1 (January-June 1980), pp. 66-70; M.M. Khan, 'Bangladesh Nationalist Party: problems and prospects,' *Asian Studies*, 4, No. 1, (1982), pp. 30-41.

16. M.M. Khan and H.M. Zafarullah, 'Innovations in village government in Bangladesh,' *Asian Profile*, 9, No. 5 (October 1981), pp. 447-53.

17. Bangladesh Bank, *Annual Report, 1981-82*. (Dhaka: Bangladesh Bank, 1982), p. 3.

17a. GPRB, *Constitution*, Articles

17b. A.F. Huq, 'Constitutional development, 1972-1982,' in Chakravarty and Narain eds., *Bangladesh*, p. 66.

18. S.G. Ahmed and M.M. Khan, 'Public administration in Bangladesh' in V. Subramaniam ed., *Public Administration in the Third World*. (Westport, Connecticut: Greenwood Press, 1987).

19. H.M. Zafarullah and M.M. Khan, 'Emerging ethos of state enterprises in Bangladesh' in S.K. Barua and T.K.Jain eds.,

State Enterprises: The Emerging Scenario. (Jaipur: Centre for Administrative Change, 1987).

20.   Ahmed and Khan, 'Public administration in Bangladesh.'

21.   K. Siddiqui ed., *Local Government in Bangladesh.* (Dhaka: National Institute of Local Government, 1984), pp. 43-60; M.M. Khan, 'Reform for decentralized development: Bangladesh's experiment with major administrative reforms/reorganizations in the '80s' in M.M. Khan and J.P. Thorp eds., *Bangladesh: Society, Politics and Bureaucracy.* (Dhaka: Center for Administrative Studies, 1984), pp. 146-67.

22.   N. Islam, *Development Planning in Bangladesh.* (Dhaka: University Press Limited, 1979), pp. 41-2.

23.   *Bangladesh Gazette Extraordinary*, 29 June 1984, p. 7947.

24.   E. Ahamed, 'Dominant bureaucratic elites in Bangladesh' in Khan and Zafarullah eds., *Politics and Bureaucracy*, pp. 163-8.

25.   M.M. Khan, 'The electoral process in Bangladesh.' Paper presented at a Regional Conference/Workshop on Comparative Study of Elections in Asia and the Pacific organized by the Eastern Regional Organization for Public Administration in cooperation with the Asia Foundation in Manila, Philippines, February 2-6, 1986.

26.   Maniruzzaman, *Group Interests and Political* Changes, p. 132.

27.   GPRB, *Constitution* (as modified up to January 1975), Articles 115 and 116.

28.   J. Alam, 'The debate over the judiciary,' *Holiday*, 20 February 1987.

29.   Ahmed and Khan, 'Public administration in Bangladesh.'

30.   M.M. Khan and H.M. Zafarullah, *Recruitment and Selection in the Higher Civil Services of Bangladesh: An Overview.* SICA Occasional Paper Second Series, No. 6, American Society for Public Administration, 1984.

31.   M.M. Khan and H.M. Zafarullah, 'Public administration training in Bangladesh: an overview,' *International Review of Administrative Sciences*, 46, No. 4, (1980), pp. 369-76; M.M.

Khan, 'Public Administration Training Centre: a critical overview' in M.M. Khan and S.A. Husain eds., *Bangladesh Studies*. (Dhaka: Center for Administrative Studies, 1986), pp. 58-80.

32. H.M. Zafarullah, 'Public administration in the first decade of Bangladesh: Observations and Trends,' *Asian Survey*, 27, No. 3 (March 1987); M.M. Khan and H.M. Zafarullah, 'Public bureaucracy in Bangladesh' in K.K. Tummala ed., *Administrative Systems Abroad*. (Washington, D.C.: University Press of America, 1982), p. 179.

33. M.M. Khan and H.M. Zafarullah, eds., *Rural Development in Bangladesh: Trends and Issues*. (Dhaka: Center for Administrative Studies, 1981), p. 151.

34. M.M. Khan, 'Experiences of rural development programmes in Bangladesh,' in Jean-Claude Garcia-Zamor, ed., *Public Participation in Development Planning and Management: Cases from Africa and Asia*. (Boulder, Colorado: Westview Press, 1985), p. 193.

35. A.S. Huque, 'The Problem of Local Government Reform in Bangladesh: The Failure of Swanirvar Gram Sarkar.' Unpublished Ph.D. dissertation. Vancouver: University of British Columbia, April 1984.

36. M.M. Khan, 'Major administrative reform and reorganization efforts in Bangladesh: an overview,' *Indian Journal of Public Administration*, 31, No. 3 (July-September 1985), pp. 1016-40; M.M. Khan and H.M. Zafarullah, 'Major administrative reforms in Bangladesh, 1972-1981: review and evaluation,' *Proceedings of the Sixth International Symposium on Asian Studies, 1984*. Vol. IV. (Hong Kong: Asian Research Service, 1985), pp. 1177-93; Zafarullah, 'Public administration in the first decade.'

37. M.M. Khan, 'Major administrative reform and reorganization efforts in Bangladesh, 1971-1985,' in C. Campbell and B.G. Peters, eds., *Organizing Governance: Governing Organizations*. (Pittsburgh: University of Pittsburgh Press, 1987).

38. M.M. Khan and H.M. Zafarullah, 'Administrative reform and bureaucratic intransigence in Bangladesh,' in G.E. Caiden and

H. Siedentopf, eds., *Strategies for Administrative Reform*. (Mass: D.C. Heath and Co., 1982), pp. 139-151.

39.   Zafarullah, 'Public administration in the first decade.'

40.   Khan, 'Major administrative reform and reorganization efforts.'

40a.   H.M. Zafarullah and M.M. Khan, 'Politics of rural development in Bangladesh,' in B. Chaudhuri, ed., *Rural Development*. (Calcutta: Centre for South and Southeast Asian Studies, 1987).

41.   M.M. Khan, 'Politics of administrative reform and reorganization in Bangladesh,' *Public Administration and Development*, 7, No. 3, 1987.

42.   For details see S.A. Khan and Z.R. Khan, *On Constitution and Constitutional Issues*. (Dhaka: University Press Limited, 1983).

43.   A Ahmed and R. Ahmed, 'A conceptual framework for political and administrative reorganization,' *Holiday*, 30 January; 6, 20, and 27 February; 6, 13, 20, and 26 March 1987.

44.   GPRB, *Administrative Reorganization and Reforms*.   (Dhaka: CMLA Secretariat, 1983), p. 7.

45.   *Holiday*, 6 March, 1 May 1987.

46.   *Bangladesh Gazette Extraordinary*, 29 July 1983.

47.   *New Nation*, 9 March 1987.

Australian National Government, 1987*

J. R. Nethercote

I.   The Confusing Face of Australian Politics, 1987

1988 will mark the bicentennial of European settlement (or invasion, as historians now again write[1]) of the continent of Australia. Australia is to have a bicentennial celebration American-style, reflecting the derivative character of so much that occurs here. The occasion is being used to review the Constitution and to open a new and permanent Parliament House. These developments, combined with reform programs in public administration and public enterprise, mean that the whole structure of national government is currently subject of active debate and examination in political, administrative and academic circles. The debate, however, is taking place in the context of much change in politics and public policy.

---

*   This is a very substantial revision of the paper presented to the IRPP Workshop in June 1987. Since the paper was written the political confusion of the earlier part of the year was essentially resolved by the double dissolution election of July 11, 1987. The advisory committees to the Constitutional Commission have reported and the Commission itself has published views on parliamentary matters. Three days after the election the Prime Minister announced major changes to administrative arrangements. He has also reopened the debate on privatisation of public enterprise. The original paper was thus very dated by the end of July 1987. This revised version endeavours to embrace the story up to October 1987.

The bicentennial itself is not a celebration meeting with the approbation of all the population. Many Aboriginals, the descendants of the original inhabitants, are either ambivalent or hostile. Graffiti on concrete supports of the new Parliament House explains their view: "White Australia has a black history – Don't celebrate in '88."

Nor are the descendants of the Europeans, long-standing or recent, at one with what is or should be celebrated. *Ethnos*, the monthly publication of the New South Wales Ethnic Affairs Commission, regards the multicultural plans as "aimlessly lacking commitment, vision and purpose, and almost certain to make non-Anglo-Saxon Australians feel excluded from the celebrations."[2]

On the other hand, conservative critique sees the official bicentennial programs, those conducted under the auspices of the Australian Bicentennial Authority, as concentrating on, among other things, religious diversity, Aboriginal culture, women's activities, contribution of unions and the bicentennial flag and logo at the expense of themes such as the work ethic, high living standards, Christian traditions, British heritage, alliance with America, the family, private enterprise, the monarchy, a workable Constitution, and the Australian flag.[3] Even radicals have hesitations, preferring a celebration in 2001, the centenary of the Commonwealth, to 1988, the bicentenary of the foundation of the penal colony of New South Wales.[4]

The controversies generated are of variable importance; even so, it is unlikely that the storms will be stilled before or during 1988. Their significance, however, lies as much in the nature of particular issues immediately in dispute as in their role as vehicles in which Australians seek to fashion their national self-perceptions in the world of the late twentieth century in which the many changes generated by the Second World War and its aftermath are coming to maturity: increasing participation of women in economy and society, the impact of mass immigration from Europe (and, more recently, immigration from Asia) greater consciousness of the plight of Aboriginals, higher levels of education, and greater diversity in our links with the world, especially the evolving relationship with Asia.

It is not, indeed, without some irony that the bicentennial should fall at a time when long-held assumptions about public policy are very much on the agenda, openly, explicitly, even ideologically. It is a verity of our politics that "Australian democracy has come to look upon the State as a vast public utility, whose duty it is to provide the greatest happiness for the greatest number. The results of this attitude have been defined as *le socialisme sans doctrines*."[5] Yet privatisation of public enterprises great and small is now a feature of the agenda, the pressures coming from both within and without government. Another handy aphorism, also longstanding, claims that

"The characteristic talent of Australians is not for improvisation, nor even for republican manners, it is for bureaucracy."[6] Nonetheless, deregulation, like privatisation, is fighting for a place on the action agenda of Australian government and possibly doing so more successfully.[7] These philosophies, supported by the Opposition before the recent election in July 1987, have been embraced by the Prime Minister and some leading members of the subsequent Government with enthusiasm.

The party political landscape is also unfamiliar in the current disposition of forces.[8] The Australian Labor Party (ALP) holds office at national level under Prime Minister Hawke and in four of the five mainland States (New South Wales since 1976; Victoria and South Australia since 1982; and Western Australia since 1983). Labor does not have a majority in the Commonwealth Senate; the Victorian and Western Australian governments also face hostile upper houses.

After a quarter of a century Queensland dispensed with coalition government in 1983. The major partner in the coalition, the National Party (previously the Country Party) now governs alone; in late 1986 the Party won a second term under its redoubtable leader, the rural religious populist, Sir Johannes Bjelke-Petersen, Premier of the State since 1968. The Liberal Party, minor partner in the defunct coalition, is but a rump in the Queensland Parliament, with little influence beyond Brisbane, the State capital (where, as it happens, it won control of Australia's largest local government in 1985).[9] Queensland has a unicameral legislature.

The other unicameral legislature in Australia is in the Northern Territory. It has been ruled since self-government in 1978 by the Country-Liberal Party, an autonomous party in the non-Labor group.

The reversal of fortunes applies to Tasmania as well. The ALP, so often in office, is now in opposition to a twice-elected Liberal Party Government which faces a powerful upper house dominated by independents, a number of whom – perhaps even a majority – have strong links with the Liberal Party.

The ruling ALP governments of the 1980s are notable for a fairly cautious policy profile and considerable party discipline through organised factions. At the national level the Hawke Government, its relationship with unions secured in the first two terms by an Accord on prices and incomes initially negotiated in 1983 before winning office,[10] has superintended a general deregulation of the financial system combined with an austere fiscal policy boasting that its 1987 budget is a balanced budget for the first time in many years (a feat which may not be realised because of the falls in stock market values in October). It has also made some important changes to taxation policy by introducing capital gains and fringe benefits taxes and, in the welfare field, an assets test on pensions. At State level the Labor governments have all displayed a measure of radicalism – this is particularly so of the long-standing New South Wales Government – but they have been in general much occupied by economic and financial matters, the fight against unemployment and the battle for solvency.

The non-Labor side of politics, long-accustomed to office nationally and in Victoria and Western Australia as well as in Queensland, is disorganised, disunited, fragmented. Faced with restrained Labor governments it has been unable to find a clear policy basis for attack; its capacity to do so has been weakened seriously by disputation particularly within the Liberal Party over whether to maintain the Keynesian-based philosophies which have served while in office[11] or to strike out on new paths favouring the market, privatisation, deregulation, lower taxes, stricter limits on unions, family-oriented welfare expenditure and small government generally. Policies in the latter vein are also being promoted by new and revitalised think tanks which have come into prominence in the past decade.[12] Their emergence has coincided with a call to Liberals "to be more overt and aggressive in the public presentation of Liberal philosophies and principles."[13]

The quest to recover office has been hampered further by the ultimately fruitless intervention in national politics by Sir Joh Bjelke-Petersen with the federal coalition rather than the Hawke Government as the immediate target. The standard for the campaign, seen at the time by some observers as a strategy to exploit a populist urge for a strong folksy leader, is one of a flat tax rate of 25 per cent. The supporting causes are total opposition to any form of general indirect (consumption) taxation of the type said to be under consideration by the Opposition and favoured by important business interests;[14] militant anti-unionism; and smaller government in the form of a reduction in the number of Commonwealth departments and return of functions such as education and health to the States.

The Bjelke-Petersen intervention brought unprecedented bitterness to coalition politics between and within the two parties. The divisions were intensified by severe economic problems in rural Australia and mobilisation of resentment against government, banks and urban interests by a united farmers' organisation, the National Farmers Federation with whom the present national leadership of the National Party has been at odds for some years.[15]

Early in May 1987 the federal coalition was dissolved under pressure from the Queensland Branch of the National Party. The double dissolution election was called shortly afterwards, ostensibly on legislation to introduce a national identity card. The Queensland Premier, in Los Angeles at the time of the announcement, failed in his bid to field his own team of candidates and did not carry out his promise to run himself. The campaigns of the two parties were essentially harmonious and the coalition was, after some reflection, restored in the aftermath of the election in which coalition performance was worst in Queensland.

The Queensland Premier's fortunes have since continued to decline. His government's record is now tarnished by allegations and admissions of police corruption, initially aired on television (ABC Four Corners) and now the subject of a royal commission, and comic incidents such as banning condom vending machines from campuses of Queensland tertiary institutions. His party has forced him to nominate a retirement date, August 8, 1988; it would nevertheless be unwise to count the Premier out until he has gone.

The Hawke Government won the election with an improved electoral position notwithstanding a drop in its share of the vote (seats in House of Representatives up from 82 to 86; vote share down from 47.55 per cent to 45.85 per cent). In the Senate, the Government lost two seats, while the National Party added one to its numbers and a new Nuclear Disarmament Party senator was elected in New South Wales. The situation in the two Houses is as follows:

	House		Senate	
ALP	86	(82)	32	(34)
Liberal	43	(45)	26	(28)
National	19	(21)	6	(5)
Australian Democrats			7	(7)
Other			3	(2)

[1984 figures are presented in brackets][16]

The immediate result of the double dissolution may be quickly told to finish the story. The election out of the way, public attention rapidly concentrated on the identity card (the Australia Card); opinion was decidedly hostile and community opposition grew, led by representatives from all sides of politics, and many without explicit partisan affiliation.

Labour had a majority to enact the legislation at a joint sitting. Implementation of the legislation, however, was contingent on the making of regulations. The Opposition, with Democrat support, announced that any such regulations would be disallowed in the Senate. The Government, after some skirmishing, withdrew with relief from the battle, protesting that once again the Opposition was protecting tax evaders, placing the revenue in jeopardy, and using the Senate to frustrate the "politics of the democratically elected government."

Beyond the daily ambitions of politicians and the unending manoeuvres of parties is a profound reassessment of public policies in light of indifferent economic performance and deterioration of the international trading position.[17] The financial system has been deregulated.[18] Tariff protection of Australian industry has been reduced. Questions of equity and efficiency in the tax and welfare systems have been compounded by others about administrability which led the Government, notwithstanding grave misgivings even within the ALP, to propose introduction of an identity card (the Australia Card) as the basis of the double dissolution. Government ascendancy over tertiary education is under challenge with the eventual establishment in Queensland of Australia's first private university on the initiative of West Australian entrepreneur and America's Cup identity Alan Bond. The highly-regulated domestic aviation system is being re-evaluated and discontinuation of the long standing two airline policy has now been announced.[19] Liberalisation, if not full-scale privatisation and deregulation, is likely to pervade developments in telecommunications. The containment of crime, organised crime, is an issue calling for more serious attention from observers of government. Its penetration of Australian life has been dramatically signalled by a number of royal commissions (the latest in Queensland)[20] as well as indictment of judges, including a justice of the High Court of Australia; in the event, the judges concerned were acquitted. The national industrial arbitration system is also under the microscope. It has survived the first challenge from a committee of review which recommended its retention in all essentials.[21] But unions have lost some symbolically important contests as well as more substantial battles with the Queensland Government in particular. In foreign policy, the alliance with the United States and the tri-partite ANZUS Treaty has had to be refashioned in the wake of a rift between the US and New Zealand. Approaches to defence policy are similarly under the microscope.[22]

Institutional reform is part of this national environment of change. But few of the proposals are directly related to the deeper issues of public policy. They have an autonomy of their own, stemming in part from a desire to modernise the legacies of the past, but reflecting also the degree of academic and professional specialisation in Australia, though not unique to Australia, which limits the level of lateral thinking (the Constitution is for lawyers, the economy for economists, industrial relations for employers, unions and their advocates, the Parliament and parties for politicians, political scientists and, more proprietorially, the parliamentary Press Gallery).

II. Constitutional Reform

The Constitution of the federal Commonwealth of Australia is the product of conventions in the 1890s, the concluding one of which was directly elected, and the adoption of the text at referendum in the six colonies.[23] Its legal basis lay in a statute of the British Parliament of 1900; the link with Britain became increasingly nominal, particularly after adoption of the Statute of Westminster in 1942, though in formal terms, it was not until the Australia Act of 1986 that all links with Westminster but not with Buckingham Palace were finally and irrevocably shed. This latter event passed with little notice or comment.

The Constitution provided the structure of national government – the Executive, the Parliament and the High Court. It sought to combine responsible government based on Westminster and colonial practice with an American-style Senate virtually co-equal in powers with the popularly-elected House of Representatives (the powers of the Senate, it needs to be noted, correspond largely to the formal powers of the House of Lords prior to the Parliament Act (UK) of 1911). It also defines the powers of the Commonwealth Government, exclusive and concurrent, in relation to those of the States. This section is concerned with the latter aspect; parliamentary issues will be examined in the next section.

The Constitution has not had many admirers despite the opinion of the Governor-General, Sir Ninian Stephen, a former Justice of the High Court, that "the wonder is . . . that our Constitution has, for so long, and in times of such extraordinary change, domestically and world-wide, at all continued to serve the needs of the Australian community as a constitutional framework."[24] Rather, as one scholar has observed, "from the very start, denigration and invective poured in . . ."[25] This continues to be the case.

Nevertheless, the Constitution has proved relatively resistant to formal change. Unlike the British North America Act (UK) it has always contained provision for its own amendment by means of referendum. Amendments, which may be initiated only by the national Parliament and, in effect, only by the Commonwealth Government, require the support of both an overall majority of voters and a majority of voters in a majority of States.[26]

Thirty-eight proposals to amend the Constitution have been submitted on 17 occasions; eight have been successful; another five have secured a popular majority but failed to meet the State requirement.[27] The reluctance to support constitutional change is not

easy to explain though the present Governor-General has questioned
whether the cause may lie "in some failure of communication betwen
legislators and public?"[28] There would certainly be support for the
view that the tendency of political parties to treat proposals in a
partisan fashion has been a contributing factor.[29] History suggests
that bi-partisan support is a desirable but not sufficient condition for
change.

Failure to effect formal amendment has not, however, deterred a
search for change. The Constitution has been reviewed by a royal
commission in the late 1920s,[30] a joint select committee of the
Parliament in the late 1950s[31] and by a series of six conventions with
membership drawn from all the parliaments, the Territory assemblies
and local government from the early 1970s to 1985 (the conventions
stemmed from an initiative of the Victorian Legislative Council, the
upper house of the Victorian Parliament).[32] Referenda were conducted on a small number of proposals for change arising from the
conventions and a few were successful.[33] In addition, the Law
Foundation of New South Wales sponsored a major study with the
bicentennial year in view as an "obvious target date for the
achievement of major reforms."[34] The centenary of the Commonwealth in 2001 is now advanced as a more likely target date.

In 1985 the Commonwealth, unhappy with the progress of the
Convention which had largely coalesced on partisan lines, yet possibly
unsettled by signs of an emerging State agenda for change,
established an "expert" Commission.[35] The Chairman is Sir Maurice
Byers, a former Commonwealth Solicitor-General (a statutory, not a
ministerial, post). Former Labor Prime Minister Gough Whitlam, Sir
Rupert Hamer, a former Liberal Premier of Victoria, and two
academic lawyers, Professor Enid Campbell of Monash University,
Victoria, and Professor Leslie Zines of The Australian National
University, make up the membership.[36] The Commission's terms of
reference are:

> to inquire into and report on the revision of the Australian
> Constitution to
>
> (a) adequately reflect Australia's status as an
>   independent nation and a federal parliamentary
>   democracy;
>
> (b) provide the most suitable framework for the economic,
>   social and political develoment of Australia as a
>   federation;

(c)   recognize an appropriate division of responsibilities between the Commonwealth, the States, self-governing Territories and local government; and

(d)   ensure that democratic rights are guaranteed.

The Commission has been assisted by five advisory committees which have recently reported. Headed by prominent Australians, including a former Governor-General, Sir Zelman Cowen, a judge, two retired judges, and the Director of the Law Foundation of New South Wales, and composed of a range of opinion leaders – politicians and ex-politicians, academics, journalists, a novelist and a pop singer with a law degree, for example – the advisory committees were commissioned to report on executive government (see following section for analysis of this report), the distribution of powers, trade and national economic management, the Australian judicial system, and individual and democratic rights.

More than 40 people have been involved in the work of the Commission and the advisory committees. The review is otherwise a lean operation in both staff and financial terms. There has been a concerted effort to stimulate and inform debate on the Constitution especially through a series of useful discussion papers on the spheres of interest of each advisory committee and background papers on other matters such as trade practices and constitutional amendment.[37] Such is the humble standing of the Constitution in Australian life that one of the Commission's more successful publicity ventures has simply been to give away copies to any who telephoned and asked.[38]

Inevitably there are a host of issues before the Commission. These include whether Australia should be a monarchy or a republic,[39] vexed questions of jurisdiction between the Commonwealth and the States over industrial relations and family law, the use of the external affairs power for domestic purposes (pursuant to Australia's becoming a signatory to international conventions on such subjects as the elimination of racial discrimination and protection of the World Natural and Cultural Heritage),[40] clarification of the Commonwealth's power with respect to corporations and securities with consequential benefits through simplification of regulatory procedures, the standing of Aboriginals under the Constitution,[41] and the relationship of the Commonwealth and State judicial systems. The Constitution itself does not deal systematically with individual rights; there are many proposals as to how this perceived deficiency ought to be addressed especially in light of recent failure to enact a statutory bill of rights. There are proposals which would allow the States to levy excise (sales tax) and thereby relieve their great financial dependence on the Commonwealth (see Table 1 for some relevant details).

But the general effect of much of the discussion so far would seem to favour clarification, streamlining and fine-tuning of Commonwealth powers in addition to particular proposals which amount to clear augmentation of central powers as would be the case in respect of defamation where the Commission has already indicated support for a national power.[42]

These inclinations are apparent in what is probably the most expansionist of the advisory committee reports, that on Trade and National Economic Management. In addition to a new Commonwealth power embracing "matters affecting the national economy," and clarification of power concerning communications, the Advisory Committee has proposed a range of new concurrent powers for the Commonwealth in navigation, shipping and civil aviation, nuclear energy and ionising radiation, corporations and securities industry, trade practices of unincorporated entities and individuals, and "the protection of consumers and of their interests." The Committee favoured an amendment to remove doubt as to whether there are limits on the power of the Commonwealth Parliament to appropriate monies. The majority was "not persuaded that the federation's fiscal balance would be prejudiced if the States could levy some excise duties" and therefore supported the amendment to permit the States to impose "final consumption" taxes. The Committee favoured recognition of local government as "a firmly established part of the fabric of national government."[43]

The Advisory Committee on Distribution of Powers did not, however, support recognition of local government in the Constitution and its demeanour was generally one of greater reticence about change, for example, in fields such as the external affairs power (though it did favour a Treaties Council and other measures to improve procedures for Commonwealth-State consultation on treaties), environmental protection, occupational health and safety, national accident compensation and registration and qualification of trades and professions. It took a more positive view on industrial relations (as was to be expected from a committee so many of whose members were drawn from the industrial relations arena), family law, Aboriginal affairs, social services, industrial and intellectual property law, and posts and telegraphs, invariably in favour of the Commonwealth.[44]

The Advisory Committee on the Australian Judicial System was similarly circumspect about change: it split on a basic question of the desirability of an integrated system, the majority opposing the idea, a minority supporting the notion at superior court level. Among the Committee's proposals was support for cross-vesting jurisdiction, amendment of the Constitution to prevent restoration of appeals to the Privy Council of the United Kingdom, and a three-member Judicial Tribunal to make findings of facts when removal of judges is contemplated. The Committee opposed a High Court power to provide advisory opinions.[45]

The only really radical report came from the Advisory Committee on Individual and Democratic Rights. It has advanced propositions for a series of amendments relating to legal procedures, limitations on powers of government, private property, Aboriginals and Torres Strait Islanders, voting and elections (Commonwealth and State), and popular initiation of referenda.[46]

There can be no question that there are problems and inconveniences in the present Constitution,[47] a number of which are documented adequately enough in the advisory committee reports. These reports, however, do not as a whole present a picture of a document which has become unworkable or whose contribution to the good government of Australia has been exhausted. Few of the proposed changes would, if adopted, be a major improvement to the workings of government in Australia or the life of its citizenry. The reports as a whole devote insufficient space to explaining the inconveniences they seek to remove; there is about these documents a strong element of remedies in search of mischiefs. They have a general air of constitutional tinkering. There is an implicit but unconvincing assumption in most of this work that to get the law right will be enough to set the nation on course for the twenty-first century. Too often they have neglected to recognize that the problems derive not from lack of federal power but lack of federal will, as former Prime Minister and Commission member Gough Whitlam pointed out recently in respect of companies legislation.[48] Nor has much effort been made to fashion proposals likely to capture the imagination of the nation save in the case of the report on Individual and Democratic Rights where the attempt is unlikely to satisfy many people.

An earlier version of this paper expressed a view that the Commission's endeavors may not be sufficient to render the Constitution more amenable to change owing to its inclinations toward Commonwealth interests, the general but not total reluctance of State governments to be involved in its work, and the hostility of the Opposition. It continued by referring to the value of the Commission's educational and informational work and suggested that "it could well be the case that a Constitution less mysterious to the people will prove to be a Constitution that they will be more willing to amend."[49]

The Commission's more recent activities have probably undermined the effect of this educational work through virtually unrelieved attacks on the Constitution combined with a pronounced reluctance to report its enduring strengths and a failure to acknowledge its role in the development of Australian nationhood. The Commission's official summary of the advisory committee recommendations simply "omits subjects about which the Committees recommended that there be *no* change."[50]   It also contains cartoon material which will be interpreted as unnecessarily derisory and offensive rather than instructive or illuminating.   The Commission's unwillingness or incapacity to treat the Constitution as a serious document around which the fabric of Australian government in the twentieth century has been woven will ensure that its own proposals will be similarly and deservedly mocked.   This demeanour is as evident in the public utterances of advisory committee members as it is in official Commission publications: social observer Professor Donald Horne of the Advisory Committee on Executive Government frequently rejoices in the depth and quality and character of his Australian nationalism but remains undaunted in his denigration of the Constitution to which he gave a "national disaster award" in a recent address to the National Press Club in Canberra.   These developments simply underline the importance of counsel contained in the earlier version of this paper: ". . . there are achievements and it would be well perhaps to give more time to study of the Constitution's successes rather than its failings, and, indeed, to the capacity of Australian governments, Commonwealth and State, to make the federation work."

III. The Parliament

The Commonwealth Attorney-General, Lionel Bowen, MP, when expressing disquiet about the failure of the Constitutional Convention to make substantial progress in reforming the Constitution and foreshadowing appointment of the Constitutional Commission, said that "The real sleeper in the issue is: will the Senate continue to refuse Supply?"[51]

He thus touched on the most controversial issue in Australian government and politics: the powers of the Senate.   Nor are the questions so raised hypothetical.   Bowen was himself a member of the Whitlam Government which, denied passage of its budget legislation in 1975, was dismissed by the Governor-General, Sir John Kerr.   Kerr then commissioned Malcolm Fraser as Prime Minister, notwithstanding that he lacked majority support in the House of Representatives, on the understanding that he [Fraser] would immediately advise a double dissolution of the House and the Senate.   It was an event in Australian politics which still inspires deep resentments and fears and a determination that it should not be repeated.[52]   The powers of the Senate, and of a governor-general to dismiss a prime minister supported by a majority in the House of Representatives, accordingly stand at the centre of debate about the Constitution, though on the latter issue, despite much writing, there has been little progress even in elucidating the issues.

Equally, few people hold out hope that a referendum to deprive the Senate of its finance powers would succeed. Numerous stratagems have been sought. Among these is the idea of fixed term parliaments.[53] Other proposals to circumscribe the Senate's role include simultaneous elections so that elections to the Senate would always be held in association with general elections for the House of Representatives.[54] Proposals to this effect have been rejected at referenda in 1974, 1977 (when it enjoyed bi-partisan support) and 1984. At the time of writing there is strong support for extending the term of the House from three to four years (which means, in effect, extending the potential term of governments).[55] Similar changes have been achieved in a number of States.[56]

More recently Treasurer Paul Keating has suggested neutralising the Senate by introducing optional preferential voting.

Annoyed by Senate opposition to the Rent Resources Tax bill the Treasurer protested:

> I think the Senate's become the major problem for Australia. These low quotas have got all the flotsam and jetsam of Australian politics in the Senate. And they're not voting with any rhyme, reason or rationality. I mean, in the final analysis, the major parties are going to have to decide what to do with it. It's becoming a political swill. And I think we're really going to have to consider, in the end, an optional preferential voting system for the Senate, to clean all these irresponsible, minor parties and independents out of the place. I mean, it's just an appalling situation where something as fundamental as the Resource Rent Tax, to get a proper tax for the public from the mining of Australian resources, and we can't get the Bill through the Senate because of obstruction by these minor parties, which show no semblance of responsibility ... the Senate quotas are now very low, you know, if you've got a large family you can almost get into the Senate these days.[57]

As this paper was being finalised the Advisory Committee on Executive Government and the Commission itself added their weight to these debates. The Advisory Committee has implicitly focussed on 1975, albeit on the basis of a selective if not jaundiced recollection of the events of that year, and endeavoured to protect a future government from the problems which faced and ultimately unseated the Whitlam ministry. Thus it would simply be provided that to "maintain the confidence" of the House of Representatives should be sufficient for a government to remain in office and the Senate's power to block supply for more than thirty days would be removed so as "to avoid the destabilising consequences for executive government of the threat of a Senate denial of supply."[58]

The Commission's proposals embrace four-year terms for Parliament, a prohibition on elections within the first three years of a term, during which time the Senate would not have the power to block supply; simultaneous elections for the House and half the Senate; resolution of disputes between the Houses over money and other bills by means of a joint sitting; and double dissolutions only in the final year of a term should the Senate block supply for more than 30 days.[59] These proposals are asserted rather than argued or justified. Yet so profound would their impact be upon the elective character of the Australian parliamentary system that they warrant the most sustained exposition before they can be regarded as worthy of consideration by the Parliament and, ultimately, the community at referendum. If adopted, and for the abrupt, terse manner of their presentation alone they ought not to be, they would remove from Australian government most of the elective procedures and institutions now available to give some substance to such notions as responsibility and accountability, for policies as well as for ministries.

The Senate, it will be apparent, has a distinctive role in preservation of this quality of Australian national government and, like the Constitution itself, it has few admirers. Until 1978 its abolition was a plank in the Labor platform. In order to explain the threat posed by the Constitutional Commission's proposals, and the current of opinion of which they are a part, to responsible government in which public, elective institutions still have some role to play, it is necessary to describe the central part of the Senate in preserving a system which is not totally dominated by the Executive Government, with whose problems and concerns the Constitutional Commission is most preoccupied and whose interests it is so prone to articulate.

Senators serve terms of six years, half the Senate retiring at three yearly intervals. Senators are chosen on a State basis — twelve from each State irrespective of population. The two Territories return two senators each, though for terms which coincide with the House of Representatives. The method of election has, since 1948, been proportional and preferential[60] (it is to this method of electing Senators that the Treasurer's views, quoted above, were directed). Because of the national character of the Australian party system, and the fairly even division of the community betweeen the two main sides of politics, it has been, under the proportional/preferential system, unusual for either to win a majority in the Senate; it is also possible for minor parties and independents to win seats,[61] which they do, and they often hold the balance between the two major parties. Minor parties and independents have rarely won seats in the House of Representatives since the expansion of the Parliament in 1949; prior to that there were usually a few independents in the House.

A government cannot therefore "control" the Senate as it must "control" or, to use formal language, have the "confidence" of the House of Representatives. This is a matter of great import, for the Senate is virtually co-equal in power with the House. The main distinction is that financial legislation must originate in the House and may not be amended by the Senate though it can, nevertheless, suggest and press amendments.

The great power of the Senate is reflected in matters of smaller moment as well as in the fate of budgets and other legislation. Both houses have the power to disallow subordinate legislation (regulations, ordinances, determinations). Only the Senate has a committee to review regulations and ordinances; it does so and over the years the Senate, acting on the reports of its committee, has disallowed a sizable number, mainly on the ground that they infringe individual rights and liberties. (The prospect of this power being exercised was enough to persuade the Government not to persist with its Australia Card legislation.) The House has a negligible record in this field, even in the business of considering disallowance. The Senate has also had since 1981 a similar committee for scrutiny of primary legislation.[62]

In the past twenty years committee life has flourished in the Senate.[63] Its select committees have conducted important investigations into securities and exchange, and off-shore legislation. Since 1970 it has had estimates committees which conduct the only systematic parliamentary scrutiny of administrative matters (attempts by the House to emulate the Senate in this regard have foundered). And it has a system of standing committees on such matters as constitutional and legal affairs[64] (responsible for a major report on freedom of information legislation in the late 1970s) and finance and government operations[65] (an important contributor to scrutiny of public enterprises, statutory boards and commissions). More recently it has had select committees to review the conduct of a High Court judge.[66] The judge was subsequently indicted and, eventually, after two trials, acquitted.

These committees interest themselves in the business of government on a scale unknown in joint House-Senate committees or House committees. Their work is sometimes of high quality but there is much scope for improvement. They are too often too timid in enquiry, too formal in procedure notwithstanding the informality of hearings, and they make too little use of the considerable resources available especially from the Legislative Research Service and the Parliamentary Library. But in arresting the much-written about "decline of parliament", they are a major bulwark. The Senate's powers are, therefore, of a much more ample and constructive character than might be suggested by simple blockage of legislation.

The critics of the Senate damn it as a party house, as if partisanship in a parliamentary democracy is some sort of taint. That it does not function explicitly as a States House is seen also to be a failing, though there is every reason why Burke's precepts on representation should apply as much to the Senate as to any other house of parliament.[67] It is urged, therefore, that, as the Senate is a party and not a States House,[68] its powers, roles and functions ought to be brought more in line with those of the House of Lords (Westminster retains its lure even as the links are severed).[69]

Westminster is not, however, an appropriate guide for action in Australia at present. For if the Senate has a formally more significant role than the Lords, as it does, it is correspondingly essential to recognise that the House of Representatives has in practice a substantially less significant role than the House of Commons (itself much criticised for Executive domination).

Assessment of the Senate's role must thus be undertaken in association with an appreciation of the House of Representatives' weaknesses as a repository of responsibility and accountability in Australian government.

Party discipline in the House is rigid (it would be a short paper indeed which traced the history of breaches);[70] opportunities to test ministers are much reduced compared to Westminster, not least because of the structure of Question Time (without notice and without supplementaries, though possible under Standing Orders)[71] and the absence of provision for questions following major government statements; there are no Opposition supply days (other procedures such as the Matter of Public Importance help to bridge that difference in a small way); the Speaker has no discretion once closure is moved; and the House's committee activities are only a shadow of those of the Senate (such activities as there are are partly attributable to the desire of members to have some of the opportunities available to their Senate colleagues. A new system of committees reflecting that of the Senate was instituted after the recent election: time will show whether it fares better than the House's earlier endeavours to develop a viable committee structure but there is little reason for optimism.) To these failings it may be added that the House and the Senate are very under-worked by standards of at least some comparable legislatures elsewhere, as Table II shows.

Some commentators (including the Advisory Committee on Executive Government) argue that the Senate would function better in its review activities by "removal of the power to reject money bills for the sole purpose of precipitating an election . . ."[72] (whatever the purpose, an election will be the eventual outcome, if the Senate persists with rejection of budget legislation). A truer view is that:

> Desirable as . . . this change is on other grounds, if administrative scrutiny is to be effective it must be conducted by an institution with at least the potential to exercise power and officials would always know that they had greater influence over ministers than an impotent Senate.[73]

But to support the Senate's current powers and other aspects which sustain its vital role is not to rule out change altogether. A strong case exists for providing that where the Senate fails to pass budget legislation there should be, as a matter of course, a double dissolution of the Parliament.

Budget practices make it unlikely that critical financial legislation blocked by the Senate can be dealt with according to procedures in section 57 of the Constitution for resolving deadlocks between the Houses (an interval of three months between first and subsequent submission to the Senate of legislation passed by the House is required). In light of this feature of the working of the Constitution as it affects handling of government bills by Parliament, the Clerk of the Senate has recently stated his support for a double dissolution when this occurs:

> . . . I had, and have, no difficulty in accepting the principle that the whole Senate should accept its responsibility in such circumstances. To my mind this would fairly combine and balance the twin elements of deterrence and responsibility.[74]

At a broader level there is a case for including the proportional/preferential method of election in the Constitution to ensure that this important condition of Senate effectiveness is not changed by a government able briefly to win a majority in the upper house. And because the proportional/preferential method of election virtually guarantees substantial continuity of membership, there may in consequence be a case for doing away with split elections for the Senate providing the move is not associated with introduction of simultaneous elections. This would remove one perceived obstacle to the four-year term proposal (the obstacle is that a four-year term for the House means either that House and Senate elections will only occasionally coincide or, alternatively, that Senate terms would need to be increased from six to eight years, which is generally regarded as unacceptable).[75]

The four-year term proposal is basically an argument for government.[76] It would *prima facie* do little to address the weaknesses of the House of Representatives outlined above. The claim that it would allow more time for government programs to take effect is only partially true; in any case, not since 1931 has a government failed to win a second term (the only other case was 1914). And if stability is the goal then there is much that governments can already do without extending the term of Parliament such as limiting the number of changes in the departmental machinery of government, a disruptive practice very evident in the records of recent governments.[77]

Although not on the agenda, democratisation of the party system might also add to the effectiveness of Parliament. Compulsory voting is convenient for party managers but dulls the edge of husbandry.[78] Of itself, it amounts to a substantial government subsidy to the parties by taking over from them the job of getting voters to the polls. The case for choosing party leaders by conventions of delegates elected by party members rather than members of parliamentary parties alone could also be examined. And public funding of parties which took effect in the 1984 general election has had little apparent impact of value: one suspects that it simply increases the role and cost of advertising in election campaigns.[79] The parties would also do well to foster a more substantial capacity for policy development.

It may seem that reform of Parliament has been laboured in this essay. Yet in studying the governance of democracies it is too easy to do so from the perspective of governors and administrators to the neglect of the parliamentary, elective and other democratic components. The failings of Parliament are many and there for all to see; but it is an illusion to think that government and administration deprived of a democratic and parliamentary context would be superior.

There is another reason in Australia for being concerned about the capacity of elective institutions of the nation to scrutinise the doings of government. It has hitherto been the practice that policy is guided by the platform and commitment of the victorious side in a general election, even if in the event there may be substantial reversals in the life of a parliament. Prime Minister Hawke has now taken this characteristic a step further.

Immediately following the 1987 election, the Prime Minister announced significant changes to the departmental machinery of government. Later the Prime Minister asked his party to bring forward its next national conference to discuss the agenda of his third government and specifically a program of privatisation of public enterprises: the agenda of the third term should have been largely settled by the campaign, particularly if it was proposed to embark on a program of selling government enterprises contrary not only to

Labor's traditions but also to the recent pronouncements of almost all ministers of the government (Minister for Finance Peter Walsh has generally been equivocally pragmatic[80]). Within another four days the Prime Minister revived the issue of a treaty with the Aboriginals.[81] These are all matters which should have been before the electorate during the campaign, as one Labor backbencher in fact said when commenting on the machinery of government changes. They should, accordingly, be the subject to rigorous parliamentary scrutiny when legislative measures are introduced to give effect to them. Party conferences, even if conducted in public, cannot be regarded as a substitute for debate and decision in the electorate and in the Parliament.

These, then are lively matters in Australia, and not only because of controversy about the Senate. The Parliament in Australia is an Executive-dominated institution.[82] Within the life of the last Parliament both presiding officers took ambassadorial appointments; not a voice was to be heard on the wisdom or propriety of people occupying ostensibly impartial offices in the Parliament vacating them mid-term for prestigious posts in the gift of the Executive Government.[83]

Next year the Commonwealth Parliament will move to a "new and permanent" building. It dominates the central Canberra landscape like a Minoan palace in ancient Crete. Unlike a Minoan palace, however, it is not a community centre but an executive citadel, designed as much to meet the needs of ministers as of members and Senators. Its very structure will probably compel change in procedure. Most of such change, however, is unlikely to be in the interests of democratic scrutiny of administration and legislation.[84] Neither house has chosen, unfortunately, to prepare for 1988 by reviewing its procedures: the Parliament's contribution to the bicentennial is taking the form of two histories and a guide to its workings.[85]

IV. Public Administration

The four years of the Hawke Government have brought extensive change in the administrative and public service personnel system of Australia. These changes are mainly embodied in legislation enacted in 1984,[86] 1986,[87] and in 1987 following the double dissolution election.[88] Their effect has been to underwrite the capacity of ministers to control departments, to establish conditions for enhancing the management capacity of the senior echelons (now designated the Senior Executive Service), to streamline the personnel system by elimination *inter alia* of all but essential rights of appeal, and to strengthen the career service by applying equal employment opportunity concepts to the operation of the merit principle, and introduction of explicit prohibitions on patronage and discriminatory practices. The objectives, if realised, will leave Australia with a leaner, more competitive, more responsive public service.

Important institutional dimensions of the changes have been a relative diminution after 1984 in the responsibilities of the central management and personnel agency, the Public Service Board, and its eventual abolition in 1987. Its resource allocation functions were transferred to the Department of Finance (the budget agency) and, in part, to secretaries of departments (that is, the officials responsible under ministers for the general working of departments). Upon its abolition the Board's industrial relations responsibilities were vested in the Departmment of Industrial Relations, though the exact shape of the new arrangements has still to be worked out fully.

The Board has been replaced by a single member Public Service Commission with responsibility for general personnel management policy and the administration of the Senior Executive Service (introduced in 1984). There is also to be an Australian Public Service Management Advisory Board, chaired by the Secretary to the Department of the Prime Minister and Cabinet, and including the Public Service Commissioner, the secretaries for Industrial Relations and Finance, two secretaries from line departments on rotation, and two members, one with private sector experience, the other nominated after consultation with the Australian Council of Trade Unions (ACTU).

The Board's abolition was accompanied by a major change in the departmental machinery of government. The number of departments has been reduced from twenty-seven to eighteen, sixteen of which are represented by cabinet ministers. At the same time the ministry has been expanded to thirty, thirteen of whom are outside the cabinet: the idea of a ministerial hierarchy in departments is new in recent times and, on the present scale, an innovation.

The new arrangements have been justified as further enhancing ministerial authority and increasing democratic accountability through Ministers, as improving departmental management and policy making and as eliminating overlaps and duplication. Significant changes include the creation of a merged Department of Foreign Affairs and Trade, a new Department of Employment, Education and Training, combination of Community Services and Health in a portfolio which embraces the autonomous Department of Veterans' Affairs and the Department of Aboriginal Affairs whose functions are eventually to be vested in a statutory commission, and amalgamation of the former departments of Aviation, Transport and Communications in a Department of Transport and Communications. The new arrangements have been much characterised as super-ministries and giant departments because of their affinity with developments in Britain during the first Wilson and Heath governments. This is not generally the case, however; only about half a dozen of the departments are in the "giant" class and most of them are small in numerical terms.[89]

The immediate media coverage given to the announcement of the new departmental structure on 14 July 1987, three days after the election, was much in the vein of the claims made by Prime Minister Hawke about what was involved. Reporting to Parliament he described the changes as "perhaps the most far-reaching reshaping of the Federal machinery of government and of public administration in our history".[90] One leading journalist described the changes as actually warranting "the Prime Minister's favourite word — historic . . . It is administratively daring and politically cunning." The same journalist later saw the reorganisation as "revolutionary." Another saw the change as "a bold initiative of profound importance."

Yet there have been reservations. The *Canberra Times* speculated that the new Department of Transport and Communications would "in fact prove difficult to manage on any common theme." The Opposition itself feared "ministerial overload" in Transport and Communications. A month later at least one journalist was wondering if the Prime Minister "fully appreciated the chaos, discord and loss of morale he would create by his dramatic reorganisation of the bureaucracy." It remains to be seen whether the transition to the new structure can be achieved smoothly, involving as it does a reduction of an estimated three thousand public service jobs (though there are to be no involuntary retrenchments).[91]

It would not have been possible to devise a plan entirely logical and satisfying all interests and individuals. The plan that has been devised has, in that light, as much to commend it as any feasible alternative. It may not have been necessary or desirable to make these changes but the issue now is their prospects of durability. The departmental system in Australian government has for the last decade and a half been notoriously unstable, a product of a quaint faith that policy problems can be solved by reorganisation combined with the arbitrary character of departmental creations, abolitions and mergers, a process which is confined to the Prime Minister and the Governor-General. The experience of the last decade and a half clearly indicates a need for a process which is more responsible and accountable.[92]

The decision to abolish the Public Service Board and fragment the central management and personnel functions is difficult to justify, and the report of the Efficiency Scrutiny Unit on which the successor arrangements are based is one of the poorest to be published by any Australian government. As one observer has written, it "has all the appearance of a predetermined solution in search of a justification ... The plain intellectual slackness of the document makes it a disappointing and unsatisfying read."[93]

The Australian government no longer has an institutional focus for managerial and administrative development. The personnel and industrial functions have been organisationally separated. The central efficiency programs have been terminated (a constructive approach would have been to place them on a cost-recovery basis[94]), and the equal opportunity programs which have done so much to invigorate personnel administration in the past twenty years have been reduced to a monitoring role.[95]

It appears that the Scrutiny program itself has virtually run its course. Although established for a three-year period, the Prime Minister has already announced that scrutinies will henceforth be run by individual departments.[96] The private sector head of the agency has been given a number of specific assignments and has also accepted a similar role with the New South Wales Labor Government.

Because the Scrutiny program has been largely conducted in secret, it is difficult to offer a useful assessment of its contribution. The lack of publicity surrounding the results of many of the single round of scrutinies commissioned in 1986, the apparent decision to wind the program down after only one such round, and the indifferent quality of the one report which has been released publicly suggests that it is but one more episode in the growing history of attempts to find ways of beneficially importing private sector inspirations into the public sector.

One important but generally unnoticed consequence of the post-election administrative reshuffle has been a major enhancement of the place of the Department of the Prime Minister and Cabinet within the government structure. Where little more than a decade ago it stood as one of three in presiding over administrative policy and arrangements, it has successively seen the Treasury split (in 1976 with the creation of the Department of Finance) and now the Public Service Board fragmented. Its Secretary has taken over the Board Chairman's responsibilities for advising on departmental secretary appointments. The Secretary also heads the new Australian Public Service Management Advisory Board. The new Public Service Commission is administratively within the orbit of the Department of the Prime Minister and Cabinet. The new arrangements combined with the Department's advisory role on machinery of government matters unquestionably leave it in a commanding position at the centre with a pre-eminence over other participants (and potential rivals) unprecedented in the previous history of Commonwealth administration. These changes in the bureaucratic pecking order are of as much significance as the rather indeterminate steps to enhance ministerial authority and control.

The reform program, largely bipartisan in its progress, has changed its character in the four and a half years of Hawke Government. The 1984 measures, and also the reforms of expenditure management and control,[97] essentially represented a revival of the recommendations of the Coombs Royal Commission on Australian Government Administration, 1974-76, in which efficiency, equity, productivity and quality of government services were the predominant themes. The 1984 measures although purposefully implemented were never significantly supported with staff and funds and action was heavily oriented towards the senior ranks of the public service and the central offices of departments.

The 1986 and 1987 changes are more in the mould of the Fraser Government's public service policies which stressed management efficiency, curtailment of tenure and a challenge to the union role; they represent in many respects a refinement and sophistication of those Fraser policies. The abolition of the Public Service Board indeed symbolises the decline of personnel management and the recovery of managerial prerogatives, from both central agencies and unions on the one hand, and the ascendancy of budget-based approaches to administration on the other. The later changes in many respects reinforce the elitist and centralist character of the 1984 reforms — centralist in the sense that policies of devolution seem to have greater application to central agency-departmental relations than to intra-departmental management, especially the still largely unaddressed question of relations between a central office and regions.

The centralising inclinations of the APS are evident in the increasing concentration of senior posts in Canberra, up from 69.9 per cent in 1975 to 77.8 per cent in 1985.[98] This in itself has a detrimental effect on capacity to recruit outsiders to the Senior Executive Service, all vacancies in which are now open for general application, to the extent that potential recruits are reluctant to come to Canberra. As it happens, most of those appointed from outside the public service have been from other parts of the public sector; this characteristic is probably also evident in those State public services which seek recruits externally on a reasonably frequent basis. In the interests of organisational effectiveness, as well as of attracting a broader range of candidates for senior posts, there are hence strong reasons for devolving a much greater proportion of higher level management work away from Canberra towards regional branches in which three quarters of the public service are actually employed.

The reassertion of the managerial/economy agenda over the efficiency/productivity/equity agenda leaves a number of priority matters still to be addressed. The whole business of fostering *esprit de corps* and professional leadership at senior levels remains an undeveloped aspect of the reform program, notwithstanding the existence of major management development programs for middle level staff and renewed efforts at higher levels. For many staff the effort is left too late in careers. Even by their early thirties, officers are so moulded in the habits of hierarchical operation as to impede successful later transition to management as a role rather than a skill (the effective though generally unacknowledged assumption behind much current policy being very much that it is a skill which can be learned whereas it is essentially a role calling upon personal qualities such as leadership, professional example and team-building developed by experience which may be enhanced by whatever knowledge and command of technique an individual may have or be able to acquire).

Similarly, policy formulation, review and evaluation have been somewhat neglected by the reform agenda. One aim was to redress stress on policy skills which were said to have had too much influence on promotions under previous arrangements at the expense of management abilities (the actual stress had been, if anything, on dealing with ministers).[99] The Government's 1984 policy paper, *Reforming the Australian Public Service*, did promise periodical meetings of ministers to review strategy but these have not really taken root.[100] Except for establishment of the Office of the Economic Planning Advisory Council in 1983[101] and imaginative use of consultants by some ministers,[102] the tone is one which puts general policy analysis (as opposed to quantitative analysis) at a discount. This is reflected in staff development programs which favour, by a large margin, job exchanges and special assignments in range and number of opportunities, and in financial benefits, over higher level study at universities and elsewhere.[103] The consequence of this inclination in the short-term will be to strengthen finance-based examination of issues (in contrast to broader analysis embracing social and even simply practical considerations); in the long term Commonwealth capacity to handle policy on a qualitative basis will not be as deep as it ought to be.

A related comment goes to the very restricted role in the reform program of a doctrinal and ethical component about the contemporary role of the public service in government. The old doctrines evolved to meet the needs of a regulatory state; the new doctrines are very instrumentalist in character. They are about how business should be conducted and how resources should be managed. They do not give much guidance about what or whether the public servant should, within the framework of political responsibility and accountability, contribute to the nature, purpose and direction of government.[104] This would be an easier task if some agreement about the tasks of government is restored; even so it may be hoped that as the changes settle there will be some place for the ethics and philosophies of modern government to be discussed more fully even if only in the many training courses now offered.

Reform of public administration has not only been about management and budgetary practice. Recent years have witnessed institution of a general system of administrative law, the genesis of which is to be found in the very early 1970s and which did not finally take shape until the early 1980s with the proclamation in 1982 of the Freedom of Information Act. The other arms of the "new administrative law" have been creation of an office of Ombudsman in 1977 (an ombudsman is now a typical feature of most Australian governments), simplification of access to judicial review of administrative decisions, and establishment of an Administrative Appeals Tribunal able to review decisions on the merits and in many instances, unlike the Ombudsman, to substitute its own decision (Victoria alone has followed the Commonwealth with freedom of information legislation and an Administrative Appeals Tribunal). These reforms were adopted in the face of criticisms mainly based on the likely costs involved, which have not for the most part been supported by experience.[105]

In the past few years, however, the momentum behind the new administrative law has been waning. Since 1986 fees have been levied on certain applications under the Administrative Appeals Tribunal and Freedom of Information legislation. The fears expressed by people such as former Liberal Attorney-General Bob Ellicott, QC, and the late Liberal Senator for Victoria, Alan Missen, about the durability of these reform achievements and their general accessibility to the population as a whole are therefore justified.[106]

Democratic administration and accountability have two elements: service to ministers who are responsible to Parliament, and responsiveness to citizens. Some of the changes surveyed above bear witness to progress on these fronts.

But straitened economic times have severely restricted scope for reform. Australian national public administration now has many attributes of a holding operation. In these circumstances the need is very much for astute leadership in effectively establishing the new structure of administration and maintaining and fostering quality and capacity.

V. Public Enterprise

The unfinished agenda in the Government's program of reform lies in the field of public enterprise. The Commonwealth is represented in many fields — banking, telecommunications, postal services, broadcasting, aviation, railways, shipping and marketing of primary produce. Its role has been shaped as much by needs of national development and service to dispersed and isolated communities as by social, welfare and distributional objectives. But there has never been an explicit general policy to guide action and performance in this field.[107]

Absence of such a general policy has increasingly become a serious gap as criticism about the size, cost, control, and performance of government has grown and public enterprise has been portrayed as a factor in the deterioration of Australia's economic performance. The criticisms have gained added potency when linked to apprehension about the number of other bodies outside the conventional departmental framework exercising regulatory powers of various types. The Coombs Royal Commission, which first attempted to map the field, was sufficiently concerned to recommend "caution in the creation of statutory bodies."[108] In the late 1970s the Senate Standing Committee on Finance and Government Operations made much of the absence of any authoritative listing of public bodies outside the departmental system and has itself sought to remedy the deficiency.[109] Fears were further confirmed by a series of scandals mainly in the marketing authorities but not altogether leaving the public service untouched.[110] The "new right," its think tanks and economists in the rational mould brought new questions about the efficiency of public enterprises.[111] Privatisation came actively into the debate particularly in light of the Thatcher Government's programs in the United Kingdom.

While the National Party with its dispersed rural constituencies has been almost as much a patron of public enterprise in Australia as the ALP, it was inevitable that the Hawke Government would wish to redress the debate and sustain the legitimacy of public enterprise. Early in its term it offered evidence of its *bona fides* through major capital injections for the Commonwealth Bank, Qantas, TAA (now Australian Airlines) and the Australian National Line. Yet the essential problem remained that there was no general policy; of the responsible ministers only the Minister for Primary Industry (now Primary Industries and Energy) seemed determined to set the house in order. In other cases refuge was taken in the long deficient "arm's length" doctrine fashioned in the 1930s and 1940s in Britain as a means to cope with newly-nationalised industries, and an unwarranted tendency to assume that government ownership automatically ensured service to the public.

A major contribution came from Adelaide historian Hugh Stretton in an eloquent paper resonant with conviction about the value of public enterprise.[112] It met the needs of higher level political debate, though it was not exploited at that level, but did not cover a number of important government issues. This purpose was addressed in what finally emerged in the face of much attack from the enterprises and their sponsor departments as a "policy discussion paper" from the Minister for Finace.[113] It endeavoured to place relations between government and enterprises on a firmer footing by means of concerted management focussed on strategic plans spanning three to five years supplemented if the enterprises wished by annual performance plans.[114] Service obligations would be balanced by efforts to yield a rate of return on assets "sufficient to justify the long-term retention of those assets in that enterprise rather than in some alternative use"[115] (this approach to public enterprise performance derived from Victorian Government policy[116]). The paper's proposals met with continuing opposition from the enterprises though not from the many administrative boards and agencies to which it was also directed. Telecom spoke for many of the enterprises when it claimed that

> The paper describes a kind of prison in which prisoners — the [Telecom] Commission and management of Telecom — are to be shackled like Gulliver in Lilliput with a multitude of intrusive restraints which negate and stifle the initiative and strength of the enterprise.[117]

(It should be stressed that apart from a general ministerial power of direction the discussion paper, as a policy framework, does not foreshadow creation of any new powers for ministers in relation to enterprises, a point which might not be obvious from the criticisms. The arrangements outlined in the Minister for Primary Industry's policy paper[118] and already implemented in a number of cases are stricter but it has not met with the same hostility. He is the only minister with significant enterprises in his portfolio to have formulated a general policy. It would be valuable if the Minister for Finance's paper were to be complemented in other fields by a policy document of the kind produced by the Minister for Primary Industry.)[119]

Whatever the value of the policy discussion paper as a foundation for systematising relations with the enterprises it has had relatively slight impact in assuring their efficient and accountable management. Although ministers, in the context of attacking the Opposition's then formally unannounced policies on privatisation, have entered rhetorical defences of public enterprises,[120] they have stressed the need for efficiency in other contexts. Finance Minister Walsh has stated unambiguously that he has

... no ideological preference for public or private ownership. In my view, what is important is not whether a business is public or private, but whether it delivers the goods and services required by the public efficiently, that is, at lowest cost.[121]

His thinking is not far removed from that of the then Opposition Shadow Treasurer Jim Carlton who, "grateful to Senator Walsh for his attempt... to cut a swathe through this haze of intellectual humbug," stressed that

... the real criterion for privatisation is consumer benefit, and the most important method of achieving better benefit is through competition. Competition is the key factor.[122]

And the enterprises, while they stress service obligations as a shield against the quest for more sustained financial performance, have come under the critical eye of the consumer movement whose representative on the Economic Planning Advisory Council has said

The consumer movement's hope is that the privatisation debate will have the effect of making these public monopolies live up to their claims about protecting consumers in a way that profit-making concerns would never do.[123]

The enterprises may in practice acquiesce a good deal more in the proposals of the Minister for Finance's paper than their public response would suggest. Already they are being brought by special legislation within the ambit of equal employment policy with little public protest on their part. This may not prevent moves towards privatisation short of actual disposal of the enterprise. For example, throughout the public sector greater use of such devices as "contracting out" may be expected. And the pressure on public finance is likely to see increasing flexibility in funding arrangements so as to keep additional financing outside the public sector. In a tight situation, according to one observer, "the next step in resolving the problem of restrictions on public sector activity is to move from the transfer of expenditure and debt from the public and private sector to the transfer of equity in order that organisations can be defined as private. This amounts to denationalisation."[124]

As has already been noted, the Government's approach to privatisation changed sharply once the election was out of the way. Less than two months after the election the Prime Minister called on the ALP "to embark on a comprehensive debate of the issue of public ownership." He continued: ". . . we are obliged as a Government to ensure that our resources are not being misdirected . . . . [We] are a Government and a Party deeply committed to social progress and equity. As such we should ask ourselves whether public resources are being efficiently directed towards achieving those goals." He went on:

> In the public ownership debate the two tests we must apply are these:
>
> First, does public ownership of a given enterprise mean that significant functions are undertaken that would not be if the private sector had the responsibility for funding, owning and operating the enterprise?
>
> If the answer is "no" then, second, what are the disadvantages and advantages of retaining public ownership of that enterprise, as opposed to transferring it to the private sector.
>
> In other words, the question should be not "Why should we sell a given enterprise?" but "Why should we continue to tie up our resources in it?"[125]

The Prime Minister has subsequently compared his approach to the public enterprise debate with the ALP's decision to drop its long-standing White Australia immigration policy twenty years ago. Others may well find a similarity between his present strategy on public ownership and that adopted by war-time Labor Prime Minister John Curtin when he successfully persuaded the Party to reverse its long-standing opposition to overseas military service by conscripts in certain specified circumstances.

Even as the debate proceeds, the Prime Minister has declared his

> . . . firm position that it would not be appropriate in Australia to sell those government business enterprises which operate as natural monopolies – I refer in particular to Telecom and Australia Post.
>
> The main activities of these enterprises require a costly supply network that cannot be profitably replicated by a competitor.
>
> I doubt too that the Australian community would – and in my opinion, they certainly should not – accept private monopolies that denied telephone and mail services to much of the country – services currently provided through cross-subsidisation.[126]

In due course the Government announced its first steps in changing aviation policy, ending the two-airline policy and opening the way for sale of the government-owned domestic carrier. By early October, less than three months after the election, a leading journalist could write:

> ... the word [privatisation] slips comfortably from the lips of Labor leaders and the concept is presented as being an essential matter for discussion as part of the process of achieving the efficient allocation of economic resources.[127]

Deregulation in other fields is well underway in Australia, a feature of government-business relations vividly demonstrated by extensive restructuring of media ownership following Rupert Murdoch's takeover of one of the country's other media groups. The Government held aloof despite having power to intervene had it wished to do so, and as urged to do by former Liberal Prime Minister Malcolm Fraser and the then Opposition spokesman on communications, Ian Macphee, until his views were overtaken by market-oriented Liberal Party leader John Howard.

A comprehensive review of regulations has been entrusted to a Business Regulation Review Unit in the Department of Industry, Technology and Commerce. Its mandate embraces review of new regulations as well as the many inheritances from the past: submissions to cabinet with significant business regulatory implications must be accompanied by a regulatory impact statement.[128] Ironically, one new source of regulations can be privatisation, where a government wishes to maintain oversight of standards even if ownership is relinquished.

VI. Capacities of Institutions of Government

The 1980s have been trying times for Australia. Visions of improved conditions for such disadvantaged sectors of the population as Aboriginals and single-parent families have receded. Neither governments nor markets can hold out promise of a secure future. But the challenges have not been ignored or evaded. And in the process the political institutions of the nation have had to adapt. This essay is in large part an account of that process of adaptation; it is also an argument for purposeful adaptation rather than adaptation for its own sake. Business and unions have also been affected and this has been very evident in a spate of takeovers and mergers affecting even BHP, "the big Australian."

It has been a story less of success than of holding ground. Nor is the end in sight. So far we can say that the institutions of government have proven capable of containing if not solving the problems. Policies once thought to be settled, even entrenched, have had the searchlight upon them. And whether the field be tax, welfare, industry, tariffs, education, foreign policy or defence, hard options have been faced and often taken. But the search for new public policies goes on occupying governments, political parties, and a broad range of other organisations in business, the unions and the voluntary sector of welfare. The task is as much one of managing change as of discerning its direction and rhythm.

For all its vicissitudes, Australia has nevertheless remained a nation not given to flamboyant or ideological politics. The response so far to crises which, if anything, have increased in intensity has been reasonable and robust; there have been signs of urgency but little of panic. There are thus grounds for confidence that the nation's political institutions of government will continue to prove capable of meeting challenges and crises of decidedly greater magnitude without a breakdown of democratic order or recourse to proffered great man solutions.

Table I
Selected Data on Public Sector Finance

(a) Expenditure, Revenue and Borrowing, 1983-84

	$m	Prop'n %
Expenditure		
State and local	41111	51.7
Commonwealth	38390	48.3
Total Expenditure	79501	100.0
Revenue		
State and local	15480	23.8
Commonwealth	49551	76.2
	65031	100.0
Borrowing		
State and local	4760	32.9
Commonwealth	9710	67.1
	14470	100.0
Revenue and Borrowing		
State and local	20240	25.5
Commonwealth	59261	74.5
	79501	100.0

(b) Commonwealth payments to the States as proportion of State expenditure, 1985-86

	State Expend- iture $m	Common- wealth Payments $m	Proportion Common- wealth %
New South Wales	15193	6753	44.4
Victoria	12099	5100	42.2
Queensland	7986	3556	44.5
South Australia	4103	2182	53.2
Western Australia	4883	2240	45.9
Tasmania	1736	887	51.1
Northern Territory	1084	929	85.7
Total States	47084	21647	46.0
Local Government	4280	94	2.2
	51364	21741	42.3

Table II
Sitting Record of Selected National Legislatures in Australia, Canada, Great Britain and the United States

Year	Australia		Canada		United Kingdom		United States	
	House	Senate	House	Senate	House	Lords	House	Senate
1981	62	72	}175	92	177	149	163	165
1982	53	73		96	175	147	140*	147*
1983	49*	63*	}av.	70	154	119	146	150
1984	52	63	}*	69	174	149	120*	131*
1985	66	74		85	173	135	152	170
1986	79	86	n.a.	n.a.	167	156	129**	143**

* Denotes an election year.   ** to October only.

Additional notes:

Average length of sittings in Australia: House (1985-86), 8 hours 24 minutes (excludes meal breaks); Senate, 8 hours.

In Canada, the House of Commons sits for about 5.5 hours per day.

The United Kingdom House of Commons had average sittings of 9 hours, 1984-85.

The US Congress: Average sitting times were: House, 6 hours 21 minutes (1985) and 6 hours 25 minutes (1986); Senate, 7 hours 23 minutes (1985) and 8 hours 53 minutes (1986).

This table should be regarded as indicative only. Information has been drawn from a range of parliamentary and Congressional sources.

VII.   Endnotes

1.   Part III of D.J. Mulvaney & J. Peter White, eds., *Australia to 1788* (Sydney: Fairfax, Syme & Weldon Associates, 1987) is entitled "The Invasion". Interestingly, W.K. Hancock, *Australia* (Brisbane: The Jacaranda Press, 1930) titled chapter 1, "The Invasion of Australia". Writing three decades later, multi-volume historian C.M.H. Clark headed the relevant section of volume I, "The Foundation" – *A History of Australia* (Melbourne: Melbourne University Press, 1962).

2.   Peter White, "1988 multicultural plans under attack", *Sydney Morning Herald*, May 23, 1986, p. 5.

3.   Ken Baker, "How to rescue our Bicentennial", *The Weekend Australian*, September 21-22, 1985, p. 13.

4.   A view expressed for example, by Professor Donald Horne in an address to the National Press Club on 14 October 1987.

5.   Hancock, *Australia*. p. 55.

6.   A.F. Davies, *Australia Democracy*, (Melbourne: Longmans, Green and Co., 1958), p. 3. In the second edition Davies added: "We take a somewhat hesitant pride in this, since it runs counter. . . to the archaic image of ourselves as an ungovernable, if not actually, lawless, people. . . Being a good bureaucract is, we feel, a bit like being a good forger." *Australia Democracy*, 2nd ed., 1964, pp. 4-5. For a critique of Davies' view, see S. Encel, "The Concept of the State in Australia Politics", in Colin A. Hughes, ed., *Readings in Australian Government* (St Lucia: University of Queensland Press, 1968), p. 36.

7.   A comprehensive survey of privatisation and deregulation in Australia may be found in *Canberra Bulletin of Public Administration*, 13, no. 3 (Spring 1986).

8.   As Australia's leading political journalist Paul Kelly has observed: "Labor is now the party of power and government and the Liberals are the party of ideas and reform – a reversal of the historic pattern of Australian politics". *The Weekend Australian*, April 25-26, 1987, p. 19.

9. See Scott Prasser "Queensland Liberals – the Party's Over", *Current Affairs Bulletin*, 63, no. 10 (March 1987).

10. See Paul Kelly, *The Hawke Ascendancy*, (Sydney: Angus & Robertson, 1984) pp. 72-4, 350, 398-9, 405-6, 440-2. For a critical assessment, Frank Stilwell, *The Accord . . . and Beyond* (Sydney: Pluto Press, 1986); a more sympathetic view is found in Robert Castle and Jim Hagan, "The ACTU and the Accord", *Current Affairs Bulletin*, 63, no. 10 (March 1987), pp. 4-11.

11. An argument for historical Liberalism was published by Ian Macphee after being dropped from the shadow cabinet on 21 April 1987 – *Sydney Morning Herald*, April 23, 1987, p. 13. The apostles of the new creeds have nevertheless staked a claim to the Menzies' record: David Kemp, "How to Reform the Liberal Party", *Quadrant*, XXX, No. 5 (May 1986).

12. Organisations usually include the old Right – the Australian Association for Cultural Freedom (publishers of *Quadrant*) and the revitalised Institute of Public Affairs (Victoria, New South Wales and Western Australia); and newer entrants, the Centre for Independent Studies (NSW), the Australia Institute of Public Policy (WA) and the Centre of Policy Studies, Monash University. Other bodies promoting similar views are the H.R. Nicholls Society (industrial relations) and the Council for the National Interest (foreign affairs and defence). A number of retired senior public servants are associated with the IPA including the former Secretary to the Treasury John Stone (also an adviser to Queenland Premier Bjelke-Petersen), former head of Defence Sir William Cole and the former Under-Treasurer of Western Australia Les McCarrey. Most often these bodies have links with counterparts overseas, especially in Britain and the USA. Ideas for a left wing think tank have been floated but nothing has yet materialised: Stephen Mills, "Left stumbles late into the think tank race", *The Age*, April 8, 1983, p. 3; David O'Reilly, "Left considers polishing image with a think tank", *The Weekend Australian*, May 3/4, 1986, p. 6.

13. Liberal Party of Australia, Report of the Committee of Review, *Facing the Facts* (Canberra, 1983), p. 60.

14. According to Eric Mayer of the Business Council of Australia on ABC radio's *PM*, April 24, 1987.

15.   Mike Steketee, "Coalition's end-of-turmoil feeling can't last long", *Sydney Morning Herald*, April 17, 1987, p. 7.

16.   This paragraph is based on Peter Coaldrake, "Prelude — the Sixth Double Dissolution Election, 11 July 1987", *Canberra Bulletin of Public Administration*, No. 52 (October 1987).

17.   An informed view on the current state of the Australian economy is that —

> . . .the Australian economy is showing some long-awaited signs of strength. A year ago the Australian dollar was in shock, interest rates were being pushed up and output was falling. But after a difficult and uncertain year things are better. Growth is up, the overseas deficit is down, employment is increasing and inflation has peaked. There is still plenty of discomfort ahead, particularly in the May 14 mini-budget. There are also continuing signs of trouble in investment, export prices, housing and the motor vehicle industry. There are still several years of low growth and tight policies ahead before Australia's foreign debt stabilises. But the widespread anxiety and confusion about our economic health is no longer justified by the facts.

John Edwards, "The State of the Economy — More Good than Bad", *The Bulletin*, April 21, 1987, p. 16. Some relevant references on the economy are F.H. Gruen, "How Bad is Australia's Economic Performance and Why?" *Economic Record*, 62 (June 1986); Richard E. Caves and Lawrence B. Krause, eds., *The Australian Economy — A View from the North* (Sydney: George Allen & Unwin, 1984); Barry Hughes, "Brookings on the Australian Economy", *Economic Record*, 61 (March 1985); and Cliff Walsh, "A View from the South on: The Australian Economy: A View from the North", *Economic Record*, 61 (March 1985).

18.   See T.J. Valentine, "The Campbell Report", *Current Affairs Bulletin*, 58, no. 9 (February 1982); and Ian R. Harper, "Financial Deregulation in Australia — Experience, Problems and Prospects", *Canberra Bulletin of Public Administration*, XIII, no. 3 (Spring 1986).

19.   Australia, Independent Review of Economic Regulation of Domestic Aviation, *Report*, (Canberra: Australian Government Publishing Service, 1986). The directions of future policy are

set down in a speech by Senator Gareth Evans, QC, Minister of Transport and Communications to the Senate on October 7, 1987, pp. 752-72.

20. Australia, Royal Commission on the Activities of the Federated Ship Painters and Dockers Union, *Final Report*, 5 vols, (Canberra: Australian Government Publishing Service, 1984). Australia, Royal Commission of Inquiry into Drug Trafficking, *Report*, (Canberra: Australian Government Publishing Service, 1983). The current Queensland inquiry is being conducted by Mr. T. Fitzgerald, Q.C.

21. Australia Committee of Review into Australian Industrial Relations Law and Systems, *Report*, (Canberra: Australian Government Publishing Service, 1985).

22. Australia, Review of Australia's Defence Capabilities, *Report to the Minister for Defence*, (Canberra: Australian Government Publishing Service, 1986).

23. On the Constitution see W.G. McMinn, *A Constitutional History of Australia*, (Melbourne: Oxford University Press, 1979), chs. 5-6; R. Else-Mitchell, ed., *Essays on the Australian Constitution*, 2nd ed. (Sydney: Law Book Co., 1961); Gareth Evans, ed., *Labour and the Constitution 1972-75 – the Whitlam Years in Australian Government* (Melbourne: Heinemann, 1977); Colin Howard, *Australia's Constitution* (Ringwood: Penguin, 1978); Colin Howard, *The Constitution, Power and Politics* (Melbourne: Fontana/Collins, 1980; John McMillan, Gareth Evans, Haddon Storey, *Australia's Constitution: Time for Change?* (Sydney: George Allen & Unwin Australia, 1983).

24. Sir Ninian Stephen, Opening of Convention, *Proceedings of the Australian Constitutional Convention*, 29 July – 1 August 1985, p. 10.

25. Rufus Davis, "The Living Constitution: A Critique of the Federal Critiques", Opening Paper, Third Federalism Project Conference, The Australian National University, 1983.

26. Section 128.

27. Regarding amendment of the Constitution, see R.S. Parker, "The People and the Constitution", in Geoffrey Sawer et al., *Federalism in Australia* (Melbourne: Cheshire, 1949); Australia, Constitutional Commission, Background Paper

No. 12, *Amending the Constitution* (Sydney: 1986); and "In defence of section 128 of the Constitution", *Australian Law Journal*, 57, no. 7 (July 1983).

28.   As quoted in *Australian law Journal*, 59, no. 4 (April 1985), p. 196.

29.   See, for example, R.S. Parker, Memorandum to Advisory Committee to Constitutional Commission on Executive Government, p. 35: ". . . the great obstacle to successful referendums has not been the voters, but the politicians. By their almost invariable treatment of referendum campaigns as mere party contests . . . the political parties (often divided within themselves) have succeeded in confusing the voters except when the advantage of change was overwhelmingly obvious".

30.   Australia, Report of the Royal Commission on the Constitution (Canberra: Commonwealth Government Printer, 1929).

31.   Australia, Parliament of the Commonwealth of Australia, Report of the Joint Committee on Constitutional Review (Canberra: Commonwealth Government Printer, 1959). Some reflections on this review are to be found in J.E. Richardson, "The Parliamentary Joint Committee on Constitutional Review", *Canberra Bulletin of Public Administration*, XIII, no. 2 (Winter 1986).

32.   Some background material on the conventions may be found in Don Blackwood, Peter Ford with Anne Schick, *A Short Historical Survey of the Activities of the Australian Constitutional Convention 1973-78* (Adelaide: 1983).

33.   In 1977, a referendum was held at which four questions were put: simultaneous elections for the House and the Senate; filling of casual vacancies in the Senate by the nominee of the party of the senator whose death or resignation caused the vacancy; a provision that residents of Territories could vote in referenda; and a provision that judges should retire at age 70. The latter three proposals succeeded with support from all States and with percentages of 73.30, 77.70 and 80.10 respectively. The simultaneous election proposal was endorsed by 62.20 per cent of voters with majorities in three States (increase from 48.32 and two States when submitted in 1974). At the 1984 general election the proposal was again submitted. Opposed on this occasion as in 1974 by the Liberal and National

parties, it was supported in two States and by 50.60 per cent of voters. The other proposal was for the Commonwealth to have power to refer powers to the States; it was defeated in all States and secured only 47.10 per cent of the vote. Australia, Constitutional Commission, *Amending the Constitution*, Background Paper No. 12 (Sydney: Constitutional Commission, 1986), p. 7.

34. McMillan et al, *Australia's Constitution*, p. x.

35. Some explanation of the desirability of a commission of experts may be found in Lionel Bowen's address to the Australian Legal Convention on 8 August 1985. Australia, *Commonwealth Record* (Canberra: AGPS, 1985), pp. 1264-1267. A critical view may be found in Rufus Davies, *The Constitutional Commission — the inescapable politics of constitutional change* (Perth: Institute of Public Affairs State Policy Unit, 1987).

36. Mr. Justice Toohey was a member until his appointment to the High Court of Australia early in 1987.

37. The issues papers, published in 1986, do not have distinctive titles. The Advisory Committee on the Australian Judical System also published a "Statement of Preliminary Views". Background Papers include "Trade Practices" (No. 2, by the Advisory Committee on Trade and National Economic Management), "Deadlocks: Constitution Section 57" (No. 8), "The Senate and Money Bills" (No. 9), "Issues Affecting Local Government" (No. 11), and "Amending the Constitution" (No. 12).

38. See "Gavel Giveaway great success", *Constitutional Commission Bulletin* (No. 3 March 1987), p. 5.

39. A recent book on this topic is George Winterton, *Monarchy to Republic — Australian Republican Government* (Melbourne: Oxford University Press 1986). Winterton, author also of *Parliament, the Executive and the Governor-General* (Melbourne: Melbourne University Press, 1983), is a member of the Advisory Committee on Executive Government, together with David Solomon, author of *Elect the Governor-General!* (Melbourne: Nelson, 1976) and Donald Horne, author of "What Kind of Head of State?" in S. Encel, D. Horne and E. Thompson, eds., *Change the Rules! Towards a Democratic Constitution* (Ringwood: Penguin, 1977). Other members are Sir Zelman

Cowen, Sir James Killen, Minister for Defence, Susan Kenny, John Wheeldon, a minister in the Whitlam Government.

40.   See P.H. Lane, "The Federal Parliament's External Affairs Power: Koowarta's Case", *Australian Law Journal*, 56, no. 10 (October 1982) and "The Federal Parliament's External Affairs Power: The Tasmanian Dam Case", *Australian Law Journal*, 57, no. 10 (October 1983).

41.   There are moves to persuade Australians to settle a new relationship with the Aboriginal inhabitants through negotiation of a Treaty. See Bryan Keon-Cohen, "The Makarrata — a treaty within Australia between Australians — some legal issues", *Current Affairs Bulletin*, 57, no. 9 (1981).

42.   Australia, Constitutional Commission, *Defamation: One Law for Australia?*, Background Paper No. 1 (Sydney, 1986).

43.   Australia, Advisory Committee on Trade and National Economic Management, Report to the Constitutional Commission (Canberra: AGPS, 1987), pp. 1-12.

44.   Australia, Constitutional Commission, Advisory Committee on the Distribution of Powers, *Report*, (Canberra: AGPS, 1987), pp. xix-xxii.

45.   Australia, Constitutional Commission, Advisory Committee Report, *Australian Judical System* (Canberra: AGPS, 1987), pp. xi-xvi.

46.   Australia, Constitutional Commission, Report of the Advisory Committee on Individual & Democratic Rights Under the Constitution (Canberra: AGPS, 1987), pp. xv-xx.

47.   A practical guide to the inconveniences of the Constitution is contained in McMillan, *Australia's Constitution*, pp. 3-7; for a more conceptual elucidation of its failings see Howard, *The Constitution, Power and Politics*, chapter 2. A different analysis may be found in Davis, "The Living Constitution".

48.   Gough Whitlam, "Where Hawke went wrong", *Sydney Morning Herald*, 2 May 1987, p. 41.

49.   It has been written that: "The Constitution remains something of a mystery to most Australians. It is very little taught in

schools, and very little talked about elsewhere. Press and public discussion of the Constitution is rare, and then usually only in moments of political crisis". McMillan, *Australia's Constitution*, p. 3.

50. Australia, Constitutional Commission, *Australia's Constitution — Trade to Update* (Canberra: AGPS, 1987), p. 1.

51. Australia, *Proceedings of the Australian Constitutional Convention*, 29 July-1 August 1985, p. 298.

52. On the background to the constitutional and parliamentary crisis of 1975 see Paul Kelly, *The Unmaking of Gough* (Sydney: Angus and Robertson, 1976), reissued in 1983 as *The Dismissal*; Richard Hall and John Iremonger, *The Makers and the Breakers — the Governor General and the Senate vs the Constitution* (Sydney: Wellington Lane Press, 1976); Colin Howard and Cheryl Saunders, "The Blocking of the Budget and the Dismissal of the Government" in Evans, ed., *Labor and the Constitution*, Chapter 8; Alan Reid *The Whitlam Venture* (Melbourne: Hill of Content, 1977); Geoffrey Sawer, *Federation Under Strain: Australia 1972-75* (Melbourne: Melbourne University Press, 1978); John Kerr, *Matters for Judgement* (Melbourne: Macmillan Company of Australia, 1978); Gough Whitlam, *The Truth of the Matter* (Ringwood: Penguin, 1979); and Garfield Barwick, *Sir John Did His Duty* (Wahroonga: Serendip Publications, 1983).

53. Papers on the issues are contained in Alan Cumming Thom and Anne Lynch, eds., *Fixed Term Parliaments* (Canberra: Australasian Study of Parliament Group, 1982).

54. See Senator Gareth Evans, "'The Machinery of Government' Constitutional Referendum Bills", *Australian Law Journal*, 57, no. 12 (December 1983); Campbell Sharman, "Referendum Puffery", *The Australian Quarterly*, 56, no. 1 (Autumn 1984); and Peter Ford, "Referendums and the Public Interest", *The Australian Quaterly*, 56, no. 3 (Spring 1984).

55. Business Council of Australia, *Towards a Longer Term for Federal Parliament* (Melbourne, 1987); see also Paul Kelly, "Senate makes 'mirage' of 4-year term", *The Australian*, April 8, 1987, pp. 1-2.

56. The terms for the lower houses in New South Wales, Victoria and South Australia have been extended from three to four

years by referendum. Tasmania, where the lower house was formerly elected for a five year term, also now has a four year term.

57.   TV Interview, Parliament House, 6 May 1987.

58.   Australia, Constitutional Commission, *Report of the Advisory Committee on Executive Government* (Canberra: AGPS, 1987), p. 64.

59.   Australia, Constitutional Commission, *Media Release — Constitutional Commission Announces New Scheme on Parliament* (Sydney, 1987).

60.   For information on the method of electing senators, see J.R. Odgers, *Australian Senate Practice*, 5th ed. (Canberra: Australian Government Publishing Service, 1977).

61.   It has been argued that the expansion of the Senate in 1984, such that there will ordinarily be six rather than five vacancies to be filled at periodical elections, will make it more difficult for minor parties and independent candidates to secure representation in the Senate: Campbell Sharman, "The Senate, Small Parties and the Balance of Power", *Politics*, 21, no. 2 (November 1986).

62.   For a review of parliamentary scrutiny of delegated legislation, see G.S. Reid, "Parliament and delegated legislation", J.R. Nethercote, ed., *Parliament and Bureaucracy — Parliamentary scrutiny of administration: prospects and problems in the 1980s* (Sydney: Hale & Iremonger/AIPA, 1982), Chapter 11.

63.   For material on the Senate's committee system, see Gareth Evans, "Scrutiny of the executive by parliamentary committees", in Nethercote, ed., *Parliament and Bureaucracy*, chapter 4. Also relevant are John H. Howard, "Preparation of committee reports: The case of the care of the aged inquiry", *Legislative Studies Newsletter*, no. 6, (March 1983); Toby Miller, "Quis Custodies Ipsos Custodet? A Review Article on the Committee System of the Australian Senate", *Legislative Studies*, 1, no. 2, (Spring 1986); Malcolm Aldons, "Promise and Performance: An Analysis of Time Taken for Commonwealth Governments to Respond to Reports from Parliamentary Committees", *Legislative Studies*, 1, no. 2, (Spring 1986). Also relevant is R.A. Herr, ed., *Party Committees — The Implications*

for Parliament (Hobart: Australasian Study of Parliament Group, 1983).

64. Now known as the Senate Standing Committee on Legal and Constitutional Affairs.

65. Now known as the Senate Standing Committee on Finance and Public Administration.

66. Australia, Parliament, The Senate, Select Committee on the Conduct of a Judge, *Report to the Senate* (Canberra: AGPS, 1984); Australia, Parliament, The Senate, Select Committee on Allegations Concerning a Judge, *Report to the Senate*, (Canberra: AGPS, 1984).

67. Edmund Burke, "Speech to the Electors of Bristol", in *Speeches and Letters on American Affairs* (London: J.M. Dent & Sons Ltd., 1908.)

68. For a sustained critique of the Senate see Richard Hall and John Iremonger, *The Makers and the Breakers*. p. 109: "The blunt fact is that . . . anyone who has eyes to see and to read, and ears to hear, knows that the Senate is . . . a party house".

69. Examples of this approach are chapters 2-6 of Patrick Weller and Dean Jaensch, eds., *Responsible Government in Australia*, (Melbourne: Drummond, 1980).

70. Studies of the UK House of Commons such as those by Phillip Norton (*Dissension in the House of Commons 1945-74* (London: Macmillan, 1975) and *Conservative Dissidents* (London: Temple Smith, 1978)) relate to a form of behaviour which is virtually unknown in any parliament in Australia.

71. Se Australia, House of Representatives, Standing Committee on Procedure, *The Standing Orders and Practices which Govern the Conduct of Question Time* (Canberra, 1986); also John Uhr, *Questions Without Answers – An Analysis of Question Time in the Australian House of Representatives* (Canberra: APSA/Parliamentary Fellow Monograph No. 4, 1982).

72. Cheryl Saunders, Submission to the Advisory Committee on Executive Government, Constitutional Commission, September 3, 1986.

73. Peter Wilenski, "Can parliament cope?", in Nethercote, ed., *Parliament & Bureaucracy*, p. 325.

74. Alan Cumming Thom, Submission to the Advisory Committee on Executive Government, Constitutional Committee, February 26, 1987, pp. 5-6.

75. Business Council of Australia, *Towards a Longer Term for Federal Parliament* (1987), p. 13.

76. The BCA pamphlet has nothing to say about reform of Parliament. Its case for a four year Parliament commences: "There is bipartisan agreement that a three-year term is too short to encourage long-term planning and decision-making by Federal Governments". See *ibid.*, p. 7. The proposal is supported by the present National Secretary of the ALP. The attitude of party managers to Parliament was expressed by his immediate predecessor, David Combe, a decade ago: ". . . there is nothing left of our program . . . to justify lengthy Parliamentary sittings. . . It has been shown repeatedly, both nationally and in the States, that Parliaments are for Opposition". David Combe, Report of National Secretary on the Bass By-Election Campaign, *The National Times*, August 11-16, 1975, p. 11.

77. See J.R. Nethercote, "Government Changes and Public Service Reform", in J.R. Nethercote, Alexander Kouzmin and Roger Wettenhall, eds., *Australian Commonwealth Administration 1984: Essays in Review* (Canberra: CCAE/RAIPA (ACT Division), 1986) pp. 2-6. See also Australia, *Review of Commonwealth Administration* (Canberra: Australian Government Publishing Service, 1983), paras 3.62-3.66, pp. 29-30; and J.B. Reid, "Inside Government — implications for business", *Canberra Bulletin of Public Administration*, XI, no. 4, (Summer 1984), p. 234.

78. Dean Jaensch writes: ". . .the people should be given the *right* to vote through the removal of compulsory voting, and the grant of the right of a citizen to decide whether or not to turn out to vote." Dean Jaensch, *Getting our Houses in Order — Australia's Parliament: how it works and the need for reform* (Ringwood: Penguin Books, 1986), p. 163.

79. For a review of the legislation, see Australia, Parliament of the Commonwealth of Australia, Joint Select Committee on Electoral Reform, *The Operation during the 1984 General*

Election of the 1983/84 Amendments to Commonwealth Electoral Legislation, Report No. 2 (Canberra, 1986). The report, however, was silent on this aspect.

80. See reference note 121.

81. See Paul Kelly, "Hawke move fraught with danger", The Australian, September 3, 1987.

82. Colin Howard gives as a reason for reforming the Constitution that "it sets up a system of central government which has enabled the executive to reduce the legislation to a cipher". Howard, *The Constitution, Power and Politics,* pp. 29-30. Unfortunately it is not the Constitution which is the real or even a contributory cause of this situation. And, as already shown, the Constitutional Commission is far more concerned to protect Executive Government from Parliament than to strengthen the Parliament in its scrutiny of the Executive.

83. Dr. Harry Jenkins, Speaker of the House of Representatives since 1983, was appointed Ambassador to Spain in 1985; Senator Douglas McClelland, President of the Senate from 1983 to 1987, was appointed High Commissioner to the United Kingdom in 1987.

84. See Terry Fewtrell, "A New Parliament House – A New Parliamentary Order", *Australian Journal of Public Administration,* XLIV, no. 4 (December 1985), pp. 323-332. Senator Gareth Evans wrote in 1981 that "Perhaps the most interesting question for lawyers and others interested in public affairs to ponder is how the new building will change over time the institution of Parliament itself. One possible, and long overdue, improvement would be to the present schoolboy rules and conventions governing divisions. With the chambers now to be a three to four minutes' walk away from the Cabinet Room and most members' offices, it is likely that the geography of the building will soon encourage moves to both electronic voting and to the holding of divisions at more or less fixed times, with huge consequent advantages in the capacity of members, and especially Government Ministers, to get on with their work without the endless frustrating interruptions that presently drive them to earlier graves than even they deserve." "The New Federal Parliament buildings in Canberra", *The Australian Law Journal,* 55, No. 1 (January 1981), p. 4; for similar views, see the Honourable Mr. Justice Kirby, CMG, then Chairman of the Australian Law Reform Commission, "To

the Thirty Third Parliament: or Summits, Bells, Whips and Other Things" (Sydney: April 1983), pp. 6-7. According to Associate Professor K.W. Wiltshire, "... the new Parliament House... has been designed for a presidential system of government. It has been designed to entrench the faults of the way our government system has evolved...I am inclined to think that architects, being fairly perceptive, have designed a Parliament House to suit the system as it works, not as it ought to work..." Evidence to Constitutional Commission, Advisory Committee on Executive Government, February 27, 1987, pp. 876-77.

85.   The histories, to be published by Melbourne University Press, are being written by the Governor of Western Australia, His Excellency Professor Emeritus G.S. Reid, and a Sydney journalist, Gavan Souter. The workings of Parliament are described in David Solomon, *The People's Palace – Parliament in Modern Australia* (Melbourne: Melbourne University Press, 1986).

86.   The reforms are described in Australia, Public Service Board, *Annual Report 1983-84* (Canberra: AGPS, 1984), pp. 3-12; Peter Wilenski, *Public Power and Public Administration* (Sydney: Hale & Iremonger/RAIPA, 1986), ch. 9 (for a shortened version see Peter Wilenski, "Administration Reform – General Principles and the Australian Experience", *Public Administration*, 64, no. 3 (Autumn 1986), pp. 257-276; articles by John Dawkins, Sir Arthur Tange, David Connolly and Peter Bailey in *Canberra Bulletin of Public Administration*, XI, no. 1 (Autumn 1984); J.R. Nethercote, "Public Service Reform: Its Course and Nature", and Mary Dickenson, "Personnel Management and Industrial Relations in the Public Service", in Alexander Kouzmin, J.R. Nethercote, Roger Wettenhall, eds., *Australian Commonwealth Administration 1983: Essays in Review* (Canberra: CCAE/RAIPA (ACT Division), 1984), pp. 16-42 and 44-60. Later developments are covered in J.R. Nethercote, "Government Changes and Public Service Reform", in J.R. Nethercote et al., eds., *Australian Commonwealth Administration 1984: Essays in Review*, pp. 14-23; and Mary Dickenson, "Industrial Relations and Personnel Management", ibid., pp. 26-39. Other related articles may be found in *Canberra Bulletin of Public Administration:* Peter Self, "Management and Politics: a Confused Relationship", X, no. 4 (Summer 1983); articles by Senator Peter Walsh, R.D. Beale

and John Pomeroy in ibid., XII, no. 2 (Winter 1985); and articles by Anna Yeatman and Lois Bryson, XIII, no. 4.

87. The 1986 streamlining measures were announced by the Prime Minister in a statement to the House of Representatives on September 25, 1986. Australia, House of Representatives, *Debates*, September 25, 1986, pp. 1448-54. For selected press comment see *Canberra Bulletin of Public Administration*, XIII, no. 2 (Winter 1986), pp. 138-9.

88. The 1987 changes were announced by the Prime Minister at a media conference on 14 July 1987. For full details see *Canberra Bulletin of Public Administration*, no. 52 (October 1987).

89. See, in particular John Halligan, "Reorganising Australian Government Departments, 1987", *Canberra Bulletin of Public Administration*, No. 52 (October 1987).

90. Australia, House of Representatives, Debates, September 15, 1987, pp. 44-46.

91. For media coverage of the new administrative arrangements see *Canberra Bulletin of Public Administration*, No. 52 (October 1987), pp. 48-9 and 54-5. Also, p. 65 and p. 96.

92. For further comment on this issue see J.R. Nethercote, "Government Changes and Public Service Reform", in J.R. Nethercote et al., eds., *Australian Commonwealth Administration 1984: Essays in Review*, pp. 14-23. Views expressed by Michael Codd, Secretary to the Department of the Prime Minister and Caninet on 12 November 1987 are pertinent to this point: "In the last two decades, the history of machinery of government changes has not been a happy one. There have been frequent changes – often of a marginal kind. They have been costly, often difficult to justify, and inimical to good morale. It is to be hoped that the major changes now introduced, because they have the flexibility just referred to, have a better prospect of remaining stable than past structures".

93. S.R. Kellaher, "Scrutinising a Scrutiny: Reflections on the Efficiency Scrutiny Unit Report on the Public Service Board", *Canberra Bulletin of Public Administration*, No. 52 (October 1987), pp. 72-6.

94. See J.R. Nethercote, op. cit.

95. See Clare Burton, "Equal Employment Opportunities – A Future", and Lois Bryson, "Retreat from EEO", *Canberra Bulletin of Public Administration*, No. 52 (October 1987), pp. 77-81 and p. 82 respectively.

96. Prime Minister's Media Statement, July 14, 1987. Reprinted in *Canberra Bulletin of Public Administration*, No. 52 (October 1987), pp. 12-14.

97. See Australia, Department of Finance, *Budget Reform*, (Canberra: AGPS, 1984).

98. Australia, Public Service Board, *Annual Report 1985-1986* (Canberra: AGPS, 1986), p. 109.

99. See Australia, Joint Committee on Public Accounts, *Selection and Development of Senior Managers in the Public Service*, 202nd Report (Canberra: AGPS, 1982), paras 1.23-1.32, pp. 6-8, for example. For comment on this report see article by Peter Self, endnote 73 supra.

100. Australia, Department of Finance, *Reforming the Australian Public Service*, (Canberra: AGPS, 1983), paras 3.2.1-3.2.5, pp. 27-28.

101. Background information about EPAC is contained in Australia Economic Planning Advisory Council, *Annual Report 1983-84*, (Canberra: AGPS, 1985). See also, Geoff Miller, "Strategic Leadership in Economic Policy", *Canberra Bulletin of Public Administration*, XII, no. 2 (Winter 1985); and Gwynneth Singleton, "The Economic Planning Advisory Council: The Realty of Consensus", *Politics*, 20, no. 1 (May 1985).

102. See Asutralia, Department of Finance, *Reforming the Australian Public Service*, pp. 23-4.

103. A possible exception to this comment are the overseas fellowships of approximately three months' duration available to members of the Senior Executive Service.

104. This issue is briefly considered in Peter Self, "Political Theories of Modern Government – I" and Ian Castles, "Political Theories of Modern Government – III", *Canberra Bulletin of Public Administration*, XIII, no. 4 (Summer 1986), forthcoming. See

also Wilenski, *Public Power and Public Administration*, chs 1,2,3 and 8.

105. On the "new administrative law", see *Australian Journal of Public Administration*, XL, no. 2, June 1981, for several articles; Peter Bayne on "Administrative Law" in Kouzmin et al., eds., *Australian Commonwealth Administration 1983*; Wilenski, *Public Power and Public Administration* pp. 186-190; John Griffiths, "Australian administrative law: institutions, reforms and impact", *Public Administration*, 63, no. 4 (Winter 1985); and Australia, *Review of Commonwealth Administration* (Canberra: AGPS, 1983) chapter 5. The *Canberra Bulletin of Public Administration*, XII, no. 4 (Summer 1985) has more than twenty articles on the Ombudsman and related aspects of the "new administrative law".

106. R.J. Ellicott, "Law Reform", Alan Missen, "The Osbudsman's resources – a comment" and Michael Kirby, "Osbudsman – the future?" in *Canberra Bulletin of Public Administration*, XII, no. 4 (Summer 1985), are relevant to these issues.

107. Many philosophical aspects are covered in Roger Wettenhall, *Public Enterprise and National Development* (Canberra: Royal Australian Institute of Public Administration (ACT Division), 1987) (forthcoming). See also G.R. Curnow and C.A. Saunders, eds., *Quangos – The Australian Experience* (Sydney: Hale & Iremonger/RAIPA, 1983).

108. Australia, Royal Commission on Australian Government Administration, *Report* (Canberra: AGPS, 1976), para 4.4.14.

109. Australia, Senate Standing Committee on Finance and Government Operations: *First Report* (1979); *Second Report* (1979); *Third Report* (1980); *Fourth Report* (1980); *Fifth Report* (1982); *Sixth Report* (1982). See also Australia, Senate Select Committee on Statutory Authority Financing, *Report*, 2 vols (Canberra: AGPS, 1983); and Peter Rae, "The financial accountability of statutory authorities", in Nethercote, ed., *Parliament and Bureaucracy*, pp. 238-248.

110. Australia, Senate, Standing Committee on Finance and Government Operations, *Report* on The Australian Dairy Corporation and Its Asian Subsidiaries (Canberra: AGPS, 1981); Australia, Royal Commission into Australian Meat Industry, *Report* (Canberra: AGPS, 1982); Australia, Review of

Customs Administration and Procedures, *Report* (Canberra: AGPS, 1983).

111. *Quangos — the problem of accountability* (Melbourne: Centre of Policy Studies, Monash University, 1982); *The Economics of Bureaucracy and Statutory Authorities* (Sydney: The Centre for Independent Studies, 1983); Michael G. Porter, "Government Regulation and Privatisation", *Canberra Bulletin of Public Administration*, XIII, no. 3 (Spring 1986).

112. Hugh Stretton, "Directing the Australian Public Sector", *Canberra Bulletin of Public Administration*, XI, no. 4 (Summer 1984). Subsequently reprinted in Hugh Stretton, *Political Essays* (Melbourne: Georgian House, 1986), pp. 70-108.

113. Australia, Minister of Finance, *Statutory Authorities and Government Business Enterprises — Proposed Policy Guidelines* (Canberra: AGPS, 1986). Some background is outlined in Roger Wettenhall, "Statutory Authorities", in Nethercote et al., eds., *Australian Commonwealth Administration 1984*, pp. 74-9. Dr. Wettenhall's critique of the paper was published in *Canberra Bulletin of Public Administration*, XIII, no. 2 (Winter 1985-6). See also *Australian Journal of Public Administration*, XLV, no. 4 (December 1986), for several articles on the policy paper including a number by heads of public enterprises. The Minister has since issued a "policy information paper": Australia, Minister for Finance, *Policy Guidelines for Commonwealth Statutory Authorities and Government Business Enterprises* (Canberra: AGPS, October 1987).

114. Australia, Minister of Finance, *Statutory Authorities and Government Business Enterprises*, paras 3.12 and 3.15, p. 21.

115. Ibld., para 3.19, p. 22.

116. R.A. Jolly, "Quangos and Public Finance", in Curnow and Saunders, eds., *Quangos*; Jean Holmes, "Victorian Statutory Corporations in the 1980s", *Australian Journal of Public Administration*, XLIII, no. 2, June 1984 for some background; and Rob Jolly, "Privatisation: Issues, Arguments and Implications", *Canberra Bulletin of Public Administration*, XIII, no. 3 (Spring 1986).

117. Australia, Australian Telecommunications Commission, *Managing Government Business Enterprises: Control and Accountability* (Telecom Australia, 1986), p. 2.

118. Australia, Department of Primary Industry, *Reform of Commonwealth Primary Industry Statutory Marketing Authorities* (Canberra: AGPS, 1986).

119. This simply repeats Dr. Wettenhall's view that "Perhaps with Primary Industry's achievement in full view, it is still not too late for other portfolios high on the statutory authority continuum — such as Communications and Transport-Aviation — to follow suit?" *CBPA*, XIII, no. 2 (Winter 1986), p. 88.

120. See "Privatisation — what the Ministers say", *Canberra Bulletin of Public Administration*, XIII, no. 1 (Autumn 1986), pp. 31-33.

121. Peter Walsh, "Public Sector Efficiency and Finance", *Canberra Bulletin of Public Administration*, XIII, no. 3 (Spring 1986), p. 219 for a comprehensive analysis by a minister, see John Dawkins, "Privatisation and Deregulation: Myths and Practicalities", *ibid.*, pp. 222-239.

122. J.J. Carlton, "Privatisation and Deregulation", *Canberra Bulletin of Public Administration*, XIII, no. 3 (Spring 1986), p. 199 and p. 203. Other Opposition views are in *ibid.*, XIII, no. 1, pp. 34-36.

123. John Braithwaite, "Privatisation, Deregulation and the Australian Community", *Canberra Bulletin of Public Administration*, XIII, no. 3 (Spring 1986), p. 257.

124. John H. Howard, "Issues in the Privatisation Debate", *Canberra Bulletin of Public Administration*, XIII, no. 3 (Spring 1986), p. 282. A valuable study of these aspects is Howard, "Deregulation and Privatisation", *ibid.*, XIII, no. 1 (Autumn 1986), pp. 5-27.

125. R.J.L. Hawke, Address to Conference of Victorian Branch of ALP, August 23, 1987.

126. R.J.L. Hawke, Address to ACTU Congress, 9 September 1987.

127. Geoff Kitney, *Times on Sunday*, October 4, 1987.

128. See A.J. Moran, "The Business Regulation Review Unit", *Canberra Bulletin of Public Administration*, XIII, no. 3 (Spring 1986), pp. 283-287. An example of official views is Australia, Bureau of Industry Economics, *Government Regulation of Industry: Issues for Australia* (Canberra: Australian Government Publishing Service, 1987).

Toward More Effective Government in the United States

Paul E. Peterson

Policy-making in the United States is decentralized, disjointed, and incremental. Government seldom analyzes problems in a comprehensive, thoroughgoing manner and then proceed to develop effective solutions that address the issues that have been raised. Instead, problems are proclaimed, competing solutions clamor for public attention, and small steps that partially ameliorate the perceived difficulties are finally agreed upon. To avoid threatening vested interests, policies attack issues indirectly instead of head-on.

Examples of this kind of policy evasion are legion. The Carter Administration's energy policy was so divided and subdivided by industry, regional, and environmental interests that its original coherence was lost in legislative logrolling.[1] The Johnson Administration's effort to create model cities was dissipated by Congress's propensity to spend a bit of model money in every city.[2] In 1985 we witnessed an extraordinary effort to reduce a budgetary deficit by a procedure that few participants understood, endorsed, or even believed was constitutional, but that nearly everyone in Congress voted for and that the President signed.[3]

One cannot ascribe the blame for fragmented, incoherent policy-making to any particular set of political leaders. Politicians are responding to a situation defined by the competition among diverse groups and organizations in a government divided between a fractured Congress and an executive better placed to prevent government action than to achieve a coherent, overall response to major social and economic problems.

I.   Statement of the Problem

Fragmented policy-making is an old problem, deeply embedded in American constitutional structure. Over the years a number of institutional reforms designed to give more coherence to government decisions have been put in place, the most important being the formation of the Office of Management and Budget, the Federal Reserve Board, the institutionalized presidency, and the Congressional budget committees. But as the experience of the Reagan Administration demonstrates, even when the executive branch is headed by a president with a well-defined philosophy who has been elected twice by overwhelming margins, it is unable to act positively to address a wide variety of deeply felt policy concerns.

The source of this incapacity lies in the tension between the complex, interdependent problems the government increasingly faces and the fragmented, entrenched political institutions with which it must solve them. To better understand the problems posed by this institutional nexus and to provide the underpinning for a series of recommendations for institutional reform, the Brookings Institution is undertaking a study of America's major political institutions with an emphasis on the two that must ultimately negotiate solutions to contemporary problems, Congress and the presidency.

Trends. The study takes as its point of departure the increasing disjunction between the legislative and executive branches. On the one side, Congress is continuing to operate as a decentralized institution. In addition to devolving its powers to a labyrinth of committees and subcommittees, Congress is spawning a host of new *ad hoc* policy coalitions with commitments as diverse as reforming the tax system and protecting the interests of the Snowbelt. Beset by competing demands from a fragmented membership, party leaders must perform a *tour de force* each time they need to secure Congressional approval of a significant piece of legislation.[4]

Meanwhile, the executive branch is becoming increasingly centralized and responsive to presidential direction. The suspicion of White House power that developed in the aftermath of Watergate was only a brief interruption in what has otherwise been a steady trend toward more presidential authority and control, a trend that has been well in place since the New Deal. Building on the institutional framework he inherited from his predecessors, the Reagan administration has centralized executive-branch decision-making. The President's greatest successes have been in domestic policy. For example, the Office of Management and Budget has new authority to oversee regulatory policy, a new capacity to review the budgetary implications of agency expenditures, and a new willingness to use OMB tools on behalf of the President's policy agenda. In addition, the President has assembled a like-minded team at cabinet and subcabinet levels that has been unusually successful in institutionalizing the President's broad policy objectives.[5]

These trends within the legislative and the executive branches are likely to perpetuate themselves beyond the Presidency of Ronald Reagan. Within the executive branch the capacity for centralized decision-making has been enhanced by advances in communication and information processing. Thus the White House will continue to analyze, evaluate, and revise agency decisions in ways that have become standardized in recent years. Other technological innovations — television, polling, sophisticated advertising techniques, direct-mail fund-raising — will continue to help presidents form a direct, personal constituency that is quite independent of parties, groups, and legislative factions.[6] Presidents will still be expected by the news media to provide strong leadership, and the "public" style of presidential campaigning that Reagan has used so successfully could easily come to supercede the coalition building and special interest politics of the past.[7]

On the Congressional side, social and political forces are working in an opposite direction. Policy issues have become so complex that legislative instruments have become too blunt to attack them effectively. As a result, Congress must delegate to departments and agencies the responsibility for policy choices as well as administrative execution. Congress is so divided into Houses, parties, committees, and factions that it can agree upon only very broad definitions of purpose and resource allocation. The details left to administration discretion are often not very specific at all. The recent Congressional decision to give the president the power to sequester funds is only the most extreme instance of a long history of abdicating authority and responsibility.[8]

At the same time that Congress is delegating major responsibilities to the executive, it is reserving for its members the capacity to shape many details that in other countries would become merely matters of administrative concern.[9] Congressional subcommittees, with their greatly enlarged staffs, are exercising their powers of oversight with increasing frequency: appropriation bills are filled with policy provisions that give new instruction on how monies are to be spent; government bureaucracies avoid acting decisively for fear that complaints from interest groups, combined with Congressional inquiries and investigations, will cast them in the limelight.

Congress's abdication of broad responsibilities, accompanied by interference in the minutiae of administrative actions, is not simply a consequence of the partisan divisions between a Democratic House and a Republican Senate or the ideological divisions between moderate Republicans on the Hill and conservative Republicans in the White House. The fragmenting trends are much more deep-seated than that. While presidential campaigns are publicly financed, the costs of increasingly expensive Congressional campaigns are paid by interest-based political action committees. While presidents make broad appeals to the nation, members of Congress are concentrating attention on services to states and districts, enabling the members to survive overwhelming presidential landslides.[10] While presidents engage in pathbreaking initiatives, Congress protects past practices and procedures.

Assessments. Some might say these trends are not only politically inevitable but socially desirable. Technological gains in both communications and information processing permit more centralized administration and a political style that relies on direct access to the public at large. In such circumstances, power inevitably shifts from the legislative branch to the executive. Congress can deliberate, but the executive can act. Congress has many opinions about everything; the executive branch can concentrate its attention on the most important matters. With manifold ties to vested interests, Congress can preserve; with the ability to discard past encumbrances, the executive can initiate. On broad issues, Congress defers to the executive; on specific ones, members of Congress can have their say. In short, the executive is now able to promulgate a consistent policy vision, while the legislature ensures that individual firms and groups in need of special attention are not overlooked.

But this Panglossian view of the federal system overlooks the enormous social and economic costs that such a political arrangement imposes. Coherent policies designed to address important national problems are the exception rather than the rule. Even the tax reform of 1986, supposedly a triumph of the public interest over special interests, is only a partial exception to the rule. The comprehensive tax legislation originally designed by the Treasury was restructured by a politically self-conscious White House anticipating Congressional pressures and redesigned once again in the House Ways and Means Committee. Its tortuous route through the Senate Finance Committee, a veritable redoubt of tax lobbyists, resulted in numerous transition concessions and the final bill contained so many concessions that the final tax law is not so much a reform as a rearrangement of tax preferences.[11] Social policy represents an even more pressing case in point. The wealthiest nation harbors within it an underclass whose unemployment potential is negligible, whose families are fatherless, whose health is poor, and whose education is inadequate. Large public sums are spent on health, welfare, and education as part of an effort to maintain the so-called safety net, yet crime, poverty, underemployment, and family disintegration continue unabated. Hardly any policymaker believes the present grab-bag of public policies represents a coherent response to this problem, yet since the hesitant efforts of the Nixon Administration to construct a family assistance policy, no administration has even dared grapple with the issue.[12]

The fault does not lie in the politicians currently in office. Many of the more responsible political leaders are themselves concerned about these very questions. The statement is instead a function of the institutional nexus that we have just described. The executive branch is crippled by the need to assemble *ad hoc* legislative majorities for each and every policy initiative. Parties in Congress are so weak and members are so individualistic that presidents must make Herculean efforts to mobilize majorities on behalf of their programs. As a result, Congress and the president both refuse to take responsibility for major policy problems and accuse each other of frustrating effective government. For example, the president refuses to propose cuts in entitlements because he knows Congress will not enact them. Congress blames the president for fiscal deficits even though it would not pass the balanced budget he might propose. Stalemate ensues until crisis makes innovation essential.[13]

Some analysts believe that constitutional reform is the only mechanism for resolving these difficulties. The separation of powers established by the founding fathers may have safeguarded liberty, but it has also left government incapacitated. But however persuasive may be the argument that the problem is a constitutional one,[14] the political feasibility of constitutional reform remains rather dubious. Only a great national crisis could provoke two-thirds of the Congress and three-fourths of the state legislatures to adopt meaningful changes in our institutional relationships. And problems posed by the presidential-Congressional relationship do not in the short run produce tangible crises.

Because the disease inflicted by the presidential-Congressional relationship is not acute or immediately life threatening but chronic and debilitating, its resolution requires not drastic surgery but carefully prescribed medicine and thoughtfully designed therapy. Indeed, it is an open question how much of today's failure in governing is attributable to the Constitution. The foundation of American institutions is certainly established in the Constitution, but the structure of those institutions has changed substantially in 200 years. The divergence of Congress and the presidency is much greater now than ever before and its consequences for national policy exceedingly more problematic.

II. Reform Proposals

Several Brookings studies are being initiated that will enable us to examine the ways in which changes in our electoral and party systems are affecting our governing capacities and the way in which policy-making processes are shaped by both presidential and Congressional influences. A variety of reform proposals designed to overcome these problems are currently under consideration.

Party Reform

One study is examining the argument that the parties can help bridge the political gap between the executive and legislative branches of the federal government. Parties played this role, A. James Reichley, the director of this study, is contending, under such diverse twentieth century presidents as Theodore Roosevelt, Woodrow Wilson, Calvin Coolidge, Franklin Roosevelt, and Lyndon Johnson. But since the middle of the 1960s, the weakness of the parties has contributed to the growing disharmony between the executive and the legislative branches and within Congress. The partial revival of the Republican Party in the early 1980s helped President Reagan push through his economic program in 1981. Much more needs to be done, however, if the parties are to become an enduring force promoting enough consensus for consistent government action.

Perhaps the single most important way of revitalizing the parties – as well as a major target for improving presidential leadership – is to improve the process by which presidential candidates are nominated. Traditionally, the national party conventions were decision-making bodies through which presidential nominees were chosen and overall policy approaches set. Since the 1960s, various factors such as the proliferation of primaries, changes in party rules, and the growing influence of television have reduced the national conventions to little more than ceremonial functions. As a result, real power has shifted from the parties to interest groups and candidate-oriented campaign organizations.[15] Despite the success of President Reagan, the system still does not foster a sense of common involvement in a party, a sense necessary to sustain a strong government.

Various proposals have been offered for improving this situation, including a national primary, a series of regional primaries, a reduction in the number of primaries, increased representation for elected officials at conventions, and a nominating convention followed by a national primary.[16] Reichley is giving special attention to a novel proposal that he believes has not received sufficient attention: a one-day national primary to elect delegates to national party conventions, which would do the actual nominating. Unless there were an overwhelming favorite among the party's presidential candidates, this system would normally produce a convention in which no one candidate had a majority before the balloting began. State party organizations would wield increased influence. It could well be that under this arrangement the convention would once more become an effective decision-making body, giving the parties new political vitality and providing beneficial results for the entire governmental system.

Congressional Reform

In a second study Steven S. Smith is examining the dramatic changes in floor activity that have occurred over the last three decades in the U.S. Congress. During that time in the House of Representatives, the number of amendments offered to pending legislation more than tripled. The proportion of legislation subject to floor amendments more than quadrupled and the number of members sponsoring amendments almost doubled. Similar but less dramatic change has occurred in the Senate. In both chambers, the norms of apprenticeship, specialization, and inter-committee reciprocity met their demise and nearly all congressional committees faced more serious challenges on the floor. These changes represent a revolutionary change in the role of the House floor, a completion of patterns already developing in the Senate by the 1950s, and a transformation of the policy-making processes of Congress.

The developments on the floors of the House and Senate reflect a greater egalitarianism in relations among members. Over the last two decades, members not only demanded the right to hold powerful committee chairmen accountable, they also sought meaningful participation in all important policy debates. Increasingly, members turned to the floor as the one location where their formal equality could be exercised and enforced. This tendency undermined the decisiveness of committee decisions, providing a check on the extent of decentralization that occurred in both chambers. The House floor has not gone as far as the Senate floor as a location for substantive policy-making, but the change in both chambers has been great enough to alter the strategies of parties and committees, stimulate extra-committee organizational innovations, and reshape relations between the two chambers.

Smith's study will include a critical review of House procedure and proposals for reform, including the political consequences of recorded votings, the effect of bill referral to multiple committees on floor amending activity, the implications of increased use of complex rules to govern floor debate, and the effect of televising floor sessions on amending activity.

In a second study of Congress, Stephen Hess is examining in depth the effects of the news media on the legislative process. The Washington press corps can no longer be considered merely the national equivalent of a town crier or a bulletin board: what and who they cover, their priorities, their skills, and how they are used by policy players affect the functioning of government. Yet in terms of serious research, remarkably little is known about journalism's impact or the implications of the news media's role in the governing process. This void partly exists because the discipline of political science has only recently chosen to include the press in its pantheon of institutions to be studied; and even the few studies that have been conducted are rapidly becoming obsolete because technological change in the news media has outstripped scholars' ability to chart the consequences.

Although most research has focused on network news, the overwhelming increase in Washington coverage by television news over the past few years has resulted from local stations opening or expanding bureaus in the capital. Using size of the membership in the Congressional Press Galleries, the most accepted measurement of press activity, the figures in Table 1 show the extent to which local

Table 1
Growth in Congressional Coverage by National and
Local Radio and Television Correspondents

Year	Network correspondents	Local correspondents
1979	354	337
1980	376	629
1983	437	795
1985	361	930

a.   These are the non-network U.S. radio and television correspondents. This includes some correspondents who report for specialized audiences, but for the most part it consists of local correspondents.

television and radio stations are superceding the networks as the major vehicles for Congressional coverage.

In the years 1979 to 1985, while the networks' strength has stayed constant, representatives of local TV have almost tripled and, indeed, are now about three times as numerous as their more prestigious network colleagues. There are three reasons for this development: the profitability of local TV; the replacement of film with tape; and most important, the availability and affordability of satellites. Other evidence points to a decline in the networks' audience and at the same time, expanded broadcasting of news on local stations – up to two hours preceding the network evening news in some areas.

What is the news that gets beamed back home from the non-network reporters in Washington? Who gets covered? These questions are especially intriguing because we know that network news pays more attention to the president than Congress and the Senate than the House of Representatives. The networks also overwhelmingly favor legislators who are institutional leaders or are running for president and use local angles only if they illustrate national stories.

Some preliminary calculations from the data at hand suggest three differences between network and non-network news coverage from Washington that could have electoral and policy consequences:

1) While the TV audience for the House and Senate on C-SPAN is very modest, the hidden impact of televising floor proceedings is that they provide material for non-network news as reporters increasingly make use of clips from the floor speeches of their area's House members. U.S. Representatives and Senators today receive virtually the same amount of attention on local TV news. Formerly, local TV mirrored network TV in its Senate bias. The trend encourages House members to challenge Senators and, at the same time, increases the leverage of the House.

2) The substantial advantage in coverage that the president has had over the Congress on network TV – which caused some to accuse TV of creating "The Imperial Presidency" – is being reversed on local TV news. If the network news "belongs" to the president, local TV is Congress's natural domain. The White House can be expected to make some adjustments (creating more and more "photo opportunities" for local TV), but it is more likely that local TV will continue to strengthen the hand of the legislative branch in its dealings with the executive.

3)   When Senate stories on local TV are divided into "local" and "national" categories, a very clear trend line emerges (see Table 2). A local story would cover a Senator announcing a HUD grant to rebuild the 14th Street bridge; a national story would cover a Senator explaining his vote on aid to the Contras.

Table 2
Percentage of News Stories on Congress that are Locally and Nationally Focused

Year	Local	National
	(Percent)	
1981	46	54
1983	52	48
1985	55	45

These figures should be combined with the following information: (a) Most Senators rarely appear in "national" (network) stories — in 1983, for example, two-thirds of all Senators were seen four times or less on the three networks' evening news programs combined; and (b) the audience for "local" stories — on which Senators frequently appear — is made up of the voters in the Senator' own constituencies.

This example is meant to emphasize that it would be difficult (and inaccurate) to try to explain the increasing provincialization of the Senate — a development with serious consequences for how effectively the United States deals with its problems — without considering how the media interact with public officials and political institutions.

The research program will also consider the way in which the operations of the executive departments are shaped by the twin forces of Congressional fragmentation and presidential preeminence. John Chubb is exploring the extent to which the federal system reduces institutional flexibility and exacerbates contemporary American problems. Especially as it has evolved over the last quarter century, federalism represents a formidable institutional obstacle to the national government's efforts to address modern problems. Notwithstanding important changes in federalism very recently, the United States now has a complex, interdependent, centralized apparatus for formulating and implementing domestic policy in literally hundreds of distinct problem areas. From just about any normative standpoint this is not desirable: state and local governments are burdened with tasks that could best be performed by Washington, federal agencies provide services that lower-level agencies are fully capable of providing, and few goals are accomplished efficiently. More importantly, the institutional support that this system enjoys represents one of the obstacles to the national government's effort to solve a key problem of the 1980s: federal budget deficits.

Understanding the modern institution of federalism is therefore one of the keys to understanding why substantial progress in reforming domestic policy and spending has been so difficult for the Congress and the president to negotiate. In *The New Direction in American Politics*, Chubb argued that the centralized federal structure is maintained by essentially three factors:

1) Congressional reelection needs that federal aid satisfies so nicely;

2) a far-flung intergovernmental bureaucracy that pressures state and local governments to fight for central support; and

3) an electoral system that makes it difficult for a successful national party – that is, the Republicans – to succeed at the subnational level and thereby establish a coalition for significant policy change.

This structure is beginning, however, to show signs of weakness and could give way to well-conceived reform. Such a reform would likely involve a radical sorting out of responsibilities. A good example of such a sorting out is the *Report of the Committee on Federalism and National Purpose* (chaired by Senator Daniel Evans and former Governor Charles Robb). Chubb's current work is ultimately aimed at assessing these kinds of reform proposals, on the premise that the federal system has developed to a point where lower levels of government can be expected to handle a large number of responsibilities that once they could not.

Paul E. Peterson and John Chubb are also organizing a major conference examining the policy-making system formed by the relations between Congress and the institutional presidency: its development, its operation, its implications for American politics. Since the Budget and Accounting Act of 1921, which created the Bureau of the Budget, successive presidents have had at their disposal a growing, increasingly complex administrative apparatus for effectively participating in the basic functions of government – collecting and analyzing information, designing and assessing policy proposals, formulating effective programs, initiating legislation, organizing for the implementation of social policies, and ensuring administrative control and accountability, among others.

In part, presidents have been granted these institutional resources – or have energetically developed them without provoking fierce opposition – because members of Congress, social reformers, and others have implicitly recognized a fundamental truth of American government: If the many problems inevitably generated by modern society are to be attacked in even a reasonably coherent manner, the inherent fragmentation of our political system must somehow be overcome. In important respects, the institutional presidency is a direct reflection of the American system's needs for some measure of centralization and direction.

But the institutionalized presidency is also a reflection of the president's needs and interests as a political leader. Its various components – from the Office of Management and Budget and the National Security Council to the far less formal White House structures for Congressional liaison and administrative appointments – are, from the president's standpoint, first and foremost administrative tools for achieving his own political ends. Presidents have used – and, in the view of some, abused – these tools accordingly. Thus the National Security Council is sometimes at the very center of foreign policy, sometimes virtually ignored, pushed aside, and allowed to atrophy. Much the same can be said for the Council of Economic Advisors, which has demonstrated little staying power when telling the president what he does not want to hear. The Office of Management and Budget, whose proper role has long been understood by Congress and academics in terms of objective analysis and efficient management, has increasingly been used by presidents for political advocacy in the policy-making process, political control of the bureaucracy, and political expediency at the expense of rational planning.

If the institutional presidency is to serve the interests of effective government, two dilemmas must be resolved. First, while the president is more likely than any other national politician to seek effective government in the national interest, this is not his fundamental concern. More important to him is his own success and stature as a political leader – and therefore with electoral popularity, with coalition support and opposition, with logrolling and strategic trade-offs, with avoiding conflict and blame. His resources, his time, his windows of political opportunity are limited, and he must be ready and willing to strike quickly if he is to attain his goals at all. Politically, he simply cannot afford to think and act in the long-run national interest. His legacy may well depend on success in but a few areas – in tax reform or foreign policy or social welfare legislation – and his priorities may force him to put most of the government on automatic pilot. Worse, he may find it worthwhile to trade away his control over parts of government to those from whom he needs support if his priority projects are to succeed. Thus in the years since the New Deal, the institutional presidency has developed in ways conducive to presidential leadership. Above all, it has become more centralized, drawing control and coordinating power into the increasingly complex structures of the White House and the surrounding Executive Office; and it has become more politicized, with greater reliance on political appointees and greater emphasis on the presidential program at the expense of bureaucratic "neutral competence." This has given presidents greater power to impose the kind of centralized coherence and direction that is clearly needed for more effective government—but, because of the distinctive way in which American institutions operate to structure presidential incentives, presidents have often used this power toward other ends.

The second dilemma has to do with the system as a whole: its design, however ingenious for minimizing the dangers of tyranny and instability, is simply not conducive to effective government. Even if the president's incentives could be modified—and it is part of the system's very design that they cannot be—his attempts to impose coherence and direction would face inherent obstacles in the two houses of Congress, in the bureaucracy (of which he is the chief in name only), in the courts, and in the states and localities. All of these play legitimate roles in policy-making and administration, and all have their own interests and constituencies to protect. There is no institutional mechanism to guarantee that these diverse power centers will agree with the president, or indeed coalesce on any fashion behind a well-designed policy for attacking the problem at hand. "Solutions" to social problems emerge from a complex process of haggling and give-and-take that generally offers something to everyone because virtually everyone has the power to block the process. As a result, a solution is almost guaranteed to be a policy grab-bag whose "design" is not even intended to solve the social problem from which it sprang. Its "design" is necessarily a solution to a very different problem: the problem of getting agreement in a fragmented system.

Notes

1. See for example Crauford D. Goodwin, ed., *Energy Policy in Perspective: Today's Problems, Yesterday's Solutions,* (Brookings, 1981); Robert Lawrence, ed., *New Dimensions to Energy Policy,* (Lexington Books, 1979).

2. M. Carter McFarland, *The Federal Government and Urban Problems,* (Boulder, CO: Westview Press, 1978).

3. See "Congress Enacts Strict Anti-Deficit Measure," *Congressional Quarterly Almanac,* (1985), pp. 459-68, William Grider, *The Education of David Stockman,* (New York: Sutton, 1982); David Stockman, "The Triumph of Politics," (Harper and Row, 1986).

4. See Stephen S. Smith, "New Patterns of Decisionmaking in Congress," in Chubb and Peterson, *New Directions,* pp. 203-33; Alan Ehrenahlt, "In the Senate of the '80s, Team Spirit Has Given Way to the Rule of Individuals," *Congressional Quarterly Weekly Report,* vol. 40 (September 4, 1982) pp. 2175-82; Burdett Loomis, "Congressional Caucuses and the Politics of Representation," in Lawrence C. Dodd and Bruce I. Oppenheimer, eds., *Congress Reconsidered,* 2nd ed., (Congressional Quarterly Press, 1981), pp. 204-20; Norman J. Ornstein, Robert L. Peabody, and David W. Rohde, "The Contemporary Senate of the 1980s," in Dodd and Oppenheimer, *Congress Reconsidered,* pp. 13-30; Barbara Sinclair, *Majority Leadership in the U.S. House,* (Johns Hopkins University Press, 1983).

5. See Terry M. Moe, "The Politicized Presidency," in Chubb and Peterson, *New Directions,* pp. 235-71; Chester A. Newland, "Executive Office Policy Apparatus: Enforcing the Reagan Agenda," in Lester M. Salamon and Michael S. Lund, eds., *The Reagan Presidency and the Governing of America,* (Washington, D.C.: Urban Institute Press, 1984).

6. Samuel Kernell, *Going Public: New Strategies of Presidential Leadership,* (Washington, D.C.: Congressional Quarterly Press, 1987).

7. Theodore J. Lowi, *The Personal Presidency,* (Cornell University Press, 1985).

8. Kent R. Weaver, *Automatic Government: The Politics of Indexation*, (Brookings, 1988).

9. Lawrence C. Dodd and Richard Schott, *Congress and the Administrative State*, (New York: John Wiley and Sons, 1979).

10. David Mayhew, *The Electoral Connection*, (New Haven, Conn.: Yale University Press, 1974); Richard Fenno, Jr., *Home-Style: House Members in the Districts*, (Little, Brown, 1978).

11. Jeffrey Birnbaum and Alan Murray, *Showdown at Gucci Gulch* (New York: Random House, 1987).

12. Daniel P. Moynihan, *The Politics of a Guaranteed Income* (New York: Random House, 1973); the Reagan Administration has simply proposed turning the problem over to the states. *Up From Dependency: A New National Public Assistance Strategy*, Report to the President by the Domestic Policy Council, Low Income Opportunity Working Group, December 1986.

13. Allen Schick, *Crisis in the Budget Process*, (Washington, D.C.: American Enterprise Institute, 1986).

14. James J. Sundquist, *Constitutional Reform and Effective Government*, (Brookings, 1986).

15. Nelson W. Polsby, *Consequences of Party Reform*, (Oxford University Press, 1983).

16. Robert E. DiClerico and Eric M. Uslaner, *Few Are Chosen: Problems in Presidential Selection*, (NY: McGraw-Hill Book Company, 1984).

Some Issues of Governance in Canada

Richard Simeon

Introduction

Late in 1982, the Government of Canada appointed a Royal Commission, the largest, and perhaps most ambitious in Canadian history, to report on "The Economic Union and Development Prospects for Canada."[1] Central to its sprawling mandate were critical questions about the governance of Canada. In addition to mapping the country's economic future, it was to investigate "the appropriate institutional and constitutional arrangements to promote the liberty and well-being of individual Canadians and the maintenance of a strong and competitive economy," including improved relations between business, government, labour and other groups, the roles and powers of federal and provincial governments, and ways to ensure that the "institutions of national government" in Ottawa are better able to take account of the "views and needs of all Canadians and regions."[2]

The Commission was appointed after a decade of political and economic turmoil which had called into question the whole range of Canadian political institutions, and indeed the very survival of Canada as a single political community. In 1976, the *Parti Quebecois*, committed to establishing an independent Quebec in an "economic association" with the remainder of Canada, had come to power. In 1980, Quebec citizens, by a margin of 60 per cent to 40 per cent, defeated the Quebec government's referendum seeking a mandate to negotiation the new political arrangement. In the same decade of the

1970s, other regional tensions in Canada were greatly exacerbated by the dramatic shift in the terms of trade in favour of resources, especially oil and gas producers.   Both regional and intergovernmental tensions were heightened in a struggle over prices, revenues and control, and in a larger battle over the locus of power in Canada. Both sets of issues culminated in a battle over the Canadian constitution, which resulted in a 1982 agreement to patriate the Constitution of Canada from the United Kingdom, a formula for future amendment of the constitution, and the entrenchment of a Charter of Human Rights and Freedoms, which added a crucial new "pillar" to Canada's parliamentary and federal institutions.

These conflicts over the "high politics" of institutional structure were merely the most recent manifestations of Canada's historic preoccupation with the politics of region and nation, and with the fundamental character of the Canadian political community.   But other events in the turbulent decade of the 1970s and early 1980s raised other questions.   As governments grappled with a roller-coaster economy, the capacity of Canadian governments — federal, provincial and municipal — successfully to manage the economy in a highly competitive and interdependent world was threatened.   Economic forces challenged the efficacy of Canadian governments, and their ability to reconcile competing interests.   Increasingly, as well, the emergence of newly mobilized groups challenged the quality of democracy in Canada.

Thus, Canada's political institutions — parliamentary government, federalism, political parties, bureaucracy, the courts — were all challenged.   Much political discourse suggested a deep-seated "institutional failure," whether they were evaluated on the grounds of community, efficacy or democracy.[3]

By 1987, the sense of crisis engendered by Quebec, the constitution and energy had greatly diminished.   Nevertheless, the issues for governance had not disappeared.   New problems had emerged, and old ones had taken on new forms.   This paper will examine some of these contemporary issues, identify some of the many reform proposals which have been debated, and attempt to project them into the future.   We begin with a brief examination of the political, social and economic context within which Canadian institutions are set.   We then turn to an examination of the strains within each of the central institutions in Canada.

Part One
State and Society in Canada

The forces which have challenged contemporary systems of governance are, in many respects, common to all modern industrial states. Throughout the recent period all have faced their own versions of the "crisis of governability",[4] a "fiscal crisis of the state,"[5] or a crisis of the welfare state.[6] Whether articulated from the right or the left, all countries have contemplated their own versions of the "crisis of democracy"[7] or the "legitimation" crisis.[8] Similarly, while differing economic circumstances, political coalitions and institutional forms have resulted in differing governmental responses and outcomes,[9] all nations have witnessed an erosion of the broad consensus around versions of the Keynesian welfare state, and have conducted intense debates concerning the contemporary role of government, the balance between public and private power, the trade-offs between equity and efficiency. In all, economic uncertainties questioned the efficacy of governing institutions and values.

Underlying these debates, Alan Cairns has identified three fundamental sets of forces, each interacting with the others which set the context for the contemporary challenges to the modern state. First is the need to come to terms with the implications of the growth of government in all advanced societies.[10] The challenge for governance is two-fold: how can contemporary governments with their expansive responsibilities act effectively, how can they be coordinated and managed? Second, how can they be controlled, in order to be held responsive, accountable and representative?

The growth of government in the postwar period is both cause and consequence of the second of Cairns' major forces: the politicization and fragmentation of society. Cairns here refers to several dimensions: the proliferation of interest groups, and their desire to seek influence and protection through the political system; the emergence of new political movements – of gender, environmentalism and the like – which have brought to politics new sets of values and new modes of political action. The image he and others use is of the "embedded state":[11] neither the top-down model of the state-centered approach, nor the bottom-up model of government as the reflection of the underlying society is appropriate. Instead state and society are locked into a tight network of linkages and interdependencies.

The complexities of governance in such a fragmented society are further increased by the third of Cairns' factors: the diminishing importance of international borders, and the increase in international economic and political interdependence. This permeability of international borders has two kinds of effects. First, it means that international economic and political forces, as they impact on the domestic environment, increasingly shape the political agenda in advanced countries. But at the same time they limit and constrain the policies and strategies which governments can develop to manage this agenda.[12] The role of government is defined by the need to mediate between the domestic political economy and external forces.

If such forces underpin debates about governance in all advanced countries, their relative salience, the form they take, and the political responses to them all depend on the specific history, political economy, cleavage structure and institutional forms of individual countries. Several broad features have been particularly important in shaping the Canadian understanding of these forces, and in shaping the Canadian version of the debates which they have engendered.

A Small, Open, North American Economy

International interdependence is nothing new to Canada. Since its earliest days, Canadian economic and political development has been shaped by its linkages with great metropolitan powers – first with France and Britain, more recently with the United States. Only with the constitutional reform of 1982 was one of the last vestiges of British authority in Canada – the domicile of the Canadian constitution in the British Parliament – finally ended.

Today, the relationship with the United States dominates many aspects of Canadian economic political and social life. The United States is overwhelmingly its most important trading partner, capital markets are tightly integrated, and US ownership of Canadian industries – (the "branch-plant economy") – remains high in many sectors. Proximity, combined with disparities in size and strong cultural affinities, ensures that the border is permeable to all kinds of cultural and social influences. Geopolitics binds the countries militarily.

The implications of this relationship for Canadian governance are massive. In many cases, the American political agenda becomes the Canadian political agenda – whether it was the "war on poverty" in the 1960s, the rise of "neo-conservative" ideas in the 1970s, or the movement towards tax reform in the 1980s. When Canadians discuss institutional reform, it is American models – whether a Bill of Rights or an elected Senate – that they often consider first. Many of the recent political movements which have recently energized Canadian politics had their inspiration south of the border. A shared continent means massive spill-overs of US environmental problems.

Tight economic integration ensures that many, especially economic, policies are effectively made in Washington or in the great American financial centres. The freedom of action of Canadian governments in monetary or exchange rate policy, for example, is tightly constrained, both by American policies and by the dynamics of an open capital market. Such integration creates strong pressures for" harmonization" across many policy areas in order to ensure that the competitive position of Canadian industries is not weakened. Canadian governments and private interest groups, must devote large resources to attempting to monitor and influence American policy.

Such close relationships also generate many cross-border irritants.[13] Recently, with growing US protectionism, these have tended to focus on Canada-US trade, and have taken the form of US challenges to a variety of Canadian policies, ranging from stumpage fees on timber, to industrial subsidies, to regionalized unemployment benefits, which are seen to provide unfair competitive advantages to Canadian industries in US markets.[14] Such actions challenge Canadian capacities to generate domestic policy responses to domestic problems.

Not surprisingly, the relationship with the US is a major preoccupation of Canadian politics. Along with the increased bilateral integration in the postwar period have been movements seeking greater autonomy from the US. These include efforts to carve out a more independent foreign policy (including so far little successful attempts to reduce Canada's economic dependence on US markets and capital), efforts to safeguard Canadian cultural industries, and the like.

The implications of Canada-US linkages for Canadian governance are well-illustrated by the current debate over the establishment of a free trade area between the two countries. It poses such questions as whether economic integration leads inexorably to political integration; whether the rules and enforcement procedures of a free trade agreement would entail sharp restrictions on the decision-making capacity of Canadian political institutions; and whether free trade would greatly alter the relative balance of power between federal and provincial governments in Canada.

More generally the growth of international interdependence, and the consequent imperatives for international competitiveness raise some other questions about the efficacy of Canadian political institutions. First, it could be argued that effective participation in a global economy requires a high degree of domestic consensus, and a strong capacity to mobilize and coordinate domestic economic actors in pursuit of national goals. Cameron, for example, argues that countries with a heavy dependence on exports also tend to have developed effective mechanisms of concertation and coordination among labour and business at home.[15] Many worry that the high degree of fragmentation of Canadian business, labour and other groups places strong constraints on Canadians' ability to achieve such commonality of purpose.

Second, it could equally be argued that the fragmentation of authority between federal and provincial governments also hampers

Canada's effective international action. Many of the issues, especially non-tariff barriers, which now arise in international trade negotiations bear directly on the policies and practices of provincial government. Many of the policy tools often thought to be especially relevant in meeting new economic challenges fall within provincial jurisdiction. Legally, Canada suffers from a constitutional "gap" in its ability to implement international agreements: the federal government lacks the constitutional authority to implement agreements which trench on matters within provincial jurisdiction. These questions are prominent in the free trade negotiations, concerning the extent to which provinces should participate in the bilateral negotiations, the extent to which any treaty will need provincial consent in order to be implemented, and the nature of the provincial role in any enforcement mechanisms.[16] Thus domestic institutional and political fragmentation intersect directly with international forces.

A Highly Regionalized Domestic Economy

These international forces impact on a domestic economy which is highly differentiated regionally, both in terms of levels of income and wealth, and in terms of economic structure. The basic division, of course, is between the concentration of manufacturing and finance in southern Ontario and the Montreal area, and the rest of country dependent largely on resource-based industries – agriculture, oil and gas, mining and fishing. International influences therefore have a varied economic impact within Canada. Much of the history of Canada in the 1970s can be written in terms of the tensions engendered by the rapid shift in the terms of trade resulting from increasing commodity prices. Similarly, much of the history of the present decade may well be written in terms of the political and economic implications of their equally dramatic decline. In the former period, economics drove a demand for a shift of power in favour of the west and Atlantic Canada, and fuelled an aggressive "province-building" drive at the provincial level. In the more recent period, a more traditional Canadian pattern has reasserted itself: regionalist movements in east and west now seek not more autonomy from the centre, but a greater voice at the centre to assert a claim for benefits.

Domestic Political Cleavages

These underlying economic characteristics underpin the pattern of domestic cleavages around which Canadian politics is organized. Canadian politics has traditionally been the politics of language and region. The fundamental challenge of Canadian political institutions, therefore, lies in the need to achieve accommodations across these divisions. The politics of language and region also means that basic questions about the character of the Canadian political community, and its representation in political institutions, have been central to Canadian political life. On the one hand, Canadian governments have sought to forge a distinct Canadian political nationality, building common values and symbols which both distinguish Canada from its imperial forbears, and which bridge or transcend regional and linguistic differences within the country. On the other hand, there have been attempts to forge strong linguistic and regional identities centered on provincial communities and their governments. This dialectic between region and country, institutionalized and reinforced in the form of province and nation-building, was at the heart of the constitutional crisis of the 1960s and 1970s, and accounts for the apparent Canadian obsession with "national unity."

Language

The modern form of language based nationalism was rooted in the industrialization and urbanization of Quebec, especially in the postwar period. These changes, reinforced by the growth of government, meant that an earlier nationalism rooted in religion and in cultural distinctiveness was supplanted in the 1960s by a modernizing "state-based nationalism" centered on Quebec as a distinct community. It focussed on the provincial state as the instrument of economic and social development. Hence, starting in the 1960s, and culminating with the election of the independantiste Parti Québécois government in 1976, it stressed the need for Quebecers to disengage from the national community and to seek greater autonomy as the national government of French-speaking Canadians; it was a strategy of disengagement, seeking "special status", and ultimately full sovereignty for the province.

This Quebec-centered movement contended with an alternative vision of French-English relations, centered on the federal government. It contended that the community of French-Canadians was not coterminous with the political boundaries of Quebec, and that the desirable political future lay in ensuring that French-Canadians were full participants in the national political community and the national government. Hence, rather than transferring power to Quebec, the strategy focused on improving federal responsiveness to Quebec, and extending minority language rights and government services across the country: it was an integrationist strategy.

The competing views, exemplified in the persons of René Lévesque, Premier of Quebec, and Pierre-Elliott Trudeau, Prime

Minister of Canada, culminated in the victory of the federalist forces in the 1980 referendum.   The defeat of sovereignty-association appears to have ended the present phase of Quebec nationalism.   The reasons for the defeat – which was among French-speaking Quebecers razor-thin – remain unclear.   In part it was a defeat born of success: French-Canadian economic disadvantages in Quebec had been virtually wiped out; and if extension of French language rights and services in other provinces had made little progress, English-Canadian domination of the institutions and processes of the national government had been substantially ended.   But the defeat was also a result of the economic strains of the decade, which rendered a political experiment more threatening.   Moreover, it was difficult for a nationalism, now so strongly centered on the state, to survive when the climate of the time throughout the western world had become disillusioned with the efficacy of the state generally.   Indeed, it has recently been suggested that the latest form of Quebec nationalism should be described as "market nationalism" centered on enhancing French-Canadian business success in the national and international arenas. [17]

The election of the PQ called into question the fundamentals of Canadian political institutions.   The "crisis of governance" was for Canada a crisis of its federal system and of its political community, which sparked a wide-ranging national soul-searching.   Following its referendum victory, the federal government led an extraordinary effort to resolve the constitutional issue.   The settlement eventually achieved offered virtually no concessions to the Quebec based model of linguistic relations.   The Quebec government refused its assent to the constitutional settlement, and mounted an unsuccessful legal challenge to it.

This exclusion of Quebec from the national constitutional consensus had potentially important symbolic – if not legal – implications.   Many Canadians believed that it represented a crucial piece of unfinished business, which if not resolved might prove a potent rallying point for the next wave of Quebec nationalism.   The Progressive Conservative government elected in 1984 made "bringing Quebec back in" a major goal of its first term in office.   That has also been a major goal of the federalist Liberal government elected in Quebec in 1985.

Constitutional negotiations were resumed in 1986, culminating in the "Meech Lake Accord" in May and June, 1987, in which the heads of the eleven governments agreed in principle on a new set of constitutional amendments which would give explicit recognition to Quebec as a distinct society, and to the role of the Quebec government in protecting it.   It also achieved Quebec's goals of a veto over constitutional amendments, limits on the federal spending power, a constitutional role in immigration, and a role in appointments to the Supreme Court. In these aspects of the agreement, equal powers were extended to all other provinces. Indeed, in the interaction between the politics of language and the politics of region, it might be said that the previous federal government had attempted to trump Quebec nationalism with federal power, but that in the end a province-centered view of Canada trumped them both.

Regional Cleavages

Regional divisions, like linguistic divisions, are a continuing thread through Canadian history. Like them, their form and salience have changed with changing economic circumstances, changing policy agendas, and changing roles of the state. Like language, regional conflicts have been highly institutionalized in the form of inter-governmental conflict.

Regional divisions and provincial identities, were muted throughout much of the postwar period. War and depression had undermined confidence in the provincial governments, and focussed attention on the role of the federal government both in establishing the welfare state and in managing the economy. The issues related to this project tended to divide the country along class rather than regional lines and to submerge regional identities and interests.

But these divisions reemerged with a vengeance in the 1970s. They did so as a product of several of the forces discussed above. First, they were fundamentally a product of a changing external environment. They pitted the interests of western, and, with the possibility of off-shore oil development, some eastern provinces directly against each other. One part of the country has a powerful interest in moving towards world prices, and in ensuring that the resulting revenues, and the power to make development decisions remained with the provinces. Another had an equally powerful interest in maintaining lower than world energy prices, and in ensuring that the economic benefits of resource development be shared nationally. For the western and eastern provinces, that translated into an assertion of provincial power; for Ontario it meant an alliance with the federal government as the agent which could capture the rents and redistribute them across the country. That in turn reinforced western perceptions that the federal government was the instrument of the most populous regions, which driven by the most basic of political calculations , would inevitably side with central Canada. Changing terms of trade, unlike the building of the welfare state, thus pitted capitalists and workers in Ontario against capitalists and workers in the west and east.

The obvious differences in economic interest were reinforced by the much longer tradition of western resentment of central Canadian economic power, and a rich heritage of symbols and issues on which to draw. They were reinforced as well by the presence of provincial governments which provided the institutional instruments with which to challenge central Canadian dominance. Hence the regional cleavage was played out as a conflict between Ottawa and the provincial governments. The dynamics of that relationship, in turn, led the conflicts of economic interest and power inexorably to a conflict over the relative primacy of the federal and provincial communities and of the federal and provincial governments.

The growth of government also helped shape the character of contemporary regional divisions. On one hand, the extension of federal responsibility for economic well-being meant that Ottawa would be held accountable for the economic development of regions — and by the late 1960s it was clear that just as the welfare state had not eliminated income inequalities, nor had Keynesian economics eliminated regional disparities. Moreover, as policy in the late 1960s and 1970s came increasingly to focus on more direct industrial and regional policies, then the federal government's involvement in dispensing large amounts of highly visible discretionary funds to specific regions and industries, prompted a high degree of sensitivity to their regional distribution. There was a vogue for calculating "regional balance sheets" detailing federal spending and revenues by region.

More important, the postwar government growth occurred, in Canada as well as in other countries, more rapidly at the provincial/municipal levels than at the central level. Many of the new or expanded responsibilities of the state — education, health care, servicing growing urban areas and the like — fell largely within provincial jurisdiction. While the major income security programs — unemployment insurance, family allowances, old age pension — were assumed by the federal government, further moves towards centralizing economic and social responsibilities were blocked by strong provincial, especially Quebec, opposition. The postwar system of fiscal federalism — with tax-sharing, equalization payments from the federal treasury to the poorer provinces, and shared-cost programs characterized by relatively weak central controls — meant that the federal government played a large role in financing provincial expansion.

Provinces thus emerged as powerful political actors; by the 1960s, they were no longer willing to accept a federal subordinate policy or political role. Increasingly provinces came to see themselves as responsible for the economic and social development of distinct provincial societies. This tendency was reinforced by other factors. As linguistic conflict increased during the 1960s, to be joined by growing regional conflict in the 1970s, the ability of federal parties to bridge the differences declined. Faced with a regionalized party system, and a national Parliament preoccupied with political support in central Canada, citizens turned to the provincial governments as the instruments which they controlled, fuelling provincial demands not only for greater policy and fiscal autonomy, but also for a role in articulating regional interests through the mechanism of federal-provincial conferences. In 1966, E.R. Black and Alan Cairns coined the term "province-building" to describe these new political roles.[18] Regional conflict in Canada came to be seen as a kind of competitive state-building, led by federal and provincial elites, each embodying different conceptions of the relative balance between regional and national loyalties, and different images of the federal system.[19]

Just as with Quebec, there have been two broad approaches to the accommodation of heightened regional cleavages. In Canadian political science discourse, they have come to be labelled "interstate federalism" and "intrastate federalism."[20] The former focusses on the division of powers between the two orders of government, and the character of their relations, the latter on the representation of regions and provinces within the institutions of the central government. Most of the earlier debate in the 60s and 70s was cast in interstate terms. Regional identities and linguistic dualism had come to be seen by many commentators as the fundamental political characteristic of Canada. This fact was to be accepted, if not celebrated. The response, therefore, was to embrace a set of constitutional changes which confirmed and in some cases enhanced provincial authority, which gave provinces a strong voice in such areas as constitutional amendment and judicial appointments, which placed strong limits on the ability of the federal government to intervene in areas of provincial jurisdiction, and which strengthened the capacity of provincial administrations to act as spokesmen for provincial interests in national policy-making.[21]

Later, however, a quite different analysis came to be embraced by the federal government, and by many commentators. The problem, it was argued, was not that provinces had too little power, but that the federal government itself was not adequately structured to represent and accommodate regional interests. In no other modern federal country, it was argued, did the constituent units have so little weight within the operations of the central government. If federal power and legitimacy were to be restored, then ways must be found to strengthen regional representation at the centre.[22] A host of proposals followed; they are discussed in Part II.

For the federal government, and for those who wished to strengthen it, such proposals had an obvious attraction. They would challenge the provincial role as spokesmen for regional interests, and establish stronger links between the federal government and individual Canadians. The federal parliament, not the federal-provincial conference would be the central arena for accommodation. Precisely because intrastate models could be seen as a device to undercut provinces, few provincial governments were sympathetic to them. When they were, as with a British Columbia proposal for Senate reform, it was with the German Bundesrat as the model: provincial interests would be represented at the centre by delegates of provincial governments, not by elected officials independent of them. Today, several western provinces have embraced calls for an elected Senate — perhaps because in their changed economic circumstances their prime goal must now be to establish influence at the centre, rather than autonomy from it.

Nevertheless, intrastate proposals face many problems. Importing all Canada's regional fragmentation into the centre may paralyze it just as much as do federal — provincial log-jams. Moreover, to sensitize the federal government fully to regional interests may — as perhaps is the case with the American Congress — so localize the national government that its capacity to articulate and defend a national interest transcending regions and provinces is compromised. Equally important, all such proposals call into question important aspects of parliamentary democracy, especially its assumption of majority rule. All suggest national majorities should be tempered by increased weight for smaller provinces.

It has been argued that Canadians have been far too preoccupied with the salience of regionalism and provincialism. Such a focus underestimates the extent to which Canada does constitute a national political community, with common interests and identities,[23] and the extent to which economic and social changes have diminished the demographic, cultural and economic distinctiveness of provinces.[24] It was also argued in the early 1980s that regional divisions were likely to fade, for a number of reasons. The economic problems the country faced, especially in international competition, would turn citizens back to the federal government; and the important new domestic social and cultural issues built on cleavages and identities which did not neatly coincide with regional lines. Some of the major sources of regional division — especially the constitution and energy — had been resolved through political settlements. And in 1984, there came to power a federal Progressive Conservative government, pledged to a new era of "national reconciliation," and enjoying for the first time in many years strong political support in every part of the country.

However, after a brief hiatus, it appears that no such long-term shift has occurred. Intergovernmental tensions across a wide range of issues remained. The collapse of commodity prices sharpened perceptions of "two Canada's" — a wealthy heartland and threatened peripheries. Regional jealousies have been fanned by federal grants and subsidies seen to favour one region over another. Fiscal restraint, a commitment to a market-based economic strategy, and external pressures, including the possibility of a US Free Trade Agreement, all constrain the federal government's ability to mount a major attack on regional disparities. Thus regional tensions are built in to the Canadian political economy and institutional structure; they, along with region will remain central problems for governance in the future.

New Cleavages: A Rights Oriented Society?

Nevertheless, newer cleavages have recently gained prominence which also pose issues for Canadian governance. The two most important are an enhanced concern with individual and collective rights, and a related emphasis on new definitions of identity, linked to new definitions of equity. Both dimensions call into question relations between citizen and state, state and society.

The notion of a "rights-oriented society" suggests that political goals are to be formulated less in terms of bargainable interests, and more in terms of absolute, abstract, natural rights, which are themselves to be defined and legally entrenched in the form of protection against the state or legislative majorities. To a lesser extent they also embody the idea of legally mandated claims on the state. Most rights have been seen as a property of individuals; but they have increasingly come to be formulated as the rights of groups.

While Canada shares in the broad Anglo-American tradition of liberalism, rights, except for certain religious and linguistic rights, have not been an important part of Canadian political discourse. The Canadian constitution, derived from the British tradition of parliamentary sovereignty, had no Charter or Bill of Rights. Under the influence of the UN Declaration of Human rights and other forces, the first national Canadian Bill of Rights, an ordinary statute, applying only to the federal government, was enacted in 1960, and in the following years most governments introduced human rights commissions.[25]

The first proposal for a broad constitutional charter of rights emerged as part of the constitutional bargaining process, at least partly because the federal government saw it as a valuable weapon to gain public support against provincial claims. In the longer run, federal leaders felt it would strengthen the national community as against provincial communities, by defining rights as a property of citizenship in the whole Canadian community, which would be guaranteed by a national institution, the Supreme Court. By casting rights in universalist terms, it would also in the long run undermine provincial particularism.

In 1982, the Canadian constitution gained an entrenched Charter of Human Rights and Freedoms. We had become, in Cairns' terms a "chartered society," institutionalizing rights, and adding a third pillar to the Canadian governmental structure, which was likely to transform citizen identities and Canadian political culture.[26] One of the most lively debates in contemporary Canada is what the long run effect of this change will be. Several aspects have received particular attention.

First what will be its effect on federalism; is it intrinsically a centralizing, unifying device, which in the long run undermines provincial power? While it applies equally to both orders of government, are provincial actions more likely to be caught in Charter net?

Second, what are its implications for Parliamentary government and for majority rule? Some features of the Charter appear to protect these principles. Section 1 specifically permits exceptions which are "demonstrably justified in a free and democratic society;" Section 33(1) empowers governments to pass legislation "notwithstanding" certain provisions of the Charter. Yet there is a general consensus that the Charter will shift power dramatically from legislatures to the courts.[27] The courts will become politicized in the way American courts have. The character of judicial appointments will have a new political significance. Judges will be required to take account of complex economic and social factors, and to define many concepts new to Canadian jurisprudence. This shift will in turn have important implications for the strategies and resources of interest groups, and perhaps for policy outcomes. The full effects of this shift are by no means clear: much depends on the use to which Canadians put the Charter, and the way judges interpret it. Traditionally, Canadian courts have been deferential to legislatures, and sensitive to the balances inherent in federalism. But they now control a potent new tool. As the Chief Justice of Canada, Brian Dickson, has said: "The courts have accepted the new responsibility that has been thrust upon them. ... They will play a vital role in determining the kind of society Canada is and will become under the Charter. ... [They will] determine how the fabric is to be woven and cut."[28]

Third, the rights-orientation reinforced by the Charter applies not only to legislatures, but also to the executive, the bureaucracy and to the whole range of regulatory agencies and administrative tribunals. All are now subject to the discipline of the Charter. Fourth, the Charter may have effects on the relative balance of power among major social groups. The coalition in support of the Charter included most of the "progressive" forces in Canadian society — women, labour and the like. Some recent decisions, upholding the rights of individuals against collectivities such as trade unions, and giving corporations the status of "persons" under the Charter have led many to see the Charter as perhaps a more potent instrument for the defense of privilege than for challenge to it.

New Identities

Overwhelmingly the most important of the new identities to emerge in Canada, as in most other western societies is gender. Not only does the women's movement introduce a new policy agenda, such as day care, but also it transforms the debate in other policy areas, such as culture and social policy. It generates two sets of issues for governance in Canada. The first is the pervasive concern with "equity" – with gender differences in occupations, incomes and status within both government and the private sector, and the ways to overcome them.[29] This will have crucial consequences for public sector collective bargaining, for recruitment, and for overall management of the public sector. Second, it will generate further discussion of the extent to which women's concerns will become institutionalized in the governmental structure, as the interests of other groups, such as farmers, have been in the past. All governments now have "Ministers responsible" for women's issues; virtually all have advisory groups such as the federal Advisory Council on the Status of Women; others have created agencies such as the Women's Directorate to monitor and promote the status of women in government. Whether these initial steps towards entrenchment will be followed by broader attempts to organize government around gender interests is an interesting question for the future.

Even more important for the future is a broader critique of contemporary governance which has been raised by – though it is not restricted to – the feminist movement. This is the challenge to male or patriarchal forms of organization and decision-making, which are seen to be hierarchical, adversarial, rule-driven, centralized and the like. Non-patriarchal models, on the other hand, are held to be more open, more egalitarian, less conflictual, less competitive, and with greater emphasis on the self-reliance of small groups. In this sense the issues raised by gender may be truly radical, calling for a transformation in the life of organizations and decision-making processes.

Gender is not the only equity concern with which Canadian governments have been seized. It shares many characteristics with the heightened sensitivity to the handicapped, to racial minorities, and those with varying sexual orientations.

A final identity issue is not new at all; rather it is as old as Canada. This is the heightened concern with the rights of the aboriginal peoples of Canada. At one level this is an issue of economic and social policy, focused on the extraordinary levels of deprivation suffered by native communities across Canada. But, as with all the divisions we have discussed, it is also an institutional and a constitutional issue. The 1982 constitution "affirmed" without specifying aboriginal treaty rights in Canada, and committed the governments to a series of Constitutional Conferences on the related issues. The last such Conference was held in the spring of 1987, with no agreement. Aboriginal groups asserted that inherent in existing rights was the right to "self-government." This included the establishment of aboriginal governments chiefly at the band level, with formal constitutional powers. Governments were not prepared to entrench such rights until the models had been specified. It was clear that whatever form it took, aboriginal self-government would have important implications for the roles of federal and provincial governments and for the extension of their authority and services to native Canadians.[30] Some saw aboriginal self-government as fulfillment of an historic commitment, and consistent with an idea of Canada as composed of a wide variety of communities; others saw the creation of a "third order" of native governments as a challenge to Canadian federalism, and, indeed, to the idea of a unified political community.[31]

The failure to reach agreement means that native issues will continue to shape the Canadian political agenda. The aboriginal struggle is likely to continue in the courts, as treaty rights are clarified and difficult land claims settlements are sought. In the meantime more dramatic constitutional changes are likely in Canada's northern territories. A movement to divide the vast Northwest Territories between a predominantly Inuit territory, known as Nunuvut, and a predominantly Indian, Metis and White region to the west and south, is well advanced.[32] So also are moves towards responsible government both in these territories and in the Yukon territory, though full provincial status for these thinly populated regions remains controversial.[33]

Finally, we must note the challenge to remote, complex big governments. The erosion of faith in governmental institutions does not appear to have been nearly as great in Canada as it has in the United States.[34] Nor has a populist, participatory political style gained as much currency. Nevertheless, Canada has not been immune from challenge. On the one hand such challenges – as reflected in the Charter – are demands to be protected from government. On the other they are demands for greater access to and participation in government decision-making. Interestingly, this kind of critique unites both left and right against bureaucratic government and the administrative state. But the two diverge when defining a response. For the right, the goal is to reduce the size, scope and intrusiveness of the "public household",[35] and to define a larger role for the individual and market. The Canadian debate on this dimension mirrors and borrows from that in countries such as Britain and the United States.[36] However despite the election of a government committed to limited government indications are that such principled attacks on big government (as distinct from those engendered by fiscal constraints) have not changed policies as much in Canada as in some other countries.

Opposition to big government on the left tends to take the form not of a return to private or market determination, but of a call for radical decentralization to smaller, local communities. Such ideas have a rich Canadian heritage in the values associated with federalism, and with the preservation of regional communities.[37]

To conclude, the agenda of issues for governance in Canada derives from two kinds of cleavages. First are the traditional historic cleavages which have shaped Canadian political life from its earliest days. The salience of such divisions, the form they take, the ways they interact with each other, and the specific issues around which they coalesce all vary over time in response to changes in the international environment, the role of government, and domestic social, economic and cultural changes. Their impact on Canadian politics is both a result of the Canadian institutional structure and a contributor to further institutional change. There is a strong Canadian tendency to governmentalize — and thus attempt to harness and control — new movements, and for divisions such as we have discussed to focus on institutional and constitutional forms as much as on specific policies.

These traditional cleavages then interact in complex ways with the emergence of new issues, cleavages and identities — class in an earlier period, gender today. For some observers the combination of a fragmented society and divided institutions, in the context of economic uncertainty and international competition does add up to a serious challenge to governance in Canada. For Alan Cairns it consists of a thin and attenuated sense of citizenship, and a diminution in the sense of collective identity and civic duty. To this is added a sense of a loss of public purpose, stemming both from conflicting visions of the Canadian community, and conflicting images of the role and purpose of government. For others, despite a certain loss of confidence in political institutions, the image is less of crisis than it is a sense of continuing challenges to which institutions and processes must adapt.[38] The combination of a politicized society, international influences, fiscal restraint and administrative complexity suggest the most accurate image may be that of the "constrained state."

Part II
Institutional Strains; Institutional Reforms
Federalism and Intergovernmental Relations

Canadian regional and linguistic divisions have been played out largely in the arena of federalism and through the mechanisms of intergovernmental relations. They have generated many debates about the structure and operation of these institutions.[39] Much of this debate has centered around two axes. First, that of centralization and decentralization — what are or should be the relative roles of federal and provincial governments? Should change move in the direction of a more "province-centered" polity, with strengthened provincial autonomy and a larger provincial voice in national affairs; or should it move in the direction of a more "nation-centered" system, with wider federal powers. Second, given the inevitable overlapping and sharing of responsibilities characteristic of all modern federations, what is the appropriate response: should it be a collaborative model which sees governing as the joint responsibility of 11 governments, whose leaders meet in a kind of "super-cabinet" of the Federal-Provincial Conference; or, should it be a more competitive mode,[40] which sees the virtues of federalism manifested in a more adversarial bidding for public support among rival governments?

Through the 1970s and early 80s, advocates of greater federal authority argued against extensions of provincial authority and in defence of federal power on communitarian, democratic and efficacy grounds. They began with an assumption that Canada was already the most decentralized federation in the world, and that, especially since the early 1960s, decentralization measured by such indicators as spending and taxing shares had proceeded apace — so much so that Canada's integrity as a cohesive, unified state was in question. On community grounds, the centralists argued that, ultimately, the national, pan-Canadian community was the most critical one for Canadians, and that the national government was the natural political expression of that community. Increased provincial authority was cutting the links which tied individual Canadians to the federal government, leading to the danger of a "checker-board Canada," a "balkanized Canada," a country made up of little more than a string of shopping centers strung along the border. On democratic grounds, it was argued that the national parliament was the only Canadian political institution in which all parts of the country were represented, and through which national majorities could be manifested. Moreover, it was argued that increased federal financing of provincial activities, with few, if any, federal controls over how the funds were spent limited the direct accountability of both federal and provincial governments to their citizens.

Finally, it was argued on the grounds of effectiveness that modern circumstances, including such forces as technological change and growing international interdependence rendered decentralized, fragmented institutions incapable of effectively dealing with contemporary challenges. This analysis echoed that made in the 1930s, when another generation of writers had argued that federalism was incompatible with the emerging needs of the modern state. Then it was felt that federalism was incongruent with the increasing spill-overs and externalities among regions, and with the emergence of nationwide organization of business and labour. Small, weak governments found themselves unable to deal with the economic crisis of the Depression. The developing consensus on the Keynesian welfare state could only be implemented by strong central governments.

The modern version of this argument, is that in a world of increasing international competition, it is imperative that the country be able to speak with one voice in international arenas, that the ability to compete internationally requires an internally united economic market, and that managing Canada's performance in the world requires a central government with broad powers, especially over the economy and international economic relations. Moreover it is felt that in many fields, such as financial institutions, or communications, technological change is rendering obsolete any attempt to divide powers along provincial lines. Modern exigencies, in this view, seem to suggest that federalism may be a luxury that can no longer be easily afforded.

An agenda for reform flows from this perspective. Its most recent manifestation occurred in the "new federalism" advocated by the Liberal federal government which held office from 1980 to 1985. Having defeated provincialism on its home ground in the Quebec referendum, the Trudeau government set out to reverse what it saw as a dangerous trend towards decentralization. It did so through its constitutional initiatives, which sought to restore the primacy of the national community through enactment of the Charter and the assertion of a unilateral federal power to amend the constitution without provincial consent. It extended to a variety of other programs, such as a National Energy Program, which asserted federal control over resource management, revenues and pricing. In social policy it took the form of imposition of strict new conditions in the shared-cost Medicare program, and an attempt to gain greater federal control over the use to which provinces put fiscal transfers in aid of higher education. Ottawa asserted its direct link with citizens, stressing federal program delivery over shared responsibility with provinces. While Ottawa did not claim increased powers in many areas, "concessions" which had previously been offered to the provinces were withdrawn, and a determined effort was made to force a discussion of "powers over the economy" designed to solidify federal authority and weaken provincial powers, which, it was held, were balkanizing and weakening the economy.[41]

A more decentralized federation was also defended on principled grounds, though the variation in size, economic circumstances, and dependence on federal financial support meant a considerable variation in provincial positions. However, provinces tended to argue for the legitimacy and integrity, if not the primacy, of the provincial community and society, and in particular for the right of provinces to control their own natural resources for their own benefit. Canada, as then Conservative Party leader Joe Clark put it, should be seen as a "community of communities." On democratic grounds, provinces not only tended to argue for the greater responsiveness of small provincial communities, but, more important, that the federal claim to represent the whole country was fatally flawed. On one hand, political imperatives meant that inevitably the federal government would be responsive to the interests of the most populous provinces, Ontario and Quebec. On the other, the party system was so regionally polarized that, under the Parliamentary system, whole regions could be frozen out of effective representation in the governing cabinet and caucus. Finally, on effectiveness grounds, it was argued that the greater homogeneity and manageability of provincial political economies meant that it was easier for provinces to develop effective policy responses. Federalism permits provinces to experiment with different strategies, at a time of great uncertainty about policy effectiveness.[42]

From this provincialist conception there also followed a clear agenda for change — one which would have strengthened provincial authority in a number of areas, such as natural resources, communications, and the like, and which would have placed strict limits on the discretionary powers which Ottawa could constitutionally use to intervene in areas of provincial jurisdiction.

The constitutional settlement of 1982 was, roughly, a standoff between these two models. Ottawa gained its nationalizing Charter; the provinces gained a future amending formula geared to the defence of provincial government interests, including the right of individual provinces to opt-out of any amendment transferring power from them to Ottawa. Apart from a slight strengthening of provincial control over natural resources, no other powers were transferred to provinces; but nor was Ottawa able to win greater power to regulate the economy.

Following the election of the Mulroney government, much of the thrust of the last Trudeau government — including some its policies most offensive to the provinces, as such — was reversed. There was also a transfer of considerable authority over off-shore resources to the provinces. The 1987 constitutional settlement continues the trend towards provincialism – extending the requirement of unanimity to amendments to major national institutions, giving provinces for the first time a formal voice in federal appointments of Supreme Court Judges and Senators, and winning a provincial voice over the use of the federal spending power in areas of provincial jurisdiction, through a right to "opt-out," with a compensating fiscal transfer from Ottawa for any non-participating province. The last provision, however, is less provincialist than it might seem, since it also for the first time gives explicit constitutional recognition to the federal spending power, and requires that opting-out provinces "meet national objectives."

Nevertheless, insofar as there is change recently, it is in a provincialist direction. It now appears that the determined attempt to reverse direction in 1980-83 was a temporary phenomenon.

The competitive/collaborative dichotomy coincides to some extent with the centralist/decentralist one. To the now classic question "Who speaks for Canada?" one side says "Ottawa must;" the other that, "Eleven governments, acting together, do." Assertive federal spokesmen have tended to argue for free-wheeling use of federal initiatives, even when they step on provincial toes. They have also argued that a collaborative model inevitably gives too much visibility and influence to provincial premiers, who are thereby cast into the public role of national decision-makers. Provinces, on the other hand, have tended to advocate the collaborative model – at least when it comes to federal action. They have been less willing to accept federal constraints on their own actions.

In general, the collaborative model argues that the extraordinary meshing of federal and provincial responsibilities, and the extent to which all modern problems cut across constitutional lines of authority, makes shared, or joint decision-making a require-ment. For them, collaboration is consistent with a conception of Canada as a collection of communities with distinct needs and interests. It is democratic mainly because it ensures the regional interests not adequately represented by the federal parliament and bureaucracy will be effectively injected into policy discussions. And it is functionally effective because it is the only way of avoiding duplication and contradiction in policy responses.

Critics of the collaborative model argue that it suffers on all grounds. It undermines the national community because it places provincial governments, especially their Premiers, in a position to challenge federal responsibility for national issues. It is undemocratic because in fatally blurring federal and provincial responsibility it greatly reduces accountability. The arcane language and closed door nature associated with "executive federalism" have also been held to diminish citizen knowledge and participation.[44] These critics argue that each government should be fully responsible for developing, funding and implementing its own programs, and for responding to its own interest group environment; the federal government should not pursue its own policies through the intermediary of provinces.

Finally, advocates of the competitive model argue that the collaborative model is undesirable on effectiveness grounds. It leads to a policy process which places far too great an emphasis on consensus. It is thus the enemy of innovation. Policy development in a collaborative process is likely to be slow, to be contaminated by too much log-rolling, and to tend towards the lowest common denominator. Moreover, to build the decision-making process so much around federal-provincial collaboration, it is argued, tends to "freeze out" other, non-territorial groups and interests in the policy-making process.

In Canada, the trend, as in other federations, has been to increase the scope of collaboration, especially since the 1960s. The number and scope of federal-provincial conferences — official, ministerial, and First Ministers — has increased. All governments established specific machinery to manage their intergovernmental relationships. The present government has given the model new impetus. Indeed, as a result of the recent constitutional agreement, annual First Ministers Conferences on the constitution, and on the economy, have become constitutionally required. Councils of Ministers now meet regularly in a wide variety of fields. Extended consultation will now be required on Senate and Court appointments, and on shared cost programs. While no decisions have yet been made on the provincial role in ratifying and implementing any Free Trade Agreement with the United States, elaborate collaborative mechanisms have been set up for the conduct of the free trade talks. These include mirror committees of officials, regular meetings of Ministers responsible for Trade matters, and meetings of the First Ministers to review progress every 90 days. (A competitive model for such negotiations would argue that Ottawa is responsible for international trade, that it alone should conduct the negotiations, and then, when it had an agreement, it would fight politically to overcome any provincial objections which emerged.)

It is unclear how the dialectic between centralization and decentralization, or between competition and collaboration will play out in the next generation. Many of those who see an international and economic imperative to centralize will be countered by those who argue that the real loser from these forces will be central governments which have diminishing control over the main levers of economic policy. Citizens may well then turn to smaller, provincial governments, which control many of the newer tools of economic development and which are seen to be more responsive.[45] The recent increase in economic development aspirations by US states and cities may be seen in this light.[46]

Within these broad alternatives, a number of specific issues will confront Canadian federalism in the next few years.

As the free trade issue demonstrates, reconciling Canadian federalism with the exigencies of the international environment is perhaps the most crucial. On one hand is the issue of how much the division of powers and the machinery of intergovernmental relations might inhibit the conduct of Canada international economic relationships – and, on the other hand, is the question of what pressures international forces will bring to bear on the federal institutions. Should Ottawa have greater ability to implement international treaties; should there be limits on provincial economic activities abroad?

Closely related are a number of other issues concerned with the management of the economy within a federal system. The federal trade and commerce power in Canada has much less scope and flexibility than does the US trade and commerce power, and there may well be pressures, perhaps endorsed by the court, to broaden it. In any case the careful judicial balancing of federal and provincial powers may become increasingly difficult.[47] Management of the economy also bears heavily on Canadian policy towards regional disparities and regional economic development. It might be argued that international developments will simultaneously exacerbate existing regional disparities and constrain the policy tools which can be brought to bear on them. The present government is strongly committed both to a high priority for regional development, and to the greater reliance on market forces (including free trade) to drive future economic development. It is becoming increasingly difficult to reconcile these two objectives.

Similarly, large and probably continuing deficits at both federal and provincial levels, will continue to place strains on the mechanisms of fiscal federalism. About one fifth of federal spending is in transfers to the provinces; a similar proportion of provincial revenues derive from Ottawa: as each tries to gain control of its budget, the pressures to divert fiscal problems to the other will be great. In addition, interests hurt by restraint measures at one level will increasingly turn to the other for redress. Further strains are likely to appear in the federal system of equalization, whose principle was constitutionalized in 1982. Finally, federal and provincial tax systems are deeply intertwined. As both levels of government increasingly look to the tax system as the instrument for achieving economic and social policy goals – and specifically as the federal government now seeks major tax reforms – the challenge to collaborative mechanisms will be great.

Despite these challenges, the record suggests that the institutions of Canadian federalism have been able to adapt to changing circumstances. They may have played some role in slowing down the emergence of the Canadian welfare state, and thus to have a conservative or delaying effect on policy change, but the effects were not dramatic.[48] It may be that some recent constitutional developments have increased the rigidity of the institutional system, but again, not dramatically so. While the agenda of strains and of reform initiatives is long, the inherent flexibility of the federal form will remain.

Parliament and Electoral Institutions

Most discussions about enhancing the quality of democracy in Canada have assumed the model of representative, party, parliamentary government,[49] though there have been some advocates of more direct democracy.[50]

Two issues have dominated discussion of reform to Canada's parliamentary institutions. First, how to render them more responsive to all regions of Canada, and therefore more capable of reaching accommodations among them and of maintaining the national legitimacy essential to effective federal authority. Second, how to ensure an effective role for the elected Commons in a system characterized by party discipline and executive dominance? The former has provoked by far the most literature and debate; the latter has recently seen some genuine reform.

"Reforming the Centre"

Early proposals to respond to the growth of Quebec nationalism and of regionalism focussed almost entirely on proposals for reform of the institutions of federalism: the constitution, the machinery of intergovernmental relations and the like. In the late 1970s, however, an alternative prescription arose: the solution to such tensions lay not in a decentralized federalism which would further institutionalize the differences, but in a reformed federal government. Reformers focussed on three institutions: the electoral system, the House of Commons, and the Senate.[51] The last has remained the focal point of most proposals.

Proposals for electoral reform locate the fundamental problem in a party system which, for most of the modern period, has been highly regionalized.[52] Until the 1984 Conservative sweep no party in recent years had been able to maintain support in all regions. The west was a desert for the governing Liberals; Quebec for the Tories. No party seemed capable of bridging the differences. Many reasons for this regional polarization were advanced, including the ideology of the leaders, the decline of parties as coalitions of regional factions, and their replacement by leader centered politics, and so on. But one institutional factor was singled out: the Canadian first-past-the-post single member district electoral system. Its most obvious flaw was that it vastly exaggerated regional disparities in seats as compared to votes. The Liberals' 20-25 per cent of the votes in the West yielded no seats. This in turn exacerbated the unrepresentative character of the parties' regional caucuses, and increased the sense in the regions of being excluded from the seats of power. Moreover, such an electoral system rewarded smaller parties whose votes were regionally concentrated, and hurt those whose votes were more widely spread. And the system created an incentive for parties to pay more attention to regions where they were already strong, and to neglect regions where a gain in votes would have little pay-off in seats. Hence the electoral system was held to exacerbate regional tensions.[53]

The natural solution was to advocate some form of proportional representation, bringing seats more in line with votes, and eliminating the damaging incentives to party leaders. No proposal for full blown PR was widely discussed. But a host of proposals aimed at creating a pool of extra members who could be used to "top up" a party's representation when the seats it won fell short of its proportion of vote in a given region were advanced[54] by both scholars and political leaders. The advantage of electoral system reform was that it utilized the existing mechanisms of voter representation – the party system and the House of Commons. There were, however, many critics. Electoral reform did nothing to alleviate the basic problem – the huge differences in population among regions. It would, in top-up schemes, create a "two-tiered" Commons membership, those elected as single members and those selected from party lists, which many thought incompatible with the traditional party model. PR could also have the opposite effect from that intended: encouraging the formation of regionalist splinter parties, rather than encouraging existing parties to become more national. And it was argued that the closer the system approached true PR, the greater the danger of minority or coalition governments, both of which were felt to be outside Canadian parliamentary norms. In the end, despite widespread academic interest, none of the major actors in the constitutional debates advocated electoral reform. The election of the Conservatives with support from all regions dampened advocacy of the idea, at least temporarily.

Those who focussed on the House of Commons singled out tight party discipline as the problem — often contrasting the Canadian system to the US Congress, where loose party discipline allows members to act as local representatives, and majorities are as much regional as party coalitions. Hence it was suggested that if party lines were loosened, Canadian MPs could play a larger role as regional representatives; and they could form regional coalitions across party lines. While national parties do have strong regional caucuses, it was argued, MPs should be more visible in their advocacy role.[55] It has also been suggested that significantly expanding the size of the House of Commons might ensure better representation of all regions, as well as of other minorities.[56]

There have been a host proposals for reform of the Senate which in all other federations plays a major role in bringing the federal principle into the organization of the national government. The Canadian Senate has not effectively played this role, primarily because its members have been appointed by the governing party in Ottawa.

Early proposals for Senate reform, by the Government of British Columbia, the Pepin-Robarts Task Force[57] and others took the German Bundesrat as their model: the Senate should be turned into a body in which provincial *governments* were represented. Senators would be appointed the provinces and be responsible to them. The Senate would become an extension of the Federal-Provincial Conference. Such proposals were soon rejected on several grounds. It was argued that such a provincialized Senate would hopelessly confuse the representative role of parliament with the executive role of governments. It would strengthen provincial governments, when many advocates of Senate reform were trying to find a way to by-pass provinces as the privileged spokesmen for regions. Any kind of appointed Senate seemed increasingly inappropriate in a democratic age.

The boomlet in Senate reform proposals waned after the 1982 constitutional settlement and the election of the Conservative government. But it has recently enjoyed a new prominence. It was a centerpiece of the institutional reform proposals of the Macdonald Commission. But its political force has recently come from the West. Disillusioned by their progress under a Tory government, many westerners have embraced Senate reform as the panacea. Its fundamental attraction is that it provides a way of tempering the weight of numbers in the House of Commons. In a region with a long history of distrust of party government, it also offers a way to by-pass party. The Alberta government and a host of western groups have now embraced proposals for the "Triple E" Senate — elected, equal and effective. Senate Reform has been inscribed as the first order of business in the next round of constitutional discussions.

But the idea faces many hurdles; a complex set of questions would have to be answered. First is the issue of numbers: how heavily weighted in favour of the smaller provinces should Senate representation be? Advocates of "Triple E" assert a clear principle: the house of Commons represents numbers; the Senate should represent provinces. Each province should have equal representation, as in the US Senate. The more "effective" – or powerful such a Senate, the greater the opposition to be expected from the larger provinces. Other proposals have suggested something in between equal provincial representation and "rep by pop", as in Germany, Australia and the present Senate, but there seems no principled stopping place between the two polar concepts.

Second in the method of election. Again proposals vary. Most are hostile to party government – they would try to prevent candidates running under party labels, and when elected would bar them from participation in party caucuses and cabinet. The Macdonald Commission, however, argued that there is no escaping that democratic government is party government, and that the real need was to strengthen the representativeness of party caucuses and cabinets – hence it would build election into the party system. In addition, the Macdonald Commission, like some others, would have used Senate elections to experiment with proportional representation devices. Timing of Senatorial elections and length of term would also be issues. If elections coincided with federal elections, then Senate membership would likely reproduce the partisan composition of the Commons and inject members oriented to a federal policy agenda; if they coincided with provincial elections, the reverse would occur. Reflecting the nervousness about a strong Senate, and the hostility to party government running through many of the proposals, some call for very long senatorial terms – nine years in the view of a Joint Committee of Parliament.

Third, and most crucial is the power of the Senate. With the exception of originating money Bills the existing Senate's authority is co-equal with the House of Commons, but by convention it is clearly subordinate. Reform advocates would wish to change that. Proposals vary considerably in how far they would go. Some are tilted to preserve the power of the Commons – giving a new Senate only limited power to delay legislation. Others would allow the Senate to be overridden only by special Commons majorities, or perhaps not at all. Some, such as the Joint Committee on Senate Reform have called for special majorities of both English- and French-speaking members in matters of linguistic significance.[58] Whatever the formal powers granted, it seems clear that the greater the democratic legitimacy of the Senators, the stronger the challenge it will be able to make to the House of Commons. It would be inconsistent to seek to please advocates by making it highly democratic – and then try to keep it in check through trying to limit its power.

Proposals such as these face many hurdles, not least because their adoption would now require unanimity of eleven legislatures. The two most fundamental criticisms lie in the departure from majority rule; and in the challenge to the existing norms of Commons supremacy. How could the responsibility of the government to the Commons be maintained – and how would deadlocks be resolved? Many critics point to the Australian constitutional crisis of 1975 as an illustration of the difficulties which might lie ahead. Nevertheless, Senate reform has now emerged as the touchstone of western aspirations.

Restoring Power to the House of Commons

Executive dominance of the Commons in Canada exceeds even that of Britain. Not surprisingly MPs themselves have been leaders in the search for a more effective role; reform of the House of Commons is a perennial theme in Canadian political debate. While much discussion focusses on the need for greater "efficiency" in debate and the processing of legislation – and thus is oriented to giving the government greater control over proceedings – most recent discussion would like to liberate the Member.

The most influential and far reaching exploration of legislative reform was carried out by a Special Committee on Reform of the House of Commons (the McGrath Committee), which reported in June, 1985. "Canadian politics," it argued, "has become too dominated by the ethic of party solidarity." It sought to "bring a modest balance to the tension between independent judgement and party discipline."[59]

One such thread, linked to regional representation is to provide MPs freedom from the rigors of party discipline. Free votes – as in the one on capital punishment – are very rare at the moment. Very few, however, argue for an American style Congress with limited party discipline and no direct responsibility of the government to the Commons. But the McGrath Committee suggested that members' independence could be increased by ensuring that only matters central to the government's programs and administration be considered as matters of confidence, on which strict party discipline would be imposed.

The most important proposed reforms focus on the committee system and its role in the legislative process – in investigating issues, developing policy, and monitoring government activity. The number and size of committees would be reduced, and the committee structure should more closely mirror the structure of government departments. Committee resources to conduct comprehensive departmental evaluations would be increased. Committee independence would be strengthened by preventing ministers' parliamentary secretaries from serving on standing committees, by referring Estimates to committee before they went to the House and by giving the Commons Board of Internal Economy greater financial autonomy. Committees would also be given more freedom to monitor the administration and to call on officials for testimony. The appropriate standing committees would be empowered to question newly-appointed Deputy Ministers. Nominations of members of regulatory agencies such as the National Energy Board, of officers of the Commons and of such officials as the Auditor-General would be subject to Committee scrutiny, and veto. Both Commons and committee review of delegated legislation would be enhanced.

The committee also recommended a series of procedural and administrative reforms designed to increase the autonomy of the House, including the election of the Speaker by secret ballot (a procedure which first occurred in 1986), granting him or her greater disciplinary powers, facilitating discussion of private members bills, and the like.

Finally, it was recognized that effective, independent Committee work was much more likely in early stages of consideration – before the government's position has hardened. Thus it was suggested that there be "wider use of Parliamentary Committees to review draft legislation, to conduct general enquiries when policy choices have not yet been made, and to bring in draft bills."[60]

Most of the Committee's proposals have been adopted; and most MPs appear to be pleased with them. Several committees have vigorously utilized the wider powers they now possess. On some issues, the Committee's expertise has come to rival that of the government. Much, however, depends on the interests and abilities of Committee members – one analysis suggests that most committees have failed to capitalize on their new freedom to conduct "more purposeful enquiries."[61] [62] Peter Dobell suggests that further committee reform is necessary, including the convening of *ad hoc* committees on each legislative Bill, and reorganization to permit analysis of broad policy questions, such as intergovernmental relations, crown corporations, or level of public expenditure.[63] The Macdonald Commission added that the separation of legislative and investigative committees would facilitate policy-making by providing policy analysis and guidance distinct both from that of the bureaucracy and of interest groups. Similarly, James Gillies has argued that Parliament and its committees need to be much better equipped to deal with economic and other policy issues effectively in a changing world environment.[64]

The Institutions of Executive Government

Two distinct but interwoven themes dominate debate about the bureaucracy and the executive in Canada. The first is what might be called "control and accountability." It is based on the contemporary distrust of government and its agents. Its thrust is to ensure that bureaucracies are rendered sensitive and responsive to societal and political norms. It seeks to restrain and tame bureaucracy. The second is effectiveness — the search for governmental organization, machinery and management techniques which will ensure effective policy development and implementation in a period of intense fiscal restraint and rapid technological and economic change. Both drives place intense pressures on the public service and its traditional view of itself as the bearer of a relatively autonomous "public interest." The title of a recent collection of articles from Canadian Public Administration on public sector management is *Fear and Ferment*.[65] For some, there is a direct conflict between these two thrusts.

Control and Accountability

The demand for a more accountable and responsive executive and bureaucracy takes many forms. First is the concern for "representative bureaucracy" which will more faithfully mirror the society in which it is embedded. In the 1960s and 1970s, with the passage of the Official Languages Act, establishment of the Office of the Commissioner of Official Languages and other measures, the focus was on increasing the capacity of the federal bureaucracy to serve Canadians in both official languages, and to ensure strong representation of francophones, especially in the upper levels of the public service.[66] Some attention has recently been focussed on regional and provincial dimensions of representation in the public service. Indeed, given the centrality of bureaucracy in the administrative state, it might be argued that this is where "intrastate federalism" reformers should place their emphasis, in order to strengthen the federal presence in all regions, and to combat the sense of Ottawa as a responsive bastion of central Canadians.[67]

Most such debate has focussed on how the federal government should structure its organization to take account of regional interests. At the cabinet level, in addition to the historic Canadian pattern of ensuring representation of all provinces, there has been renewed attention recently to the role of "regional ministers" managing the federal political role.[68] In the bureaucracy, the federal government created the role of Federal Economic Development Coordinators — FEDC's — to coordinate the bureaucratic presence.[69] The organization of the federal government to deal with regional development has undergone almost constant flux since the 1960s. Should regional development be the responsibility of a specific agency or Department — or should regional development be integrated into the responsibilities of all economic development agencies? In the 1960s the Department of Regional Economic Expansion was created; in the early 1980s, it was merged with the Department of Industry Trade and Commerce to form the Department of Regional Industrial Expansion (DRIE); in 1987 plans were announced to merge DRIE with Science and Technology to form the Ministry of Industry, Science and Technology (MOIST). At the same time specialized agencies to foster Atlantic development and Western diversification were announced, the latter to be headquartered, with a Deputy Minister, in Edmonton.[70]

Other proposals have continued an age old debate concerning centralization versus deconcentration in federal government operations, and have advocated enhancing federal regional responsiveness by requiring senior federal officials to gain greater experience in regional offices.[71]

Recent social changes have vastly increased alternative claims to representative bureaucracy. The most important of these is the claim to gender equity, both in terms of equal pay for work of equal value, and in terms of recruitment of women to more senior positions in the public service. It has been argued that governments must take the lead in this field, both serving as a model for the private sector, and using contract compliance and other regulatory actions to promote equality.[72] Similar concerns have been raised about representation in the bureaucracy of aboriginal peoples, the handicapped and visible minorities. While all governments have responded in various ways to these pressures, progress has been hampered by a climate of restraint, which limits new employment.

Legal Restraints

The Charter of Rights is likely to have pervasive effects on the bureaucracy and the public service. All governments have had to review their legislation seeking to ensure its provisions are consistent with the Charter; this will be an equally important criterion in designing new legislation. Perhaps more important, the Charter subjects the whole administration, including the cabinet itself, to a new set of procedural rules. The requirements of non-discrimination, "fairness", "due process" and "natural justice" will be used to subject a wide variety of discretionary bureaucratic action to much greater judicial scrutiny.[73] The right to privacy, embodied in the Privacy Act, and the office of the Privacy Commissioner is another example of recent movements towards protecting the rights of individual citizens against arbitrary government action. Additional legal issues are a continuing debate over the political rights of public servants,[74] and over continuing attempts to formalize and entrench a workable code of conflict of interest for ministers and officials.[75]

The other side of the coin is to ensure citizens greater access to government. Several Canadian jurisdictions now have Access to Information legislation, though there has been widespread criticism that it permits far too many exemptions (such as cabinet documents, national security, and federal-provincial relations).[76]

Accountability

Few of the current concerns are as confused as the debates about "accountability." Confusion abounds about the accountability of whom, to whom, and indeed about the very meaning of the term in an era of complex government and plural institutions. Bureaucrats are now held accountable to a bewildering number of masters. First is the accountability of officials to Ministers. This has taken the form of a debate about the political role of senior public servants. Some have argued that Canada should move in the direction of the United States, with a higher proportion of public officials considered as explicitly political appointments, whose role is primarily to uphold the interests of the party in power. In Opposition, the Conservatives had been highly critical of what it saw as a close alliance between civil servants and the Liberal party, and were suspicious about the loyalty of the public service.[77] The government announced that ministerial cabinets would be expanded and political "chiefs of staff" would play a greater role. "A new government," argued Hugh Segal, "should not be constrained by civil service tenure in shaping its direction." He recommends that all senior civil servants should serve in contract positions with terms no longer than three years, and that on a change in government, all Deputies should submit their resignations, to allow the government a free hand in appointments.[78] In reply, senior public servants, such as Gordon Robertson, Mitchell Sharp and Donald Savoie have made an impassioned defence of the anonymous, impartial, professional career public service, with a duty which extends beyond that of keeping the government in power.[79]

Second is accountability to Parliament and its agencies. The Commissioners of Human Rights, Official languages, Privacy and Information, are all recently created agents of Parliament with extensive investigative and regulatory powers. Committee vetting of senior appointments, and the ability to require officials to testify further underline a responsibility to parliament distinct from the traditional route of ministerial accountability.

Third, the most important of the agents of Parliament is the Office of the Auditor General, focussed on financial accountability. In recent years, successive Auditors-General have defined a wider role for themselves. Concepts such as "value for money," and especially "comprehensive auditing" bring the office close to analysis and comment on the substance of policy rather than simply analysis of the legal authority for spending public funds. Critics argue that the Auditor General – reporting to Parliament in general – is himself unaccountable, and that the line between auditing and policy has already been crossed.[80] Sutherland and Doern argue that the system has become "unnecessarily overwhelmed" by such autonomous "non-democratic/non-electoral based" control agencies, and that the more traditional parliamentary mechanisms for accountability – parties, cabinet, and legislative committees – should be strengthened.

Finally, within the bureaucracy itself, various avenues have been explored to render deputies more accountable for the performance of their own agencies. In Ontario, for example, Deputies now sign "contracts" specifying performance objectives with the Premier, and salary increases are being tied to performance.

Several important concerns have been raised about this complex network of mechanisms for control, accountability and representation. H.L. Laframboise argues that such "external" controls undervalue the most important mechanism of all: the sense of civic duty and adherence to the public interest inherent in civil service norms.[81] Competing models of accountability leave public servants confused and demoralized. The tendency to use the public service as a "social policy laboratory" subjects it to conflicting pressures and may impede effectiveness.[82] Freedom of information is held to inhibit the flow of unvarnished policy advice. Gallant concludes that the recent changes in the public service designed to make it more sensitive to a changing society, more accountable, and more open to citizens may have made the public service "more in tune with the priorities and values of our times." But "it also appears to be losing more and more of the features that used to be the definite sources of its strength."[83] The individual counterpart of the constrained state is the corsetted bureaucrat.

Effectiveness

The extraordinarily complex public agenda, fiscal restraint, and fundamental questions about the role of government have, of course provoked an equal – and sometimes competing – concern with the effectiveness of government organizations and of the public service. These issues have been raised at several levels.

First, they have taken place at the level of government structure and organization. The 1960s and 1970s were periods of experimentation and rapid changes in institutions and techniques of policy analysis. The rapid proliferation of activities and agencies in the 1960s and 1970s provoked an imperative for improved coordination and coherence. There was and remains a constant tug of war between fragmentation and centralization. Under the Trudeau government, a more formalized cabinet committee system was designed to reduce the autonomy of individual ministers and ministries and to develop a more collective cabinet responsibility. This was accompanied by a proliferation of central agencies. The Privy Council Office was greatly strengthened. Strong coordinating ministries, notably the Ministries of State for Economic and Regional Development and Social Development, were created. These were integrated with the Public Expenditure Management System (PEMS) which forced coordination of the spending of different ministries within broad policy envelopes.

Some elements in this structure have been dismantled by the Mulroney government, which in a variety of ways has reverted to a more brokerage and ministerial style of policy-making. The policy development and coordination role of the PCO was reduced (largely in favour of a stronger Prime Minister's Office) — though recent indications are that the political difficulties of the government are resulting in a flow of power back to the PCO. The major Ministries of State were abolished. The dialectic between central coordination and decentralized decision-making continues, but it seems likely that the period of virtually continuous *ad hoc* changes in government organization is over, at least for the moment.

Second, this has been a period of extensive review of the purposes and effectiveness of policy in particular areas. The Macdonald Commission provided a comprehensive assessment of economic and social policy over the previous two decades — arriving at pessimistic conclusions about their general effectiveness. Shortly after its election in 1984, the Mulroney government launched a comprehensive review of government programs, the Nielsen Task Force, reflecting the government's concern about "waste, duplication and red tape in federal departments and agencies," and its desire to overhaul government programs so that they would be "simpler, more understandable and more accessible to their clientele."[84] Nineteen "study teams" made up of private sector representatives with strong bureaucratic support reviewed 989 federal programs.

The summary Task Force Report recited a familiar litany — the "pervasive forces of the *status quo*," which makes it virtually impossible to terminate programs; the lack of "institutional memory" which means that the wheel is continually being reinvented; ineffective program evaluations; the inability to get a true picture of government spending, especially because of the difficulty of integrating direct spending and tax expenditures; and the perverse effects of the use of subsidies. There has been no comprehensive response to the Task Force Reports, but they have no doubt been important elements in the "downsizing" efforts of individual departments.

Third, in Canada, as in all other western countries, there has been extensive debate about the effectiveness of different policy instruments. This debate has also been cast in the framework of constraint, and of a neo-conservative agenda. One element is "privatization," and the reconsideration of role and purpose of public enterprise. The Mulroney government has created a Ministry of State for Privatization. Several federal – and provincial – crown corporations have been privatized, but there has as yet been little movement to divest from major corporations, such as Air Canada, Petro Canada, or the provincial electricity utilities. All governments have experimented with contracting-out and "user fees" but what seems striking is not the extent, but the modesty, of such efforts.

Similarly, there have been important moves to deregulation in fields such as financial services and transportation, but little indication of a frontal attack on regulation generally. A 1980 Commons committee on Regulatory Reform[85] argued that in its view, the primary issue was not deregulation itself, but rather reform of the processes through which regulations were developed and enforced especially the need for full consultation. In the same way Roderick Macdonald argues that, given the impossibility of returning to a regulation-free world, the proper phrase is "re-regulation."[86]

Finally, there has been extensive debate over the utility of tax expenditures. On the one hand, there is considerable interest in using the tax system as an instrument for achieving social and economic policy goals; on the other is the sense (backed by some horrendous examples) that tax expenditures "representing a huge hidden budget in the financial affairs of Canada,"[87] are an inefficient subsidy, distort equity, are not subject to adequate Parliamentary scrutiny, and have been in recent years the major source of increased government expenditures.

In these areas of policy and instrument change, substantive change has fallen far short of the rhetoric. Indeed, compared with the United States and Britain, Canadian moves in these directions seem modest. Moreover, provincial governments, such as British Columbia, Alberta and Quebec appear to have been far more aggressive than has the federal government. There appear to be several reasons. First,

Canadians have traditionally accorded governments a major role in nation-building and economic and social development: US-style populist conservatism has had little resonance in Canadian public opinion. Second, since so much of its spending is tied up in transfers to individuals and provinces, it has relatively little room for discretionary cuts. Cuts in both kinds of transfers are exceptionally difficult to achieve politically. Where there is discretion – as in spending on economic and regional development – the federal concern for maintaining support across regions frequently trumps its market-oriented rhetoric. Provinces are less constrained by fixed transfers, and by the need to balance contending regional interests. They also lack the ability to deal with their fiscal problems by printing money. It is possible that the major impetus for change in both policy and instruments may soon come from from outside the country – in the pressures for "harmonization" in the context of a Canada-US free trade agreement. Indeed, one little stated objective for many advocates of such an arrangement is precisely that it will bind the hands of Canadian governments, preventing them from undertaking what are seen as inefficient and distorting measures.

Public Sector Management

Two rather contradictory thrusts have marked debate about the strength and effectiveness of the public service. On one hand has been the concern with "downsizing;" on the other a concern with "renewal and revitalization." Limiting public sector growth and in the case of several governments, achieving substantial reductions in the size of the public service has become a constant theme.[88] In several cases, this has led to serious confrontations between governments and public service unions. In others, cuts in specific agencies have resulted in mobilization of clientele groups. In the middle and upper levels, all governments have been experimenting with various forms of "termination" of redundant employees. However "humane" the techniques used, this along with other strains, such as the implications of new technologies for many strata in middle management, have contributed to a pervasive problem of morale in the public service.

Downsizing conflicts with "renewal and revitalization" in several ways. It provides a hostile context for recruitment of groups such as women into more senior positions. At the junior level, recurrent hiring freezes have meant that little new, young blood has been recruited in recent years, creating fears of the loss of a crucial cadre of leaders in the future. At the middle level, on the other hand, there is a large demographic bulge, with little room for advancement and resulting frustration. This also is the group most threatened by new technologies. At the senior level, there is the problem of easing senior public servants into early retirement, along with a concomitant desire to stimulate the flow of new ideas, by recruiting more senior officials from outside the public service. While Public Service Commissions or their equivalents, are addressing all three problems, the "fear and ferment" referred to by Langford seems an appropriate description of the public service. The skills needed by public service managers today are, suggest Langford and Huffman, "survival skills." It is impossible to measure the effect on performance. On one hand is the view that a leaner public service, more driven by private sector management techniques and incentives, will be more effective.[89] On the other is the view that the current context of loss of confidence in the public service, the "starvation effect of restraint," the constraints imposed by a rights-seeking population and new and confusing set of accountability rules, and the "demise of rational analysis" in favour of political sensitivity and "marketing" will have long-term effects not only on the morale of the public service, but also its ability to act in the public interest.[90] Such critics argue for going "back to the future" of a more traditional model of a neutral, expert public service.

Conclusion

Prime Minister Mulroney recently ruefully restated an old Canadian cliche: is Canada a country somehow impossible to govern? For a Prime Minister who so recently had won the most sweeping victory in Canadian history, and now contemplated third place for his party in the public opinion polls, he can hardly be blamed for asking the question. Indeed, it is not simple: bridging the differences between language and regions, and managing the relations between federal and provincial governments do indeed present a major challenge to leaders and institutions. Doing so in the context of economic uncertainties, fiscal restraint, and a sometimes threatening world and North American environment is even more difficult. But to call this ungovernability is a kind of conceit in which one's own country's problems are somehow special and marvelously difficult. In a comparative context, despite the constant challenges, Canadian institutions have been highly adpatable.

Moreover, the "institutional conservatism" which stands in the way of adaptation to new circumstances should not be exaggerated. Canadian political institutions responded effectively to the new roles of the state in the postwar period. Recently, Canada has undergone a remarkable round of constitutional innovation: a Charter of Rights, an amending formula, and a reasonable, careful compromise among the province, Quebec and Canada-centered views of the country. The changes of 1982 and 1987 do not so much choose among the competing models, but sets the stage for the continuing dialectic among them. Support for the current government has indeed plummeted, but there is little evidence that this signifies any fundamental loss of legitimacy.

Nevertheless, the challenges to governability remain. They are likely to focus on the nexus between the need for Canada effectively to manage its international relationships and the management of a highly plural society. One force pulls in the direction of coordination, centralization, harmonization; the other in the direction of diversity, decentralization, difference. Closely related is the tension between the societal thrust towards greater participation, towards a defence of the welfare state and the preservation of poorer regions and towards the extension of new values into public affairs on one hand, and the thrust towards economic efficiency and economic growth on the other. Postwar social democracy provided a reconciliation of such tensions effective for its own time; the need is for another such integrative blueprint, or public philosophy, suited to contemporary circumstances. In the meantime the debates will be played out among citizens, politicians, and officials at all levels. Governing won't be easy; but it won't be impossible.

Notes

1.   Royal Commission on the Economic Union and Development Prospects for Canada. *Report* (Ottawa: 1985).

2.   *Report*, Appendix A. Vol. III. pp. 562-3.

3.   For an elaboration of these three perspectives on institutions, see Simeon, "Criteria for Choice." *Queen's Law Journal* 8:(1982-1983) 131-157.

4.   Anthony King, "Overload: Problems of Governing in the 1970s," *Political Studies* 23: ;(1975) 293-96.

5.   James O'Connor, *The Fiscal Crisis of the State.* (New York: St. Martin's Press, 1973).

6.   R. Mishra, *The Crisis of the Welfare State.*

7.   Michel Crozier, et al. *The Crisis of Democracy* (New York: NYU Press, 1975).

8.   Claus Offe. *Contradictions of the Welfare State.* (London: Hutchison, 1984); A. Wolfe, *The Limits of Legitimacy: Political*

Contradictions of Contemporary Capitalism. (New York: The Free Press, 1977).

9. David Cameron, "The Growth of Government Spending: The Canadian Experience in Comparative Perspective, in Banting, ed. *State and Society*, 21-51.

10. Cairns, "The Embedded State: State Society Relations in Canada," in Keith Banting, ed. *State and Society: Canada in Comparative Perspective.* (Toronto: University of Toronto Press, 1985) 53-84.

11. Alan Cairns, op. cit., and Keith Banting, "Images of the Modern State," in Banting, ed. *State and Society: Canada in Comparative Perspective.* (Toronto: University of Toronto Press, 1985) Introduction.

12. Andrew Martin, "The Politics of Employment and Welfare: National Policies and International Interdependence," in Banting, op. cit.

13. For the best survey, see Stephen Clarkson, *Canada and the Reagan Challenge.* Second ed. (Toronto: James Lorimer, 1986).

14. See US ruling on lumber, summarized in United States Embassy, Ottawa, News Release 86-181, 16 October, 1986.

15. Cameron, op. cit.

16. For a survey of this issue, see Richard Simeon, "Federalism and Free Trade," in P.M. Leslie, ed., *Canada: The State of the Federation: 1986.* (Kingston: Institute of Intergovernmental Relations, 1987) 189-214.

17. Thomas Courchene, "Market Nationalism," *Policy Options* 7: (October, 1986) 7-12.

18. Edwin R. Black and Alan C. Cairns, "A Different Perspective on Canadian Federalism," *Canadian Public Administration* 9: (1966) 27-44.

19. Alan Cairns, "The Governments and Societies of Canadian Federalism" *Canadian Journal of Political Science* 20: (1977) 693-725. See also his "The Other Crisis in Canadian Federalism," *Canadian Public Administration* 22: (1979).

20.   For a detailed analysis of the concept, and the recommendations which flow from it, see D.V. Smiley and R.L. Watts, *Intrastate Federalism in Canada*. (Toronto: University of Toronto Press, 1985) Vol. 39.

21.   See, for example, Task Force on Canadian Unity, *A Future Together: Observations and Recommendations*. (Ottawa, 1979).

22.   Smiley Watts, op. cit., fully review this literature. For an analysis which argues that it is the institutional difference between US and Canadian federalism, rather than a sociological difference based on stronger regional interests and identities in Canada, see Roger Gibbins, *Regionalism: Territorial Politics in Canada and the United States*. (Toronto: Butterworths, 1982).

23.   See, for example, "Canada as a Political Community," Introduction to R. Kenneth Carty and John Wards, eds. *National Politics and Community in Canada*. (Vancouver: University of British Columbia Press, 1986).

24.   Roger Gibbins, *Prairie Politics and Society: Regional Differences in Decline*. (Toronto: Butterworth, 1980).

25.   For an excellent survey of this history, see Cynthia Williams, "The Changing Nature of Citizen Rights," in Alan Cairns and Cynthia Williams, eds. *Constitutionalism, Citizenship and Society in Canada*. (Toronto: University of Toronto Press, 1985). Vol. 33, 99-132.

26.   See Cairns and Williams, "Constitutionalism, Citizenship and Society in Canada: An Overview," in Cairns and Williams op. cit. 1-50.

27.   See A. Wayne MacKay and Richard W. Bauman, "The Supreme Court of Canada: Reform Implications for an Emerging National Institution," in C.F. Beckton and A.W. MacKay, *The Courts and the Charter*, (Toronto: University of Toronto Press, 1985) 37-131; and Guy Tremblay, "The Supreme Court of Canada: Final Arbiter of Political Disputes," in I. Bernier and A. Lajoie, eds. *The Supreme Court of Canada as an Instrument of Political Change*, (Toronto: University of Toronto Press, 1985) Vol. 47, 179-201.

28.   Cited in Cairns and Williams, op. cit.

29. For the most important government study of these questions, see the Royal Commission on Equality in Employment (Abella Commission), *Report* (Ottawa, 1985).

30. For detailed analyses of these issues, see the publications of the Aboriginal Self-Government Study, published by the Institute of Intergovernmental Relations, Queen's University, Kingston, under the direction of David Hawkes.

31. For the former view, see Special Committee on Indian Self-Government in Canada, *Report* (The Penner Report), (Ottawa, 1983). For an analysis which raises the latter issues, see Roger Gibbins and J. Rick Ponting, "An Assessment of the Probable Impact of Aboriginal Self-Government in Canada," in A. Cairns and C. Williams, ed., *The Politics of Gender, Ethnicity and Language in Canada*, (Toronto: University of Toronto Press, 1985) Vol. 34, 171-245.

32. For a review of these issues see Michael S. Whittington, ed. *The North*, (Toronto: University of Toronto Press, 1985).

33. Gordon Robertson, "Northern Political Development Within Canadian Federalism," in Whittington, op. cit. 23-131.

34. See A.H. Birch, "Political Authority and Crisis in Comparative Perspective," in Banting, ed., *State and Society in Comparative Perspective*, 87-128.

35. The term is Daniel Bell's. See "The Public Household," *The Public Interest* 34: (1974) 29-68.

36. See George Hermer, ed. *Probing Leviathan: An Investigation of Government in the Economy*, (Vancouver: The Fraser Institute, 1984).

37. See Charles Taylor, "Alternative Futures," in Alan Cairns and C. Williams, eds., *Constitutionalism, Citizenship and Society*, (Toronto: University of Toronto Press, 1985); George Woodcock, "Confederation as a World Example," in Keith Banting and Richard Simeon, eds., *And No one Cheered: Federalism, Democracy and the Constitution*, (Toronto: Methuen, 1983). For a general survey of these issues, see Richard Simeon, "Considerations on Centralization and Decentralization," *Canadian Public Administration* 29: (1986) 445-61.

38.   For an analysis in this vein, see Richard Johnston, *Public Opinion and Public Policy in Canada*, (Toronto: University of Toronto Press, 1985), Vol. 35.

39.   For a recent review, see Kenneth Norrie, "Richard Simeon and Mark Krasnick. *Federalism and the Economic Union*, (Toronto: University of Toronto Press, 1985) Vol. 59.

40.   Albert Breton, "Supplementary Statement." *Report*, Royal Commission on the Economic Union. Vol. III, 486-526.

41.   Hon. Jean Chretien, *Securing the Canadian Economic Union in the Constitution*, (Ottawa: 1980).

42.   For a generally decentralist view of federalism by a market-oriented economist, see Thomas Courchene, *Economic Management and the Division of Powers*, (Toronto: University of Toronto Press, 1985), Vol. 67.

43.   Gordon Robertson, "The Role of Interministerial Conferences in the Decision-Making Process," in Richard Simeon, ed. *Confrontation or Collaboration: Intergovernmental Relations in Canada Today*, (Toronto: Institute of Public Administration of Canada, 1979).

44.   D.V. Smiley, "An Outsider's View of Federal-Provincial Relations among Consenting Adults," in Simeon, op. cit. *Confrontation or Collaboration*.

45.   See Simeon, "Federalism and Free Trade," in Peter Leslie, ed. *Canada: The State of the Federation: 1986*, 189-212.

46.   Peter Eisinger, paper presented at Queen's University, January 1987.

47.   John Whyte, "Constitutional Aspects of Economic Development Policy," in Richard Simeon, ed. *Division of Powers and Public Policy*, (Toronto: University of Toronto Press, 1985), 29-70.

48.   For a careful survey of the literature on the policy consequences of federalism, see F.J. Fletcher and Donald Wallace, "Federal-Provincial Relations and the Making of Public Policy in Canada," in Richard Simeon, ed. *Division of Powers and Public Policy*, 125-206.

49. See, for example, the *Report* of the Macdonald Commission, Part VI, The Institutional Context, Introduction and The Institutions of the National Government, Vol. III, 1-97.

50. Such ideas have a strong tradition in the prairie provinces. For a recent defence of direct democracy through referendum, see Vincent Lemieux, "The Referendum and Canadian Democracy," in Peter Aucoin, ed. *Institutional Reforms for Representative Government* (Toronto: University of Toronto Press, 1985), 111-159.

51. Three studies prepared for the Macdonald survey these issues: Peter Aucoin, ed. *Party Government and Regional Representation in Canada*; Aucoin ed., *Institutional Reforms for Representative Government*; and D.V. Smiley and R.L. Watts, *Intrastate Federalism in Canada*, (Toronto: University of Toronto Press, 1985), Vols. 36, 38, 39.

52. See David E. Smith, "Party Government, Representation and National Integration in Canada," in Aucoin, *Party Government and Regional Representation*, 1-68.

53. Alan Cairns was the first to explore the electoral system, in detail. See "The Electoral System and the Party System in Canada, 1921-65," *Canadian Journal of Political Science* 1: (1968) 55-80. For a thorough review of various reform proposals, see William P. Irvine, "A Review and Evaluation of Electoral System Reform Proposals," in Peter Aucoin, ed. *Institutional Reforms for Representative Government*, (Toronto: University of Toronto Press, 1985), Vol. 38, Royal Commission Studies, 71-109.

54. For a summary, see Irvine, op. cit., and Smiley and Watts, *Intrastate Federalism in canada*, 102-3.

55. For a discussion of the role of regional caucuses, see Paul G. Thomas, "The Role of National Party Caucuses," in Peter Aucoin, ed., *Party Government and Regional Representation in Canada*, (Toronto: University of Toronto Press, 1985) 69-136. Thomas recommends improved links between federal and provincial wings of parties, and establishment of all-party regional caucuses.

56. John C. Courtney, "The Size of Canada's Parliament: An Assessment of the Implications of a Larger House of Commons,"

in Peter Aucoin, ed., *Institutional Reforms for Representative Government,* (Toronto: University of Toronto Press, 1985) 1-39.

57.   Task Force on National Unity, *Report: A Future Together,* (Ottawa: 1979).

58.   Special Joint Committee on Senate Reform. *Report,* (Ottawa: 1984). This was also recommended in the Macdonald Commission's proposal for an elected Senate, among others.

59.   *Report,* p. 60.

60.   p. 22.

61.   Peter Dobell, "Some Comment on Parliament Reform," in Peter Aucoin, ed., *Institutional Reforms for Representative Government,* (Toronto: University of Toronto Press, 1985), 41-70. p.58.

62.   See also Paul Pross, "Parliamentary Influence and the Diffusion of Power," *Canadian Journal of Political Science* 18: (1985) 235-66.

63.   Dobell, p. 70.

64.   "Economic Policy and Institutional Reform," *Canadian Parliamentary Review* 9: (Spring, 1986) 10-13.

65.   John W. Langford, ed., *Fear and Ferment: Public Sector Management Today,* (Toronto: Institute of Public Administration of Canada, 1987).

66.   For a modestly approving survey of the effects of the first 15 years since passage of the Official Languages Act, see Commissioner of Official Languages, *Annual Report,* (Ottawa: 1984).

67.   For a review of these issues, see Kenneth Kernaghan, "Representative and Responsive Bureaucracy: Implications for Canadian Regionalism" in Peter Aucoin, ed., *Regional Responsiveness and the National Administrative State,* (Toronto: University of Toronto Press, 1985) 1-50.

68.   Bakvis.

69.   Peter Aucoin and Herman Bakvis, "Regional Responsiveness and Government Organization: The Case of Regional Economic

Development Policy in Canada," in Aucoin, ed. *Regional Responsiveness and the National Administrative State*, 51-118.

70. See Donald Savoie, *Regional Economic Development: Canada's Search for Solutions*, (Toronto: University of Toronto Press, 1986); and Aucoin and Bakvis, op. cit., for recent reviews.

71. Kernaghan, op. cit., 45-6.

72. The best and most complete analysis of these issues is the *Report* of the Royal Commission on Equality in Employment (the Abella Commission), (Ottawa: Supply and Services, 1984) and its *Research Studies* (Ottawa: 1985).

73. See Mary Eberts, "The Equality Provisions of the Canadian Charter of Rights and Freedoms and Government Institutions," in Beckton and MacKay, *The Courts and the Charter*, 133-221.

74. Kenneth Kernaghan, "Political Rights and Political Neutrality: Finding the Balance Point," in Langford, ed., *Fear and Ferment*, 131-144.

75. See Jean-Pierre Kingsley, "Conflict of Interest: A Modern Antidote," in Langford, ed., *Fear and Ferment*, 77-84.

76. For an assessment of these issues, see the articles by Sharp, Mann and Cassidy in Langford, ed., *Fear and Ferment*.

77. For an impassioned critique of alleged manipulation by the civil service in the 1979 Conservative government, see Hon. Flora MacDonald, "The Minister and the Mandarins," in Gallant, ed., *The Future Public Service*, 4-7.

78. "The Accountability of Public Servants," *Options*, 21.

79. Articles by Sharp, "The Role of the Mandarins," and "Neutral Superservants;" Robertson, "The Deputies' Anonymous Duty;" Savoie, "Putting Deputies Through the Hoop;" and Kenneth Kernaghan, "The Hired Help," all in Edgar Gallant, ed., *The Future Public Service*, (Ottawa: Institute for Research on Public Policy, n.d.)

80. See Sharon L. Sutherland and G. Bruce Doern, *Bureaucracy in Canada: Control and Reform*, (Toronto: University of Toronto Press, 1985), Vol. 43; and P.M. Pitfield, "The Office of the

Auditor General as a Way to Parliamentary Reform," *Optimum* 15: (1984) 22-32.

81.   H.L. Laframboise, "The Future Public of Public Administration in Canada, *Canadian Public Administration* 25: (1982).

82.   Sutherland and Doern, Ch. 4.

83.   In *Options*, special issue, 1.

84.   Ministerial Task Force on Program Review (Nielsen Task Force) *Report*, (Ottawa: 1986), p. 1.

85.   Special Committee on Regulatory Reform. *Report*, (Ottawa: 1980).

86.   "Understanding Regulation by Regulations," in I. Bernier and A. Lajoie, eds., *Regulation, Crown Corporations and Administrative Tribunals*, (Toronto: University of Toronto Press, 1985), Vol. 48, 81-154.

87.   Auditor General of Canada, *Report*, 1985.

88.   Experience among governments varies widely. British Columbia reduced its public service by 25 per cent between 1983 and 1985. See L.R. Jones "Coping with Revenue and Expenditure Constraints in the Provincial Government Context," in Langford, *Fear and Ferment*, 20-33.

89.   For an expression of this view, see Michael Horsey, "Taking Care of Business: The Public Official as Entrepreneur," in Langford, ed., 173-177.

90.   John Langford and Kenneth Huffman, "Fear and Ferment: Public Sector Management Today," in Langford, ed., *Fear and Ferment*, 3-19.

Members of the Institute

Board of Directors

The Honourable John B. Aird, O.C.,Q.C. (Honorary Chairman)
Aird & Berlis, Toronto
Roger Charbonneau, O.C., (Chairman)
Président du conseil, Président et Chef de la Direction Interim
NOVERCO, Montréal
Rosalie Abella
Chairman, Ontario Labour Relations Board, Toronto
Dr. Robert Bandeen
President and Chief Executive Officer, Cluny Corporation, Toronto
Nan-Bowles de Gaspé Beaubien
Vice-présidente, ressources humaines, Télémédia Inc., Montréal
Larry I. Bell
Chairman, B.C. Hydro & Power Authority, Vancouver
Marie Bernier
Montreal
Catherine Callbeck
Callbeck Limited, Central Bedeque, PEI
Allan F. (Chip) Collins
Special Advisor, Provincial Treasurer of Alberta, Edmonton
Peter C. Dobell
Director, Parliamentary Centre for Foreign Affairs and Foreign Trade, Ottawa
Dr. Rod Dobell
President, The Institute for Research on Public Policy, Victoria
Peter C. Godsoe
Vice Chairman of the Board, The Bank of Nova Scotia, Toronto

313

George Cooper, Q.C.
McInnes, Cooper and Robertson, Halifax
James S. Cowan, Q.C.
Partner, Stewart, MacKeen & Covert, Halifax
V. Edward Daughney
President, First City Trust Company, Vancouver
Dr. H.E. Duckworth, O.C.
Chancellor, University of Manitoba, Winnipeg
Dr. Stefan Dupré, O.C.
Department of Political Science, University of Toronto
Marc Eliesen
Chairperson and Executive Director, Manitoba Energy Authority, Winnipeg
Emery Fanjoy
Secretary, Council of Maritime Premiers, Halifax
Maureen Farrow
C.D. Howe Institute, Toronto
Dr. James D. Fleck
Faculty of Management Studies, University of Toronto
Dr. Allan K. Gillmore
Executive Director, Association of Universities and Colleges of Canada, Ottawa
Margaret C. Harris
Past President, The National Council of Women of Canada, Saskatoon
Michael Hicks
Principal, Centre for Executive Development, Ottawa
Dr. David Hopper
Washington, D.C.
Richard W. Johnston
President, Spencer Stuart & Associates, Toronto
Dr. Leon Katz, O.C.
Saskatoon
Dr. David Leighton
Director, National Centre for Management Research and Development
University of Western Ontario, London
Terrence Mactaggart
Managing Director, Sound Linked Data Inc., Mississauga
Judith Maxwell
Chairman, Economic Council of Canada, Vanier
Milan Nastich
Canadian General Investments Ltd., Toronto
Professor William A. W. Neilson
Dean, Faculty of Law, University of Victoria
Roderick C. Nolan, P.Eng.
President, Neill & Gunter Limited, Fredericton
Robert J. Olivero
United Nations Secretariat, New York
Gordon F. Osbaldeston, O.C.
Senior Fellow, School of Business Administration, University of Western Ontario,
London
Garnet T. Page, O.C.
Calgary
Jean-Guy Paquet
Vice-président exécutif, La Laurentienne, mutuelle d'Assurance, Québec
Professor Marilyn L. Pilkington
Osgoode Hall Law School, Toronto
Eldon D. Thompson
President, Telesat, Vanier

Dr. Israel Unger
  Dean of Science, University of New Brunswick, Fredericton
Dr. Norman Wagner
  President and Vice-Chancellor, University of Calgary
Ida Wasacase, C.M.
  Winnipeg
Dr. R. Sherman Weaver
  Director, Alberta Environmental Centre, Vegreville
Dr. Blossom Wigdor
  Director, Program in Gerontology, University of Toronto

Government Representatives

Roger Burke, Prince Edward Island
Joseph H. Clarke, Nova Scotia
Hershell Ezrin, Ontario
Allan Filmer, British Columbia
George Ford, Manitoba
Ron Hewitt, Saskatchewan
Barry Mellon, Alberta
Geoffrey Norquay, Canada
Eloise Spitzer, Yukon
Barry Toole, New Brunswick
Gérard Veilleux, Canada
Louise Vertes, Northwest Territories

Institute Management

Rod Dobell   President
Peter Dobell   Vice-President and Secretary-Treasurer

Yvon Gasse   Director, Small & Medium-Sized Business Program
Barry Lesser   Director, Information Society Studies Program
Jim MacNeill   Director, Environment & Sustainable Development Program
Shirley Seward   Director, Studies in Social Policy
Murray Smith   Director, International Economics Program

Jeffrey Holmes   Director, Communications
Parker Staples   Director, Financial Services

Tom Kent   Editor, *Policy Options Politiques*

Fellows- and Scholars-in-Residence:

Edgar Gallant   Fellow-in-Residence
Tom Kent   Fellow-in-Residence
Eric Kierans   Fellow-in-Residence
Jean-Luc Pepin   Fellow-in-Residence
Gordon Robertson   Fellow-in-Residence
David Cameron   Scholar-in-Residence
Alan Maslove   Scholar-in-Residence
Eugene M. Nesmith   Executive-in-Residence
Dennis Protti   Scholar-in-Residence
James Taylor   Scholar-in-Residence

317

Publications Available
—February 1988

Order Address

The Institute for Research on Public Policy
P.O. Box 3670 South
Halifax, Nova Scotia
B3J 3K6

Leroy O. Stone & Claude Marceau	*Canadian Population Trends and Public Policy Through the 1980s.* 1977 $4.00
Raymond Breton	*The Canadian Condition: A Guide to Research in Public Policy.* 1977 $2.95
J.W. Rowley & W.T. Stanbury (eds.)	*Competition Policy in Canada: Stage II, Bill C-13.* 1978 $12.95
C.F. Smart & W.T. Stanbury (eds.)	*Studies on Crisis Management.* 1978 $9.95
W.T. Stanbury (ed.)	*Studies on Regulation in Canada.* 1978 $9.95
Michael Hudson	*Canada in the New Monetary Order: Borrow? Devalue? Restructure!* 1978 $6.95
David K. Foot (ed.)	*Public Employment and Compensation in Canada: Myths and Realities.* 1978 $10.95
Raymond Breton & Gail Grant Akian	*Urban Institutions and People of Indian Ancestry: Suggestions for Research.* 1979 $3.00

Thomas H. Atkinson — *Trends in Life Satisfaction Among Canadians, 1968-1977.* 1979 $3.00

W.E. Cundiff & Mado Reid (eds.) — *Issues in Canadian/U.S. Transborder Computer Data Flows.* 1979 $6.50

Meyer W. Bucovetsky (ed.) — *Studies in Public Employment and Compensation in Canada.* 1979 $14.95

Richard French & André Béliveau — *The RCMP and the Management of National Security.* 1979 $6.95

G. Bruce Doern & Allan M. Maslove (eds.) — *The Public Evaluation of Government Spending.* 1979 $10.95

Leroy O. Stone & Michael J. MacLean — *Future Income Prospects for Canada's Senior Citizens.* 1979 $7.95

Richard M. Bird — *The Growth of Public Employment in Canada.* 1979 $12.95

Richard J. Schultz — *Federalism and the Regulatory Process.* 1979 $1.50

Richard J. Schultz — *Le fédéralisme et le processus de réglementation.* 1979 $1.50

Elliot J. Feldman & Neil Nevitte (eds.) — *The Future of North America: Canada, the United States, and Quebec Nationalism.* 1979 $7.95

David R. Protheroe — *Imports and Politics: Trade Decision Making in Canada, 1968-1979.* 1980 $8.95

G. Bruce Doern — *Government Intervention in the Canadian Nuclear Industry.* 1980 $8.95

G. Bruce Doern & Robert W. Morrison (eds.) — *Canadian Nuclear Policies.* 1980 $14.95

Allan M. Maslove & Gene Swimmer — *Wage Controls in Canada: 1975-78: A Study of Public Decision Making.* 1980 $11.95

T. Gregory Kane — *Consumers and the Regulators: Intervention in the Federal Regulatory Process.* 1980 $10.95

Réjean Lachapelle & Jacques Henripin — *La situation démolinguistique au Canada: évolution passée et prospective.* 1980 $24.95

Albert Breton & Anthony Scott — *The Design of Federations.* 1980 $6.95

A.R. Bailey & D.G. Hull — *The Way Out: A More Revenue-Dependent Public Sector and How It Might Revitalize the Process of Governing.* 1980 $6.95

David R. Harvey — *Christmas Turkey or Prairie Vulture? An Economic Analysis of the Crow's Nest Pass Grain Rates.* 1980 $10.95

Donald G. Cartwright — *Official Language Populations in Canada: Patterns and Contacts.* 1980 $4.95

Richard M. Bird	*Taxing Corporations.* 1980 $6.95
Leroy O. Stone & Susan Fletcher	*A Profile of Canada's Older Population.* 1980 $7.95
Peter N. Nemetz (ed.)	*Resource Policy: International Perspectives.* 1980 $18.95
Keith A.J. Hay (ed.)	*Canadian Perspectives on Economic Relations With Japan.* 1980 $18.95
Dhiru Patel	*Dealing With Interracial Conflict: Policy Alternatives.* 1980 $5.95
Raymond Breton & Gail Grant	*La langue de travail au Québec : synthèse de la recherche sur la rencontre de deux langues.* 1981 $10.95
David M. Cameron (ed.)	*Regionalism and Supranationalism: Challenges and Alternatives to the Nation-State in Canada and Europe.* 1981 $9.95
Heather Menzies	*Women and the Chip: Case Studies of the Effects of Information on Employment in Canada.* 1981 $8.95
H.V. Kroeker (ed.)	*Sovereign People or Sovereign Governments.* 1981 $12.95
Peter Aucoin (ed.)	*The Politics and Management of Restraint in Government.* 1981 $17.95
Nicole S. Morgan	*Nowhere to Go? Possible Consequences of the Demographic Imbalance in Decision-Making Groups of the Federal Public Service.* 1981 $8.95
Nicole S. Morgan	*Où aller? Les conséquences prévisibles des déséquilibres démographiques chez les groupes de décision de la fonction publique fédérale.* 1981 $8.95
Raymond Breton, Jeffrey G. Reitz & Victor F. Valentine	*Les frontières culturelles et la cohésion du Canada.* 1981 $18.95
Peter N. Nemetz (ed.)	*Energy Crisis: Policy Response.* 1981 $10.95
James Gillies	*Where Business Fails.* 1981 $9.95
Allan Tupper & G. Bruce Doern (eds.)	*Public Corporations and Public Policy in Canada.* 1981 $16.95
Réjean Lachapelle & Jacques Henripin	*The Demolinguistic Situation in Canada: Past Trends and Future Prospects.* 1982 $24.95
Irving Brecher	*Canada's Competition Policy Revisited: Some New Thoughts on an Old Story.* 1982 $3.00
Ian McAllister	*Regional Development and the European Community: A Canadian Perspective.* 1982 $13.95

Donald J. Daly	*Canada in an Uncertain World Economic Environment.* 1982 $3.00
W.T. Stanbury & Fred Thompson	*Regulatory Reform in Canada.* 1982 $7.95
Robert J. Buchan, C. Christopher Johnston, T. Gregory Kane, Barry Lesser, Richard J. Schultz & W.T. Stanbury	*Telecommunications Regulation and the Constitution.* 1982 $18.95
Rodney de C. Grey	*United States Trade Policy Legislation: A Canadian View.* 1982 $7.95
John Quinn & Philip Slayton (eds.)	*Non-Tariff Barriers After the Tokyo Round.* 1982 $17.95
Stanley M. Beck & Ivan Bernier (eds.)	*Canada and the New Constitution: The Unfinished Agenda.* 2 vols. 1983 $10.95 (set)
R. Brian Woodrow & Kenneth B. Woodside (eds.)	*The Introduction of Pay-TV in Canada: Issues and Implications.* 1983 $14.95
E.P. Weeks & L. Mazany	*The Future of the Atlantic Fisheries.* 1983 $5.00
Douglas D. Purvis (ed.), assisted by Frances Chambers	*The Canadian Balance of Payments: Perspectives and Policy Issues.* 1983 $24.95
Roy A. Matthews	*Canada and the "Little Dragons": An Analysis of Economic Developments in Hong Kong, Taiwan, and South Korea and the Challenge/Opportunity They Present for Canadian Interests in the 1980s.* 1983 $11.95
Charles Pearson & Gerry Salembier	*Trade, Employment, and Adjustment.* 1983 $5.00
Steven Globerman	*Cultural Regulation in Canada.* 1983 $11.95
F.R. Flatters & R.G. Lipsey	*Common Ground for the Canadian Common Market.* 1983 $5.00
Frank Bunn, assisted by U. Domb, D. Huntley, H. Mills, H. Silverstein	*Oceans from Space: Towards the Management of Our Coastal Zones.* 1983 $5.00
C.D. Shearing & P.C. Stenning	*Private Security and Private Justice: The Challenge of the 80s.* 1983 $5.00
Jacob Finkelman & Shirley B. Goldenberg	*Collective Bargaining in the Public Service: The Federal Experience in Canada.* 2 vols. 1983 $29.95 (set)
Gail Grant	*The Concrete Reserve: Corporate Programs for Indians in the Urban Work Place.* 1983 $5.00
Owen Adams & Russell Wilkins	*Healthfulness of Life.* 1983 $8.00

Yoshi Tsurumi with Rebecca R. Tsurumi	*Sogoshosha: Engines of Export-Based Growth.* (Revised Edition). 1984 $10.95
Raymond Breton & Gail Grant (eds.)	*The Dynamics of Government Programs for Urban Indians in the Prairie Provinces.* 1984 $19.95
Frank Stone	*Canada, The GATT and the International Trade System.* 1984 $15.00
Pierre Sauvé	*Private Bank Lending and Developing-Country Debt.* 1984 $10.00
Mark Thompson & Gene Swimmer	*Conflict or Compromise: The Future of Public Sector Industrial Relations.* 1984 $15.00
Samuel Wex	*Instead of FIRA: Autonomy for Canadian Subsidiaries?* 1984 $8.00
R.J. Wonnacott	*Selected New Developments in International Trade Theory.* 1984 $7.00
R.J. Wonnacott	*Aggressive US Reciprocity Evaluated with a New Analytical Approach to Trade Conflicts.* 1984 $8.00
Richard W. Wright	*Japanese Business in Canada: The Elusive Alliance.* 1984 $12.00
Paul K. Gorecki & W.T. Stanbury	*The Objectives of Canadian Competition Policy, 1888-1983.* 1984 $15.00
Michael Hart	*Some Thoughts on Canada-United States Sectoral Free Trade.* 1985 $7.00
J. Peter Meekison Roy J. Romanow & William D. Moull	*Origins and Meaning of Section 92A: The 1982 Constitutional Amendment on Resources.* 1985 $10.00
Conference Papers	*Canada and International Trade. Volume One: Major Issues of Canadian Trade Policy. Volume Two: Canada and the Pacific Rim.* 1985 $25.00 (set)
A.E. Safarian	*Foreign Direct Investment: A Survey of Canadian Research.* 1985 $8.00
Joseph R. D'Cruz & James D. Fleck	*Canada Can Compete! Strategic Management of the Canadian Industrial Portfolio.* 1985 $18.00
Barry Lesser & Louis Vagianos	*Computer Communications and the Mass Market in Canada.* 1985 $10.00
W.R. Hines	*Trade Policy Making in Canada: Are We Doing it Right?* 1985 $10.00
Bertrand Nadeau	*Britain's Entry into the European Economic Community and its Effect on Canada's Agricultural Exports.* 1985 $10.00
Paul B. Huber	*Promoting Timber Cropping: Policies Toward Non-Industrial Forest Owners in New Brunswick.* 1985 $10.00

Gordon Robertson	*Northern Provinces: A Mistaken Goal.* 1985 $8.00
Petr Hanel	*La technologie et les exportations canadiennes du matériel pour la filière bois-papier.* 1985 $20.00
Russel M. Wills, Steven Globerman & Peter J. Booth	*Software Policies for Growth and Export.* 1986 $15.00
Marc Malone	*Une place pour le Québec au Canada.* 1986 $20.00
A. R. Dobell & S. H. Mansbridge	*The Social Policy Process in Canada.* 1986 $8.00
William D. Shipman (ed.)	*Trade and Investment Across the Northeast Boundary: Quebec, the Atlantic Provinces, and New England.* 1986 $20.00
Nicole Morgan	*Implosion: An Analysis of the Growth of the Federal Public Service in Canada (1945-1985).* 1986 $20.00
Nicole Morgan	*Implosion: analyse de la croissance de la Fonction publique fédérale canadienne (1945-1985).* 1986 $20.00
William A.W. Neilson & Chad Gaffield (eds.)	*Universities in Crisis: A Mediaeval Institution in the Twenty-first Century.* 1986 $20.00
Fred Wien	*Rebuilding the Economic Base of Indian Communities: The Micmac in Nova Scotia.* 1986 $20.00
D.M. Daly & D.C. MacCharles	*Canadian Manufactured Exports: Constraints and Opportunities.* 1986 $20.00
Gerald d'Amboise, Yvon Gasse & Rob Dainow	*The Smaller, Independent Manufacturer: 12 Quebec Case Studies.* 1986 $20.00
David J. Roy & Maurice A.M. de Wachter	*The Life Technologies and Public Policy.* 1986 $20.00
David Feeny, Gordon Guyatt & Peter Tugwell (eds.)	*Health Care Technology: Effectiveness, Efficiency, and Public Policy.* 1986 $20.00
International Symposium	*Les répercussions de l'informatisation en milieu de travail / The Impact of New Information Technologies on the Workplace.* 1986 $20.00
N.G. Papadopoulos	*Canada and the European Community: An Uncomfortable Partnership?* 1986 $15.00
W.T. Stanbury (ed.)	*Telecommunications Policy and Regulation: The Impact of Competition and Technological Change.* 1986 $22.00
James Gillies	*Facing Reality: Consultation, Consensus and Making Economic Policy for the 21st Century.* 1986 $15.95

International Seminar	*The Management of Water Resources — Proceedings / La gestion des ressources en eau — Actes.* 1986 $20.00
William J. Coffey & Mario Polèse (eds.)	*Still Living Together: Recent Trends and Future Directions in Canadian Regional Development.* 1987 $25.00
Bryan Schwartz	*First Principles, Second Thoughts: Aboriginal Peoples, Constitutional Reform and Canadian Statecraft.* 1987 $25.00
G.E. Salembier, Andrew R. Moroz and Frank Stone	*The Canadian Import File: Trade, Protection and Adjustment.* 1987 $20.00
Emer Killean	*Equality in the Economy: A Synthesis of the Proceedings of a Workshop / L'égalitarisme et l'économie : synthèse des débats d'atelier.* 1987 $10.00
Barry Lesser & Pamela Hall	*Telecommunications Services and Regional Development: The Case of Atlantic Canada.* 1987 $20.00
Stephen Brooks	*Who's in Charge? The Mixed Ownership Corporation in Canada.* 1987 $20.00
Richard W. Wright with Susan Huggett	*A Yen for Profit: Canadian Financial Institutions in Japan.* 1987 $15.00
Thomas Gunton and John Richards (eds.)	*Resource Rents and Public Policy in Western Canada.* 1987 $20.00
Shirley B. Seward and Mario Iacobacci (eds.)	*Approaches to Income Security Reform.* 1987 $10.00
Louis Raymond	*Validité des systèmes d'information dans les PME : analyse et perspectives.* 1987 20,00 $
Edward R. Fried, Frank Stone and Philip H. Trezise (eds.)	*Building a Canadian-American Free Trade Area.* 1987 $15.00
A.R. Riggs & Tom Velk (eds.)	*Canadian-American Free Trade: Historical, Political and Economic Dimensions.* 1987 $15.00
Robert M. Stern, Philip H. Trezise and John Whalley (eds.)	*Perspectives on a U.S.-Canadian Free Trade Agreement.* 1987 $17.00
Jacques Saint-Pierre and Jean-Marc Suret	*Endettement de la PME : état de la situation et rôle de la fiscalité.* 1987 $15.00
Shirley B. Seward (ed.)	*The Future of Social Welfare Systems in Canada and the United Kingdom.* 1987 $22.00
Michael B. Percy and Christian Yoder	*The Softwood Lumber Dispute and Canada-U.S. Trade in Natural Resources.* 1987 $20.00
Allan M. Maslove and Stanley L. Winer (eds.)	*Knocking on the Back Door: Canadian Perspectives on the Political Economy of Freer Trade with the United States.* 1987 $20.00

Alexander Kemp (with postscript by Campbell Watkins)	*Petroleum Rent Collection around the World.* 1987 $30.00
Murray G. Smith and Frank Stone (eds.)	*Assessing the Canada-U.S. Free Trade Agreement.* 1987. $15.00
David W. Conklin and France St-Hilaire	*Canadian High-Tech in a New World Economy:* *A Case Study of Information Technology.* 1988 $25.00
John W. Langford and K. Lorne Brownsey (eds.)	*The Changing Shape of Government in the Asia-* *Pacific Region.* 1988. $22.00